First Nations, Museums, Narrations

Alison K. Brown

First Nations, Museums, Narrations

Stories of the 1929 Franklin Motor Expedition to the Canadian Prairies

UBCPress · Vancouver · Toronto

22 21 20 19 18 17 16 15 14   5 4 3 2 1

Printed in Canada on FSC-certified ancient-forest-free paper
(100% post-consumer recycled) that is processed chlorine- and acid-free.

Library and Archives Canada Cataloguing in Publication

Brown, Alison K. (Alison Kay), 1971-, author

   First Nations, museums, narrations : stories of the 1929 Franklin Motor
Expedition to the Canadian prairies / Alison K. Brown.

Includes bibliographical references and index.
Issued in print and electronic formats.
ISBN 978-0-7748-2725-6 (bound). – ISBN 978-0-7748-2726-3 (pbk.)
ISBN 978-0-7748-2727-0 (pdf). – ISBN 978-0-7748-2728-7 (epub)

   1. Franklin Motor Expedition (1929). 2. Ethnological expeditions – Canada,
Western – History – 20th century. 3. Native peoples – Antiquities – Collectors and
collecting – Canada, Western – History – 20th century. 4. Indians of North America
– Antiquities – Collectors and collecting – Canada, Western – History – 20th century.
5. Anthropology – Canada, Western – History – 20th century. 6. Ethnological
museums and collections – Social aspects – History – 20th century. 7. Ethnological
museums and collections – Political aspects – History – 20th century. 8. Native
peoples – Museums – Great Britain – History – 20th century. 9. Museums and Indians
– Great Britain – History – 20th century. 10. Museums – Acquisitions – History –
20th century. 11. Canada, Western – Antiquities. I. Title.

AM21.A2B76 2014   305.897'0712075   C2014-900714-0
                                                          C2014-900715-9

Canadä

UBC Press gratefully acknowledges the financial support for our publishing program
of the Government of Canada (through the Canada Book Fund) and the British
Columbia Arts Council.

This book has been published with the help of a grant from the Canadian Federation
for the Humanities and Social Sciences, through the Awards to Scholarly Publications
Program, using funds provided by the Social Sciences and Humanities Research
Council of Canada. Additional funding was provided by a grant from the Foundation
for Canadian Studies in the United Kingdom.

UBC Press
The University of British Columbia
2029 West Mall
Vancouver, BC V6T 1Z2
www.ubcpress.ca

To Joy Brown, who encouraged me to write this book,
and in memory of Tom Brown and Iain Brown

Contents

List of Illustrations / ix

List of Abbreviations / xi

A Note on Terminology / xiii

Acknowledgments / xvii

Introduction / 1

1 Community Contexts: Reserve Life in the 1920s / 36

2 Collecting on the Prairies: "A Splendid Collecting Field" / 62

3 Collecting in Action: The Franklin Motor Expedition / 99

4 Representing Collecting: Images and Narratives / 133

5 Reflecting on the Franklin Motor Expedition: First Nations
Perspectives / 156

6 Curating the Rymill Collection: The Prairies on Display / 194

7 Building Relationships: British Museums and First Nations / 236

Notes / 253

References / 270

Index / 298

Illustrations

Photographs

1 The Franklin Motor Expedition team, 1929 / 5

2 . Blackfoot farmers putting up hailed wheat, Siksika Nation, c. 1930 / 42

3 Students at the St. Mary's Roman Catholic Residential School, Kainai Nation, c. 1920 / 48

4 RCMP officer with participants at a ceremony, File Hills, June 1926 / 55

5 Portrait of Louis Clarke by P.A. Laszlo, 1906 / 82

6 Selling beadwork at the Regina Fair and Exhibition, 1925 / 97

7 Robert Rymill's inventory, showing the codes he used to organize artifacts / 102

8 Ajidamoo's house, Swan Lake Nation, June 1929 / 116

9 Three generations from File Hills with Indian Commissioner William Graham, c. 1914 / 121

10 Headdress owned by *mostāhtik* / 121

11 Cougar hide painted with war deeds / 127

12 *Immoyiikimii* at the wheel of the Franklin, August 1929 / 130

13 Robert Rymill and Swan Lake men examine the Franklin, June 1929 / 139

14 Posing for the camera at the Star Blanket Nation, July 1929 / 140

15 Profile view of *atim kâ-mihkwasit,* July 1929 / 141

16 Front page of *Air-Cooled Adventure among the Aborigines* / 142

17 Robert Rymill with *kâ-mostoswahcâpêw,* File Hills, July 1929 / 143

18 Encountering bears, August 1929 / 145

19 Robert Rymill collecting at the Piikani Nation, August 1929 / 146

20 Dog modelling a travois, Piikani Nation, August 1929 / 147

21 "Red Dog at teepee door. Bob emerging from teepee" / 153

22 *atim kâ-mihkwasit* and his daughters, *mihkostikwân* and Hortence, Star Blanket Nation, July 1929 / 170

23 Storage bag, used for food / 174

24 Girl's outfit, identified by Robert Rymill as Plains Cree / 178

25 Trade cloth banner with beaded designs, used with backrest / 209

26 Floor plan showing the organization of space in the Maudslay Hall, c. 1960 / 212

27 Display case with Blackfoot artifacts, c. 1960-70 / 213

28 The "Plains Indians" case, following the 1990 redisplay / 221

29 The "Plains Indians" case, following the 2004 redisplay / 225

30 Bowl and spoon collected at the Wahpeton Dakota Nation, August 1929 / 231

Map

1 The route taken by the Franklin Motor Expedition / 113

Tables

1 Rymill Collection artifacts catalogued by nation / 101

2 Rymill Collection artifacts proposed for display by Robert Rymill / 205

3 Artifacts in the 1981 Plains display / 216

4 Rymill Collection artifacts in the 1990 Plains display / 222

Abbreviations

AMNH	American Museum of Natural History
CF	Cadzow Family
CMC	Canadian Museum of Civilization
DIA	Department of Indian Affairs
GAI	Glenbow-Alberta Institute
LAC	Library and Archives Canada
MAA	Museum of Archaeology and Anthropology, University of Cambridge
MAI	Museum of the American Indian, Heye Foundation
NMAI	National Museum of the American Indian, Smithsonian Institution
PRM	Pitt Rivers Museum, University of Oxford
SAB	Saskatchewan Archives Board
UCCA	United Church of Canada Archives

A Note on Terminology

THE NAMES USED to refer to the Aboriginal peoples of what is now Canada have undergone changes and shifts throughout history. In 1929, the time of the Franklin Motor Expedition that is the focus of this book, "Indian" was the most commonly used descriptive term for indigenous people. It is still used in legislation, such as the Indian Act. Many people now prefer the collective term "First Nations," which includes status and non-status persons and is currently applied to federally recognized bands. Given that the narrative of this book moves between past and present, I have chosen to use "First Nations" throughout, unless I am quoting. At times I use the more inclusive "Aboriginal," which encompasses all three groups of original peoples and their descendants recognized in the Canadian constitution: Indians (First Nations), Métis, and Inuit. I also use the nations' own names for themselves, wherever possible, though they may differ from those with which the expedition team was familiar. For example, Bungay, Saulteaux, and Plains or western Ojibwe were all used historically to refer to Anishinaabe peoples who moved to the Plains region of Western Canada. The autonym "Anishinaabe" is now relatively common in spoken and written English, whereas the equivalent Cree and Blackfoot autonyms, *nehiyaw* and *Niitsitapi*, are used less frequently. It is for this reason that I have chosen to use the collective names "Cree" and "Blackfoot" in this book, rather than "*nehiyaw*" and "*Niitsitapi*." Naming is a political act, and I appreciate that my decisions on this matter raise problems of historical accuracy, to which some readers may object.

There are no adequate English translations of the indigenous words for the materials that museums call "objects" or "artifacts." According to the Royal Commission on Aboriginal Peoples (RCAP 1996, 592), "In many cases, Aboriginal people consider the term 'artefact,' with its connotations of dusty relics tagged and catalogued, inappropriate. Sacred objects such as medicine bundles and totems still speak to the people; they are still used in traditional ceremonies." Some First Nations colleagues prefer "holy things," which comes from their own language; others are uncomfortable with the words "object" or "artifact" but, given the need to find a suitable English term, prefer the latter. Museums often use the generic "sacred objects," "ceremonial artifacts," or "sacred-ceremonial artifacts," which are used in repatriation legislation and in guidelines for the care of such materials. Though I acknowledge the difficulties with all these terms, I have chosen to use "ceremonial artifacts" in this book.

I also acknowledge that "community" is a contested and complex term that, if applied uncritically, suggests a bounded group rather than many shifting relationships. I use it as imperfect shorthand with the understanding that it encompasses a range of social relationships, rather than a unified, cohesive group. At the same time, I appreciate that it is used by many people of indigenous descent, who find it a helpful way to identify collective relationships, both historically and in the present day. Likewise, "mainstream society" is problematic and equally homogenizing. It generally refers to Eurocentric values and assumptions that, at the time of the Franklin Motor Expedition, characterized much of the policy decisions and institutional structures that affected the interactions of Aboriginal peoples with the state. The term is less useful today, given that Canada is a much more culturally diverse nation than it was in 1929, but as with "community," since no suitable alternative exists, I have reluctantly chosen to use it.

Finally, attempts to standardize style and format in a publication that uses multiple First Nations languages can inadvertently gloss over the cultural complexities embedded within the words themselves, and the variant spellings. First Nations linguists continue to debate how best to represent their languages on the page. This book uses Plains Cree, Ojibwe, and Blackfoot words throughout. I have followed the guidance of colleagues who speak and write these languages fluently, and who frequently publish in their respective language. Basing my approach on their advice, I have used the following conventions in this book: all Plains Cree words are in lower case and in italics; all Blackfoot words are in italics and use upper case for the first letter of proper nouns; Ojibwe words also use upper case for the first letter of proper nouns but are not italicized.

Acknowledgments

THIS BOOK HAS BEEN many years in the making, and I am most grateful to colleagues, friends, and family who have encouraged me along the way. In particular, I acknowledge the support of Anita Herle at the Museum of Archaeology and Anthropology (MAA) at Cambridge University, who has provided intellectual guidance and friendship since I began the research while employed in the Anthropology section of the MAA. I am grateful to other MAA staff – former and current – for their assistance as the research progressed: Robin Boast, Wendy Brown, Gillian Crowther, Jocelyne Dudding, Mark Elliot, Rachel Hand, the late Peter Gathercole, Imogen Gunn, John Osbourne, Gwil Owen, and Deborah Swallow. I also thank the director of the MAA, Nicholas Thomas, for permission to quote from and to illustrate material in the museum's collections. Funding for the research was provided by a number of sponsors to whom I am indebted: the UK Economic and Social Research Council; the Crowther-Beynon Fund; Aberdeenshire Educational Trust; the Robert Nicol Trust; Linacre College; the University of Oxford Committee for Graduate Studies; the Peter Lienhardt Memorial Fund; the Alistair Buchan Fund; the Beit Fund; and the Cyril Foster Fund.

The initial research was undertaken between 1997 and 2000, when I was based at the Pitt Rivers Museum and the Institute of Social and Cultural Anthropology, University of Oxford. This was an exciting time to be at the Pitt Rivers Museum. Many of the staff and graduate students were concerned with better understanding what collections acquired during the colonial era meant to indigenous peoples and with finding ways to increase access to these materials. I am especially grateful to Laura Peers, Chris Gosden, and the late Donald Taylor for their suggestions and encouragement. Jeremy Coote, Elizabeth Edwards, Trudy Nicks, and Michael O'Hanlon supported the project as it developed, and their recommendations improved this book. I wish to thank Joshua Bell, Cecily Crampin, Sarah Hill, Gwyneira Isaac, David Odo, Emily Stokes-Rees, and Nicole Zitzmann for their collegiality and continued friendship. The book was drafted at the University of Aberdeen, where many colleagues gave sound advice on various aspects of its development. In particular I thank Tanya Argounova-Low, Tim Ingold, Johan Rasanayagam, and Nancy Wachowich.

Outside the United Kingdom, many people assisted with locating archival materials, fieldwork logistics, and other aspects of the research. I especially acknowledge the support of Susan Pender, the late Gladys Rymill, Peter Rymill, Robert Rymill Jr., and Thomas Rymill in Australia, and Jane Buhrman, Nannette Buhrman, and Hugh Cadzow in the United States, for granting access to their family papers and welcoming me into their homes. I was also fortunate to have the support of a great many people in Canada who generously offered assistance, friendship, and advice as the project developed. I would like to thank staff (and former staff) of the Glenbow Museum in Calgary for allowing me to participate in museum activities and for answering my numerous archival queries: Seema Bharadia, Beth Carter, Doug Cass, the late Gerry Conaty, Clifford Crane Bear, Irene Kerr, and Pat Molesky. I am especially grateful to Gerry Conaty, who supported the many museum projects in which I have since been involved and whose guidance, knowledge, and gentle humour will be very much missed by museum and Blackfoot colleagues alike; and to Beth Carter and Irene Kerr, who encouraged me to write this book and discussed many parts of it with me on the countless occasions that we drove through Southern Alberta. Sarah Carter and Pat McCormack of the University of Alberta offered sound advice in the early stages of fieldwork and have also advised on later projects. Colleagues whom I met in Regina and with whom I enjoyed many discussions about issues arising from the research include Lorne Carrier, Rebecca Gibbons, Margaret Hanna, David R. Miller, Sherry Farrell Racette, and Danette Starblanket. In Winnipeg, Jennifer and Wilson Brown made me most welcome in their home, and Jennifer also arranged a visiting fellowship in the Department of History of the University of Winnipeg from 1998 to 1999. I also thank Diane Haglund, Jennine and Blair Krauchi,

Anne Lindsay, Maureen Matthews and Charles Feaver, Jenny Meyer, Katherine Pettipas, Darrell Racine, Corey Whitford, and the staff of the Hudson's Bay Company Archives, all of whom offered support at various stages of researching and writing this book. Morgan Baillargeon and Benoit Theriault of the Canadian Museum of Civilization provided access to collections data and archival materials. In the United States, Betty Prisch facilitated access to the collections of the Rochester Museum and Science Center in Rochester, New York, and Kathryn Murano assisted with subsequent queries; Kristen Mable from the Division of Anthropology at the American Museum of Natural History provided access to the correspondence of David Mandelbaum. Allison Jeffries hosted a research visit to the Museum of the American Indian in New York City before the collections were incorporated into the National Museum of the American Indian (NMAI), Smithsonian Institution. She and Lou Stancari assisted with archival and photographic queries during the early stages of the research, and NMAI media archivist Michael Pahn helped with more recent enquiries. Frank Hantak of the Thomas Hill Hubbard/H.H. Franklin Foundation enthusiastically answered my questions about the Franklin automobile that plays such a key role in this story. I also acknowledge the permission of the various archives listed in the References to consult and cite documents, and to reproduce photographs.

It has been a privilege to get to know so many First Nations people as this project has developed. I am particularly indebted to members of the Star Blanket Cree Nation, Swan Lake First Nation, and the Piikani Nation for their friendship and generosity over the years. Some individuals who supported the initial research have since passed on, but I sincerely hope that they would have been satisfied with this book. There are too many people to mention individually, but I am especially grateful to the late Donald Bigknife, Narcisse Blood, Jenny Bruised Head, Don Daniels, Alvine Mountain Horse, Allan Pard, Elizabeth Pinay, Mike Pinay, Jerry Potts Jr., Pat Provost, Irvine Scalplock, Wayne Scott, Danette Starblanket, Noel Starblanket, the late Gilbert Starr, and Herman Yellow Old Woman, many of whom continued to advise on the book during the writing process.

I have tried, where possible, to use the names by which First Nations individuals are known in their own communities and have been helped in this matter by several colleagues. Assistance with the editing and interpretation of Cree names was provided by Arok Wolvengrey and Doreen Oakes of the Indian Languages Programs at First Nations University of Canada

(Regina), Barry Ahenakew of the Saskatchewan Indian Cultural Centre (Saskatoon), Neal McLeod of Trent University, and Noel Starblanket. Alan Corbiere, Roger Roulette, and Wayne Scott assisted with translation and interpretation of Anishinaabe names; Shirlee Crowshoe, Alvine Mountain Horse, and Duane Mistaken Chief advised on Blackfoot spellings.

I am indebted to Darcy Cullen, of UBC Press, for her encouragement over the years, and to her colleagues Ann Macklem and Deborah Kerr for guiding me through the publication process. Prior to publication, parts of the manuscript were read by Jenny Bruised Head, Jane Buhrman, Nannette Buhrman, Jane Burkinshaw, Lorne Carrier, Beth Carter, Gerry Conaty, Don Daniels, Anita Herle, Alexander King, Jonathan King, Allan Pard, Susan Pender, Jerry Potts Jr., Johan Rasanayagam, Wayne Scott, Danette Starblanket, Noel Starblanket, and Deborah Swallow, as well as by two anonymous reviewers. I am grateful to them all for their thoughtful comments and take full responsibility for any outstanding errors.

First Nations, Museums, Narrations

Introduction

Now or never is the time in which to collect from the natives what
is still available for study. In some cases a tribe has already practically
given up its aboriginal culture, and what can be obtained is merely
that which the older men still remember or care to impart. With the
increasing material prosperity and industrial development of Canada,
the demoralisation or civilisation of the Indians will be going on at an
ever-increasing rate. No short-sighted policy of economy should be
allowed to interfere with the thorough and rapid prosecution of the
anthropological problems of the Dominion. What is lost now will
never be recovered again.

> – Edward Sapir, "An Anthropological Survey
> of Canada," 1911

WITH THESE WORDS, Edward Sapir, director of the newly established
Anthropological Division of the Geological Survey of Canada, concluded
an article in which he discussed the organization's intellectual agenda
and research priorities. The following year, Alfred Cort Haddon (1912, 598),
the eminent University of Cambridge anthropologist, quoted Sapir in an
article that summarized the division's work and outlined the involvement
of British scholarly institutions and societies in anthropological research
in Canada.[1] In the pages that follow, I draw upon the history of anthropological practice in Canada as well as upon current approaches in museum

anthropology to address the changing meanings and continued significance of artifacts that left First Nations communities decades ago and are now in museums in the United Kingdom. My key aim is to demonstrate how the analysis of historic collections can inform awareness of the legacy of colonialism as it relates to the revitalization of cultural heritage and to improving relations between indigenous people and museums. Both these processes have ramifications for the health and well-being of First Nations, and to building mutual respect. If understanding the history of relations between mainstream Canada and Aboriginal people is essential for reconciliation, as many commentators claim, museums, which continue to symbolize colonial power but are well positioned to contribute to public debates, can play a crucial role in this process. Many Canadian museums are now responding to this task, but those in Europe, which contain a great deal of the earliest Aboriginal heritage items, also have a responsibility to end what Wayne Warry (2007) calls the denial of the colonial actions that sustain the social and economic disparities between mainstream society and Aboriginal people. This book lays out some of the ways in which museums located at a considerable geographical and cultural distance from Aboriginal communities might approach this challenge.

The focus of *First Nations, Museums, Narrations* is a 1929 collecting expedition to Western Canada, informally known as the Franklin Motor Expedition, which was sponsored by Cambridge University's Museum of Archaeology and Anthropology (MAA). At the time, First Nations people were subject to extremely invasive policies aimed at assimilation, which, in turn, stimulated an extensive program of ethnographic salvage. The collection that resulted is known as the Rymill Collection, after Robert Rymill, the team member who initiated the expedition. Ethnographic salvage and the professionalization of anthropological expeditions came together in the late nineteenth and early twentieth centuries, a merging manifested in research expeditions that were aided by new technologies such as light-weight movie cameras and other portable recording equipment and that took place by road, rail, airplane, and boat (Bell, Brown, and Gordon 2013). Some of these endeavours involved professional adventurers who sold their stories for personal gain and to raise the profile of their wealthy sponsors. There was money to be made in adventure travel, though funding it could be a struggle, and expedition leaders used a range of strategies to recover their costs. These included recording documentary footage for public distribution, affiliating with the wealthier museums of large North American and European cities, and participating in the lecture circuit on their return. Relationships between professional expeditionaires and museums were mutually beneficial; expedition leaders' claims to scientific respectability were legitimized, and museums built up their collections by having their staff participate directly or by having first refusal on acquired specimens. The mounting of scientific (or referentially scientific) excursions to remote places intersected with and was supported by nationalist programs of expansion – hence their frequent sponsorship by government agencies. Expeditions affiliated with museums, such as the Franklin Motor Expedition, were heavily influenced by wider societal assumptions about progress and the inevitable demise of indigenous peoples. Collecting, as a process of ordering and classification, was thus not only a means of salvaging the material traces of disappearing cultures, it was also used to confirm existing theories about social evolution.

The interwar period witnessed numerous expeditions to all corners of the globe, and anthropological training also became more rigorous during this time. In the United Kingdom, the emphasis on evolution as a paradigm for understanding society and culture, which had dominated much anthropological thought from the mid-nineteenth century, was gradually replaced by attention to social organization and function (Stocking 1999; Kuklick 2007). The new generation of university-trained anthropologists was expected to use more intensive forms of study, particularly fieldwork, to observe indigenous subjects (Stocking 1983). Whereas in the nineteenth century, museum collections and an object-centred approach had been key to the development of theory (in both the United States and the United Kingdom), by the early twentieth century scholars had begun to distance themselves from material culture as well as from the natural sciences. Franz Boas (1907, 928), for example, had come to argue that "the psychological as well as the historical relations of cultures, which are the only objects of anthropological inquiry, can not be expressed by any arrangements based on so small a portion of the manifestation of ethnic life as is presented by specimens." The shift was gradual, however, as George Stocking Jr. (1985, 114-15) notes: "The historically oriented diffusionisms that immediately succeeded [the First World War] still to some extent sustained an object orientation insofar as they conceived culture as a collection of easily transportable thing-like 'elements.' But even within the 'historical school' certain leading figures in both countries had already begun to move away from an object-oriented museum-based anthropology."

Practical as well as intellectual reasons fuelled this change, as the discipline became more secure in its move from museums to universities during the aftermath of the First World War. Colonial authorities, particularly in British territories in the Pacific region and in Africa, argued that if future unrest were to be prevented, it was essential to understand the peoples who lived in colonized areas. In consequence, anthropological studies were seen as vital to supporting the implementation of new forms of enlightened governance (Stocking 1999, 385). In the United Kingdom, courses aimed specifically at colonial officials were available at some universities, and government anthropologist posts in the colonies were often filled by men who had studied anthropology at Oxford, Cambridge, or the London School of Economics. By the 1920s, degree courses in anthropology were much more widely available; methods training and the portable recording technologies available to support data collection had become increasingly sophisticated. The professional discipline was coming into its own (Mills 2003, 2008).

Anthony Shelton (2006, 68) argues that expeditionary collecting "allowed for more controlled and better-documented acquisitions, a requirement that provided criteria for distinguishing the emergent subject position of scientific specialists from amateur collectors." But, of course, expeditions – including those sponsored by museums – took many forms. The Franklin Motor Expedition exemplifies the blurred boundaries between the "amateur" and "professional" periods of anthropology. The team consisted of Donald A. Cadzow (1894-1960), a former employee of the Museum of the American Indian (MAI) in New York who had extensive experience of making field collections and undertaking survey ethnography; Robert Riddoch Rymill (1904-90), an Australian who had recently completed his bachelor's degree in anthropology and economics at Cambridge; and his younger brother, John (1905-68), for whom the expedition was a means to gain experience to realize his ambition of becoming a polar explorer (Figure 1). The three men met in Winnipeg, Manitoba, in late June 1929 and spent much of the following three months driving westward across the Canadian prairies, stopping at numerous First Nations reserves along the way. Though the expedition was smaller in scale than many contemporary examples, the team amassed the largest single collection from the Canadian prairies now in a British museum. It encompasses several hundred artifacts from at least eight First Nations. In this book I use the sources generated by the expedition, which include visual and written documents as well as the collection itself, not only to explore how and why the venture took place, but also to show

Figure 1   The Franklin Motor Expedition team, 1929. *Left to right:* John Rymill, Robert Rymill, and Donald A. Cadzow | Reproduced by permission of University of Cambridge Museum of Archaeology and Anthropology, P45592

how the contexts that informed the creation and subsequent use of collections can shape emerging relationships between museums and First Nations. Although I have chosen to concentrate on one collection assembled at a particular time and place for a British university museum, my arguments have relevance for museums in many parts of the world, particularly those that deal with the complex legacies of colonialism.

A Shifting Museumscape

In the years following Sapir's article, the Anthropological Division of the Geological Survey of Canada, which was housed in what was then called the Victoria Memorial Museum, sent out ethnographers and archaeologists to all parts of Canada to document the languages, cultural traditions, and material heritage of the peoples they encountered.[2] Film footage, photographs, and audio recordings were made, and thousands of pages of notes were taken to detail daily life, cosmological beliefs, and relations with European newcomers prior to the onset of the reserve era. Also, artifacts were collected for the nation, and these are now located in the Canadian Museum of Civilization in Gatineau, Quebec. Together with associated field notes and images, they form an extensive archive illustrating the rich artistic, cultural, and spiritual traditions of the indigenous peoples of Canada. Since arriving in the museum, these materials and many others that were added over the past century have been used in a variety of ways to contribute to knowledge of how First Nations, Métis, and Inuit responded materially, spiritually, and artistically to their lived environment. Some artifacts are displayed and published to highlight the histories, arts, and social lives of the people who produced them; others are studied by artists and craftspeople, who regard them as irreplaceable resources from which to recover fragmented knowledge about techniques and materials; others still have been subject to repatriation requests, as part of indigenous efforts to assert political self-determination and human rights, and to heal the damage caused by the assimilation policies of the recent past.

Given that many founding collections were assembled at a time when indigenous peoples were thought to be assimilating or dying out, the use of these collections by their descendants testifies to the resilience of indigenous peoples, to their present moral and legal rights of ownership, and to the responsibility of museums to make collections accessible. In making this statement, I bear in mind that categories of museum "artifacts" differ according to both indigenous ontologies and museological classifications. Thus, though museums and/or community-run cultural centres may currently be the most appropriate place for many of them, some are living beings and may be better situated in people's homes or given as offerings.

In museums across Canada, engagements between First Nations, Métis, and Inuit people and collections are now relatively common and have resulted in numerous mutually beneficial projects. But these positive relations have not come easily.[3] Since the 1988 protest over The Spirit Sings exhibition, which was developed by the Glenbow Museum in Calgary and a team of guest curators, Canadian museums have thought very carefully about their responses to the needs of the Aboriginal people whose material heritage is in their hands. The Spirit Sings was timed to coincide with the 1988 Winter Olympics held in Calgary. It aimed to attract attention to the rich artistic heritage of the indigenous people of Canada and to highlight collections in European museums, where most of the earliest surviving First Nations, Métis, and Inuit heritage items are now housed (Harrison et al. 1987). The Olympics and the exhibition soon became the focus of a boycott, initiated by the Lubicon Lake Cree from Northern Alberta, to focus international attention on an outstanding land claim. They argued that the exhibition sponsor, Shell Oil Canada – one of the extraction companies then drilling on land they claimed – as well as the provincial and federal governments, who had contributed to the exhibition costs, were trying to appear supportive of First Nations while simultaneously destroying their land and very existence.[4]

Turning the Page: Forging New Partnerships between Museums and First Peoples, a report by the Task Force on Museums and First Peoples (Hill and Nicks 1992), was a direct response to the controversy, and it brought together museum staff and Aboriginal people from across the country to discuss and to make recommendations for the curation of collections from indigenous people. Since its publication – and that of *Gathering Strength,* Volume 3 of the Royal Commission on Aboriginal Peoples (RCAP 1996), which dealt with matters of cultural heritage – significant advances have been made in mainstream Canadian museological practice. Both reports commented on the indivisible relationship between people and the land, and the beliefs and practices connecting the two, which are manifested in material things as well as in intangible heritage. For example, the royal commission report (ibid., 107-8) stated that many Aboriginal peoples understood healing as a holistic concept that referred to "personal and societal recovery from the lasting effects of oppression and systemic racism experienced over generations." It added that "many Aboriginal people are suffering not simply from specific diseases and social problems, but also from a depression of spirit resulting from 200 or more years of damage to their cultures, languages, identities and self-respect. The idea of healing suggests that to reach 'whole health,' Aboriginal people must confront the crippling injuries of the past." Therefore, restoring access to heritage items and supporting efforts for cultural revitalization are acknowledged as crucial to recovering from the effects of colonialism and to building strong communities that could contribute to the nation as a whole.

The recommendations of these reports have been addressed to varying degrees in Canada, but as they are *recommendations* rather than *requirements,* individual museums are at liberty to implement them as they choose.[5] First Nations, Métis, and Inuit advisory committees and internships have been created in some museums (see Syms 1997; Ames 1999; Conaty 2006), whereas others have developed gallery projects in partnership with First Nations community curators and researchers (see Holm and Pokotylo 1997;

McCaffrey 2002; Conaty 2003). Some museums have facilitated knowledge revitalization projects in which historic collections have been the focus for reviving artistic skills (see Marie and Thompson 2004; Thompson and Kritsch 2005). A few have come to be regarded as keeping houses and are used to store ceremonial artifacts that cannot yet be fully repatriated (Pettipas 1993); others have become involved in digitization and online exhibition projects aimed at increasing access and revising how information about collections is generated and disseminated (see Ridington and Hennessy 2008; Phillips 2011, 277-96). In some cases, the repatriation of artifacts has become linked to land claims and the treaty process. For example, both the Canadian Museum of Civilization and the Royal British Columbia Museum have returned artifacts to the Nisga'a, through the Nisga'a Final Agreement, which came into effect on 11 May 2000 (A. Rose 2000; Laforet 2006). Chapter 17 of this treaty recognized that Nisga'a artifacts are central to the continuation of Nisga'a culture, values, and traditions. Items such as headdresses, masks, rattles, blankets, and a totem pole have now been returned to the Nisga'a and are housed in Hli Goothl Wilp-Adokshl Nisga'a, the Nisga'a Museum in Laxgalts'ap, British Columbia. More recently, through the Labrador Inuit Land Claims Agreement of 2005, it was agreed that legal title to artifacts in the Canadian Museum of Civilization would be transferred to the Nunatsiavut government. In addition, the number of First Nations owned and operated cultural centres has increased throughout Canada, though this important development is beyond the scope of this Introduction.

Despite these steps forward, many recommendations made in the reports of the Task Force on Museums and First Peoples (Hill and Nicks 1992) and the Royal Commission on Aboriginal Peoples (RCAP 1996) have yet to be seriously considered, largely due to neglect at the federal, provincial, and territorial levels of governance. Following the release of the royal commission final report, Ottawa claimed that its recommendations were too expensive to implement (Warry 2007, 60). Moreover, as legal scholar Catherine Bell (2009, 84) notes, "Canadian legislation affecting ownership and control of cultural heritage is also largely dated and fails to take into consideration developments in Aboriginal rights law and the unique interests of, and constitutional obligations to, Aboriginal peoples of Canada." In consequence, many First Nations people and museum staff in Canada would agree that more equitable working relationships, which may include the co-management of collections and better integrated indigenous concepts of collections care, are still a long way off and may not be possible or desirable. Not all First Nations are in a position to establish working relations with museums even if they want to. Many recognize that separation from heritage materials has contributed to dysfunction in their communities and that access to such items can foster healing and the strengthening of cultural identity. But these are long-term goals, and other concerns are more pressing. At a time when chronic underfunding, a lack of infrastructure, and the social divisions brought about by the nature of reserve life and its attendant systems of governance have contributed to inadequate housing, allegations of financial mismanagement, unemployment, violence, drug abuse, and other social ills, it is not difficult to see why communities focus on solving these problems rather than locating long-gone cultural artifacts. Given that the royal commission's sound recommendations relating to culture and heritage have yet to receive adequate backing, sufficient financial and practical support for tackling the international dispersal of heritage materials is unlikely to be forthcoming in the immediate future.

Many factors have hindered the sustained implementation of the Task Force on Museums and First Peoples and royal commission recommendations, but nevertheless a considerable realignment of power has occurred between Canadian museums and Aboriginal peoples during the past two decades. In Europe the situation is quite different. Given this, what are the possibilities for establishing relations between First Nations and museums outside of Canada, and what forms might these relations take? Artist and scholar Sherry Farrell Racette (2008, 63-64) points to the difficulties that indigenous people face when trying to make connections with heritage materials and stresses that curators should be aware of the constraints experienced by community researchers:

> It is critical that curators and administrators outside of Canada recognize the on-going struggles of Aboriginal people. Racism is still a daily reality. We are the most impoverished people in the country, with the greatest volume of social and economic challenges. Our struggle to revitalize and protect our cultural traditions is still just that, a struggle. We continue to be marginalized. How does this affect our relationships with museums? There are very few Aboriginal people who can afford to do research in European museum collections. There are only a handful of Aboriginal

curators working in Canadian museums who can initiate projects. Most projects that engage community are museum-centred and directed. Cultural centres are Aboriginal controlled and able to initiate projects, but they are often under-funded and struggle to meet their broad and ambitious mandates. Aboriginal researchers are rarely affiliated with research institutions, and are often unable to access the funding available to others. Funding agencies generally do not recognize community-based researchers, Elders and other traditional knowledge keepers. Even in my own position of relative privilege, this is the first year (since 1989) that I have been able to access research funding. Ironically, of the four times I have visited, two visits have been partially funded by UK sources.

Although many European museums house First Nations, Métis, and Inuit artifacts, some of which are centuries old, until quite recently there have been relatively few attempts to connect with indigenous communities in Canada. In the late 1990s, when I began the research upon which this book is based, I soon discovered that no one from the First Nations visited by the Franklin Motor Expedition had ever been to Cambridge to see the collection. This was not due to a lack of interest; people simply did not know it was there. At that time it was considerably more difficult than it is now for indigenous researchers to locate materials from their communities in British public collections. Several inventories of ethnographic collections in British museums had been printed, but these generally included only minimal information and were rarely accessible outside major libraries (see Gathercole and Clarke 1979; Kwasnik 1993; Proctor 1994; Starkey 1998; Pole 2000). As for the Rymill Collection, very few pieces had been published, and those that had were in scholarly books or journals that were not widely available (see C. Taylor 1975, 76; Brasser 1984, 56). Online collections databases were still in their infancy, and the MAA's own database did not go live until 1996.[6] Furthermore, as Farrell Racette (2008, 63) explains with reference to her own experiences of accessing historic First Nations and Métis collections, the cost of research visits to Europe was (and remains) prohibitive.

There are other concerns as well. Travelling to museums in unfamiliar places can be exciting and richly rewarding, but it can also be emotionally and physically draining, especially when it involves being confronted with stunning artworks using techniques and skills that few now have the knowledge or time to develop, ceremonial artifacts crucial to the maintenance of the spiritual strength of a community, and ancestral remains that speak to colonial injustices and the disregard of human rights. In addition, community-based researchers who have travelled to view overseas collections have spoken candidly about the expectations placed upon them by people from their own communities: that they will return with more than just images and information. Since the mid-1990s, I have participated in many First Nations and Native American research visits to British museums, either as a staff member or, since 2005, as a university-based researcher. During informal conversations, usually outside the museum space and away from curatorial staff, I have frequently been told about the pressure researchers feel to attempt the repatriation of the items they have seen. I have also been told about the difficulties they face when they explain to people at home that repatriation of ceremonial artifacts is a long process, one that some museums are not yet ready to entertain, especially if there are no legal requirements or few precedents upon which to draw, as is currently the case in the United Kingdom. Some researchers have also noted that misunderstandings about how museums operate have sometimes prompted criticism in their own communities that they have received access to artifacts that has been denied to others, the implication being that they are hoarding information or delaying the repatriation process in order to get more free trips.

Visits by indigenous researchers to European collections are still fairly unusual, although they are certainly more common than even a decade ago.[7] In consequence, dialogue between indigenous people and museum staff has been relatively infrequent and sometimes difficult to sustain. Although there are some excellent examples of successful and innovative collaborative exhibition projects, attempts to integrate alternative perspectives into collections management, policy decisions, and outreach have been limited (see Waller 2004; and van Broekhoven, Buijs, and Hovens 2010). As Laura Peers (2009, 80) states in an essay on the approaches of British museums to ancestral remains, whereas indigenous people in settler societies have been vocal in renegotiating policies and practice, in the United Kingdom "arguments have been characterized by the relative absence of overseas Indigenous groups and have effectively consisted of different groups of British people speaking to each other, with very minor input from source communities." Moreover, according to Peers (ibid., 90), the social and political distance between UK museums and originating communities has contributed to a particular colonial mindset in which museums have been hesitant to engage with indigenous people due to the possible repercussions concerning the control of collections.

Peers's comment certainly contains some truth, though her critique needs qualification. Without doubt, the pressure to engage directly with indigenous people, which has occurred in Australia, Canada, New Zealand, and the United States, has not been as strong for British museums. Nonetheless, this does not mean that UK museum staff are complacent or unaware of the issues, though it would be reasonable to say that the ethical responsibilities of working cross-culturally are unevenly understood in the sector.[8] Nor are museum staff in settler societies necessarily more inclined to favour change. My discussions with First Nations and other indigenous researchers who have visited collections in British museums suggest that many feel they have been treated exceptionally well by their hosts and that their concerns have been listened to carefully and with sensitivity. There is a sense that though most UK museum staff are less familiar than their Canadian counterparts with the challenges facing First Nations people who seek access to their material heritage and with the social problems that derive from the troubled relationship between Aboriginal people and the state, they are nevertheless willing to entertain possibilities for collaboration. They recognize that such endeavours bring uncertainty and raise questions about the future of collections, and indeed, about the purpose of museums, and so Nicholas Waller's (2004, 670) phrase – "careful enthusiasm" – is well chosen in this regard. Despite what seems to be general goodwill, there often seems to be a sticking point when it comes to acting. I would suggest that any hesitation is perhaps due less to an overt fear of losing control over collections (though this may have been true a decade or so ago) and is more to do with the fear of getting things "wrong," with being institutionally torn between the needs of originating communities and local audiences, and with concerns about the high financial costs of engaging in such work, none of which should be underestimated.[9]

For the reasons outlined above, the visits to UK museums by First Nations researchers, elders, and other community members since the 1990s have been of key importance. They have contributed to a growing realization among museum professionals that institutional relationships with indigenous people (and other community groups) have been tenuous and that the status quo of projects driven and controlled by museums should not be maintained.[10] This shift in attitude began during the late 1980s, when the so-called crisis in representation related to authority and voice was beginning to be discussed in anthropological and museological literature. The potential impact of pending repatriation legislation, such as the Native American Graves Protection and Repatriation Act, which was passed in the United States in 1990, exhibition controversies such as those surrounding The Spirit Sings, Into the Heart of Africa at the Royal Ontario Museum, and the proposed display of the *Enola Gay* at the Smithsonian's National Air and Space Museum, as well as broader trends in museum practice that aimed to increase access to marginalized groups, were beginning to affect the British museum sector.[11] Staff, particularly in those museums with sizeable collections of ethnographic artifacts, started to question how their institutions represented indigenous peoples and the impact of their curatorial choices. They also began to think more critically about their accountability to these groups, about the longer-term implications of establishing connections with originating communities, and about the responsibilities that such work entails.[12]

Today, many curators, conservators, and other staff in British museums do their utmost to learn from colleagues overseas and to implement change where they can, often working around extremely challenging institutional constraints. This is no easy task. Given Britain's history of colonial expansion, and the sheer mass of material now in British museums that is part of this legacy, staff who work with ethnographic material are usually responsible for collections that are larger and broader in geographical and cultural scope than those curated by their Canadian counterparts. At the MAA, for example, the entire collection is estimated to include some 800,000 artifacts split between Archaeology and Anthropology, almost 200,000 photographs, and an extensive documentary archive drawn from all over the world (Thomas 2011, 4). The number of items in the Anthropology section, bearing in mind discrepancies in how they might be counted and given that the collection is constantly growing, is estimated at approximately 200,000 (Anita Herle, MAA, pers. comm., 5 January 2012). Despite its size and extent, the Anthropology collection has only two curators and one collections manager, which represents an increase of two permanent staff members since the late 1990s.[13] Also, the MAA has had several grant-funded contract positions to cover various areas of collections management (including my own from 1995 to 1997). Like many university museums, the MAA draws on the voluntary assistance of graduate students, but there are limits to how far students can participate in managing collections and developing policy.

Taken together, the points above have contributed to a situation where UK museum staff do what is realistically possible, given the strain on resources, but the truth is that collaborative projects with indigenous people have involved the larger institutions that have curatorial teams with a range of regional specialties and that are often better-resourced financially. These museums currently have three dedicated curatorships for collections from the Americas.[14] In Canada there are comparatively more curatorial posts with remits for First Nations, Métis, and Inuit collections, which is to be expected given the greater immediacy between Canadian museums and Aboriginal people. Nevertheless, although Canadian museum staff may not have to juggle with quite such culturally diverse collections as their UK colleagues, they do need to be mindful of responding to the needs of their neighbours in ways that British museum staff do not. It is also worth pointing out, for the benefit of readers less familiar with the museum landscape in the United Kingdom, that British museums are governed in a variety of ways, and that this affects the availability of funding sources, staff remits, and the expectations regarding the identity of their primary audiences. Museums fall into one of three general categories – those managed and funded by local authorities (such as Exeter's Royal Albert Memorial Museum and Art Gallery); national museums (such as the British Museum); and university museums (such as the MAA). There are also private and military museums, and organizations such as the National Trust for Scotland, which own materials originating from First Nations and other indigenous groups.

Theoretical Contexts

 My approach to the changing relationships between First Nations people and British museums is informed by three closely related sets of scholarly literature: theories and histories of collecting, specifically in colonial situations; material culture theory, which explores the intersection of human and artifact histories; and the contemporary realignment of relations between museums and indigenous people, and how this fits with indigenous perspectives on scholarship more broadly. I address each of these in turn, but before doing so, I wish to make clear that my own experience of developing relationships between museums and First Nations is not based solely on scholarly literature grounded in academic theory and articulated in print. Though I acknowledge the value of this work, and I draw upon its useful parts, much of it simply does not align with the way in which many First

Nations people of my acquaintance speak about "artifacts." This is not to say that First Nations people and museums approach collections in entirely oppositional ways – differing views can sometimes rub along. However, though some critical, scholarly approaches to artifacts are helpful, I am also influenced by discussions with First Nations friends and colleagues whose theories about relationships between human beings, other-than-human beings, places, and artifacts are anchored in language and the practices of being who they are. These theories are not written, but they are experienced and are just as important (if not more so) for understanding the relations between people and artifacts, whether in museums or not. I am reminded here of an observation made by a ceremonial leader during a break at a Thunder Medicine Pipe opening I attended at the Piikani Nation in the spring of 2010. On that day, I should have been participating in a workshop about Blackfoot collections at a nearby museum. As we chatted outside the tipi about what I would have been doing at the museum, I was told, "You'll learn much more by being here anyway."

All three sets of literature upon which I draw have been influenced to varying degrees by scholarly debates regarding the politics of representation. With the reflexive turn in anthropology, which challenged dominant research paradigms based on asymmetrical power relations, researchers began to reject the realist and objectivist style that had long characterized conventional methods and assumptions of the discipline (Clifford and Marcus 1986; Marcus and Fischer 1986). At the same time, indigenous researchers worldwide critically called attention to issues of voice and the inherent problem of the silencing and thus the diminishing of perspectives of groups that mainstream society had already marginalized (see L.T. Smith 1999; Battiste 2000). Since the 1970s, with the expansion of Native American and indigenous studies programs at the university level across North America, as well as training opportunities in curatorship, there has been a florescence of scholarship in history, archaeology, anthropology, and critical art theory, which has contributed to debates on representation in museums and galleries, as well as to the discussions concerning the wider political implications of the exclusion of Aboriginal voices from these arenas (see, for example, Jessup and Bagg 2002; Sillar and Fforde 2005; Smith and Wobst 2005; and Sleeper-Smith 2009).

Indigenous scholars in Canada and elsewhere continue to call for the decolonization of research methods and outcomes, and for the recognition of indigenous conceptual frameworks so as to balance the inequalities inherent in non-indigenous intellectual traditions. They also call for a sincere commitment to include indigenous voices in arts institutions and heritage initiatives in ways that go beyond one-off projects so as to stop the continued essentialization of indigenous peoples. Lee-Ann Martin (2002), curator of contemporary Canadian Aboriginal art at the Canadian Museum of Civilization, for example, points to the long history of "othering" of Aboriginal art and calls for museum and gallery staff to critically acknowledge the historical reasons for its under-representation and exclusion from mainstream galleries. Sherry Farrell Racette (2008, 60), meanwhile, calls for a better understanding of the role that historic collections can play in processes of decolonization. Drawing upon these processes, as outlined by the Native Hawaiian lawyer and activist Poka Laenui, she writes that "for many of us, the process of rediscovery and recovery includes work with museum collections, and our encounters there move us into the second stage of mourning. People visiting museum collections are often at different stages of the process of decolonization, and some have not begun the process." Though this point is made in relation to physical engagement with historic collections in museum storerooms and galleries, photographs of artifacts and the stories of their accumulation can also play a part, as I hope will become clear from this book.

Collecting Practices

What does it mean to collect? Sharon Macdonald (2006, 94-95) reminds us that collecting is "a set of distinctive – though also variable and changing – practices that not only produces knowledge about objects but also configures particular ways of knowing and perceiving." Moreover, collecting is a deeply political activity and is never neutral. It raises questions related to the power of one culture to collect from another, to who grants that authority, and to what images of a culture are constructed through the collecting process. Being a collector is about being in control, and building a collection involves conscious decisions about arranging its contents. Collecting is a profoundly human activity related to how people construct the world around them. It is "classification lived, experienced in three dimensions. The history of collections is thus the narrative of how human beings have striven to accommodate, to appropriate and to extend the taxonomies and systems of knowledge they have inherited" (Elsner and Cardinal 1994, 2). Or, as Susan Stewart (1993, 151, 160) puts it, the act of collection "seeks a form of self-enclosure" in which the collector "can gain control over repetition or series by defining a finite set ... or by possessing the unique object." "The collection," she writes, replaces history with classification, with order beyond the realm of temporality" (ibid., 151). Thus, in museums, as order is imposed upon artifacts, space and time are collapsed, with all time "made simultaneous or synchronous within the collection's world" (ibid., 151). Susan Pearce (1992, 1995, 1998) also examines ideas about control in a series of influential volumes concerning the psychology of collecting. Her work draws heavily on semiotic analyses to consider how meaning is formed during collection making and how collections are related to personal narrative and identity. Consider, for instance, the following comment from Pearce (1992, 38):

> The crucial semiotic notion is that of metaphor and metonymy, a key which helps us to unlock one fundamental aspect of the nature of collections. Everything which goes into a collection of whatever kind has done so as a result of selection. The selection process is the crucial act of the collector, regardless of what intellectual, economic or idiosyncratic reasons he may have when he decides how his selection will work, what he will choose and what he will reject. What he chooses bears an intrinsic, direct and organic relationship, that is a metonymic relationship, to the body of material from which it was selected because it is an integral part of it. But the very act of its selection adds to its nature. By being chosen away and lifted out of the embedding metonymic matrix, the selected collection now bears a representative or metaphorical relationship to its whole. It becomes an image of what the whole is believed to be, and although it remains an intrinsic part of the whole, it is no longer merely a detached fragment because it has become imbued with meaning of its own.

Stewart and Pearce offer useful insights into how material things are used in various ways by the people who assemble collections (see also Alsop 1982; Elsner and Cardinal 1994; Belk 2001; Pearce and Martin 2002; and MacGregor 2007). Their work is most concerned with the selection processes inherent in collecting and how they are shaped by values, desires, and ways of thinking about the world. Although their studies deal with European collecting habits rather than the motives for acquiring the cultural materials of non-European peoples (though see Pearce 1995, 327-51), their approach to collecting culture can be applied to collecting of many forms and has had a lasting influence on how scholars theorize museum objects (Dudley 2012, 2). Indeed, together with the work of other scholars who have explored collecting as a phenomenon, it has enabled the construction of a typology of collecting praxis that is relevant to how we understand the linkages between collecting and colonialism, and in turn, between collecting, colonialism, and anthropology. Ruth Phillips (1998), for example, has focused on the collecting of souvenir arts produced by First Nations and Native Americans in the Great Lakes region. She identifies four types of collector. Professional ethnologists and their students, often based in museums, viewed ethnicity and material culture as "isomorphically related" and attempted to secure "representative" collections that fit pre-determined categories of use while excluding evidence of acculturation. Native agents used their community connections to supply external collectors – especially those associated with museums – with examples of artifacts required to fill gaps, thus assisting the project of creating representative series of material culture. Rare art collectors, motivated by the pursuit of "authenticity," valued age and rarity over the recent and the common. Tourists, who saw Native-made souvenir arts as trophies to be consumed, displayed them as "a sentimental brush with an exotic and noble past" (ibid., 65). Of course, as Phillips (ibid., 66) observes, there is fluidity between these ideal types, and as I show in this book, the men who participated in the Franklin Motor Expedition cross-cut them all.

Collecting Histories

In her study of the 1948 American-Australian Scientific Expedition to Arnhem Land, Sally May (2010, 11) writes that, in the past, ethnographic collections were believed to provide objective information about human societies, in that objects "stood" for cultural "facts." In her view, ethnographic collections assembled on expeditions are more representative of cross-cultural encounters than of the indigenous societies from whom they were acquired. With this point in mind, I turn to how scholarly literature has addressed collecting as it relates to indigenous peoples. The act of amassing non-European things by Europeans has long been regarded as a manifestation of the antiquarian imagination and, during the colonial era, as a search for the "exotic" Other (Hooper-Greenhill 1992; Barringer and Flynn 1998). By the beginning of the twentieth century, the collecting impulse had taken on new dimensions as a result of increasing cross-cultural encounters commensurate with processes of colonialism. Historians and anthropologists have described this development as a "scramble" for art and artifacts (Cole 1985; Schildkrout and Keim 1998) in which material culture, thought [trophies] to encapsulate the arts, beliefs, and traditions of indigenous peoples, was [helping/valuing] valued more highly than the people themselves. Following from traditions [indigenous] of collecting in the natural sciences, anthropological collecting was couched [lives] in scientific terms, and artifacts came to be seen primarily as specimens. Although objects were central to the development of anthropological theory in the United Kingdom, disciplinary histories tell us that during the first half of the twentieth century, museums and material culture studies fell from favour in British anthropology. This was due partly to the uncomfortable and outdated association between evolutionary thought and displays of material culture from non-Western societies but also to the turn to structural functionalism, in which anthropologists began to use social structure, language, and belief as analytical frames for understanding the world (Stocking 1985). In Britain the study of material culture was revived with the development of Marxist anthropology and archaeology, in which debates over production, exchange, technology, and consumption were closely tied to analysis of the networks in which artifacts circulated. At the same time, with the growth of what has been referred to as "the new museology" (Vergo 1988), museums began to be viewed less as dusty storehouses full of the detritus of past civilizations and more as dynamic spaces in which engagements with artifacts could shape political, cultural, and aesthetic values. These theoretical shifts in anthropology and archaeology more broadly contributed to the reassessment of how collections were assembled and the judgments implicit in their formulation.

Many scholars who have looked at collecting as a social phenomenon have concentrated on its relationship with colonialism. Much of the resulting literature has examined natural history collecting, but many excellent studies have explored the development of ethnographic collections by focusing on the biographies of collectors and situating their collecting habits within the impact of colonialism more broadly (see Krech and Hail 1999; O'Hanlon and Welsch 2000; Gosden and Knowles 2001; Shelton 2001a, 2001b; Penny 2002). This is unsurprising, given that as museology was emerging as a specific field of study allied to established disciplines such as anthropology, archaeology, art history, and psychology, anthropologists were questioning the colonial origins of their own discipline and the validity of its representational approach. Thus, anthropology, history, and museology came together as scholars and curators sought to make sense of the holdings in museums.

As collections began to be seen as artifacts in themselves, and the analysis of artifacts broadened out beyond functionalism, studies of collecting practices started to emphasize how social relations were mediated by the exchange and circulation of artifacts. Early collecting studies tended to privilege the experience of collectors and glossed over the dialogic nature of acquisition processes. This resulted in an uneven understanding of ethnographic collecting as a dynamic relational process. Though we now know a great deal about the intellectual rationale that drove collectors of ethnographic materials from the Enlightenment onward, we know considerably less about what indigenous people made of their activities. There are, of course, exceptions. Two of the most influential scholars to scrutinize the complexities of collecting are Douglas Cole and Nicholas Thomas. Cole's *Captured Heritage* (1985) examines the rivalry between collectors on the Northwest Coast of North America who operated on behalf of metropolitan museums during the heyday of anthropological collecting, and the role of Aboriginal people in their exchanges. Thomas's *Entangled Objects* (1991) studies the circulation of artifacts in the Pacific to show that indigenous people shaped the content of collections in a significantly greater manner than surface-level analysis might suggest. These two works have influenced later studies, such as Ruth Phillips's *Trading Identities* (1998), which deals with the lengthy participation of First Nations and Native Americans in the production of souvenir arts for the Great Lakes tourist trade. Similarly, Jenny Newell's (2005, 2010) studies of how Polynesians collected European goods just as Europeans collected from Polynesians, challenge the conventional view of collecting as a one-way extractive process. Indeed, many scholars working on collecting histories in the Pacific, where there is a long tradition of anthropological theorizing on exchange – of which collecting could be considered an extension – have been influenced by Thomas's early work (see, for example, Küchler 1997; Herle 1998, 2003; Venbrux 2001; and Henare 2005). Of particular relevance to this book is Sally May's *Collecting Cultures: Myth, Politics, and Collaboration in the 1948 Arnhem Land Expedition* (2010). May also addresses multiple perspectives on a particular ethnographic collecting expedition by drawing upon oral histories as well as written and photographic sources. In so doing, she underscores the differing perspectives and interests of the people who have a stake in the resulting collection, as well as the varying motives of those who contributed to its creation in the past. Together, the studies cited above reveal that as social relations are mediated by material culture, a focus on agency in collecting exchanges can also critically inform how we understand the lived experiences of colonialism. I draw upon these ideas in my approach to the Rymill Collection, and in particular, in my efforts to understand how the First Nations people who encountered the Franklin Motor Expedition responded to its colonial collecting project. Works such as these have conclusively shown that cross-cultural collecting is a process of constant negotiation and that ethnographic collections are the outcome of multiple and sometimes contested conversations (see also Adams 2009; and Beck 2010).

In part, the hesitancy of early studies to address indigenous experiences of collecting may have been due to the biases of historical documentation. Unfamiliarity with the cultural contexts from which collections derived has also contributed to representations of collecting as an extractive process, which denies agency to other participants in the transactions. Certainly, such studies have added greatly to what is known about collecting as a social process, and in turn, how the display of artifacts has shaped popular imaginaries of indigenous peoples, but we must nevertheless ask what value they have for marginalized people who seek access to artifacts to tell their own histories. Whose interests are served by studies of collecting? Are collecting histories of more value to museums and historians of science and anthropology than to anyone else? Do they continue to add to entrenched processes of what Julie Cruikshank (2000, 71-96) terms "cultural erasure"? Most historical studies of collecting encounters have evaded these questions, but I raise them in hopes that thinking about collecting and how it is conceptualized will be moved forward.

Collecting in Regional Contexts

In the Canadian context, much of the literature on collectors and collecting has focused on the Northwest Coast and the connections between the development of museums and the discipline of anthropology, particularly as it related to the Boasian salvage paradigm (see Fenn 1996; Duncan 2000; Jacknis 2002; Wickwire 2005; Nyce 2008). There is also a sizeable literature on collecting in the Arctic and Subarctic, with scholars discussing the interactions between collectors and Inuit and Aboriginal people, and the treatment of artifacts as commodities made specifically for sale (see Ross 1984; Hail and Duncan 1989; Krech 1989; Oberholtzer 1996, 2002, 2008; Krupnik and Fitzhugh 2001). These works consider how amateur and professional collectors sought to acquire and categorize artifacts, and they provide a broad framework for the intellectual currents driving collecting activity in the late nineteenth and early twentieth centuries. All these approaches have proven helpful points of departure for this book. Not all studies have dealt with collecting in the past, however. Patricia McCormack's (1991) reflections on her experience of making a museum collection at Fort Chipewyan in Northern Alberta offers a useful contrast to historical studies and provides insights into indigenous agency and decision-making processes that are less speculative than those found in many historical studies (see also J.C.H. King 1991b; and Tracy 1991).

Surprisingly, there are fewer studies of collecting on the Canadian Prairies than one might expect, given the long-standing practice of collecting from First Nations in this area. This phenomenon is now being examined in a small (but growing) number of historical studies that reflect recent trends in museum-based research and ethnohistorical scholarship (see Peers and Pettipas 1996; Brownstone 2002, 2008; S. Pratt 2006; Berry 2011). These works give valuable historical context for my own research, although most deal with nineteenth-century collections that were assembled earlier than the Rymill Collection. Nonetheless, some scholars have touched upon collecting as conducted during the early twentieth century. Katherine Pettipas's (1994) analysis of anthropological activity on the Prairies in the context of ceremonial repression, for example, is a key source for understanding the impact of colonial assimilation policies on some of the First Nations visited by the Franklin Motor Expedition. Through an extensive reading of archival documentation, she shows that First Nations people viewed some anthropologists as sympathetic listeners, just as some government officials regarded them as meddlesome. Less extensive in their discussion, but still extremely helpful for understanding the range of materials acquired on the prairies during the late nineteenth and early twentieth centuries, are James VanStone's catalogues of Plains Cree (1983) and Blackfoot (1992) collections in the Field Museum, Chicago. Both include introductory chapters that situate the collections within the wider social and political context of assimilation that made collecting on the Prairies possible. Complementing these studies is Hugh Dempsey's (2011, 163-99) autobiography, which describes his experiences of collecting Blackfoot artifacts for the

Glenbow Museum from the 1950s until his retirement in 1991. He reflects upon his mixed feelings when Blackfoot people who were keepers of sacred artifacts, or who otherwise had access to them, requested that he buy them for the museum's collection. Finally, Michelle Hamilton's (2010) study of relations between First Nations and museums in Southern Ontario in the later nineteenth and early twentieth centuries offers a nuanced discussion of the intellectual rationale for collecting in this part of Canada and how First Nations from that region are now involved in projects of self-representation with the development of their own museums and cultural centres. Though her emphasis is on the motivations of collectors to acquire, rather than the reasons that First Nations people chose to engage in these exchanges, her work points to the complexities of collecting in terms of ideology and practice, and demonstrates that it was a negotiated process rather than one in which Euro-Canadians were pitted against Aboriginal people.[15]

This book builds upon the literature outlined above. It also builds upon what Cory Willmott (2006, 212) characterizes as "colonialist" and "nationalist" traditions in academic research, which she discusses in relation to their intersection with collecting practices and the subsequent exhibition strategies of museums. She states that much scholarly literature on the development of North American anthropology, and on collecting culture specifically, has conflated these models and that her own comparative study of museum anthropology in the United States and Canada facilitates reflection on their differences. Willmott (ibid., 213) summarizes the two traditions as follows:

> The colonial model is characterized by aristocratic participation and elitist principles; physical and symbolic distance and 'otherness'; personal and sovereign trophies of conquest; and relative autonomy from state support and policy-making. In contrast, the nationalist model consists of mercantile participation and democratic principles, especially with regard to knowledge possession; collapse of physical and symbolic distance and 'otherness'; personal and state emblems of collective national identity; and an intimate relationship with state support and policy-making.

Whereas Willmott examines North American collecting institutions and their relationship with the politics of nationalism and identity, my focus on a British museum adds an international dimension to this topic and reminds us that at the time of the Franklin Motor Expedition, Canada was still very much tied to the United Kingdom through its status as a self-governing dominion. These points are explored in more depth in Chapter 2.

This book is also concerned with the issue of voice. Most scholarship on ethnographic collecting, regardless of regional focus, concentrates on the perspectives of collectors and often remains silent regarding other viewpoints. Although locating evidence of the opinions of indigenous participants can be difficult, a nuanced reading of collections can offer insights into the range of their concerns and priorities, as well as into why certain artifacts and not others were sold. Moreover, the reflections of First Nations people on historic collections and collecting as a practice can challenge how museums have conventionally associated collections with the production of knowledge. Consider, for example, this statement from Jerry Potts Jr., a Piikani ceremonial leader: "They sent people over here in 1929 to collect this stuff, but going through the descriptions here, it is pretty clear that they don't have an explanation of what they have" (Jerry Potts Jr., author interview, Fort Macleod, 18 August 1999). Comments like this – which I have heard many times during the past twenty years – force museums to confront their own lack of knowledge about collections, and call into question their authority to speak for other people. A further comment from the same interview concerns how First Nations people can utilize collections to enhance their own knowledge in ways, and for reasons, that may not be immediately obvious to museums. Potts described his own artistic practice and the difficulty of learning the traditional techniques that so few people now remember:

> I didn't have anyone here I could go to ask how you mix paints to paint designs on rawhide. I've done years of experimenting with pigments and oil mixtures and that kind of a thing to try and capture that same finish, so you see that's why I'm saying that I've had to go to museums and study and look. There's stuff you can feel and touch. You know you can look at a photograph of a parfleche, but when you see it for real, there's something about it that comes at you.

My approach in this book is to incorporate contemporary reflections on historic exchange processes, such as those offered by Jerry Potts, into my analysis of collections and collecting as much as to highlight the dialogic nature of collection making as to reflect upon how the knowledge-producing activities of museums (whether in settler societies or not) have shaped representations of indigenous peoples. In this sense, the book responds to questions raised by Mary Louise Pratt (1992, 4-5) in relation to how European travel writing created the "domestic subject" of imperialism – specifically, "How has travel and exploration writing produced 'the rest of the world' for European readers at particular points in Europe's expansionist trajectory?" Making collections and displaying them were akin to collecting travel experiences and putting them onto a page. As I show in Chapters 4 and 6, the words and images produced during and after the Franklin Motor Expedition, and the collection itself, were used to construct narratives about First Nations people over which they had little control but which had a lasting impact.

Narratives and Biographies

A second body of literature from which I work, which continues to influence scholarly approaches to collecting histories and contemporary museology, concerns the social dimensions of things. This literature borrows from the scholarship in archaeology and material culture studies of, for example, Ian Hodder (1987, 1989, 2012) and Daniel Miller (1987, 2005, 2007, 2010), both of whom address how artifacts are embedded in social relations and, as such, are active players in the making of cultural meanings. Hodder's and Miller's approaches have transformed how scholars think about the material world. Indeed, Miller's work, which is grounded in extensive ethnographic fieldwork and draws upon universal experiences of the everyday (such as love, death, grief, and social isolation), has reached an audience far beyond the academy (Geismar 2011, 213). Similarly, Arjun Appadurai's edited collection *The Social Life of Things* (1986), particularly the chapter by Igor Kopytoff (1986), has influenced scholars in a range of disciplines interested in how the lives of people and things are mutually constituted, but has been especially relevant for how material culture theory can be extended to museum collections. The basic premise is that artifacts cannot be fully understood at just one point in their existence; processes of production, of circulation, and of consumption must all be taken into account. For Kopytoff (ibid., 68), a cultural biography approach focuses on the chain of events through which an object becomes culturally marked and unmarked as a particular type of thing. He writes, "A culturally informed biography of an object would look at it as a culturally constructed entity, endowed with culturally specific meanings, and classified and reclassified into culturally constituted categories." In essence, the meanings and values of objects change as they age and move between various locales. Thus, an artifact acquires a patina of histories, and its current significance is related to the people who have interacted with it over time. This way of thinking has implications for how museum collections are theorized, as Sandra Dudley (2012) has recently observed. Although museum objects have commonly been treated as *de*contextualized and indeed as "dead," this view constrains the possibilities for thinking about objects in their new or *re*contextualized locations. In contrast, the cultural biography approach allows us to see that "museum objects continue to participate in socialised relationships and interactions and to be attributed particular – and changing – meanings and values as a result" (ibid., 2).

Studies that trace the trajectories through which artifacts travel, from the idea that first prompts their creation, to the process of manufacture, to their acquisition and subsequent consumption and use by successive owners, are now found throughout the social sciences literature (see, for example, Hoskins 1998; Gosden and Marshall 1999; Jackson 2000; and DeSilvey 2006). The literature on consumption, on agency, and what is termed "materiality" has also been influential in the wider field of material culture studies (see D. Miller 1987, 2005; and Gell 1998), though as Tim Ingold (2007, 3) observes, it has so privileged objects over processes of making and consideration of how materials themselves shape an artifact's final form that "the concept of materiality, whatever it might mean, has become a real obstacle to sensible enquiry into materials, their transformations and affordances." For Ingold (ibid., 9), many "so-called studies of material culture" are based in "a world of objects that has, as it were, already crystallized out from the fluxes of materials and their transformations." Indeed, few studies that claim to be framed by a biographical approach take the production of artifacts as their starting point. Instead, they begin with the fully formed object and thus neglect the changeability of things and the environmental factors that contribute to continual processes of change. Rosemary Joyce (2012, 124) also critiques the presumed linearity of the biographical approach, remarking that despite its usefulness as a model, the concept of biography does not always fit well with what she terms "the situation of everydayness." "Biographies," she writes, "are supposed to have distinct beginnings and ends. But objects actually move in and out of relationships, from treasure to trash and back again." Joyce's comment relates to how archaeologists have used the biographical approach, but it could easily be applied to museological research and would raise similar problems. A more useful model, she suggests, would be to consider "the itinerary of things" as "evident in the traces of their passage." Ian Cook and Divya Tolia-Kelly (2010, 111) identify further limitations of the biographical approach. The first concerns its impression that artifacts are discrete, stable, and bounded, "with simple, identifiable 'origins' and destinations, rather than more complex assemblages." The second concerns the emphasis on consumption, which (for some scholars) overshadows the role that material things play "in other aspects of (other) people's lives, producers in particular."

As I show throughout this book, despite its limitations, a biographical approach can clarify thinking about how artifacts have contributed to particular representational tropes in museum displays. Nevertheless, the model is far less helpful for considering how the indigenous people who made the items may have related to them historically, and how (and indeed, *if*) the meanings these artifacts have for their descendants do change over time. In part, the problem may arise from trying to fit indigenous artifacts into theories developed in a very specific intellectual tradition, without taking sufficient care to understand how they articulate with indigenous ways of knowing. However, some recent publications have attempted to overcome these problems by critiquing and offering challenges to dominant taxonomies. These works relate very closely to this book as they are based on ethnographic research undertaken in the Northern Plains of North America. First, Kenneth Lokensgard's (2010) study of the consequences of cultural commoditization of Blackfoot ceremonial items uses both Maussian concepts of gifts and commodities and Blackfoot concepts of *pommaksiistsi* (ritual transfer) to think through the wider impact of colonization on Blackfoot communities and how it relates to contemporary engagements with museums. Second, Maria Zedeño (2008, 363) has looked at indigenous meanings of ceremonial bundles so as to "refine or build classificatory criteria that allow for culturally contextual understandings of object worlds." By considering the concepts of animacy and agency, she addresses the power that resides within ceremonial bundles and how it relates to the biography of an individual bundle as a whole and to the object-persons it contains. Both writers draw upon discussions with Blackfoot individuals who are themselves ceremonial leaders with the authority to speak about such matters, so the works are also excellent examples of emergent collaborative research practice, which makes up the third body of literature informing my own study.

Collaborative Curation

There is now a growing literature on collaborative anthropology and archaeology, and how it fits with attempts to decolonize research more broadly (see Lassiter 2005; Colwell-Chanthaphonh and Ferguson 2008; and Starn 2011). Within this framework, the assumed right to know, implicit in anthropological research since its genesis, is questioned, and asymmetric power relations are repositioned. Related to this is a demand for recognition that indigenous epistemologies and research protocols have validity and for transparency regarding the control of data. In practical terms, this means that some topics are off limits for external researchers; this will be apparent in the following pages, particularly in Chapter 5, where I discuss the responses of people from the communities visited by the Franklin Motor Expedition to the artifacts that it acquired.

Much of this literature is relevant to museum anthropology. Working with historic collections is rarely confined to questions about the past; rather, it can raise questions and challenges for social relations in the present. This point is made explicit by James Clifford in his much-cited essay "Museums as Contact Zones" (1997), which identifies factors that have contributed to tensions between indigenous people, museums, and museum audiences. He begins by describing an encounter in the basement of the Portland Museum of Art, Oregon, between a group of Tlingit elders, museum staff, and the museum's Northwest Coast collection. The elders responded to the historic artifacts by relating them to ongoing political struggles concerning access to resources. The stories told around the artifacts became starting points from which to negotiate new sets of relationships with non-Native people. Clifford (ibid., 192, emphasis in original) adapted the concept of a contact zone from Mary Louise Pratt (1992) and suggested that "when museums are seen as contact zones, their organizing structure as a *collection* becomes an on-going historical, political, moral *relationship* – a power-charged set of exchanges, of push and pull."[16] Within this framework, competing agendas collide, but as Clifford (1997, 213) notes, "all sites of collection ... seem like places of encounter and passage"; he adds that "by thinking of their mission as contact work ... museums may begin to grapple with the real difficulties of dialogue, alliance, inequality, and translation."

Clifford's essay contributes to a growing body of work that advocates the renegotiation of relationships between museums and indigenous communities worldwide (see Tamarapa 1996; Ames 1999; Kreps 2003; Hirsch and

Pickworth 2005; Janes and Conaty 2005; and Gabriel and Dahl 2008). Related to this is an emerging literature that evaluates the potential for sharing ethnographic and curatorial authority through the use of new technologies (see Christen 2006, 2011; Basu 2011; Geismar and Mohns 2011; and Salmond 2012). These "virtual repatriation" or "digital repatriation" projects have brought unprecedented access to many items that were previously out of reach for indigenous communities. These labels and the processes involved have been somewhat contentious and have been described as providing "lip service to an idealized concept" (Houghton 2010), though Christen (2011, 187) cautions against making assumptions about what they imply, noting that "while some may assume on first glance that the digital object – as a surrogate – is meant to replace the physical object, no one, standard definition, nor agreed-upon terminology, characterizes the multiple practices of collecting institutions, individuals, or local community groups surrounding the return of cultural and historical materials to Indigenous communities in their digital form." Such initiatives certainly raise difficult questions regarding open access, indigenous copyright, the control of information, and whether the artifact is of greater importance than its associated knowledge. Nevertheless, community responses to virtual repatriation and its possibilities for creating, recording, and preserving information for future generations have often been very positive. Institutional participants in these initiatives are not blind to the problems of working digitally with cultural heritage items. Many collaborate with originating community and diaspora colleagues to develop technologies that address cultural protocols and also challenge the legacies of colonial collecting practices and existing institutional structures so as to enable interpretation of heritage materials that takes account of alternative knowledge systems. Indeed, the potential of these projects to reconfigure how collections and museums are thought of, but also to underscore how the balance of power in relationships between museums and communities might shift, is one of the most exciting developments in contemporary museum practice.

Tracking the Franklin Motor Expedition

In these changing professional and theoretical contexts, I embarked on research into the Rymill Collection of Northern Plains material. After having received qualifications in history, museum studies, and social anthropology, I worked as a documentation assistant in the Anthropology section of the MAA and, in 1996, was awarded a grant from the Crowther-Beynon Fund to document the Rymill Collection and produce an illustrated catalogue (Brown 1998), an in-house document that was not intended to reach out to First Nations. As I familiarized myself with the collection, the question of how to proceed became increasingly challenging. One area of tension concerned the many items associated with ceremony. I was not sure whether they should be photographed, and indeed, whether I could even handle them. Traditional care practices that were being incorporated into North American museums under the guidance of elders and ceremonial leaders, such as storing sacred artifacts separately, smudging by burning sweetgrass or other plants before approaching ceremonial material, and ensuring that menstruating staff did not touch it, were not yet being implemented in the United Kingdom (see, for example, Pettipas 1993, 93; Conaty and Dumka 1996; Hanna 1999, 46-47; Clavir 2002; Ogden 2004; and Dignard et al. 2008). Although the MAA would have considered taking on such practices where feasible, doing so without having received proper instruction from persons who had the authority to teach was clearly problematic.

Matters were complicated by the large number of communities with ties to the Rymill Collection as well as its high percentage of ceremonial material; indeed, in the early stages of the catalogue project, no MAA staff (myself included) had any comprehension of the potential power of some of these items. We suspected that cultural protocols might need to be addressed, but we did not know what they were or how to proceed. This situation is common to many museums that are far from the communities they represent; curators frequently have only the most superficial understanding of artifacts and very little idea of whom to ask for help (assuming they even know which communities they should approach in the first place).[17] In Britain many staff working with world cultures collections have quite limited or even *no* direct experience of traditional care. That said, many are familiar with the concept through the growing literature on the topic and also through discussions with overseas colleagues and indigenous visitors to UK collections. British museums are now aware that there may be cultural protocols to observe when curating and conserving indigenous heritage materials (even if knowledge of what those protocols are remains hazy). By contrast, in the late 1990s the idea of traditional care was still very new. For guidance on this issue, I consulted with curatorial staff in three of the largest museums in the Prairie provinces (Winnipeg's Manitoba Museum, Regina's

Royal Saskatchewan Museum, and Calgary's Glenbow Museum) and with Laura Peers, then a post-doctoral researcher at the University of Winnipeg, who had visited the MAA in 1996 to view the Anishinaabe collections.[18] We concluded that although photographing ceremonial artifacts was potentially problematic, images were more helpful than written descriptions for identifying what was in the collection. If First Nations people were to learn about what was in the MAA, there were few viable alternatives.

The resulting catalogue followed the format devised by Gillian Crowther (1993) for her catalogue of the MAA's Northwest Coast collections. Produced on a shoestring budget, at a time when cut-and-paste meant just that, it contained a brief overview of the Franklin Motor Expedition and its participants, followed by a record for each artifact arranged by nation. Every record included the accession number, a black-and-white image, Robert Rymill's collection notes and identification number, a more extensive (but still relatively brief) description of the item written by myself, the keywords used in the MAA's computerized database, and the dimensions. Records for items that could not be located or had been destroyed by moth damage several decades previously were included, though obviously without illustrations. To restrict the circulation of images of ceremonial material, only five copies of the catalogue were produced. I used two of these during my fieldwork, and the remaining three are kept by the MAA, along with the negatives and original colour photographs, which are stored in three large and rather unwieldy binders. The catalogue had a number of shortcomings, the most significant of which was the use of black-and-white photography. Even though the photos were as good as permitted by the funding, colour shots would have been more helpful. The images predated the proliferation of digital photography, which would have allowed for a far more useful document. Nonetheless, as many First Nations people who studied the catalogue observed, black-and-white photos were better than nothing. It was a start.

The Rymill Collection, which consists of some seven hundred items acquired primarily from Anishinaabe, Plains Cree, and Blackfoot First Nations living on reserves in Manitoba, Saskatchewan, and Alberta, includes tools, clothing, medicines, furnishings, domestic utensils, and ceremonial artifacts. Unlike many expeditions of the 1920s, the Franklin Motor Expedition did not have a formal title and was identified in contemporary newspaper reports simply as a joint venture of the Cambridge University Museum and the British Museum.[19] The name "Franklin Motor Expedition" is derived from the automobile used by the expedition and was coined by the family of its leader, Donald A. Cadzow, to distinguish it from the many other expeditions in which he participated.

A striking aspect of the Franklin Motor Expedition is the extent to which its story had been submerged, if not quite forgotten, within the broader history of the MAA. In "The Case of the Misplaced Ponchos," Nicholas Thomas (1999) compares the challenges of working with museum collections to those of a detective attempting to solve a mystery. Because so little may be known of the histories of collections, he argues, researchers who work with artifacts must first disentangle the layers of clues embedded in evidence that has become obscured with the relocation of collections to museums. Using the case study of bark cloth in nineteenth-century Polynesia to show how some forms of clothing were adapted in the process of materializing social change, Thomas (ibid., 7) notes that "we will always be led away from the artefact and then back to it, in a succession of movements and speculations around implicit effects and meanings." Thus, if the unruliness of artifacts and their ability to generate multiple situational meanings are inescapable, we must develop a theoretical framework that allows us to be empowered by artifacts themselves rather than being disempowered by the lack of contextual information.

The 1999 publication of Thomas's article was serendipitous. By this time I had begun my doctoral studies and felt frustrated by the lack of documentation to explain how the Rymill Collection came to be in the MAA. I was also struggling to understand it as an assemblage, as my museum training indicated I should do. I continued my search for sources beyond the museum, and the breakthrough came when I located the families of Donald Cadzow in the United States and of Robert and John Rymill in Australia. They had numerous documents relating to the expedition, which they made available to me, with the result that I was able to follow Thomas's suggestion and use them in conjunction with the artifacts to reconnect the collection with several First Nations communities. During thirteen months of fieldwork from September 1998, I visited as many of these communities as possible to speak about the collection with people who were actively engaged with museums and cultural revitalization, using photo-elicitation as my primary methodology. I describe these processes in Chapters 3, 4, and 5, not just to historicize the expedition and collection, but to indicate the richness of contextual information that may be uncovered when museum archives documentation is brought together with knowledge located beyond it.

I was initially based at the Glenbow Museum, where I undertook archival work over three months to find evidence concerning the impact of government assimilation programs on First Nations and how these programs presented opportunities for collecting. As the Glenbow was developing its new Blackfoot gallery, Niitsitapiisinni: Our Way of Life, I was invited to attend planning meetings and to visit sites of significance with the community curators. By participating as an observer and a volunteer, I was able to watch the dynamics of an unfolding relationship between museum staff and Blackfoot people, which was crucial to my own understanding of the possibilities for using museum collections in community-centred projects.[20] I then spent four months based in Winnipeg, during which I met with individuals from Swan Lake First Nation and Long Plain First Nation, and undertook further archival research in the Manitoba Museum, the Provincial Archives of Manitoba, the Hudson's Bay Company Archives, and the United Church of Canada Archives. This was followed by three months based in Regina, most of which I spent talking to people from Star Blanket and Peepeekisis Cree Nations, two of the four First Nations known collectively as the File Hills. I also undertook a comparative study of artifacts collected from the File Hills communities in the 1920s and 1930s, which are now in the Royal Saskatchewan Museum. Finally, I spent a further three months based in Calgary, during which I interviewed people from the Piikani and Siksika Nations about the Rymill Collection. Bringing together the voices of community members, collectors' descendants, and museum staff – all of whom reflected upon the expedition and the collection in different ways – enabled me to better appreciate how and why the collection was assembled. It also allowed for a deeper understanding of the meanings of its artifacts to First Nations people today and the implications of this for European museums that hold similar collections.

Since 1998, I have participated in cross-cultural work with museum collections as a focus, and as my research has taken me to the Prairies on a regular basis, I have been able to continue the conversations I began in the late 1990s with many of the individuals who contributed to the initial research. Most of this work has been with Blackfoot people, particularly those of Kainai and Piikani, and I have visited colleagues and friends in all four Blackfoot nations at least once a year since 1998. Regrettably, my visits to the Star Blanket and Swan Lake Nations have been less frequent, though I made short follow-up visits to both in 2005 and to the former in 2006 and 2007. I also met frequently with a main supporter of this project from

Swan Lake, who spent several years in Calgary during the early 2000s. Many of these individuals helped me to develop my thinking by commenting on drafts of this book and by patiently answering my numerous e-mail and telephone enquiries.

THE METAPHOR OF "the expedition" is useful for thinking about this book. Expeditions set out with a destination in mind and with clear expectations about what they will find. Along the way, they encounter unexpected twists that might take them in new directions or at least make them pause and reflect before regrouping and carrying on. This has certainly been my experience of trying to understand the Franklin Motor Expedition and its museological legacy. Like most researchers, I started with certain objectives in mind, but these shifted as the research progressed and I became more familiar with the artifacts and other documentary sources, and, most importantly, with their social, historical, and cultural contexts. Similarly, my views on the development of relations between First Nations and British museums also changed, and I expect they will continue to do so as more museums and First Nations people find ways of getting better acquainted.

I have adopted a referentially biographical approach to follow the Franklin Motor Expedition from its inception to how the Rymill Collection is conceptualized by First Nations people. I wish to stress, however, that as my focus is on the *collection* as an artifact, I address neither the manufacture of its individual pieces nor their use prior to being commoditized. Accordingly, I am not concerned with tracing the biographies of individual objects except in relation to how they contribute to the collection as a whole. I reached this decision in part due to my concern with the limitations of applying a biographical approach to indigenous artifacts, which I have discussed above, but also because a study of creative processes was beyond the scope of the initial research. Furthermore, as many of the collection's artifacts are associated with ceremony, this restricted the kinds of questions that were permissible to ask, and these included technical questions about their manufacture.

To set the scene, I begin with an overview of how Indian policy was manifested in the 1920s with specific reference to its implementation on the reserve communities visited by the Franklin Motor Expedition. It is important to note that unlike some contemporary expeditions that had similar adventurous overtones and in which the participants set forth to places and peoples entirely new to them, the Franklin team members had all visited Western Canada previously. In 1925 and 1926, Donald Cadzow had made two substantial collections for the Museum of the American Indian at communities subsequently visited by the Franklin Motor Expedition; Robert and John Rymill had less direct experience with First Nations, though they had encountered Nakoda people from the Morley reserve during a 1928 camping holiday near Banff. All three, therefore, had some familiarity with the social and political context of relations between First Nations and the state, though their understanding of the daily realities of reserve life was limited. My opening chapter thus serves as an introduction to these realities by describing how First Nations people were responding to government-imposed policies of assimilation in an era of social, cultural, and economic transition. The chapter also introduces the communities of Swan Lake First Nation (Manitoba), Star Blanket Cree Nation (Saskatchewan), and the Piikani First Nation (Alberta), whose experiences of collectors and museums inform this book. Chapter 2 examines the lure of the Prairies for collectors in the context of anthropology's development as an academic discipline. Citing the experiences of museums in Canada, the United States, and the United Kingdom, I survey institutional collecting practices and explore the professional networks that assisted the acquisition of First Nations artifacts. I also discuss the role of the Department of Indian Affairs in controlling anthropological research and collecting during the 1920s and point to the often contradictory nature of official intervention into these matters. Chapters 3 and 4 examine the intentions and practice of the Franklin Motor Expedition, using family histories and archival documents such as correspondence, press reports, and visual sources. These chapters expose the multiple narratives of the expedition, with a view to understanding issues of agency in the collecting process. Chapter 5 repositions the Rymill Collection; based on interviews with First Nations people, it examines how they talked *around* the collection so as to express their views on museums and on the role of collections in cultural and spiritual revitalization processes and in supporting community history. The biographical approach to collections is most explicit in Chapter 6; by tracing how the Rymill Collection was used in and beyond the MAA, it explores representations of First Nations people in British museums. My concluding remarks point to what I see as a necessary shift in how collecting histories are conceptualized in museum contexts, and the implications of this for museological practice, particularly in Britain.

1
Community Contexts
Reserve Life in the 1920s

1929? That's a long time ago ... You want me to tell you about it?
There's not much to tell. Nothing very special. Mostly farming. In 1928,
that's when I was elected to council on the reserve. I tried to work for
the management on the reserve, but it was very hard to be an Indian
because of Indian Affairs. It was very hard to convince them. But
anyway, we were able to get through all right. We started the Band
Farm in 1929. We got a tractor and a plough, which we managed,
and we started to farm our land.

               – Sam Cameron, author interview, 5 April 1999

IN THE EARLY SPRING of 1999, Wayne Scott, an elder from Swan Lake First
Nation, took me to visit his community to talk about the Rymill Collection in the Museum of Archaeology and Anthropology (MAA) at the
University of Cambridge. We spent an afternoon sitting at the kitchen table
of (the late) Sam Cameron, who was then in his late eighties, looking at
photographs taken by the Franklin Motor Expedition seventy years previously and talking about life at Swan Lake at the time of its visit. Sam
Cameron described the band's agricultural achievements and the involvement of government officials in its business, and then spoke about some of
the individuals in the photographs. He recalled that during the late 1920s,
people "from museums out east" came to meet with these elders at least
twice. As he was only in his late teens, he had not been party to the discus-

sions, but he knew that some items had been taken to a museum in the United States and that several years later Chief Matoas had tried unsuccessfully to get them back.[1] That Swan Lake artifacts had also gone to a British museum was news to him. He ended our conversation by asking what purpose was served by having them so far from home: "It would be nice to have them back where they belong. It would be a great thing to have them back. It's no use to them. Queen Elizabeth can't use them" (Sam Cameron, author interview, Swan Lake Nation, 5 April 1999).

Such comments from First Nations people about how museums do (or do not) use historic collections are not unusual. A goal of this book is to address how First Nations past experiences of museums can inform decisions about the appropriate future care of heritage materials. During the late nineteenth and early twentieth centuries, museum collecting was facilitated by legislation that was designed to assimilate First Nations into the mainstream population. Prohibitions on the expression of spiritual and cultural ways and wearing traditional clothing, as well as the deliberate attempt to wipe out indigenous languages, created an environment in which the use and circulation of ceremonial artifacts, in particular, were threatened. It is important to note that colonial policies were not implemented consistently and that First Nations responses to them were not uniform, but in order to contextualize the Franklin Motor Expedition, I explore below how some of the First Nations it visited coped with social, cultural, economic, and political change during the interwar period.

Administration on the Reserves

During the last quarter of the nineteenth century, a shift occurred in the balance of power between First Nations and settler communities on the Prairies. Until this time, First Nations controlled immense territories and vastly outnumbered the Europeans who had come to the area to trade. In the years that followed, as small towns were established and grew in size, the resources of First Nations and Métis people were gradually depleted, processes that continue today with the spread of urban development and natural resource extraction. The decimation of the bison – which some First Nations people view as "a deliberate act to crush resistance" – as well as exposure to diseases to which they had no immunity, brought extreme physical and emotional suffering, and disrupted life for clans and bands throughout the region (Narcisse Blood, author interview, Kainai Nation,

6 December 2001). First Nations leaders were attentive to the bitter experiences of Native American peoples with US government and military forces, and were concerned about the implications of the settler influx in their territories. Having already established numerous alliances with European traders, they began to consider the benefits of new agreements through which the land and resources would be equitably shared and the future safety, well-being, and autonomy of their own people would be secure.

The impact of Confederation in 1867, the transfer of Rupert's Land to the newly formed Canadian government in 1870, and the formation of the North-West Territories further compromised the traditional lands of First Nations. From 1871 to 1921, eleven numbered treaties (with adhesions) were confirmed between the Government of Canada (representing the Crown) and many First Nations in what are now Alberta, British Columbia, Manitoba, the Northwest Territories, Ontario, and Saskatchewan. The First Nations visited by the Franklin Motor Expedition adhered to Treaties 1 (1871), 3 (1873), 4 (1874), 6 (1876), or 7 (1877). As part of these agreements, land was set aside for the creation of reserves for each band or nation. Oral accounts of the treaty-making process emphasize that First Nations signatories anticipated that the relocation of their people to reserves would allow their gradual adaptation to the transitions taking place and eventually to participate as equal citizens of the new nation of Canada. The specifics of the numbered treaties varied, but they generally included provisions for annuity payments of five dollars for each enrolled band member, with a larger sum for the chief and headmen; they also provided for land entitlement, farming supplies, a school on each reserve, and triennial suits of clothes for chiefs and headmen.

From the start, those involved in the negotiations held differing views on what the treaties represented and what had been decided. For First Nations, the treaties were sacred agreements that were sealed by the smoking of the pipe, and they encompassed reciprocity and mutual obligations that were to be upheld in perpetuity; they were made in good faith as acts of friendship and as a means of establishing peaceful relationships between nations. First Nations leaders anticipated that treaty promises, such as the provision of health care and access to education, assistance with resource development, and the maintenance of hunting and trapping rights, would be honoured for current and future generations. First Nations historians have repeatedly explained that the leaders agreed not to surrender the land, but to share its resources with the newcomers. As land is a gift from the

Creator and a source of survival and knowledge for all who inhabit it, human beings cannot own it. Though the leaders recognized tribal territories, the concept of property in land as it was understood in a European legal framework made little sense to them (J.R. Miller 1991, 165). Cessation of land title was therefore meaningless (see, for example, Treaty Seven Elders et al. 1996; Venne 1997; Price 1999; Ray, Miller, and Tough 2000; and N. McLeod 2009). In contrast, the Crown viewed the treaties as land surrenders and saw reserves as a temporary measure. As federal policy was geared toward the assimilation of First Nations into mainstream society, it was assumed that the need for separate reserves would eventually diminish and that reserve land would become available for Euro-Canadian settlement. Following from this view, the agreement of First Nations leaders to accept annuity payments and gifts was a concession that the land had been surrendered. Land sales and legislation passed in subsequent years, such as the Soldier Settlement Act and amendments to the Indian Act, further alienated First Nations from their territories (Tobias 1976, 23; J. Taylor 1984; K.D. Smith 2009).

Long before the numbered treaties were negotiated, a series of legislative measures was passed to control the lives of First Nations people, initially by the British government and then by the Government of Canada. With the establishment of reserves, these laws became easier to enforce, though they encountered considerable resistance from many First Nations people. The Gradual Civilization Act (1857), for example, aimed to enfranchise First Nations individuals and to remove their status as "Indians" (J.R. Miller 1991, 114). The Indian Act was passed in 1876 and, with its subsequent amendments, consolidated and revised all previous legislation relating to status Indians in the provinces and territories. Indians were treated as wards of the government, yet they were not represented in Parliament and had no input into legislation that affected them. Euro-Canadian education and health care standards were imposed upon peoples who had their own practices for dealing with these matters (see, for example, Shewell 2004; and Burnett 2010), and values such as economic individualism were promoted in an effort to break down traditional social structures. Policies that, from the start, were invasive and unsympathetic to the needs of people adjusting to significant transitions in their way of life, and that took little account of their concerns, gradually became more repressive. In the years immediately following the First World War, the hardships experienced by First Nations communities were exacerbated by the impact of diseases, especially influenza, the limitations on their attempts to farm reserve land, the prohibitions on ceremonial expression, the distress caused by the enforced separation of families, and the subsequent collapse of traditional social and cultural organizations (Pettipas 1994; Titley 1995).

Policy was administered through the Department of Indian Affairs (DIA), which was founded in 1880 as a branch of the Department of the Interior and was transferred to the Department of Mines in 1936. From 1913 to 1931, the deputy superintendent general of Indian Affairs was Duncan Campbell Scott (1862-1947), who favoured moral suasion over legislation to resolve the so-called Indian problem (see Scott 1931), but who nevertheless oversaw a period in which the rights and freedoms of First Nations people were consistently undermined by laws designed to limit spiritual and cultural expression. The DIA was responsible for the management of reserves, trust funds, treaty obligations, health care, education, welfare projects, and enfranchisement. At the local level, business was conducted through its agencies; by 1930 there were 116 of these scattered across the country. The number of bands in each agency varied from one to thirty, and staff levels were determined accordingly (Department of Indian Affairs 1930, 47). Each agency was coordinated by an Indian agent, a government official with the power to control access to resources, who acted as an intermediary between chiefs and more senior DIA administrators. Agents came to their posts with a wide range of experience and vastly differing attitudes toward First Nations. Some were hired because they were familiar with local conditions; for example, George Gooderham was offered the job when his father, Indian agent at the Gleichen, Alberta, Blackfoot Agency, died unexpectedly.[2] Although many agents respected First Nations people and worked hard to help them prosper economically despite adversarial conditions and the almost impenetrable bureaucracy, others were inefficient and sometimes corrupt, and were hired only because the remoteness of many reserves made it difficult to retain competent staff. Others took great pains to enforce DIA policies and showed little compassion or comprehension of their impact on their charges. Depending on the size and needs of an agency, other employees might include a medical officer or nurse, a farming instructor and stockman, and a constable and a clerk. In Western Canada, the DIA was further represented by two Indian commissioners who oversaw the running of the agencies; one was based in Victoria, and the other in Regina. Commissioner William Graham, who was responsible for the Prairie provinces during the 1920s, was known for his harsh methods and his belief that Ottawa-based civil servants underestimated the extent of the "Indian problem." He spent much of the 1920s in conflict with his superior, Duncan Campbell Scott, and implemented his own solutions to curb ceremonial and cultural expression, using threats, coercion, and harassment to such an extent that even many Indian agents thought him "dictatorial."[3]

Indian agents worked closely with First Nations leaders and helped introduce new forms of leadership. Some reserves were still nominally governed by hereditary lifetime chiefs; for example, *atim kâ-mihkwasit* (Chief Red Dog), the eldest son of *acâhkosa k-ôtakohpit* (He Who Has Stars as a Blanket, Chief Starblanket), led the Star Blanket Nation from 1917 to 1940.[4] However, this arrangement was gradually replaced with the elective system that incorporates a chief and a band council, which remains in place today. It was not unknown for a DIA official to favour an amenable individual as chief, or to remove those whom he found troublesome, and the influence of chiefs varied from community to community. While visiting the Tsuu T'ina Nation near Calgary, Oxford University anthropologist Beatrice Blackwood commented on changing leadership roles during this period, noting that "they still have a Chief, but he has little power. The Agent tries to foster a sense of responsibility in the Chief and consults him on minor matters. He is supposed to help keep up the roads. (Most of these are tracks across the country, made by the passing of the ever-present Ford)."[5]

The interference of DIA officials certainly limited the extent to which chiefs could respond to the needs of their people, but many continued to exercise their traditional role as much as possible. For instance, *atim kâ-mihkwasit* is remembered as a respected and good leader who cared deeply for his people and resisted government pressure to assimilate. In spite of the enforced changes to governance structures and leadership roles, many Prairie First Nations continued to practise situational forms of leadership, in which the most appropriate leaders were selected depending on the circumstances, as far as was possible.

Earning a Living

Agriculture was central to the federal government's goal of economic self-sufficiency for First Nations. By the late 1920s, many reserve communities in Western Canada had been farming for several decades, despite challenging climatic conditions and limited access to the appropriate machinery (Figure 2). The summer of 1929 was unusually hot, and as the Franklin Motor Expedition drove across the prairies, the team would have noticed

Figure 2 Blackfoot farmers putting up hailed wheat, Siksika Nation, near Gleichen, c. 1930 | Glenbow Archives, NA-2966-18

that some crops were beginning to suffer from lack of moisture, with farmers in Southern Saskatchewan facing the most difficulty. Total yield was estimated at 52 percent of what was considered normal (Livesay 1929, 10). Though poor harvests caused problems for everyone working in agriculture, First Nations farmers were less equipped than their neighbours to deal with the consequences of fluctuating environmental conditions. They also had to cope with government policies, which aggravated rather than ameliorated the situation (Carter 1990, 13; Buckley 1993).

Commercial farming and stock raising had been introduced to many First Nations following the signing of the treaties. With the decimation of the bison and restrictions on hunting and trapping, other strategies for food production were needed. Horticulture and ranching were regarded by both government officials and First Nations as viable means of attaining economic independence, particularly in those areas with rich soils or abundant grazing land. Though the specifics varied with each treaty, Ottawa was obligated to supply bands with some farm equipment, grain and livestock, and a farming instructor, and many communities worked hard in the post-treaty years to develop the skills required for successful crop production and stock management (Carter 1990, 12). Despite the unpredictable conditions, First Nations farmers persevered, pooling resources to acquire machinery and supporting each other when times were hard. Oral accounts and written records indicate that crop production and ranching were successful on many reserves during the years immediately following the treaties, with good harvests and quality livestock commanding competitive prices on the market. In contrast, only a decade or so later, production decreased and crop quality varied due to factors outside the control of the farmers.

The first three decades of the twentieth century were characterized by increased interference by DIA officials and, in some cases, the deliberate obstruction of First Nations efforts to succeed as farmers and stock raisers. The instructors hired to advise trainee farmers were sometimes inexperienced and lacked the necessary qualifications; others worked hard and were supportive but were hindered by bureaucracy and disagreements with the Indian agent. With the DIA consistently failing to provide even the most basic equipment for extensive agricultural operations, First Nations farmers could not compete with their Euro-Canadian neighbours, and some chose more profitable work as farmhands in the agricultural belt (Treaty 7 Elders et al. 1996, 149). Inevitably, this meant that some farmland was neglected, providing further evidence for officials that First Nations people were work-shy and that their land should be sold or leased to individuals who, from their perspective, would use it properly.

The poor quality and unreliability of much DIA-provided machinery hindered the development of First Nations farming in Western Canada. Equipment was often outdated and in poor condition, and though arranging repairs involved cumbersome bureaucracy, farmers were sometimes prevented from undertaking the task themselves. In addition, they were forbidden to buy their own tools and machinery without the prior agreement of the Indian agent. Those who overcame these obstacles and raised healthy crops were then unable to sell their produce without a permit. DIA control extended to managing the profits made on a crop, which were often kept by the Indian agent on behalf of the farmer's family and could only be withdrawn a few dollars at a time by special request. Not all agents were quite so heavy-handed, but many genuinely believed that First Nations people didn't know how to conduct their own affairs, a misconception that persists today and is perpetuated by widely available neo-conservative commentary.

The DIA considered its control of First Nations business affairs to be "kindly supervision," a term that repeatedly appears in its reports and correspondence of the period.[6] Although its aim was ostensibly to protect First Nations from unscrupulous traders and to ensure that they got a fair price for their crops, Aboriginal people themselves unsurprisingly saw this interference as degrading and counterproductive. In Edward Ahenakew's (1995, 101) allegorical account of reserve life in the 1920s, for instance, the narrator, Old Keyam, argues that

> this may be "kindly supervision," but it is most wretchedly humbling to many a worthy fellow to have to go, with assumed indifference, to ask or beg for a permit to sell one load of hay that he has cut himself, on his own reserve, with his own horses and implements. I say again, it may be right for some, but that is no reason why those who try to get on, and who do get on, should have to undergo this humiliation.

At the Swan Lake reserve in Southern Manitoba, people were doing their best to "get on" and were developing an economic base from which to raise revenue for the community. A band farm was begun in 1929 and many young men who worked for immigrant farmers nearby were pleased to be able to concentrate their efforts for the benefit of their families instead (Daniels 1981, 256). In the opinion of United Church missionary-teacher Reverend James Donaghy, who worked at Swan Lake from 1920 to 1927, these men were far better qualified than the farming instructor, Mr. Oliver, who had recently arrived to supervise the development of the band farm. Donaghy also reported that the wheat harvested by band member Charles Tanner in the mid-1920s was of such high quality that the government held it for seed purposes.[7]

At Swan Lake, and most of the Saskatchewan reserves visited by the Franklin Motor Expedition, farmers concentrated their efforts on cereal production, but other agricultural pursuits were also undertaken. At the File Hills reserves some men were involved in mixed farming and raising horses and cattle, whereas others cleared the bush, made pickets, stoked crops, worked on the roads in the summer, and trapped in the winter (Donald Bigknife, author interview, Piapot Nation, 25 June 1999, cited in Brown 2000, 30). In Southern Alberta, wheat and sugar-beet cultivation was common, but cattle ranching predominated, with animals and raw hides being sold to companies such as J.E. Love and Sons in Calgary. First

Nations people in this region raised their own stock, and bands also issued grazing permits or leased part of their reserves to ranchers from nearby settlements. The Department of Indian Affairs (1930, 10) described stock raising in the three Prairie provinces as "in a very flourishing condition" in 1929, with cattle to the value of $140,117.64 being sold that year by First Nations people.

Across the Prairies there were opportunities to work in industries other than agriculture, both on and off the reserves. In Southern Alberta, many Siksika sold coal from drift mines along the Bow River to neighbouring settlements and to the Canadian Pacific Railroad. By the late 1920s, the market demand for coal had increased, and in 1931 a cooperative mining business was established on the Siksika reserve, which employed many local people and labourers from the nearby towns of Milo and Cluny. Contract work could also be found in the sugar-beet fields or in picking fruit, by digging bones for fertilizer, or in shipping "canner" horses to Montana (Regular 2008, 103-25). Manual work was also available at the schools and hospitals or construction projects in the expanding settlements close to reserves.

Men were the main wage-earners at this time. Women's work centred largely on the home and involved food preparation, tending small gardens, sewing clothes for the family, and child rearing. Some women sold beadwork or other crafts at summer fairs to raise additional income; others worked as cooks or cleaners in agency buildings or went into domestic service. When they were not in school, children who had learned English also helped at home by translating for their elders, who either knew little English or preferred to speak through an interpreter. They also helped care for younger siblings or elderly relatives and contributed to food supplies by fishing or snaring small animals. Per capita income of status First Nations people in 1929 was reported to be eighty-seven dollars, an increase of twenty-eight dollars since 1916, a statistic that was celebrated by the DIA as "remarkable progress" (Dominion Bureau of Statistics 1930, 1041).

Promoting "Civilization": Education and the Church

> Among the forces that must be overcome are the Sun Dance; the Medicine Man; and a number of social customs, especially that of marriage. They do not take an active stand against the Church, but they have a great silent influence that it would not be wise to make

war against. The young are already tiring of some of these customs, and leave them to the old folks, but for them to openly rebel would be a serious matter.

– J.A. Donaghy, "History of the Swan Lake Indian Reserve"

With these words the Reverend James Donaghy, missionary-teacher at Swan Lake, expressed his belief that the most effective way of assimilating First Nations people was to convert younger generations to Christianity. He was not alone. Assimilation policies were made manifest through a range of "civilization" programs that aimed to expose First Nations people to Euro-Canadian moral values (see, for example, D.G. Smith 2001). Schools were the logical place to begin this process. During treaty negotiations, First Nations leaders had expressed their recognition of the value of formal schooling, which, in their view, would provide young people with equal access to social advancement and prosperity like that of immigrants to the region. They stressed that children should learn English, and they encouraged the foundation of schools in their communities so that these new skills could supplement existing systems of knowledge transfer and pedagogy.

In the years immediately following the treaties, various Christian denominations established day schools on many reserves. Children attended classes during the day and returned home to their families in the evenings. At the suggestion of the missionary or Indian agent, some children attended industrial schools located at a distance from their reserve, where they learned a trade or skills for domestic service. It soon transpired that neither day schools nor industrial schools were able to maintain good attendance rates. If a child were needed to help at home or to attend a ceremony, that child was simply kept from school. Missionaries and nuns failed to understand the centrality of the "parallel educational system" that existed on reserves, which was based on First Nations values and traditions (Gresko 1975, 175). They blamed falling attendance figures on First Nations lifestyles, parents' dislike of corporal punishment, and their indifference to the job prospects that a formal education would bring their children. The structure and content of Euro-Canadian schooling, in which children participated for several hours a day, threatened the dissemination of First Nations cultural knowledge and skills, which were transmitted through informal learning processes such as listening to stories and observing and participating in the daily tasks necessary for survival. Teachers dismissed and often ridiculed traditional knowledge, and they actively discouraged the use of First Nations languages. Some parents who had initially seen the schools as improving communication between the two groups felt betrayed and refused to allow their children to attend regularly. Others who remained keen for their children to receive a Euro-Canadian education objected to their lack of choice regarding the school they attended. Eleanor Brass (1987, 4, 20), from Peepeekisis First Nation, Saskatchewan, for example, recalled in her memoirs that her father, Fred Deiter, "had no use for Indian schools." Although he wanted his children to attend school in the nearby town, he was told that all status Indian children must go to the Presbyterian boarding school at the File Hills Colony, the experimental model community founded on the Peepeekisis reserve in 1898.

Parental resistance to such controls convinced the authorities that firmer measures were required to push on with the assimilation program. Across Canada, they created boarding schools both on and off reserves, and children were forcibly sent to them (Milloy 1999). Here they spent months, if not years, separated from their families and being taught a limited range of skills that were deemed appropriate for what Indian Commissioner Amédée E. Forget described in an 1897 Sessional Report as "the youth of a people who one generation past were practically unrestrained savages" (quoted in Legacy of Hope Foundation 2003, 17). These skills included cookery, sewing, and cleaning for girls, and farming and carpentry for boys. Children were also taught basic arithmetic and most importantly, how to speak, read, and write in English (Figure 3). They remained at school for varying times, with boys often leaving at about age fourteen and girls staying until they reached marriageable age.

The accommodation and facilities in residential schools were often inadequate, and numerous contemporary commentators criticized their management. In his report on the Alberta schools, for example, Dr. F.A. Corbett wrote scathingly of the unsuitable and poorly maintained buildings. Of the Old Sun School on the Siksika reserve, he remarked,

> The children of this school are generally below par in health and appearance. There are fifty pupils and 70 percent of them have somewhat enlarged lymphatic glands of the neck. Five of these have scrofulous sores requiring active treatment: first surgical and afterwards tonics and fresh air ... Sixty percent of the pupils have scabies or itch, many of them in an aggressive

Figure 3   Students at the St. Mary's Roman Catholic Residential School, Kainai Nation, c. 1920 | Glenbow Archives, NC-7-1030

form. The condition has been neglected or unrecognized and has plainly gone on for months ... The building in which these children are housed is far short of ideal. The dormitories are overcrowded and the ceilings are low ... There is no infirmary in the building and only two small balconies, but as these are off the staffroom they are not available for the pupils. This constitutes a very serious defect in the building as an Indian School, for an abundance of fresh air is essential for the health of all children, and much more so for the Indian, who has been for many centuries an out of doors animal and who, in the process of becoming a house dweller, suffers so severely from these diseases which may be classed as *house diseases,* among these, particularly, Tuberculosis.[8]

Corbett made similar comments about other residential schools and stressed that the substandard living conditions exacerbated poor health among students. In another example, anthropologist Beatrice Blackwood commented on the health of schoolgirls at St. Mary's Roman Catholic Residential School on the Kainai reserve: "The children were not a very healthy bunch, several had open wounds, and others had swollen ones which they had not reported. ('They don't say anything about them till they hurt'). They are treated with iodine."[9] At a time when the DIA made every effort to justify its policies and assure the public of their success, accounts such as these highlight the tensions between the realities of life on Western Canadian reserves and how they were reported.

Once they were at school, many First Nations children were told by their instructors that there was nothing for them on the reserves and that the beliefs of their elders were wicked and akin to "Devil worship."[10] In an environment where their languages and cultural expression were actively forbidden, students often became demoralized and struggled to maintain a sense of cultural identity. Upon leaving school, many found it difficult to readjust to life outside of a controlled institutional environment and to cope with the pressures of working and raising families, having received so little experience of parenting. Often no longer fluent in their own language, and therefore unable to fully understand ceremonial teachings, they found that the spiritual observances of their elders seemed alien. In addition, the secrecy that surrounded the teachings contributed to their ambivalence and feelings that they were wrong (Pettipas 1994, 227). Anthropologists who witnessed these changes sometimes commented that elders were worried about the generational divisions in their communities and were concerned for the future of their spiritual ways and for the material embodiments of their beliefs. Lucien and Jane Hanks (1950, 167), for example, who undertook fieldwork at the Siksika Nation between 1938 and 1941, noted that younger people would "lampoon the older men and dismiss their sacred bundles as museum relics, which they would be glad to sell for cash." These divisions became greater as the twentieth century progressed, but they had their roots in the belittling of First Nations spiritual beliefs that was common to the residential school experience for thousands of children.

Assimilation by Legislation

The residential school system was possibly the most significant factor in the disruption of cultural and spiritual knowledge in First Nations communities, and this is now acknowledged by the federal government and the various religious denominations that implemented educational policy. The culture stress experienced by First Nations during the late nineteenth and early twentieth centuries was intensified by legislative measures that challenged their rights and freedoms. One of the first of these was an 1884 amendment to the Indian Act that became known as the Potlatch Law (Cole and Chaikin 1990).[11] This amendment stated explicitly that participation in potlatches

and *tamanawas* (healing ceremonies) was illegal and punishable by a custodial sentence of between two to six months. Some DIA officials criticized
the amendment on the grounds that it was harsh and difficult to enforce.
They were supported by Euro-Canadian traders who operated near
Northwest Coast communities, although their reaction was arguably motivated by economic self-interest rather than concern for First Nations rights
(Pettipas 1994, 96). Many First Nations requested that the law be repealed,
but it was revised in 1895 and became part of section 114 of the Indian Act.
The law also targeted Prairie First Nations and was intended to curb the
perceived extravagance of the ceremonial distribution of money and other
goods, to shield First Nations from immoral activities, which were associated with large gatherings, and to prohibit certain ceremonial activities that
officials found objectionable. The latter included the piercing ceremonies
and the consumption of dog flesh practised by some Plains groups as well
as the "cannibalistic-related rituals" of the Hamat'sa of some Northwest Coast
peoples (ibid.).

Across the Prairies, people found ways to subvert the legislation. Some
conducted the "offensive" ceremonies in secret, ignored the law, or simply
informed the DIA that they intended to proceed with ceremonies and other
events because they saw no reason to do otherwise. In 1915, for example,
following a meeting called by Chief Bull Plume, Piikani leaders wrote to
the DIA, reminding the authorities of Piikani loyalty to the Crown following the signing of Treaty 7, questioning the section 114 amendment of the
Indian Act, and noting that "presents" would be given to guests at a forthcoming dance. These would include "dancing outfits, Indian made coats,
Indian made pants, Indian made moccasins, beaded belt, neck beads, stone
pipe, tobacco, pocket knife, handkerchief, a blanket that we can do without."
The letter added that those who were giving the presents did not "have
much use for" them. To emphasize the point, it listed items that would *not*
be gifted: "wagon, harness, rigs of any kind, saddle, horses, cattle, furniture,
stoves." Moreover, no "money exceeding two dollars" would be given away.[12]

At Swan Lake by the 1920s, fewer younger people were actively involved
in the teachings of the Midewiwin, the religious belief system of Anishinaabe
people, but spiritual leaders continued to observe Sun Dance ceremonies.[13]
During this difficult period, people sought for various solutions to problems
and for support. Swan Lake elder Rosie Scott, for example, recalled her own
preference for traditional healers:

I was baptized as a Catholic; my dad was Catholic, but I raised my kids in the Indian way because I thought when my kids were sick, the Indian was there. Where was my priest, the Catholic priest? They didn't come in and help you. All they'll do is bring in the holy water ... That's what they used to do, because I saw them. That's all they'd do. The Indian would sit there and support you, and the medicine man would help, and that's the way I raised my kids. (Rosie Scott, author interview, Swan Lake Nation, 5 April 1999)

Although some DIA staff and missionaries prevented traditional healers from practising, the healers nonetheless did what they could to help, and as Rosie Scott's remarks reveal, some people considered their skills to be more effective than introduced methods.

To circumvent the Potlatch Law and lessen the likelihood of interference from officials, some spiritual leaders reduced the length of ceremonies or dropped certain rituals. At Swan Lake, the piercing ritual of the Sun Dance, which the authorities particularly abhorred, was removed from the ceremony. As James Donaghy explained,

We know the authorities had to forbid it some years ago on account of the cruelty practised in it. In making braves one deserved the title if he were able to stand the test right through. But now all that has been deleted, and it consists in a strong service of praise; prayer and thanksgiving to Manitou for his care of his children. They say that Manitou told them to keep up this rite for all time or they would not prosper. So for that reason the old men feel that they are bound to keep it up. There is still a certain amount of trial in its present form as those taking part neither eat nor drink until it is finished. It lasts just one day, but if it is very hot that is quite enough.[14]

In this instance, the ceremony was adapted but its integrity remained intact. Elsewhere across the Prairies, ceremonies were modified so that they could proceed within the law. Numerous press reports of "public" ceremonies from the 1920s and 1930s highlight the "progress" being made by First Nations but show little understanding of the ceremonial significance. For example, a 1929 article about the Siksika circle camp (referred to as a Sun Dance), claimed,

Each year the Indians show improvements in their tepees and the general layout of the encampment. This year the improvement is particularly noticeable and it is a picturesque sight indeed with varied coloured tents of all dimensions quite artistically arranged. The Indians, too, are changing gradually in many ways, both in dress and otherwise. This, of course, is due to the education they are receiving and the younger of both sexs [sic] quite cheerfully enter into conversation with visitors answering many questions and explaining many things to the white visitors. A few years ago it was most difficult to get more than yes or know [sic] from any of them, but now they use excellent English. (Anon. 1929d, 1)

Such reports illustrate the belief of some observers that the long-term goal of civilization was being achieved, although correspondence in the DIA files reveals that many who were involved in the assimilation program thought otherwise. Missionaries often asserted that ceremonies were immoral expressions of paganism and were especially detrimental to the children who witnessed the participation of their parents and grandparents. Occasionally, they put aside their theological differences to secure converts and to criticize the DIA for not rigorously enforcing policy. One co-authored letter opined that

> to the Indians the "Sundance" is not merely a sport or a dance, but, specially a revival of their pagan traditions, the return to their ancient customs, the raising up of the old paganism with all its evil consequences, moraly [sic] and materially, a challenge to our common christian [sic] principles and a setting up of the old barbarian order on the ruin of our common civilization.[15]

These concerns were strengthened by the complaints of Indian agents and farming instructors who claimed that many valuable hours were wasted when people participated in ceremony rather than working in the fields. Associated cultural activities also came under attack and were frequently characterized in economic terms that misinterpreted their meaning. At Blackfoot transfer ceremonies, for example, the gifting of blankets, money, horses, and other goods recognized the sacrifices of previous bundle holders, but critics (and anthropologists) mistook it for payment (Lokensgard 2010, 54). Giveaways in other communities – which might include food, clothing, horses, household goods, tobacco, and money – were frowned upon as wasteful and a cause of impoverishment.

Throughout the interwar period, missionaries and government officials lobbied the DIA about the unwillingness of First Nations to abandon their beliefs. In response, further legislation was passed to control cultural expression. First Nations participation in the summer fairs and agricultural exhibitions that flourished throughout the Prairies was also cause for concern. These events, which brought entertainment to rural residents and helped promote the nascent tourist industry, also provided opportunities for collectors of First Nations arts and crafts. Indian Days celebrations, stampedes, Wild West shows, and many historical pageants required a First Nations presence, which had to be approved by DIA officials (see Geller 1996). Historian Blair Stonechild (2010) discusses the 1925 Lebret Historical Pageant and notes that 3,500 First Nations people from the surrounding area participated in it. According to Stonechild, historical pageants were often held near residential schools to symbolically reinforce the policy aspects of these institutions. The 1925 pageant commemorated the landing of Samuel de Champlain, the exploration of La Vérendrye, and the arrival of Father Hugonard at Lebret in 1875. Stonechild suggests that "the greeting of Champlain, while geographically dislocated, nevertheless would have symbolized the acceptance by Indians of white presence. At the same time, Indians in full dress could be displayed like trophies, standing in straight and unthreatening lines."

First Nations participants in historical pageants and parades were expected to play the part of their ancestors and dress accordingly in beaded buckskin outfits and feather headdresses. These events contributed to sanitized and stereotyped characterizations of First Nations, though some historians have argued that negative criticism of parades, fairs, and pageants must be considered alongside their positive benefits. For instance, in his study of the lengthy history of First Nations involvement in the Calgary Stampede, Hugh Dempsey (2008, 49) writes,

> While the exhibitions were organized for the entertainment of the townspeople, the Indians thoroughly enjoyed the chance to participate. They performed social dances and war dances; had tug-of-war contests, races, and other athletic events; showed off their finery; and visited friends from other reserves. The trip to the fair gave them an opportunity to relieve

the monotony of reservation life, to get away from the boredom of farming and gardening, and to relive some of the exciting days of the past.

Dempsey uses oral narratives to show that many First Nations participants (especially in more recent years) viewed the Calgary Stampede favourably and as an opportunity to educate people about their cultural heritage. He also outlines the history of disputes between Stampede organizers, who asserted that First Nations involvement was popular and generated income, and many missionaries, who believed that it harmed First Nations people. The general secretary of the Methodist Church, for example, claimed in 1912 that

> permitting these Indians to take part in the Stampede at Calgary will result in hundreds of acres of grain being neglected. Besides, there is all the degrading, disgusting immorality which is so openly practised upon these Indians, who are wards of the Government, by immoral and vicious white men. Many of the Indians ... are [so] ruined by these parades that they are never restored to the position and character they formerly held.[16]

Whereas missionaries maintained that taking part in summer celebrations jeopardized the work of residential schools and prevented First Nations from progressing toward civilization, many Indian agents complained that their charges spent more time visiting friends and relatives at organized summer events and at ceremonies and social dances on other reserves than they did working in their fields. If the "Indian problem" were to be resolved, this behaviour must be stopped. To tackle the concerns of church leaders and government officials in the field, section 149 of the Indian Act was amended in 1914 to restrict First Nations' involvement in summer celebrations. Participants and organizers alike were targeted:

> Any Indian in the province of Manitoba, Saskatchewan, Alberta, British Columbia, or the Territories who participates in any Indian dance outside the bounds of his own reserve, or who participates in any show, exhibition, performance, stampede or pageant in Aboriginal costume without the consent of the Superintendent General of Indian Affairs or his authorized Agent, and any person who induces or employs any Indian to take part in such dance, show, exhibition, performance, stampede or pageant, or induces any Indian to leave his reserve or employs any Indian for such

Figure 4 RCMP officer with participants at a ceremony, File Hills, June 1926 |
National Museum of the American Indian, Smithsonian Institution, N11766

a purpose, whether the dance, show, exhibition, stampede or pageant has taken place or not, shall on summary conviction be liable to a penalty not exceeding twenty-five dollars, or to imprisonment for one month, or to both penalty and imprisonment.[17]

This restriction was extended in 1933 when a further amendment removed "in Aboriginal costume," which meant that *any* participation could result in charges (Pettipas 1994, 164). In practice, the amended legislation and the heightened RCMP presence during celebrations did little to curtail First Nations involvement in social and ceremonial events on reserves, or to prevent organizers of town and city festivities from requesting it (Figure 4). Instead, strategies were developed to circumvent the law. For example, people who lived on adjacent reserves, such as the Poundmaker and Little Pine reserves near North Battleford, held dances on the boundary between them; others simply disregarded the legislation and continued to attend off-reserve dances and ceremonies.[18]

First Nations people forcefully objected to the restrictions on their freedom to participate in social occasions, which they perceived as little different from those enjoyed by settlers in nearby towns. Although secular gatherings such as powwows were becoming more common than ceremonial dances by the 1920s, many First Nations people continued to exercise their right to celebrate and to worship according to their own traditions. Their requests to officials to participate in such events were skilfully framed in terms that could hardly be regarded as subversive. Chief *atim kâ-mihkwasit* of the Star Blanket Nation wrote to D.C. Scott in early 1918, requesting permission to hold a dance at his community. He explained that on the few occasions when Agent George Dodds had permitted dancing, the people had collected money for the patriotic fund, which was then sent to Regina. Should they be allowed to hold a weekly circle or tea dance, they would happily donate to the fund each time.[19] The letter was forwarded to the inspector of Indian agencies at Balcarres, who was instructed to reply to *atim kâ-mihkwasit* directly. Unfortunately, his response cannot be located in the DIA files, but it is probable that *atim kâ-mihkwasit* had shrewdly judged that the dances could go ahead if he highlighted their contribution to the war effort.[20] He did not ask permission to dance as a reward for his community's patriotism, however. From his point of view, dancing was a right, and the support of the war effort was never in question.

Section 149 of the Indian Act enabled officials to restrict movement between reserves, thus limiting First Nations participation in celebrations, but there were other means of curtailing mobility. Following the North-West Rebellion of 1885, those who wished to leave their reserve were required to possess a pass, signed by the Indian agent, which stated the purpose and duration of their journey. Ostensibly, the pass system was implemented to protect First Nations people from immoral influences, such as alcohol, prostitution, and theft, but it also separated them from the settler population, as tensions between the two groups were still running high (Barron 1988, 25). Some arrests were made for unauthorized movement between reserves, particularly before the turn of the century, but many people simply ignored the system, which was not legally enforceable, and some agents turned a blind eye to the comings and goings of their charges. Despite its ineffectiveness, the pass system was used during the 1920s to bolster government authority and as a threat to monitor First Nations mobility (ibid., 38).

A significant consequence of repressive legislation and increased government interference in daily life was the development of political astuteness among many First Nations people regarding their relations with settler communities. It is no coincidence that in the years following the First World War, pan-Indian organizations, such as the League of Indians of Canada, had an active membership on the Prairies. These groups lobbied for improved housing, health care facilities, and hunting and fishing rights, and attempted to prevent further land sales, which had reduced the economic base of many reserves during the first decades of the twentieth century. In this atmosphere of political change, where young people were beginning to employ their Euro-Canadian education in service of their communities, many felt caught between two worlds and found it difficult to reconcile the spiritual beliefs of their elders with the economic values that were becoming more prevalent in reserve communities (Brass 1987). Some who found their loyalties divided shunned their background. Others continued to express their Indian-ness, despite opposition from the DIA and relatives who had converted to Christianity. Renewing ties at gatherings, such as Sun Dances, was a means of reaffirming identity during a period when it was constantly undermined (Cuthand 1991, 389).

Anthropologists and Assimilation

In their field notes and private correspondence, anthropologists who worked on the Prairies during the early decades of the twentieth century often noted the effects of government policy on ceremonial expression as well as First Nations resistance to it. Furthermore, they were sometimes asked to advocate on behalf of the communities that hosted them (Pettipas 1994, 172), though not all were willing or able to do so. In one case, David Mandelbaum, a doctoral student working on an ethnographic study of the Plains Cree during the mid-1930s, was asked to support the Little Pine First Nation in its efforts to exercise ceremonial expression. In his field notes, he wrote, "How precious and sacrosanct the sun dance is to many of the Indians after fifty years of intensive and steady missionising may be realized only in the face of the manifold pleas addressed to me to help the Indian protect his religion against the church."[21] He also reported that members of the Sweet Grass First Nation had asked Leonard Bloomfield, who studied Cree linguistics during the early 1930s, to write to the DIA in support of their right to religious freedom.[22] These comments indicate that although First Nations continued to defy the legislation, its repressive effects were being felt in the Prairies. Around the same time, Donald Cadzow wrote to D.C. Scott at the request of Chief Matoas of Swan Lake Nation in support of the community's proposed Sun Dance.[23] He enclosed a copy of the chief's letter, which explained why the dance had to go ahead:

This winter one woman was sick and we appealed to our religion the Sun-dance. And when we told Mr Waite the Indian Agent about having the dance, he said, no, the Indian Department doesn't allow it. When this was told to the woman she was very sorry as she put her trust in getting well in joining the dance. She grew worse after that and finally pass away on the 10th of this month. And we are asking you very kindly to please make arrangement with our Canadian Government to allow us the freedom to have our Sun dance, and our religion.

Every different nations have their own religion and they use it as they like. And we, Indians, are not allowed to have ours as we like. And we would like to know if this is made in the Department, as the Indian Agent says, if so we want you to ask our Department to allow our religion. We are not going to give up, as there are some more that promised to join the dance, when we do have it, this summer.[24]

In his own letter, Cadzow stated that "the Sun Dance, as it is held today, is a harmless affair and would do much to uphold the morale of the Bungi." He added that "the psychological effect of preventing this dance would have affect upon their minds and would, as in the case mentioned in the letter, cause serious complications."[25] In response, A.G. Hamilton of the Manitoba Inspectorate dismissed his concern that the Swan Lake people were unhappy with the "severe methods" of the Indian agent and upheld the decision to prohibit the ceremony.[26]

Some researchers were pointedly told by DIA officials that their interest in traditional practices hindered the advancement of First Nations people as it encouraged them to resist department policies. Oxford University anthropologist Beatrice Blackwood encountered this view in conversation with W.E. Ditchburn, the Indian agent in Victoria, British Columbia. She wrote in her diary that he "has no use for anthropologists because he says they try to keep the Indians back when the Indian Department is doing its best to civilise them (!?!). (Harlan I. Smith claims he has done more to control the Indians in three months than the Department in as many years)."[27]

Despite the willingness of some anthropologists (and other concerned citizens) to support First Nations pursuit of religious freedom, DIA officials usually made it plain that they had no business meddling with departmental policies. Nonetheless, one should not assume that all anthropologists were prepared to advocate for First Nations or that anthropological research was necessarily intended to highlight their concerns. The reticence of some anthropologists to support First Nations, as well as the invasiveness of some anthropological research, the lack of time spent with communities, and the use of ethnographic data against indigenous peoples (see, for example, Beaulieu 1984) contributed to tensions between First Nations and the discipline that persist to this day. Anthropology was deeply embedded within colonial processes, and as Chapter 2 discusses in more detail, the relationship between the Canadian government and ethnographic collecting was ambiguous. Anthropologists were not permitted to conduct research on reserves without the consent of the deputy superintendent general of Indian Affairs, and their work was often facilitated by Indian agents and other officials.[28] As a result, their views regarding the legitimacy of assimilation programs often remained private.

THE DISCUSSION ABOVE has introduced the historical landscape into which the Franklin Motor Expedition entered, but it is crucial to note that the colonial policies and assumptions of this period continue to affect relations between indigenous peoples and the state. The impact of the residential school system, in particular, cannot be exaggerated. In Canada today there is growing acknowledgment of the devastating human cost of a system ostensibly designed to ease assimilation, cut expenditure, and increase school attendance, but which resulted in a painful legacy of mistrust, distress, and disjunction (Milloy 1999). Though care must be taken not to characterize all schools as unwavering totalitarian regimes and all staff as monstrous abusers, the trauma of forced separation, the cultural repression, and the physical and sexual abuse endured by generations of children have filtered into their home lives and had continuing repercussions. Residential school survivors have described the suffering, brutality, loneliness, hunger, and feelings of abandonment, inferiority, and confusion that they experienced. Many also recall that only the support of friends or siblings enabled them to get through their school years and begin to heal from the cycle of abuse. A compensation package for survivors was announced in 2005, intended to contribute to healing in First Nations communities, and in 2008 Prime Minister Stephen Harper formally apologized to residential school survivors on behalf of the federal government for its role in creating and maintaining the schools. The Truth and Reconciliation Commission of Canada has since been established as part of the Indian Residential Schools Settlement Agreement to research residential school histories, to inform all Canadians about their impact, and to work toward reconciliation and renewed relationships based on mutual understanding and respect. It is in this context that efforts are being made to connect with First Nations who have been dispossessed of the material heritage now in museums.

In addition to the residential school system, the assaults on land, freedom of religious expression, citizenship, and status also continue to reverberate in Aboriginal communities. First Nations culture, lands, and livelihoods are constantly under threat, particularly for communities affected by actual or proposed resource extraction, such as the Keystone Pipeline, fracking, and other drilling operations. Rapid urban growth also threatens cultural and historic sites. The construction of housing developments in the southern Prairie provinces has destroyed many sites that First Nations people are only now starting to reconnect with, having been forcibly separated from them by the imposition of residential schools and the pass system. Though the mobility restrictions were lifted around the mid-twentieth century, a generation had already been unable to visit these sites and became disconnected to some degree from the knowledge associated with them (Chambers and Blood 2009). Legislation is in place to protect some archaeological sites, but it came too late for others, and the devastation and desecration cannot be reversed (Yellowhorn 1999). Unfortunately, the deliberate despoliation of such sites continues and is sometimes symptomatic of the uneasy relationship between First Nations and settler communities. In the late summer of 2012, for example, ancient pictograms and petroglyphs near Pincher Creek in Southern Alberta were destroyed by vandals who used a power drill, acid, and a power washer to erase them. This act was likened to the Taliban's destruction of Buddhist statues in Afghanistan and was seen as a deliberate attempt to destroy evidence that the Blackfoot had a written language before European settlement (Humphreys 2012). Certainly, many sectors of society expressed concern regarding the act, but it is not an isolated incident.

Some First Nations people assert that the combination of disenchantment, widespread financial difficulties, and the effects of residential schools meant that many of their ancestors felt threatened and chose to give up certain ceremonial artifacts in the hope they would be cared for outside their communities until it was safe for them to return. This argument goes some way toward explaining why anthropologists and others collected so many items on the Prairies in the 1920s and returns to First Nations a measure of control in collecting exchanges, but it also points to the future-focused outlook of those individuals during a period of repression. The following chapters build upon this theme, first by looking at the institutional and intellectual contexts that enabled collecting and then by turning to the Franklin Motor Expedition and its many encounters.

2
Collecting on the Prairies
"A Splendid Collecting Field"

At that time, the beginning of [the] century and the early part of the twenties, people honestly thought that First Nations cultures were dying out, so there was a rush to go and get artifacts and get a record of them. And in most cases, people didn't think, because they didn't see or understand the ceremonies that were going on. They couldn't comprehend what was going on, so I guess they assumed it was unimportant to First Nations people. And these items were taken, sometimes illegitimately, and put on display, and bundles were opened and people looked inside, which you're not supposed to do. Only the individual who owns that has the right to do it. So, there were a lot of things going on in the early part of the century, and we have to take that into consideration today.

– Lorne Carrier, author interview

Maybe they knew that some day the people were going to need them. Who knows? No matter how wrong we might think it might seem at that point in time, the circumstances might have forced people into doing it that way, taking that method. They might have thought, "My grandchildren are going to need this forty years, fifty years, eighty years after I'm gone. And I know if I give it to my son, he's going to destroy it, so I'm giving it to the museum now for safekeeping." Who knows? Maybe.

– Wayne Scott, author interview

COLLECTORS OPERATING throughout North America in the later nineteenth and early twentieth centuries are often said to have been driven by an unshakable assumption that indigenous peoples would soon disappear due to the impact of modernity and "technology's transcendent progress" (Cronin 2013, 57). This supposition had become normalized by the time the Franklin Motor Expedition traversed the prairies, but as the comments above from Lorne Carrier, of the Piapot Cree Nation and former community development manager of the Museums Association of Saskatchewan, and Wayne Scott of Swan Lake Nation make clear, not only was it misplaced, it took little account of how First Nations people themselves may have perceived their encounters with collectors. In this chapter, I address collecting from the perspective of museums and academic institutions to show how the "disappearing" peoples argument was sustained during the early twentieth century. In the Introduction to this book, I suggested that, by its very nature, collecting is a dialogic process, one influenced by many factors. The present chapter will establish a framework for the subsequent chapters, in which First Nations responses to the Franklin Motor Expedition are considered in depth.

The idea that indigenous people were disappearing was accompanied by theoretical developments in evolutionary science and the emergence of anthropology as a discipline in Europe and North America. It was further shaped by contexts of political and colonial control, economic conditions on reserves, and First Nations responses to the assimilation policies outlined in Chapter 1. Indeed, as Jonathan Peyton and Robert Hancock (2008, 49) state, the development of anthropology in Canada cannot be separated from the "hegemonic project that sought to assimilate Indigenous peoples into a constantly developing liberal state." Institutional collecting, whether undertaken by newly established Western Canadian museums or their larger, wealthier counterparts in Europe and the United States, was thus stimulated by concerns that First Nations were abandoning their cultural practices and that soon there would be nothing left to collect. It is important to note, however, as does Andrew Nurse (2006, 53), that though institutional collecting in Canada drew upon the practice of anthropological research as it developed in the United States and Britain, "the dominance of 'salvage ethnography' in the first half of the twentieth century made Canadian anthropology different from other national anthropological traditions."

The Franklin Motor Expedition was part of a wider project of museum-sponsored collecting that began during the later nineteenth century and continued to the mid-twentieth century. Although museums acquired items for somewhat differing reasons, their predominant motive was to save the remnants of "traditional" or "authentic" cultures, thereby preserving them for posterity. These remnants, as understood by scholars, administrators, and church leaders, predated the reserve era and took the form of artifacts (especially ceremonial ones), oral histories, songs, and images. Scholars had little interest in material reflective of transitional or contemporary First Nations lives; instead, collectors sought older pieces that were increasingly difficult to acquire and that supposedly showed less evidence of interaction between indigenous people and settler society. Professional anthropologists were aware of the limitations of salvage ethnography but persisted in it nonetheless. Marius Barbeau, a government anthropologist who worked for the Anthropology Division of the Geological Survey of Canada, wrote on this matter in 1917: "The ethnologist is a fool who so far deceived himself as to believe that his field notes and specimens gathered in the raw from half-breeds or [the] decrepit survivors of a past age, still represent the unadulterated knowledge of the prehistoric races of America" (52).

Museum-based anthropologists may have been concerned about the social conditions on reserves and the impact of assimilation policies, but their collecting activities had long contributed to the trope of the "disappearing Indian," just as their exhibition strategies foregrounded cultures for whom time seemingly stood still (see Phillips 2011, 113). Franz Boas (1907, 929-30) stated that the preservation and scientific study of indigenous societies through artifacts were primary functions of large museums:

Museums are the storehouses in which not only must the material be preserved by means of which deductions of scientists can be checked, but they are also the place where scientific materials from distant countries, vanishing species, paleontological remains, and the objects used by vanishing tribes, are kept and preserved for all future time, and may thus be made the basis of studies which, without them, would be impossible. We are spending vast sums year after year to bring together evidences of life forms of distant countries and of past ages, to accumulate the monuments of the past and objects used by remote tribes. We collect these because they are the foundation of scientific study. Should we be unwilling to provide adequate means for keeping intact the results of our expensive inquiries? It is the essential function of the museum as a scientific institution to preserve for all future time, in the best possible way, the valuable material that has been collected, and not to allow it to be scattered and to deteriorate.[1]

Although Boas had left his position at the American Museum of Natural History by 1907, his influence remained strong and his words no doubt resonated with his former student Edward Sapir as he formulated plans for the Geological Survey's Anthropological Division. As is revealed by the Sapir quotation that heads the Introduction to this book, the highest echelons of Canada's emerging anthropological community believed that many "primitive cultures" were moribund. A language of salvage, which stressed the urgency and competitiveness of the collecting mission, permeated museum correspondence, academic publications, and newspaper reports of the time: as Donald Cadzow put it, "the archaeology for the time being will be safe under the ground, the ethnology is disappearing fast"; the *Edmonton Journal* noted that George Heye, founder of the Museum of the American Indian, was "anxious that all pertaining to the Indian should be gathered before it is too late"; and a headline in the *Calgary Albertan* read "French Scientists Gather Relics of Indian Tribes; Fear Historical Losses."[2]

Remarks of this sort frequently underscored the apparent decline of First Nations cultural beliefs and practices, and the associated loss of material heritage, but seemingly disregarded the impact of the relocation of artifacts to museums and private collections, and the ability of First Nations people to withstand intense external pressure. The salvage paradigm also failed to recognize the complex survival strategies employed by many indigenous people to nurture and pass on traditional knowledge. Although expressions of cultural identity and belief became less visible, they were not necessarily abandoned; instead, they went underground or were modified to suit given situations. An example of such subversive action is provided by Ruth Phillips (1998, pl. 3, 195), who writes that seamstresses in the Great Lakes region incorporated visual expressions of spiritual beliefs, such as the "Tree of Peace" or floral imagery, into moccasins and beaded ornaments produced for sale. Similarly, Sylvia Kasprycki (2007) suggests that the ribbon work appliqué on clothing sewn by Menominee women during the late nineteenth century may have been a subtle attempt to maintain traditional values.

Salvage ethnography peaked on the Canadian Prairies in the first three decades of the twentieth century, though it was certainly not a new phenomenon, as George Stocking Jr. (1987, 1992, 1999) reveals in his historical accounts of the anthropological endeavour. The impact of economic expansion and settlement on the future prospects of indigenous people in the British colonies had long been of concern to philanthropic and learned societies. The Aborigines Protection Society, for example, successfully lobbied for an official investigation into British colonial policy and practice toward indigenous peoples (British and Foreign Aborigines Protection Society 1837). In 1837 the Select Committee on Aboriginal Tribes (British Settlements) published a report that, as Jacob Gruber (1970, 1292) notes,

> with all of its detail and in the fullness of its understatement, emphasized for all who had the interest to read it the imminence of the racial destruction that lay in the immediate future, and for those who were concerned not only with the human questions but with the scientific ones as well, the conditions that the report exposed made necessary remedial action.

The Aborigines Protection Society published numerous reports on the welfare of indigenous peoples during the following years (see British and Foreign Aborigines Protection Society 1856), yet according to Ronald Rainger (1980, 708-9), it saw no conflict between promoting science and advocating civilization. Its publications collated and distributed ethnographic information while calling for missionary involvement in the colonies and for the more humane treatment of indigenous peoples.

Jacob Gruber (1970, 1295) writes that throughout the later nineteenth and early twentieth centuries, the refrain was the same – "the savage is disappearing; preserve what you can; posterity will hold you accountable." Staff at the new Canadian museums took this message to heart and practised a "colonialist" model of collecting to preserve First Nations heritage for future generations (Willmott 2006, 17). For museum administrators and government officials, these future generations would not include First Nations people, but some anthropologists privately saw their collecting activity as a means of preserving artifacts for the communities in which they worked. Despite this, they probably would not have predicted the levels of access to these collections now sought by First Nations individuals and communities. It is also unlikely that they would have anticipated the rise of keeping houses and cultural centres managed by First Nations, or that ceremonial items would be repatriated and looked after in people's homes.

Institutional Collecting in Canada

Most disciplinary histories date salvage ethnography and the rise of *institutional* collecting in Canada to the mid-nineteenth century, although less structured collecting occurred beforehand for many years, particularly where the fur trade and whaling industries had established links between Europeans, Inuit, and First Nations. From the seventeenth to mid-nineteenth centuries, collecting activity was mostly undertaken by missionaries, North West and Hudson's Bay Company traders (Racine 2009), and military men such as Thomas Whyte and his contemporary Jasper Grant, who was stationed in Upper Canada from 1800 to 1809 (Phillips 1984; Brown 2009). Europeans involved in surveying and exploration also amassed natural and "artificial curiosities"; on the Northwest Coast, the crews of Captains James Cook and George Vancouver traded for furs, other natural resources, and artifacts (Kaeppler 1978; J.C.H. King 1981, 1994). Many such artifacts are now housed in European and American museums, and are among the earliest surviving examples of First Nations creativity. Though many were collected with specific goals in mind – to illustrate First Nations artistic skills, to demonstrate the economic utility of particular materials, or to support the ideology of empire – others were acquired via gift exchange and as indicators of particular social relations rather than within scientific frameworks that emphasized their educational or economic potential.

On the Prairies before the mid-nineteenth century, most collectors were fur trade personnel who lived at trading posts or explorers travelling through the region. The artifacts they accumulated were often sent home and subsequently acquired by natural history societies, curiosity collectors, and museums in cities farther east, or even overseas.[3] As in other parts of the world, where collecting was bound up with colonization (Penny 2002; Henare 2005; MacKenzie 2009; Newell 2010), the gathering of First Nations artifacts often complemented surveying or missionary endeavours and fed the curiosity of European audiences who were keen to learn more about indigenous people. Although early exploratory expeditions had scientific goals, collecting cultural information about First Nations people was secondary to obtaining knowledge about the physical landscape, particularly its potential to support settlement and natural resource extraction. As museums began to expand from cabinets of curiosities to public institutions with rigorous scientific agendas, many European curators were supplied with new artifacts by their contacts in Canada and elsewhere (see D. Lindsay 1993; Knowles 2007). Systematic collecting informed by colonial ideologies began to take hold. Earlier motives for collecting became blurred with the concept of ethnographic salvage; where the collecting of First Nations artifacts had initially been concerned with the otherness of indigenous peoples, new forms of organized collecting were informed by emerging scientific theories of categorization (MacKenzie 2009).

Anthropology and the Development of Museums in Canada

The Canadian Museum of Civilization, whose origins date from the 1842 founding of the Geological Survey of Canada, has a lengthy history of collecting First Nations cultural materials.[4] Following Confederation and the incorporation of Manitoba, the North West Territories, and British Columbia into Canada, Geological Survey staff focused on charting these areas and finding the best route for a transcontinental railroad. Though they often photographed First Nations people as they undertook this work, a concerted effort to record information regarding them did not occur until the 1870s. The stimulus for change came with the 1875 appointment of George Mercer Dawson to the Geological Survey. Dawson had worked in Western Canada from 1872 to 1874 for the British North American Boundary Commission and was then employed by the Geological Survey until 1901. Greatly influenced by the work of his father, Sir John William Dawson, who was curator of the Geological and Natural History Museum in Montreal, he conducted linguistic and ethnographic research among BC First Nations and played an important role in developing ethnological collections for the survey's museum (Zaslow 1975; Hall 1983, 51). According to Douglas Cole (1985, 79), the Geological and Natural History Museum had "no pretensions to universality," and Dawson was keenly aware that the financial constraints faced by the survey, in comparison with better-funded museums in the United States and Europe, limited its ability to build up its own collections of ethnological specimens even within Canada.

In 1881 the Geological and Natural History Museum moved to Ottawa, and staff began systematic ethnological research that focused on the Northwest Coast. The research program was supported by the British Association for the Advancement of Science (BAAS), which had advocated a policy of ethnographic salvage in Canada for some time (Avrith 1986; Stocking 1999, 85-86). At the 1884 Montreal meeting of the BAAS, for instance, it was suggested that the need for research among Canadian First Nations was even more pressing than in the United States (Darnell 1998b, 156), and a Committee on North-Western Tribes was established, under the guidance of George Dawson, Edward Burnett Tylor, then keeper of the University Museum in Oxford, and Daniel Wilson, president of the Royal Society of Canada. Its aim was to record "as perfectly as possible the characteristics and conditions of the Native tribes of the Dominion before the racial peculiarities become less distinguishable through intermarriage and dispersion, and before contact with civilised men has further obliterated the remains of their original arts, customs, and beliefs" (BAAS 1887, 173).

Over the next fourteen years, the BAAS supported the fieldwork of Franz Boas, A.F. Chamberlain, and others, publishing their findings in its annual reports (McIlwraith 1930, 135). Although this research produced vast amounts of ethnological data on BC First Nations, concerns were raised that other Canadian First Nations should be subjected to equally intensive study before time ran out. Accordingly, the BAAS formed a second committee at its 1896 Liverpool meeting whose task was to organize a comprehensive ethnographic survey of the dominion. Modelled on the BAAS Racial Survey of the British Isles, this committee aimed to address urgent issues in salvaging folk customs that were rapidly disappearing due to industrial expansion (Urry 1984; Sillitoe 2004, 12). Appointed its first chairman for a three-year term, George Dawson enthusiastically began to coordinate the project, but his untimely death in 1901 threw it into disarray before much headway could be made. Anthropological enquiry on the grand scale envisioned by the committee was no longer possible as "the field-workers fell out of touch with one another and with the subject; the instruments were scattered, and in 1904 the Ethnographic Survey Committee was not recommended for renewal" (J.L. Myres, Presidential Address to Section H of the BAAS Winnipeg meeting, 1909, quoted in Haddon 1912, 597).

In the event, this collapse did not spell the end of anthropological research in Canada. In 1907 changes to the coordination of scientific research and new economic developments pursued by the state led to the founding of the Department of Mines, and the Geological Survey was included in its remit. The survey's mandate was now broadened to include collecting, cataloguing, and displaying information about First Nations people. Furthermore, at the 1909 BAAS meeting in Winnipeg, a third committee was appointed to reinstate the ethnographic survey of Canada. The recommendations jointly made by this committee, the Royal Society of Canada, and the Canadian branch of the Archaeological Institute of America were fundamental to the development of a separate division for ethnographic research within the Geological Survey. Anthropology was becoming a national concern (Zaslow 1975, 279). Fired by the realization that state-sanctioned assimilation policies were reducing the opportunities for serious academic study, scientific associations also successfully lobbied for the creation of a central repository where the collections and associated information belonging to the Geological and Natural History Museum could be stored. With the construction of the new Victoria Memorial Museum in Ottawa, which opened to the public in 1911, the new Anthropological Division became the "only fully professional anthropological organization in Canada [at the time]" (Darnell 1998b, 158). Its foundation was considered a tremendous boost to scientific knowledge, and contemporary reports in Canada and Europe heralded a new age for the professionalization of the discipline and the hope that similar developments would be implemented throughout the colonies (Haddon 1912, 597).

The goals of the Anthropological Division were ambitious. Staff were expected to conduct fieldwork among a wider range of First Nations than ever before and to disseminate the results through publication and display at the Victoria Memorial Museum. In the Geological Survey's 1910 annual report, Director Reginald Brock (1911, 7) outlined the division's work in the years ahead: "field work among the Native tribes of Canada for the purpose of collecting extensive and reliable information on their ethnology and linguistics, archaeological field work, the publication of results obtained in these investigations, and the exhibition in the Museum of specimens illustrative of Indian and Eskimo life, habit and thought."

Jonathan Peyton and Robert Hancock (2008, 49) argue that Canadian anthropology was dominated by two parallel trends during the interwar period: the Boasian tradition, in which localized case studies were used to explore the particularities of individual cultures; and the social evolutionism characteristic of British anthropology from the later nineteenth century to the First World War. The establishment of the Anthropological Division was regarded as a means to tackle the "problems" of ethnographic salvage, but it was also a response to criticisms of scientific apathy. During the late nineteenth century, the Northwest Coast had been a hub of anthropological interest, with comparatively less scientific investigation undertaken elsewhere in Canada. With the turn of the century, fieldworkers from the United States and increasingly from overseas began to conduct ethnological research among First Nations in other parts of the country. This caused consternation in Canada's small, but vocal, academic community, many of whose members saw the research activity of external organizations as an encroachment and whose concerns were entwined with an emergent nationalism. In her discussion of "colonial" and "nationalist" models of collecting, as exemplified by the practices of US and Canadian museums, Willmott (2006) suggests that the traditions established by private gentlemen collectors, travellers, and Hudson's Bay Company (HBC) personnel continued to dominate in Canada, whereas the United States had a lengthier tradition of public education through the museum movement and a fuller integration of anthropology and museums in universities. Furthermore, she notes, as financial and other government support for collecting from indigenous North Americans was intertwined with policy development, this affected the respective abilities of scientific institutions in Canada and the United States to develop museums and collections. Willmott (ibid., 224) also points to the significance of the relationship between national identity and the concept of "possessive individualism" (Handler 1985), which characterized the nationalist model of collecting. In Canada, indigenous peoples were treated as "other," and in consequence their material heritage was viewed with indifference. Handler (ibid., 213) observes that by the mid-1980s, this relationship had shifted in response to competing nationalist claims of minority groups and the federal government. With reference to the Applebaum-Hébert Report on museum and cultural policy, which recommended greater attention be paid to Aboriginal arts in Canada's national institutions, he writes, "This involves changing the status of Native material culture from artefact to art – that is, from being viewed as the remains of a vanquished 'Other,' to being included as part of the 'high culture' of the mainstream."

In the 1920s, though, First Nations arts and material culture were still very much seen as different yet worthy of study as artifacts in themselves. At least from the 1890s, the Canadian press condemned the flow of such objects to the museums of other countries. Critics complained that the government had allowed foreign anthropologists to collect too much and too widely, and they questioned Canada's ability to assert its own scientific interests. The authors of such opinion pieces claimed that this situation was indicative of Canada's institutional apathy toward studying First Nations, though they rarely exhibited any concern for the welfare or rights of First Nations people. For example, a *Fort Macleod Gazette* article titled "American versus Canadian Enterprise" (Anon. 1897, 1) noted that George Dorsey of the Field Columbian Museum of Chicago had spent several days in May 1897 at the Kainai reserve, Southern Alberta, collecting "ancient relics that have been in the possession of the tribe for many generations" before moving to British Columbia to make further collections.[5] Noting that Canadian museum provision compared unfavourably with that of the United States, the author complained that

> sometime during the next century perhaps, Canada will awaken to the fact that she has had within her borders one of the most extensive and interesting fields in the world for anthropological research, but it will then be too late for original investigations and the study of Canadian ethnology will have become to a large extent the study of the literature and museums of the US.

In the face of such criticism, the Anthropological Division staff set to work. Founding director Edward Sapir led the organization until 1925, when he accepted a teaching position at the University of Chicago. A former student of Franz Boas, with research experience on the Northwest Coast, Sapir proved an extremely capable and resourceful leader who, according to Regna Darnell (1998, 157), "shared Boas's near fanaticism about the need for professional training of anthropologists and systematic organization of anthropological research on a broad, in this case, national, scale." He separated the division into four branches to fit with the Boasian "four-field" approach – archaeology, ethnology, linguistics, and physical anthropology – and he immediately sent staff into the field to collect data and artifacts from First Nations who were not represented in the museum's collection. He set high standards for data collection, and unlike many of his contemporaries, he insisted that his staff gather material that reflected everyday life, not just the visually striking or culturally valuable (Hall 1983, 55). The achievements of Sapir and his staff are all the more remarkable when the lack of funding and government support is taken into account. Like most other Canadian museums at this time, the Victoria Memorial Museum struggled financially but was also hampered by bureaucratic interference; as government employees, its staff had less freedom to determine research priorities than would have been the case in a university. In addition, the weak infrastructure for anthropology as an academic discipline in Canada afforded fewer means through which to lobby for greater support. In his study of the politics of Arctic archaeology in Canada during the early twentieth century, Barnett Richling (1995, 109-10) observes that "a government policy that accorded little importance to anthropological work of any kind meant that survey and museum personnel found themselves on the sidelines all too often, while scientists from foreign institutions investigated what were then the central problems in Canadian (and North American) prehistory and ethnology." For Willmott (2006, 220), this approach conforms to the colonial model of collecting, in which "the federal government consistently failed to see the potential of ethnological data for policy development." Furthermore, as Canada had few wealthy patrons who were prepared to support the development of museums and ethnographic research more broadly, the *only* professional anthropology institution in Canada struggled to establish itself throughout the first half of the twentieth century.

Given the lack of domestic opportunities for aspiring anthropologists in Canada, the Anthropological Division retained strong links with the United Kingdom during its early years, a fact that reflected "its ideological and geographical position within the British colonial empire" (ibid.). Sapir initially saw its role as similar to that of the Bureau of American Ethnology, but many division staff had studied anthropology at British universities and were less familiar with the Boasian approach, which Sapir took for granted. Charles Marius Barbeau became associate ethnologist in 1911, having recently completed a diploma in anthropology at Oxford, which he followed by graduate study at the Sorbonne with Marcel Mauss. He was joined by his Oxford classmate Diamond Jenness, a New Zealander who had participated in the Canadian Arctic Expedition (1913-16) led by Vilhjalmur Stefansson (Jenness 1991). Jenness undertook fieldwork for the division, spending two months during the summer of 1922 on the Tsuu T'ina reserve near Calgary, where he collected clothing, tobacco bags, and domestic utensils that were no longer frequently used, such as hide scrapers and fleshers and pemmican pounders (Jenness 1938). After Sapir's departure in 1925, Jenness became the museum's chief anthropologist, supervising the fieldwork of the assistant staff and publishing prolifically (see, for example, Jenness 1937, 1938, 1996).

By the interwar years, British anthropology was characterized by the lone fieldworker model, in which a researcher undertook extended study, using participant-observation methods. Although this approach was appropriate in many of Britain's overseas colonies (particularly in the Pacific Islands and parts of Africa), it was less suited to locations where the form of colonialism had shifted. Accordingly, most anthropologists in Canada undertook field-work in short bursts over the summer months before returning to their institutions to teach and write. They commonly visited several reserves during a season, usually staying for a few weeks at most and often for far shorter periods. Research staff at the Anthropological Division were no exception to this trend and were given precise instructions at the beginning of each field season. The brevity and tone of these glossed over the complexities of both making field collections and the relationships between First Nations and anthropologists, as the 1928 fieldwork instructions for Harlan I. Smith show:

> Your field work this year will consist of three duties: (1) Purchasing ethno-logical specimens; (2) Securing motion pictures; (3) Discovery and examination of archaeological remains. These operations should be carried on together wherever possible ... Accompanying this letter you will find: (1) A copy of your estimate approved for the expenditure of sums up to $2,250; (2) Booklet of information; (3) Instrument list; (4) Equipment list; (5) Employment and separation forms.[6]

Smith, who had responsibility for the Archaeology Section, spent the field seasons of 1928 and 1929 at the Siksika reserve, where he collected artifacts and took motion picture film for a 1928 documentary titled *The Blackfoot Indians of Alberta*. Other significant collections made by Anthropological Division staff include those assembled by Wilson D. Wallis, also Oxford-trained, who undertook research among the Teton Dakotas of Portage, Manitoba (Richling 1990), and those of William J. Wintemberg, who spent the summer of 1925 in Western Canada at the Bobtail, Duck Lake, Ermineskin, and Paul reserves, and with Nakoda people at Morley.

Archival documents in the Canadian Museum of Civilization indicate that staff felt that the lack of Prairie material hampered their ability to represent First Nations diversity. Consequently, even if employees were sent into the field to conduct archaeological research, they were also expected to collect ethnological material to fill gaps in the collection. A letter from Sapir to L.L. Bolton, acting director of the museum, regarding William Wintemberg's 1925 fieldwork, illustrates this concern. Sapir wrote, "I am venturing to suggest that Mr Wintemberg be asked to purchase about $250 worth of ethnological specimens. We are not very well of [sic] for Plains ethnology, and it would be a pity to miss this opportunity to get further material."[7] Wintemberg's instructions did not refer to carrying out detailed ethnological research, merely to gathering materials.

This stance characterized the activities of many collecting institutions at this time and was related to notions of authenticity and the perceived role of the anthropologist as cultural authority. In his study of the relationship between salvage ethnography and the work of the Anthropological Division, Andrew Nurse argues that, during the 1920s, Marius Barbeau believed that an anthropologist's role was to reconstruct "authentic" Aboriginal cultures as they would have been prior to interaction with settler society. Barbeau thought that First Nations people had been so affected by this interaction that they no longer remembered their culture and that the task of the anthropologist was to do this for them. As he explained, "The present-day Indians of the western prairies and Rocky Mountains are no longer what they used to be. They have dwindled in numbers; their ancient customs are gone, their character is lost. They are a vanishing race" (Barbeau 1924, 6, quoted in Nurse 2008, 15). According to Nurse (2008, 18), Barbeau "lamented the demise of 'authentic' aboriginal cultures, but he seemed to feel that there was little that could be done about it." His views were shared by virtually all his colleagues.

Establishing Museums on the Prairies

During this period of ethnographic salvage, most Prairie artifacts collected by Canadian museum staff were sent to Eastern Canada. Gradually, as small towns and larger cities were established, accompanied by civic pride, the museum movement spread west. Although cities such as Ottawa and Montreal had enjoyed public museums for some time, Winnipeg, Regina, and Calgary, comparatively recently settled, had fewer cultural institutions. The development of museums on the Prairies was partly an attempt to show that Western Canadian cities would not be left behind by their eastern counterparts, and the push for the creation of "provincial museums" was closely linked, in Saskatchewan and Alberta at least, with their new status as provinces.

The Provincial Museum of Natural History in Regina, known today as the Royal Saskatchewan Museum, was the first provincial museum to be founded in the Prairie provinces. It was established in 1906 with the mandate "to secure and preserve natural history specimens and objects of ethnological interest" (Borden 1986, 5). Launching an ethnology program in 1913, the museum appealed to the public to donate any First Nations artifacts it might find, and its collection grew through donations and purchase (ibid., 6). Farther east, Manitoba did not have its own provincial museum until 1970. The Museum of Man and Nature (now the Manitoba Museum) opened in Winnipeg that year, though its origins lie in 1932, when six local doctors formed a museum association for the city to collect and display items of human and natural history (Anon. 1970; Dubois 1991). Manitobans had access to formal and informal displays of First Nations material long before this, however, which is unsurprising, given the demographics in the province and the complex backgrounds of many families. Most HBC fur traders who retired to the Red River Settlement had accumulated material made by Aboriginal people (including their own wives and daughters), which they would have arranged in their homes with varying degrees of formality and visibility.[8] These displays would have included utilitarian items, such as clothing and snowshoes, as well as decorative silk-embroidered cushions and beaded wall pockets.

Winnipeg did not have a publicly accessible museum-style exhibition until the twentieth century, after several retired fur traders proposed a permanent collection of HBC historical artifacts (Pettipas 2009, 59). Their plan was authorized by the HBC in 1919, with the intent of commemorating the company's 250th anniversary the following year. In 1922, the Hudson's Bay Company's Historical Exhibit opened in the HBC Main Street store in Winnipeg. This display, organized thematically with sections titled "Early History," "Life in the Service," and "Indians," was relocated in 1925 to the new HBC retail store on Portage Avenue (ibid., 60), where the Franklin Motor Expedition team may well have visited it. It remained open until 1959, when it was transferred on permanent loan to the Province (Hudson's Bay Company 1923; Coutts and Pettipas 1994). In 1994 the loan was converted to a donation, and a new Hudson's Bay Company Gallery was opened in the Manitoba Museum in 2000.

By the turn of the twentieth century, Calgary's leading citizens were troubled by Alberta's lack of a provincial museum, and they lobbied hard for the funds to build one in their city, rather than Edmonton, where the provincial government was located. In their view, the museum would not only draw donations from local people, who would willingly offer their prized collections, but would also boost Calgary's image, branding it as a cultural centre rather than a rough frontier town. Indeed, a contemporary report noted that a new museum would secure Calgary's place as "one of the most interesting cities of the west from an historical point of view alone."[9] The museum was expected to build upon the work of the small museum established by the Calgary Natural History Society, which had opened to the public in 1911 and was presented as a trust to the City of Calgary in 1927.

Like many museums during this period, the Calgary Museum collected and displayed specimens of natural and human history, which were acquired largely through donation and occasionally through purchase. Around the late 1920s, it began to collect directly from First Nations people, albeit on a limited scale, motivated as much by salvage concerns as by the increased prices of First Nations handiwork. In a 1929 lecture, for example, its curator, J. Thurston, emphasized the need for speed in developing the collection:

> Quick action will be necessary in order to secure an accurate record of the crafts and customs of the Indian tribes of Alberta ... The Indians now are not engaging in the primitive crafts of their fathers and it is becoming increasingly difficult to obtain specimens of their work. Ten years from now the cost of making a collection of Indian relics will be much greater than it is today.[10]

Despite the museum's intention of generating a more systematic approach to collecting, acquisitions were mostly left to chance, as is revealed by a 1931 letter from a resident of Big Valley, Alberta, which included a deceased rodent: "We were interested visitors at the Museum in November but I cannot remember if you have a specimen of the pocket gopher or mole. We found this in a stack a few days ago and I send it as I think it is a good specimen. If you already have one your cat will no doubt relish this tidbit."[11] The Calgary Museum operated until 1935, when financial hardships forced its closure and ended plans to develop a provincial museum in the city. Not until 1967, with the opening of the Provincial Museum of Alberta in Edmonton – known today as the Royal Alberta Museum – was a museum finally established for the province.[12]

The values and opportunities that museums were believed to encapsulate were promoted throughout Canada, though collecting styles differed according to the size and remit of institutions, funding, and staff expertise. Comments in 1920s visitor books, including those of the Calgary Museum, suggest that most visitors saw museums as valuable educational establishments that were unquestionably worthy of support. Clearly, visitors and administrators alike saw museums as a vehicle through which Canadians could take pride in a growing sense of nationhood and could showcase the cultural and natural heritage that was unique to the country. Canadian responses to collecting by researchers and museums from other countries were shaped by this context.

British Museums and Collecting in Canada

First Nations were not affected solely by the actions of Canadian and American collectors. During the late nineteenth and early twentieth centuries, British museums assembled substantial ethnographic collections on an unprecedented scale. Artifacts deemed to show the progress of technological and cultural evolution, as well as botanical and zoological specimens and human remains, were gathered from around the world, especially from regions where British colonial authorities asserted political power and military interests or where settler societies had established themselves. During this period, First Nations cultural materials entered British museums through a number of routes: as donations, bequests, or purchases from former colonial officers, traders, missionaries, and tourists who had visited or lived in Canada, or from their descendants. Others were purchased, often with scant provenance, from specialist dealers, auction rooms, or house sales. With the exception of the Museum of Archaeology and Anthropology (MAA) at Cambridge University, whose collecting activities will be addressed in subsequent chapters, few British institutions had the resources – or the inclination – to support collecting activity like that of Canadian or American museums. Instead, their First Nations research and collecting projects were (and are) on a much smaller scale, and were primarily undertaken by people employed by or associated with university or national museums.

This by no means implies a lack of interest at the popular or scholarly level or that UK museums rarely exhibited First Nations artifacts. Indeed, British museums, art, and literature have a long history of representing the indigenous peoples of North America (see, for example, S. Pratt 2005). Moreover, throughout the nineteenth century, with increased travel and emigration, and the resulting global circulation of Native-made arts, the British public was not unfamiliar with First Nations artifacts or with the images and descriptions of them that appeared in journals, newspapers, and letters from friends and relatives.[13]

The perception that First Nations ways of life were dying out was common in Britain, although concerns about the future of indigenous peoples throughout the colonized world were voiced principally in academic circles. Between 1900 and 1930, almost every meeting of the BAAS stressed the need to invest in anthropological study and the importance of having trained observers in colonial outposts (Fortes 1953, 12; Stocking 1999, 379; see also Mills 2003; and Sillitoe 2004). The call came from academics and civil servants, who believed that indigenous people must be studied to ascertain the best means of controlling them. The teaching of anthropology was still in its infancy at this time, although courses were available at several universities throughout the United Kingdom (Kuklick 2007), with Cambridge being a main centre for the discipline's development. The comparative lack of tuition at Canadian universities meant that students with anthropological interests were compelled to study in Britain or the United States. In consequence, links between anthropologists working in Canada and their former departments in the United Kingdom played an important role in the sharing of theory and practice, and were also a factor in the movement of First Nations artifacts between institutions. Examples of this appear in the correspondence between Diamond Jenness and MAA curator Louis C.G. Clarke. In one letter, Jenness wrote that he had "picked out a dozen little specimens illustrating the Cape Dorset culture and am forwarding them in a little box. It is a very tiny gift, but the specimens are carefully selected and very typical, illustrating some of the most marked features in that culture."[14] Several years later, Jenness compared British- and American-trained research staff, noting that he could "get any number of assistant archaeologists in the US, but would prefer an Englishman with old world training."[15]

Professional ties were strong, and anthropologists sometimes acquired material for several museums, seemingly without any conflict of interest. Indeed, Louis Clarke approached Edward Sapir in 1923 to set up just such an arrangement on behalf of the MAA. He had learned that the Victoria Memorial Museum planned to send Thomas F. McIlwraith, former student of the Faculty of Archaeology and Anthropology at Cambridge University and a founding member of the University of Toronto's Department of Anthropology, to collect among the Nuxalk Nation (Bella Coola).[16] Sapir replied that he had no objection to McIlwraith collecting for the MAA as well, adding that he should be able to "secure a rather good general collection," though neither museum should expect to obtain anything other than "ordinary staples."[17] Other correspondence indicates that some items were sent overseas due to anxiety regarding their care. Writing to A.C. Haddon in Cambridge, McIlwraith suggested that the Victoria Memorial Museum was too bureaucratic, a flaw that would adversely affect staff's ability to curate collections. Prior to his appointment with the Victoria Memorial Museum, he had collected artifacts for the Canadian government, some of which he sent to the MAA with a request that their source remain anonymous. In McIlwraith's view, they would receive better care in Cambridge than in Ottawa, where the museum "would not have the sense to appreciate them" (quoted in Rouse 1996, 189).

British university museum staff maintained an interest in North America throughout the early decades of the twentieth century, but by the late 1920s collecting agendas lay largely elsewhere, partly due to shifting colonial policies and responsibilities, but also because much of the "best" material was no longer available. Indeed, the heyday of museum collecting had ended by the early 1930s, as financial problems exacerbated by the Depression reduced the number of expeditions that could be funded. Prior to this, large amounts of First Nations material had entered the United Kingdom for exhibition outside university environments, and some of it found its way into museum collections. Beginning with the Great Exhibition of 1851, a series of displays and expositions held in cities throughout the United Kingdom promoted Britain's overseas interests and introduced the public to indigenous peoples from the colonies in ways that museums could not replicate (Coombes 1994a, 112; Qureshi 2011). These expositions were designated both as "scientific demonstration" and "popular entertainment," and as Annie Coombes (1988, 57) writes, they were "the physical embodiment of different and sometimes conflicting imperial ideologies" and were intimately bound up with notions of social class. They usually offered information about a country's natural resources and industrial potential, but they also presented packaged cultural narratives through the use of reconstructed villages inhabited by people representing particular nations, which were intended to introduce the public to the lives of colonial subjects. First Nations people often participated in these displays, sometimes living for weeks at a time in tipi villages and demonstrating cultural practices that, by this time, were rarely found on reserves (J.C.H. King 1991a, 41). Like the ever-popular Wild West shows that toured Europe from the 1880s to around the 1930s, these cultural representations fulfilled the expectations and fantasies of an undiscriminating British public, allowing it to make judgments about indigenous people based on identifiers such as the clothes they wore and the artifacts they used. Some of these artifacts were produced specifically for exhibition; others were loaned by Canadian museums. During the late 1920s, for example, the National Museum of Canada sent photographs of First Nations people for display at London's Royal Colonial Institute, and in 1929 it loaned ethnological material to the Native Exhibit of the Canadian Section of the Imperial Institute to create "an exhibit worthy of a prominent position in the halls of the Imperial Institute and one in which the National Museum of Canada can take pride. The material is excellent, representative and valuable, and a great deal of it could not be replaced."[18]

British museum curators made the most of opportunities to acquire First Nations materials that entered the country with the participants of travelling shows or as contributions to larger expositions, but the collection of First Nations objects was generally rather haphazard.[19] The personal interests and experience of staff often dictated the areas in which a museum would collect, but even museums that actively amassed ethnographic materials rarely had the resources to undertake field trips abroad. Those that did were generally associated with the wealthier universities and benefited from collections gathered on university-sponsored scientific expeditions. For instance, artifacts collected on the British Arctic Air Route Expedition (1930-31) and the Wordie Arctic Expedition (1934) are now in the MAA, and materials assembled during the Oxford University Ellesmere Land Expedition (1934-35) are in the Pitt Rivers Museum. During the first half of the twentieth century, the MAA was the only British museum that consistently supported fieldwork in North America. This was due largely to the research interests and generosity of Louis C.G. Clarke (1881-1960), who was its curator from 1922 to 1937. Independently wealthy, having inherited a fortune from his family's coal-mining interests, Clarke frequently paid for new acquisitions and museum furnishings, and he often sponsored the collecting endeavours and academic aspirations of students studying anthropology and archaeology (Elliott and Thomas 2011, 13) (Figure 5). His protégés included Graham Rowley and Thomas Paterson (archaeologists who worked in the Canadian Arctic), and Geoffrey Bushnell, a natural historian who subsequently switched disciplines to Central American archaeology.[20] In his obituary of Clarke, Bushnell (1961, 192) referred to his mentor's legendary generosity: "Among the Museum's possessions is a rubber stamp saying Clarke Gift, and it is interesting to speculate on how much time has

Figure 5   Portrait of Louis C.G. Clarke by P.A. Laszlo, 1906 |
Reproduced by permission of University of Cambridge Museum of Archaeology
and Anthropology, 1971.40

been saved by its use in the accessions books and catalogue cards. There is
hardly a show case in the building which does not contain some gifts from
him, and some have many."[21]

As a result of Clarke's efforts, the MAA acquired artifacts from Plains
people through auction, exchange, and donation. Clarke actively sought to
expand the Plains holdings throughout his curatorship, but most UK museums had neither the resources nor the inclination to compete. Though
the larger museums that actively collected ethnographic artifacts did accept
donations of North American material, they were less likely to solicit it or
to contribute to field trip costs. British anthropologists and museum professionals undoubtedly regarded salvage ethnography on the Prairies as an

important task but generally felt that it was the responsibility of Canadian museums. Certainly, once the Anthropological Division and the Victoria Memorial Museum were established, correspondence between UK anthropologists and their overseas colleagues makes less reference to the urgency and need to collect, although British anthropologists, and the BAAS in particular, remained interested in anthropological research in Canada, as in all parts of the empire.

American Museums and Collecting in Canada

The prolific collecting of the Anthropological Division of the Geological Survey did much to raise the profile of anthropology and museums in Canada. Nevertheless, Canadian scholars remained concerned that valuable resources for the future study of First Nations were being removed by collecting institutions in the United States. Some critics suspected that their neighbours to the south regarded collecting from First Nations in Canada as a legitimate extension of their efforts to collect from Native Americans. It is not difficult to see why such assumptions were made. Until the creation of the Anthropological Division, there had been no framework to coordinate research in a nation as geographically and culturally diverse as Canada. Furthermore, political leaders were far more concerned with the prospects for settlement, economic growth, and resource extraction than with the cultural resources of First Nations. Even though Canadian museums indisputably benefited from government policies regarding First Nations people – policies that ultimately facilitated collecting – supporting museums financially was less of a priority for the federal and provincial governments. Canadian museums were consistently underfunded in comparison with those in the United States (Willmott 2006).

Near the close of the nineteenth century, Canadian critics became increasingly antagonistic toward American collectors. British competition for the limited number of specimens seemingly caused rather less alarm, due to the professional relationships and mutual support between Canadian and UK-based scholars, and the political ties linking the two countries. In an 1897 letter to Edward Tylor at Oxford University, for instance, George Dawson complained bitterly about the numbers of artifacts being collected by American institutions. In his view, Franz Boas was the major culprit. Much of Boas's fieldwork on the Northwest Coast had been funded by the BAAS, and he was by then curator of ethnology at the American Museum of Natural History (AMNH). Dawson, who believed that these activities were strengthening American collections at the expense of both Canadian and British museums, wrote,

> It is to be regretted that it means a further concentration of what little remains of our West Coast ethnological material in the New York museum, there being already there, in Washington and in Berlin, far better collections of the remarkable works of the British Columbia Indians than exist in the British Museum or in any Canadian museum. It has almost been a weakness in our connection with Dr Boas, that while we supplied the funds, or most of them, his collecting went elsewhere.[22]

Charles Harrison, a missionary, collector, and amateur ethnologist living at Massett, Haida Gwaii, voiced similar sentiments and also wrote to Tylor, claiming that British scientific institutions had some catching up to do: "The Smithsonian Institute [sic] has had photographers and skeleton hunters here already. In this respect the English Societies are behind the Americans, and allow them to obtain the best specimens."[23] Such statements were not uncommon in the private correspondence of Canadian and British scholars at this time, and they contributed to the discourse of ethnographic salvage that marked anthropological practice in the early twentieth century. They also point to the collegiality between Canadian-based anthropologists and their UK colleagues. As we have seen, they occasionally shared resources and sometimes collaborated on the development of collections. By contrast, American anthropologists were regarded with some mistrust, and their presence as staff in the National Museum and other Canadian institutions was viewed as a "take-over," albeit the result of "both conscious and unconscious choices made by Canadians themselves" (Avrith 1986, 285).

Most difficult for Canadian-based anthropologists to accept was the gap in funding opportunities between Canadian and American museums and research institutions. More numerous than their Canadian equivalents, American museums were better resourced and organized, and Canadian museums simply could not compete. Their efforts to collect were also hampered by the fact that anthropology's professional development had occurred much earlier in the United States than in Canada (see, for example, Hinsley 1981; Bieder 1986; and Harrison and Darnell 2006). Ethnological research, including philology, technology, mythology, and collecting the material culture of Native American tribes, had been part of the Bureau of American Ethnology's mandate since its inception in 1879 (Judd 1967, 4); all the metropolitan centres had public museums and scientific societies, and other museums developed in tandem with the discipline itself in the universities (Bronner 1989). Academic institutions devoted to the study of Native Americans were generously funded through government resources or philanthropy. Moreover, there were more university anthropology programs in the United States than in Canada and many more job opportunities for anthropology graduates. Although some Canadian universities offered anthropology courses during the 1920s, it was not until 1936 that the first independent Department of Anthropology was founded, at the University of Toronto (Darnell 1998, 158).

Like their British and Canadian colleagues, US-based scientists who undertook ethnographic fieldwork, collecting, and research in Canada initially focused on the Northwest Coast and the Arctic, with Franz Boas being the most prominent scholarly authority on these areas (Cole 1985; Darnell 1998a; Jacknis 2002). The large-scale expeditions funded by American museums to these regions were never replicated on the Canadian Prairies, though several American anthropologists conducted individual research and collecting projects there as part of their doctoral studies or on a contract basis for US museums. Like National Museum staff, US-based anthropologists working on the Prairies during the first three decades of the century tended to spend short periods of up to three or four months at reserves, and depending on the aspirations of their employers and their own academic goals, their work ranged from survey collecting to more detailed ethnographic study.

David Mandelbaum (1911-87) was one such anthropologist. He spent the summers of 1934 and 1935 at a number of Plains Cree reserves in Southern Saskatchewan, undertaking fieldwork for his doctorate (Mandelbaum 1940, 1996). Though his focus was the impact of environmental change on Plains Cree cultural practices, he also collected artifacts, some of which are now in the AMNH in New York.[24] Mandelbaum's fieldwork followed the solitary participant-observer model, which involved spending a lengthier period in a chosen field site rather than moving comparatively rapidly and gave him the time to make extensive ethnographic field notes; in contrast, the Franklin Motor Expedition team recorded only superficial information about the artifacts they purchased and, as far as can be ascertained, no written records other than an inventory of items acquired were made. That such different styles of fieldwork could occur within a five-year period is indicative of the complexities of collecting histories on the Prairies, as well as of the methodological approaches adopted by field collectors.

A further form of museum collecting in the early twentieth century was that supported by Mandelbaum's supervisor, Clark Wissler (1870-1947). Every summer between 1902 and 1905, while employed as an AMNH ethnology assistant, Wissler undertook brief ethnographic research and collecting visits to the Northern Plains. He subsequently succeeded Boas as AMNH ethnology curator and took on teaching responsibilities at Yale and Columbia (Freed and Freed 1983). Wissler's research was heavily influenced by his long-term partnership with David C. Duvall, the son of a French Canadian father and a Piikani mother, and resulted in six volumes in the AMNH Anthropological Papers series, based primarily on Duvall's observations (Wissler 1910, 1911, 1912, 1913, 1918; Wissler and Duvall 1995; Wissler and Kehoe 2012). This relationship was largely conducted through correspondence, and Wissler rarely engaged directly with Blackfoot people, as Allan Pard of the Piikani First Nation has remarked in an interview concerning changes in curatorial practice:

> I think that now museums have become more sophisticated and advanced in their thinking. They are now coming out into the communities and into the areas where they have collected artifacts, and are now collecting the information. A lot of the information was collected really haphazardly at the time. Probably by shoddy fieldworkmanship, that type of thing, for whatever reasons. But none of the leading people were really out in the community. For example, Clark Wissler of the Museum of Natural History in New York. The majority of his fieldwork was done by a person from that community [David Duvall], and that information was sent to New York. He didn't have an understanding or first-hand, direct involvement with the people, so he was making all his conclusions away from the community. (Allan Pard, author interview, Fort Macleod, 6 August 1999)

Wissler relied on Duvall for ethnographic information, and he also encouraged him to collect artifacts on his behalf. Some of these items were commissioned; others were sought as existing examples of specific artifact types. In a letter updating Wissler on his purchases, Duvall wrote, "I have old man Boy, making the bow, arrows and the rattle for $6.00. And Heavy Breast is making the robe. The willow, water bag, whistle Leader's feather and one lance for twenty dollars. Lazy Boy has got the shirt for me any time I want it. I offered him six dollars for it."[25] Although Duvall conducted the bulk of the field collecting during his lengthy association with the AMNH, decisions about artifact selection were made in consultation with Wissler, who would identify gaps in the collection and ask Duvall to fill them. Wissler drew upon this experience when guiding Mandelbaum's collecting three decades later.

George Heye's Museum of the American Indian

Despite the protests and suspicions of the Canadian media and museum staff, American anthropologists were probably less preoccupied with collecting from First Nations than was sometimes implied. They were probably outnumbered by private collectors, whose actions were less visible. Furthermore, although American scholars certainly collected in Canada, many preferred to focus their efforts on Native American reservations within their own national boundaries. Finally, by the 1920s, research funding tended to be more closely linked to US foreign policy interests overseas, which enabled museums to broaden their collections by sending scientific expeditions to areas that had previously been less accessible, most especially in Africa, Asia, and the Pacific (Schildkrout 1998, 175; May 2010).

The broadening of US ethnographic interests allowed one American museum to continue its efforts with very little competition: the Museum of the American Indian (MAI), located in New York City. Its founder, George Heye (1874-1957), has been described as "probably the most intensely driven and acquisitive collector of the material artefacts of native cultures who has ever lived" (Bruhac 1994, 42). According to Bruhac (ibid.),

When Heye ... descended upon a native community, he bought everything in sight, sending boxcars full of artefacts back to New York. Contemporary Native people, whose parents remember his visits, have said, "If he left us with our underclothes we were lucky!" Heye – a man of whom my own Abenaki people might have used the phrase *gedacowaldam mziwi*, "He wants it all" – collected so extensively that almost every aspect of the material cultures of countless native communities is represented in the museum's holdings.

Heye has been branded an obsessive-compulsive collector who was driven by materialistic goals rather than a sincere interest in the lives of Native American people. According to one biographer (Wallace 1960, 118), he

> didn't give a hang about Indians individually and he never seemed to have heard about their problems in present-day society ... George didn't buy Indian stuff in order to study the life of a people, because it never crossed his mind that that's what they were. He bought all these objects solely in order to own them – for whatever purposes, he never said.

The result of Heye's compulsiveness was a collection that eventually became the largest of its kind, including approximately 90,000 photographic images and some 800,000 artifacts from across the Americas. It has since been absorbed by the Smithsonian Institution to form the National Museum of the American Indian. This consists of three venues – the George Gustav Heye Center in New York City, the Cultural Resources Center in Suitland, Maryland, and the National Museum of the American Indian, which opened in Washington, DC, in 2004. It also maintains an outreach service to bring the collections and staff expertise together with indigenous communities throughout the Americas (Jacknis 2006; Lonetree and Cobb-Greetham 2008).

Heye began to collect Native American materials as a young man, and following his mother's death in 1915 and his inheritance of the family fortune, he gave up his business interests to devote himself to his hobby. He joined the American Anthropological Association around the time he began collecting and started to correspond with scholars such as George Hubbard Pepper of the AMNH and Marshall H. Saville, an archaeology professor at Columbia University, both of whom he credited with introducing him to the science of anthropological study. In return, Heye provided financial support for several scientific expeditions to Central America, including those of Pepper and Saville (N.B. Martinez 1998, 34).

During these years, Heye continued to build up his artifact collection by sponsoring archaeological and ethnographic fieldwork, visiting reservations, buying up private collections, and arranging exchanges with museums and collectors, often in Europe (Kidwell 1999; Bernstein 2004, 53). The collection repeatedly outgrew its storage arrangements and had to be rehoused several times. Heye eventually decided to found his own museum, with himself as director and chair of the board of trustees. The MAI was established in New York City in 1916, although the US entry into the First World

War delayed its public opening until 1922. It was staffed by a team of field-workers who were attracted by the prospect of "a new dream museum," with fully-funded fieldwork, permanent salaries, and pensions (Lothrop 1957, 66). Until 1928, when the deaths of two of the museum's most generous benefactors and the subsequent Depression led to cutbacks and the loss of several positions, the staff enjoyed great freedom; they collected, researched, and published with few of the teaching or administrative duties that encumbered anthropologists and archaeologists based in universities or in other museums.

A hands-on employer, Heye was closely involved in the activities of his staff, even accompanying them on their expeditions. His presence was not always appreciated, however, and he was soon left with few experienced staff, as many of his employees disliked his interference, his "amateurism and megalomaniac collecting," and his unorthodox practices (Carpenter 1991, 15; 2005). Those who remained had little or no formal training in archaeology and anthropology, and their attitudes to record keeping and other professional standards were arguably less rigorous than those of their departed colleagues. The lack of academic training was not necessarily a hindrance, as many of the remaining staff had relevant practical skills acquired through previous work as traders or junior members of expeditions, and they learned about curatorship and research methods on the job.

Several MAI staff made field trips to the Canadian Prairies between 1914 and 1926. Alanson B. Skinner visited Anishinaabe and Plains Cree reserves in Central and Southern Manitoba, Saskatchewan, and Alberta in 1914 (Skinner 1914a, 1914b, 1914c), and several years later, during the summers of 1925 and 1926, Donald A. Cadzow travelled through the Prairie provinces and made collections at over a dozen reserves. Like other museum staff at this time, MAI fieldworkers practised a form of salvage ethnography, and as the following extracts from the museum's *Annual Reports* imply, their approach was also shaped by the need to fill gaps in the collection:

> In the latter part of June Mr Cadzow proceeded to Portage la Prairie, Manitoba, Canada, to study and collect ethnology from the Bungi Indians, a tribe not heretofore represented in our collections ... The month of August and part of September Mr Cadzow spent among the Prairie Cree in south and central Saskatchewan, Canada. Authentic ethnology from these people was needed badly to strengthen the Museum collections from the Canadian Northwest. (Museum of the American Indian 1926, 6)

Starting in May, Mr Donald A. Cadzow, of the Museum staff, continued his work in the Canadian northwest ... An interesting series of specimens with related data was gathered, so that the Museum now possesses as complete an ethnologic collection from these people as it is now possible to obtain. (Museum of the American Indian 1927, 5)

Staff reported their findings in *Indian Notes,* a quarterly publication that included MAI news, reviews of new acquisitions, short articles written by scientific staff on their return from the field, and details of radio talks, lectures, and film presentations given in the museum and elsewhere.

National Pride and Controlling Collecting

That the MAI and several other US institutions had the resources to be active in Canada was a constant source of irritation for Canadian-based anthropologists and curators. Archival evidence suggests that though National Museum staff and other Canadian officials did not deliberately obstruct American anthropologists, they were rather more helpful to their British colleagues. Nevertheless, if the choice were between seeing specimens in an American museum or losing them to a private collector, the former was infinitely preferable. Correspondence between Diamond Jenness and former HBC trader Phillip Godsell, for instance, shows that, on at least one occasion, Jenness advised persons seeking fieldwork contracts through the National Museum to contact the MAI instead.[26] He wrote, "Personally, I very much regret seeing so much Canadian material go to the US, but we are sadly restricted in our activities and it is better for the material to go to a reputable museum like the Museum of the American Indian than to be destroyed or lost."[27]

With concern mounting in Canada that too many First Nations artifacts were being sent across the border, museum staff devised a new strategy with the hope of reducing losses. Jenness suggested, in a letter to W.H. Collins, acting director of the Victoria Memorial Museum, that the larger Canadian museums should work together; staff would collect for more than one institution and the costs could be shared, thus preventing "many of the most valuable specimens from going to the U.S." Jenness's scheme was a direct response to the news that, once again, an American museum had sponsored field collecting on the Canadian Prairies. In the same letter he wrote, "The United States museums are finding Canada a splendid collecting field. Last year (and again this year) the Heye Museum in New York had a party gathering all the specimens it could purchase from our Prairie Indians into its store-rooms; so that probably when our Canadian museums try to make extensive collections, there will be nothing left to collect."[28]

Jenness's proprietary tone was connected to prevailing ideas of Canadian nationalism and autonomy, and was exacerbated by the frustrations of operating with limited funds. In addition, legislation had been passed that assumed a higher financial value for Northwest Coast indigenous carvings than for the cultural materials of other First Nations. Replying to a letter from Jenness, who had declined to buy his First Nations artifact collection for $10,000, Phillip Godsell wrote,

> It is too bad that Parliament is not a little more liberal in this respect, as
> it appears to me that the big American museums are pretty well cleaning
> out all the western Indian reserves of the really good and valuable stuff,
> and while the Smithsonian Institution, Field Museum, American Museum
> of Natural History and the Heye Foundation all have wonderful collec-
> tions, there is hardly any large public collection in Canada.[29]

Despite increasingly vocal public and professional anxiety about the collecting ventures of museums from outside of Canada, legislation to protect First Nations cultural property was not passed until 1927, when section 106 of the Indian Act was amended (*An Act to Amend the Indian Act*, S.C. 1926-27, c. 32, 17 Geo. V, in Department of Indian and Northern Affairs 1981, 142). Under the act, removing or altering certain cultural items such as carved house-posts, grave-houses, and rock carvings found on re-serves could result in a $200 fine, seizure of the materials, and a jail sentence in default of payment (Pettipas 1994, 165). This amendment also enabled the Department of Indian Affairs (DIA) to veto the sale of any totem pole on reserve land. Furthermore, whereas totem poles that served as tourist attractions were to be preserved in situ, the rest were to be put in museums, preferably in Canada. As few Canadian museums could afford to buy them, the legislation did little to prevent their sale to public institutions elsewhere, and the control of totem poles and their movement was effectively handed to Ottawa (Cole 1985, 278; Hawker 2003, 54). Limited as the 1927 amend-ment was, it did at least provide some protection to the material heritage of Northwest Coast First Nations, albeit under the guise of declaring monumental carvings part of Canada's national heritage. No such legislation protected the cultural artifacts of Prairie nations. Indeed, as discussed in the previous chapter, rather than encourage their preservation, legislation was enacted to disrupt expressions of ceremonial life as far as possible.

Collecting and the Department of Indian Affairs

Museum collecting on the Canadian Prairies during the early twentieth century could not have occurred without the involvement of DIA officials.[30] DIA control of reserve communities extended to managing the activities of visiting anthropologists and researchers, and Indian agents sometimes used their authority to encourage or limit First Nations participation in scientific studies. Following the 1927 amendment to the Indian Act, scholars who wished to undertake research with First Nations communities were expected to secure official permission, whereas previously an informal request for assistance had sufficed. The DIA seemed to view the 1927 amendment as a way of controlling the breadth, if not the specifics, of research projects. Deputy Superintendent General D.C. Scott claimed to be "pleased to lend any assistance that [would result] in the advancement of scientific investigations," and it appears that so long as research proposals came from reputable organizations and did not conflict with the department's assimilation policies, official approval was granted.[31] DIA officials were expected to assist researchers and to act as intermediaries between them and reserve residents. Oxford University researcher Beatrice Blackwood, for instance, who between 1925 and 1927 conducted research on issues of race and culture across North America, recorded numerous occasions in her diary and field notes when Indian agents facilitated her fieldwork. Common forms of assistance included driving her around the reserves, translating for her, and arranging for her to take photographs and physical measurements. Though Blackwood did not say that her research would have been impossible without the support of government officials, missionaries, and other reserve staff, her comments make clear that these individuals were crucial to its success (Brown, Peers, and members of the Kainai Nation 2006, 72).

Careful reading of ethnographic monographs, articles, and field notes produced at this time, such as those of Beatrice Blackwood, highlights the various responses of First Nations people to visiting researchers. Whereas some individuals and communities were deeply opposed to the presence of researchers and collectors, and resisted the efforts of DIA agents to force their compliance, others chose to cooperate. Aware of the changes taking place in their communities, some people seem to have regarded anthropologists – though not necessarily museums – as being better placed to look after ceremonial bundles and other spiritual artifacts at a time when the illegality of their use made them vulnerable. Katherine Pettipas (1994, 172) suggests that individuals who chose to work with anthropologists were resisting outside stresses and were using the opportunity to voice their concerns to potentially sympathetic listeners who might advocate on their behalf. David Martínez makes a similar point with reference to a collecting expedition led by the Dakota writer and activist Charles Eastman (Ohiyesa) and sponsored by George Heye, which visited Minnesota and Ontario in 1910. Martínez (2008, 80) reminds us that some First Nations people "willingly" participated in anthropological projects and that "we must not be blind to the fact that, 'Indian etiquette' aside, the Ojibwes who handed over the utilitarian and sacred artefacts to Eastman did so under their own volition."[32] This point alerts us to the complexities of collecting exchanges, which were rarely as clear-cut as museum documentation might imply. Martínez's essay also draws attention to the possibilities of collectors "indigenizing the collecting process." Eastman's family background made him more attuned to cultural protocols than many other museum-sponsored collectors. "Less of a scientist and more of a traveller," he "approached Indian leaders and showed them due respect, smoked the pipe with them, stayed in their camps and villages, ate with them, 'and made them presents'" (ibid., 81). As we shall see in later chapters, Donald Cadzow and the Rymill brothers followed suit, though they probably had a more limited appreciation of the wider implications of their actions.

The DIA involvement in anthropological inquiry was not confined to facilitating research activity on reserves, and staff from various levels of government worked together to further scientific knowledge about First Nations. Correspondence between Edward Sapir and D.C. Scott, for example, indicates that the Anthropological Division and the DIA collaborated to further the work of the division. On one occasion, following an introduction from Scott, Sapir arranged for four Nisga'a men who were visiting Ottawa to be shown around the Victoria Memorial Museum and for their photographs to be taken and their physical measurements documented. He also used the opportunity to record "some valuable data on the Nass River social organization." After their visit, Sapir wrote to Scott to suggest that other First Nations people visiting the capital on official business with the DIA should be encouraged to meet with the museum's research staff, who would record ethnographic information about them. According to Sapir, "There [was] no reason why an increasingly valuable storehouse of photographs and anthropometric material might not be obtained in this way, not to speak of the possibility of getting incidental data on ethnology and linguistics."[33] Scott expressed his pleasure that Sapir had enjoyed the "interview with the Nishga Indians" and said he would keep his suggestion in mind.[34] The Nisga'a visitors' perspectives on their museum experience were not recorded. This example demonstrates Sapir's willingness to work with the DIA when it suited, but his relationship with the department was complex. Peyton and Hancock (2008, 55) point to instances when Sapir spoke out publicly against the anti-Potlatch laws and advocated for the return of wampum belts that had been illegally removed from the Six Nations reserve. They note Darnell's view that "Sapir felt that the responsibility of the Division as a national anthropological research body was to act on behalf of the native people" (Darnell 1984, 171, quoted in Peyton and Hancock 2008, 54) and conclude that although "Sapir's moral standpoint on the treatment of First Nations is clear ... it is regrettable that he did not use his position of influence and expertise to initiate a persistent program of advocacy" (Peyton and Hancock 2008, 55).

DIA field staff also gathered First Nations artifacts, and many of these personal collections later entered museums in Canada or overseas.[35] Some employees maintained a regular correspondence with DIA officials about collecting on the reserves where they worked. Robert Wilson, who had assisted Clark Wissler's Blackfoot research and who was a keen amateur ethnographer, was aware of the competitive nature of institutional collecting, its effects on inflating market values, and its impact on First Nations communities.[36] In 1913, after leaving the DIA, he attempted to send a shield to an American collector, but it was intercepted by Montreal customs officials, so Wilson wrote to D.C. Scott, asking him to offer it to "that big museum in Ottawa" or any individual or institution that would pay his price of $200. Noting that, in his experience, only US museums and private collectors would pay "fair prices for valuable specimens," he said that he had already sold them many items. Should no Canadian buyer be found for the shield, Scott was to forward it to the AMNH.[37] Scott replied that he had not received the shield and could only assume that it had gone to the United States. He added,

I should like to have had an opportunity of purchasing this and would have endeavoured to buy it for my own office and afterwards have it transferred to the Museum. If you have anything else to dispose of I wish you would let me know. I can assure you it would have been no trouble to deal with this matter, only a pleasure to do anything for you.[38]

Shortly after this exchange, Wilson again contacted Scott with an offer of two further Blackfoot shields. The correspondence indicates that these were purchased by the Victoria Memorial Museum, which was prepared to pay his price "rather than lose the opportunity to secure such valuable specimens."[39]

Throughout this period, D.C. Scott frequently corresponded with Victoria Memorial Museum staff and encouraged his colleagues and acquaintances to sell or donate their collections to Canadian institutions rather than to buyers elsewhere. In one instance, he contacted Diamond Jenness to recommend that his friend Thomas Deasy should collect Haida "Jadite" totem poles for the museum.[40] Jenness replied that the museum would be happy to select carvings up to the value of $300, and he requested that Scott ask Deasy to seek out other artifacts as well, as "some of the older people on the islands must still possess a number of old house-hold things which belonged to the aboriginal life and these would be just as valuable to us as more artistic specimens."[41]

In Western Canada, DIA staff also took an active role in assisting local museums to establish First Nations collections. Correspondence in the F. Bradshaw files of the Royal Saskatchewan Museum shows that throughout the 1920s, Indian Commissioner William Graham worked directly with museum staff to acquire items such as beaded bags, clothing, and birch bark containers for display at the annual Regina Fair and Exhibition. These would later be incorporated into the provincial museum collection. Graham bought or borrowed locally made work and asked Indian agents on Prairie reserves to send him additional materials whose purchase might be negotiated at a later date. Museum staff would then create a list of pieces required for the collection, which they would submit to Graham, who arranged for them to be forwarded to the museum. Though many First Nations people did agree to the sale of items requested by Graham, others were less willing and would sell only if their price were met. When Jack Low Horn of the Kainai Nation was asked to sell a fire bag to the Royal Saskatchewan Museum, for example, the sale fell through because his asking price of fifty dollars was refused.[42]

Commissioner Graham did not restrict his assistance to Canadian museums, although they were the primary recipients of his aid. A handwritten receipt issued by Graham for a "Fire bag made by the Indians of Standing Buffalo Reserve (Sioux) near Fort Qu'Appelle," which reads on the reverse "Rec'd from Miss B. Blackwood the sum of seven dollars – Chah n haw his mark X. Witness W.M. Graham, Indian Commissioner," is stored in the Pitt Rivers Museum along with Beatrice Blackwood's diary and associated papers from her North American research trip. Blackwood visited the Regina Fair and Exhibition in July 1925 and wrote in her diary that some "excellent examples of beadwork" were available in the Exhibits Building (Figure 6).[43] A beaded and quilled fire bag that she donated to the Pitt Rivers Museum in 1935 is probably the piece referred to in the receipt.[44]

Many DIA staff mediated relations between researchers and collectors and First Nations people, but the department's official stance toward science and collecting was complex and sometimes contradictory. The DIA was not averse to research, so long as First Nations people were discouraged from talking too much about the forbidden activities that were, of course, the very subjects in which anthropologists were interested. It was not unknown for the DIA to direct researchers to particular communities, further controlling the extent of contact between anthropologists and First Nations. In one instance, Samuel H. Hooke and William Perry, from University College London, asked the DIA for advice regarding a suitable location for summer fieldwork. Scott recommended that they visit the Blackfoot reserves in Southern Alberta and explained that "we have not prohibited the Sun Dance on these reserves and you will likely be able to investigate that, and it may be that they will let you into some of the inner mysteries of their secret societies."[45] Scott's suggestion that Hooke and Perry talk to the Blackfoot about ceremonial matters is intriguing, given that researchers were usually discouraged from pursuing these topics in detail, or at least, in relation to the legislation concerning religious practices.[46] In some cases, such as with Beatrice Blackwood's mid-1920s fieldwork, DIA staff spent considerable time with visiting academics and thus were heavily involved in shaping their activities, but in other instances, researchers – and crucially First Nations people – had more freedom to participate in research as they saw fit. Accordingly, though there were many versions of the researcher-subject experience in First Nations communities at this time, the extent of DIA involvement should not be discounted.

Figure 6 Selling beadwork at the Regina Fair and Exhibition, 1925 |
Courtesy and Copyright Pitt Rivers Museum, University of Oxford, PRM BB-A3-16N

BACKED BY LEGISLATION intended to assimilate First Nations people into
mainstream Canadian society, official rhetoric supported the principles of
salvage ethnography and sanctioned the collection and preservation of
cultural artifacts, which were increasingly regarded as part of Canada's
national heritage. As collectors competed for a diminishing supply of old
and "authentic" items, and as anthropology became established as a discipline, museums in the United States and Canada, and to a lesser extent in

the United Kingdom, participated as much as they could in the structured acquisition of First Nations cultural materials. The activities of museum staff were marked, to varying degrees, by underlying tensions connected to emergent national pride. DIA officials played a significant role in shaping museum collections during this era, and many of them worked with museum staff to secure items that were considered rare and potentially vulnerable to purchase by museums outside of Canada.

The overview of institutional collecting presented in this chapter has indicated the complex relations between museums, bureaucrats, and the accumulation of First Nations artifacts during the first three decades of the twentieth century. Missing from the analysis, though, are the views of the First Nations individuals who were also involved in these transactions. In the chapters that follow, I turn to the Franklin Motor Expedition to provide insights into the perspectives of First Nations people that have largely been submerged in most analyses of collecting in Canada and to contribute to the indigenizing of this history.

3
Collecting in Action
The Franklin Motor Expedition

The time is just right for an expedition of this kind, and I know it
would be a success. We would have the cooperation of Canadian officials
because we would represent a Mother Country institution. I know just
where to go and I believe the two boys would have a glorious time and
get something out of it that they can never forget.

>   – D.A. Cadzow to L.C.G. Clarke, 1928

There was a reason behind it [the expedition]. And, when I look
back then, our people were put on reserves, very small pieces of land.
Hunting wasn't that good. They were restricted. So, even ceremonies
at that time, about the time most of that stuff was collected, our
ceremonies were banned. Churches and Indian agents took these
items away and actually sold them and put the money in their pockets
... They got a lot more money too! Whereas when the Indian agent
and the priests took them away, they [First Nations people] didn't get
anything. When the collectors came along, at least they got something.

>   – Mike Pinay, author interview[1]

THE FRANKLIN MOTOR Expedition of 1929 responded to and advocated
for ethnographic salvage. Its combination of the latest recording technologies, a top-of-the-range automobile, and the promotional strategies employed

by the team leader during and at the close of the trip shows that it corresponded to adventure travel and survey ethnography as practised by museums at the time (Bell, Brown, and Gordon 2013). A remarkable aspect of this particular expedition, though, is the extent to which its story was submerged, if not quite forgotten, at the Museum of Archaeology and Anthropology (MAA) in Cambridge. Furthermore, the collection was almost entirely unknown outside the MAA itself. North American and European researchers had studied some pieces, but the collection as a whole had not attracted much scholarly attention. Until I began the research on which this book is based, the First Nations from which the artifacts came had no knowledge of its existence. A goal of this book, then, is to restore context to the collection and the expedition that assembled it.[2]

The lack of awareness about the collection and its origins, both within and outside the museum, reflects dominant trends in scholarly research using ethnographic materials. Disciplinary histories inform us that the rise of structural functionalism prompted anthropologists to eschew the study of artifacts, although with the "material turn" of the late 1980s onward, the study of the place of things within social relations is now established as a critical field in anthropology and related disciplines (see, for example, Knappett 2005; Gosden, Phillips, and Edwards 2006; Henare, Holbraad, and Wastell 2006; and D. Miller 2009). In museums themselves, of course, research never ceased, though the demands on curatorial time and the sheer numbers of items requiring attention precluded in-depth study of many collections. Despite this, in some museums – particularly those in universities – artifacts continued to play a role in the development of theory.

Exploring the Archives

My reconstruction of the history of the Franklin Motor Expedition began with the MAA *Annual Report* for 1929. In its list of new accessions, it referred to a Mr. R.R. Rymill who had made "an extensive and valuable collection" in Canada for the museum, noted that the collection was a gift from MAA curator Louis C.G. Clarke, and added that it came from the "Bungay, Cree (Plains), Dakota, Sarsi, Assiniboine, North Blackfoot and Piegan Indians" (Museum of Archaeology and Anthropology 1930, Appendix).[3] The MAA card catalogue contains 456 handwritten records, one for every accession number (Table 1), each of which names Robert Rymill as

TABLE 1

Rymill Collection artifacts catalogued by nation

Cultural group or nation[1]	Number of artifacts[2]	Total number of artifacts[3]
Bungay (Anishinaabe)	66	97
Plains Cree	122	180
Wahpeton Dakota	38	52
Soto (Saulteaux)	5	9
Stoney	2	3
Northern Blackfoot (Siksika)	9	13
Sarsi (Tsuu T'ina)	14	23
Piegan (Piikani)	199	302
Unprovenanced	1	1
Total	456	680

Notes:
1 Based on Rymill's catalogue cards
2 Based on accession sequence
3 Based on catalogued constituent parts (e.g., pair of moccasins counted as A and B)

the collector, briefly describes the artifact, identifies the nation associated with it, and gives the acquisition date as 1929. As with many museum cataloguing systems, one accession number may have suffixes to cover several constituent parts. Thus, 1930.1062A-C refers to a pipe bag, pipe bowl, and pipestem. If all the separately *alphabetized* parts of the collection are counted, the total is 680, but even this figure is deceptive. For example, some ceremonial artifacts were catalogued as single items, though they include wrappers and contents, and some that belong together have been separated.

A search of the MAA's extensive documentary archives produced a carbon copy of a collection inventory prepared by Robert Rymill.[4] As well as listing the artifacts, this loose-leaf inventory includes three codes. The first refers to the cultural group or nation associated with each artifact; for example, "CR" refers to Plains Cree and "WD" to Wahpeton Dakota. The second code, which is inconsistently applied, is the letter "W" or "M," indicating that an artifact belonged to, was acquired from, or was used by a woman or a man. The final code is a + symbol, which is placed alongside five "Bungi" artifacts (Figure 7). Though these items are all associated with the Midewiwin,

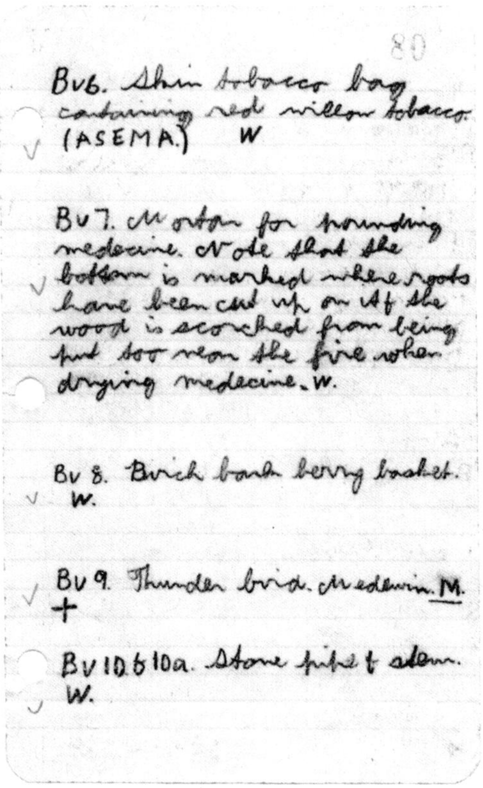
80

Bv6. Skin tobacco bag containing red willow tobacco. (ASEMA.) W

Bv7. Mortar for pounding medecine. Note that the bottom is marked where roots have been cut up on it & the wood is scorched from being put too near the fire when drying medecine. W.

Bv 8. Birch bark berry basket. W.

Bv 9. Thunder bird. Medewin. M. +

Bv 10 & 10a. Stone pipe & stem. W.

Figure 7 Robert Rymill's inventory, showing the codes he used to organize artifacts during the expedition | Reproduced by permission of University of Cambridge Museum of Archaeology and Anthropology, FA5/1/2

the documentation does not reveal whether they are linked by any other factor. No further notes created by Rymill have been located in the MAA's archives or elsewhere in the university, and no references have been found to research publications arising from the expedition. It seemed remarkable – and perplexing – that such an extensive collection could generate so little documentation in the museum archives.[5]

That said, though detailed field notes have not been located, this does not mean that none were made. Correspondence subsequently found in the personal papers of Robert Rymill suggests that he did take more extensive field notes than are now available, and his family believes that he would have recorded as much as he could, subject to the constraints on his time and the cross-cultural nature of the interaction (Robert Rymill, author interview, Penola, Australia, 5 March 1999). We must also remember that Rymill trained in anthropology at Cambridge at a time when great emphasis was placed on field research methods.[6] It seems probable that any other notes he took – including, perhaps, the original inventory – were either misplaced during the Second World War, when the museum moved some of its collections for safekeeping, or were destroyed by a house fire some years later on Rymill's property, though his family believes that "it would have been unlike him to retain anything that should properly stay in the collection" (Thomas Rymill, e-mail to author, 4 November 1997). Indeed, a comparison of the carbon copy inventory and the actual catalogue cards prepared from it indicates some discrepancies in the amount of information. Though the descriptions on most cards remain tantalizingly brief, several do contain rather more detail than is found in the inventory, and it is unlikely that Rymill was working purely from memory.

In 1996 Gillian Crowther, then acting assistant curator for anthropology at the MAA, wrote to the National Museum of the American Indian (NMAI) to ask about professional links between Louis Clarke and George Heye. The response from the NMAI was crucial in uncovering the history of the Franklin Motor Expedition. In a letter located in the NMAI archives, the author, one Donald Cadzow, referred to "a trunkfull of ethnology" that he had collected in "the Canadian Northwest for Cambridge University," which included "the famous 'Beaver Bundle' of the Piegan."[7] None of the documentation in the MAA archives indicated that Robert Rymill had worked with anyone else, and no other collecting venture sponsored by the University of Cambridge had ever gone to the Canadian Northwest. The intriguing news that someone else had encountered "the Piegan" while working for the university could only mean that Rymill had been part of a larger group. The reference to the Beaver Bundle confirmed the connection, as the Rymill Collection contains a number of items associated with Beaver Bundles that were collected at the Piikani reserve. A further search of the MAA archives unearthed several letters implying that Cadzow had first met Louis Clarke in 1923, when they worked together on the jointly funded MAA-MAI excavation at Kechiba:wa, New Mexico.[8] They stayed in touch, exchanging gifts and news of their research, as this 1926 letter from Cadzow to Clarke reveals:

> Thank you very much for the pipe. I don't have to tell you as one pipe smoker to another that it is appreciated, you know it is. I have smoked to you in the desert of New Mexico and thought of you as I puffed away on my Dunhill on the northern Prairies and in the Rockies. And if all goes well I'll puff the new one and think of you above the Arctic Circle

in Alaska next summer[9] ... Had a fine trip through northwest Canada this past summer. Made three collections and gathered a lot of interesting data. Wish you could have been with me, it was hard going in the bush country of Sask. but, that was all in the days [sic] work.[10]

Cambridge University supported numerous research expeditions during the late nineteenth and early twentieth centuries, most famously the 1898 Cambridge Anthropological Expedition to the Torres Strait (Herle and Rouse 1998), and the MAA received many important and richly documented collections as a result. The correspondence between Clarke and Cadzow indicated that the Rymill Collection had been acquired specifically for the MAA, but the lack of associated documentation suggested that it had been assembled on a survey collecting venture rather than during extended ethnographic fieldwork. Biographical research into the lives and careers of Donald Cadzow and Robert Rymill offered some answers to the collection's history and was generously supported by the families of the expedition participants. They provided access to documentary materials, including correspondence, photographs, and film footage that are key to understanding the expedition's history and to determining the provenance of some of the artifacts.[11]

The Idea of an Expedition

In 1928, following a summer hunting trip to the Canadian Rockies with his younger brother, John, and their friend Thomas Mitchell, Robert Riddoch Rymill, then an undergraduate student reading anthropology and economics at Cambridge University, discussed his experiences with Louis Clarke. The hunting party slept in canvas tipis, trekked through coniferous forests, marvelled at the scenery, and occasionally came across First Nations people, all of which added to the romance of the trip, which Thomas Mitchell later described in his unpublished memoir:

> The Rockies express the latent power of a new and larger country. This was a Scotland, a Norway, and a Switzerland all together but magnified a thousand times. There was a wildness and a primitive savagery about this land; there were no Indians in Switzerland, you did not carry rifles at Gstaad, and there were no grizzlies on the Hardanger glacier. We were a long way from Thomas Cook here.[12]

For Mitchell, the landscape was a wilderness and a hunter's playground; by contrast, Robert Rymill was profoundly affected by what he saw of the lives of First Nations people, and he became convinced that their cultural materials and knowledge would be lost if nothing were done to preserve them (Gladys Rymill, author interview, Penola, South Australia, 5 March 1999).

Clarke would have been very interested in Rymill's impressions. Though he had a wide range of academic interests, his particular specialty was American ethnology and archaeology. He was a generous supporter of research initiatives in the Americas and contributed financially to archaeological excavations led by staff of the Museum of the American Indian, at Kechiba:wa, New Mexico (1919 and 1923), and at Bee Cave Canyon in Texas (1929). During his curatorship, his many contacts and colleagues in North America helped him build up the First Nations and Native American collections, which at the time of his appointment, were the least developed part of the MAA.[13] These collections had grown sporadically since the museum's founding in 1884, with most items arriving as donations from alumni or friends of the staff, or as purchases from salerooms and specialist dealers of ethnographic artifacts and antiquities, such as W.D. Webster and William Oldman, both of whom ran mail order businesses around the turn of the twentieth century.[14] Certain cultural areas, such as the Northwest Coast and the Arctic, were well represented in terms of quantity and range of artifact type, but there were comparatively few items from the North American Plains and Prairie regions. Robert Rymill was due to graduate in June 1929 (University of Cambridge 1929, 1157), and Louis Clarke fully supported his wish to collect in Western Canada, so as to fill the gap in the museum's holdings. The expedition team would consist of Robert and John Rymill, and Clarke approached Donald Cadzow to take on the role of leader.

The social background and personalities of the Rymill brothers made them well suited for such an adventure. They were born into a successful farming family of Scots and English heritage in Penola, South Australia, and though their father, Robert, had died in 1906, they had a comfortable upbringing. Their mother, Mary, was keen that her sons be well educated and, in 1923, accompanied them to England, where they pursued their studies, Robert at Cambridge and John in London. As a boy, John had become fascinated by polar exploration and combined his academic studies with practical skills. Reflecting on his preparation for the explorer's life, he later wrote, "I did survey and navigation at the Royal Geographical Society, and went through the De Havilland School of Flying and went through their workshop, and went to college in London to do accountancy ... training myself for all the things, including cooking, that I considered necessary for the running of a polar expedition" (quoted in Béchervaise 1995, 34). Rymill, who made a significant contribution to polar exploration, joined the British Arctic Air Route Expedition to Greenland (1930-31) only months after returning from Canada. He assumed leadership of a second Arctic expedition from 1932 to 1933, after its leader, Gino Watkins, died while hunting seals. Several years later, he organized and led the British Graham Land Expedition (1934-37), the last Antarctic wintering expedition made by sail (Rymill 1938; Béchervaise 1995). A colleague from the British Graham Land Expedition, Alfred Stephenson, later recalled that John was "not particularly interested in the academic side of the Canadian expedition and went ... purely to gain extra experience of travelling in uncharted territory" (A. Stephenson, letter to author, 8 February 1998), a view confirmed by Peter Rymill, John's eldest son (author's field notes, 4 March 1999). Robert Rymill, who was rather more academically inclined, enjoyed his undergraduate studies and the opportunities that they afforded him. In 1926 he volunteered as a special constable in London for National General Strike Duty, and he mixed civic duties with a social and academic life that included spending time with Louis Clarke and other Cambridge faculty who encouraged his academic interests. Though young and inexperienced in the practicalities of ethnographic research, the Rymill brothers had enthusiasm and a love of outdoor pursuits that would assist their endeavours, and they no doubt planned to learn how to collect as they travelled.[15]

Clarke was sure that if Donald Cadzow led the expedition, the Rymills would be in safe hands and the museum would acquire a valuable ethnographic collection. Cadzow had extensive experience of collecting expeditions and excavations, and of dealing with First Nations people. He was born in Auburn, New York, in 1894 and in 1911 travelled to Rampart House on the Porcupine River in the Yukon to work at the trading post managed by his uncle, Daniel Cadzow.[16] On his return to New York in 1916, he brought "a great collection of specimens and trophies," mostly of Gwich'in and Inuinnait provenance.[17] He offered parts of this to several museums, and it was stored in the AMNH while he waited for the best price.[18] George Heye was so impressed with Cadzow's collection that not only did he buy it, he also offered him a job at his newly opened Museum of the American Indian (MAI). Cadzow's first fieldwork as a member of the scientific staff was to return to the Arctic, this time accompanied by his wife, Helen, to collect among the Inuinnait and to study their material culture (Cadzow 1920).

Having received no formal training in anthropology or archaeological techniques, Cadzow learned on the job, and the practical skills and resourcefulness he acquired during his years in the Arctic, combined with his relaxed personality, would have been as useful to a museum fieldworker as any academic qualification. His colleague Alanson B. Skinner referred to these qualities in an informal biographical sketch written while he and Cadzow worked at the MAI. Describing Cadzow's arrival at Rampart House in 1911, he wrote that

> his reception as a tenderfoot or Cheechako by his uncle was characteristic. When Don, after a long and hard journey, arrived, he had set before him two gophers or marmots, singed and roasted whole on a spit, as his dinner. They did not look very appetizing, but under the dour eye of his "Sourdough" uncle, Don concealed his scruples, sampled the meal, and pronounced it good! From that time on, his success as a northerner was assured.[19]

Following his appointment to the MAI, Cadzow worked on excavations and collecting expeditions throughout North America until 1928, when he was a victim of the staff cuts brought on by the museum's financial difficulties. He found temporary work with the Pennsylvania Indian Survey in the spring of 1929 and, after the Franklin Motor Expedition, secured a permanent position as the first state archaeologist for Pennsylvania, rising to executive director of the Pennsylvania Historical and Museum Commission. He retired from this post in 1956, four years before his death in 1960 (Anon. 1960).

Cadzow's 1925 and 1926 collecting expeditions to the Prairies made him just the man for the job. He knew exactly where to go, whom to see, how much to pay, how to acquire official permission to enter the reserves, and most importantly, how to get artifacts out. When Clarke approached him about his availability, he seems to have been considering a position at the Rochester Museum and Science Center, New York, but the chance to return to the Prairies was too tempting.[20] He jumped at the offer and told Clarke, "I think we can give your two students one of the most interesting adventures they have ever had. And at the same time impress upon them the fact that our work is very, very interesting and important."[21] Throughout this correspondence, Cadzow used the language of salvage to express the seriousness of their enterprise, noting that "many of my old friends among the tribes are dying and before they all pass on I would like to see them and collect and preserve their ancient bundles and etc. for our Museums."[22] The expedition would gather new collections and information for the museum, and Cadzow suggested that each Rymill brother concentrate on a subject that interested him, such as folklore or material culture. He himself planned to make a small ethnobotanical collection with the assistance of his First Nations contacts. Records in the NMAI show that Cadzow had already collected ethnobotanical specimens, and he told Clarke that he could

> make a collection of these things from the Cree that would be of very great interest ... It is a delicate and expensive work for they prize these things very highly even now. One has to pay high for the necessary information which would make the herbs and other objects valuable to a Museum. The Crees are famous among the Indians for their medicine men, and Keevisk their leader is one of my oldest friends in this tribe.[23]

The expedition would be hard work but would also be fun and exciting, and the correspondence hints at the adventures ahead. The men would cross three provinces in a specially adapted car, meeting First Nations people and participating in ceremonies. To Robert Rymill, Cadzow proclaimed, "I believe you will both enjoy it and carry home something with you that you will always remember. You will get closer to and see more of the real American Indian and his mode of living than some people who spend their lives near them."[24] The venture would include an element of danger, and throughout his pre-expedition correspondence with Clarke and Robert Rymill, Cadzow invoked the image of Western Canada as a last frontier, with the expedition team fulfilling the duty of preserving ethnological information for the future. This notion of the frontier is apparent in written and visual records generated by the expedition, as well as in the writing and photography of other collectors, explorers, and expedition participants during this period (Bell, Brown, and Gordon 2013). The documentation thus conformed to the genre of exploratory literature and photography connected with salvage ethnography, which were commonly used to envision cultural otherness for "the domestic audience of imperialism" (M.L. Pratt 1992, 63).

The team members spent the spring of 1929 finalizing their plans. In their correspondence, Robert Rymill asked Cadzow about the possibilities for hunting.[25] He and his brother had enjoyed this aspect of their 1928 trip to the Rockies and hoped to repeat it. Cadzow replied that he would arrange permits and recommended hiring Métis guides near Meadow Lake, Saskatchewan. He also proposed that the team collect zoological specimens, and although one contemporary newspaper report states that the expedition was also working on behalf of the British Museum's Natural History Section (now the Natural History Museum), there is no evidence to suggest that zoological specimens were acquired.[26]

Cadzow completed the administrative duties by securing DIA permission for the team to undertake its work. Regrettably, his letter requesting assistance cannot be located in DIA records; nor is there a copy in his personal papers, though permission was clearly granted for the expedition to proceed, as Deputy Superintendent General of Indian Affairs D.C. Scott supplied a letter of introduction that directed DIA officials to "extend the usual courtesies to Mr Cadzow and render him any assistance possible."[27] A further letter of introduction was signed by Louis Clarke and Ellis Minns, the Disney Professor of Archaeology at Cambridge University, which stated that Cadzow was "directing a scientific expedition and collecting specimens for [the] Museum in the USA and Canada."[28]

Cadzow made a number of logistical suggestions, which included travelling by car for the bulk of the trip and hiring horses where necessary. Early in the planning phase, he told Robert Rymill of his intent to get a new car especially for the journey: a "re-conditioned air cooled Franklyn [sic]."[29] This would be large enough to carry the men, their equipment, and their purchases. The Rymills offered to bring a canvas tipi they had acquired the year before, and Cadzow advised that a mosquito-proof tent should also be purchased. Their clothing would consist of "leather lumber jackets, dark flannel shirts, trail boots, sweaters and khaki pants."[30] The team took two portable cameras and a 16mm movie camera; visual records show that the equipment also included tarpaulins, sleeping bags, and three folding chairs and a table, all of which fitted neatly into the car, along with motoring accessories such as snow chains and tools.

Funding a collecting expedition of this scale was expensive, and Cadzow recommended that other museums be asked to purchase duplicate specimens to help offset the costs. This common practice was integral to the complex social networks of exchange that existed between museum personnel in a variety of institutions worldwide, as well as between curators and amateur ethnographers interested in indigenous peoples (Edwards 2001, 27-50; Gosden and Larson 2007; Byrne et al. 2011). These networks were essential for expanding collections, and surviving correspondence reveals that George Heye and Louis Clarke also discussed the possibility of acquiring "duplicate" materials. Heye wrote,

> It occurred to me that while he [Cadzow] was in the Piegan country that if you care to, he could collect some specimens of types of objects that we have not got in our Piegan collection, and then I could exchange these with you for ethnology, of which you have nothing; say, either Crow material or some of the feather and other ethnological work of the Pacific coast from the Karok or Yurok tribes. It would, of course, be distinctly understood that Cadzow would not send anything but duplicates to us, of things we needed. Let me know if you feel like taking this matter up.[31]

Cadzow himself believed that American museums would happily buy the expedition's artifacts and specifically proposed contacting London-based pharmacist and collector Sir Henry Wellcome to gauge his interest in adding Plains Cree ethnobotanical specimens to his collection of medical materials.[32] In the event, no other museums contributed to the expedition, which was funded almost entirely by Louis Clarke. The artifact budget was estimated at $3,000, though to save money it was suggested that some of this be used to buy consumables, which would then be traded for specimens.[33] A further $4,000, exclusive of Cadzow's salary of $300 a month, covered the costs of transport, interpreters and guides, food, and sundry expenses.[34] The Rymills would have covered their own travel and subsistence costs, and Clarke paid for the specimens, field assistants, shipping fees, and Cadzow's salary (Gladys Rymill, author interview, Penola, South Australia, 5 March 1999). Cadzow anticipated that they "would live high in town and on our own cooking in camp and that they [the Rymills] will return to England with their minds made up for another go at the northwest as soon as they can get away."[35]

Out on the Open Road

Neither Cadzow nor the Rymills published extensive reports of the Franklin Motor Expedition, but a number of sources enable us to retrace its route and determine how the team interacted with First Nations people. The surviving visual images are complemented by Robert Rymill's notebook, newspaper reports, and Cadzow's personal papers as well as his *Air-Cooled Adventure among the Aborigines,* a promotional leaflet that he wrote for the H.H. Franklin Manufacturing Company (Cadzow n.d.). His *Indian Notes* articles relating to his 1925 and 1926 MAI expeditions also provide useful context, as they give names and information about several individuals whom the Franklin Expedition visited and who contributed in various ways to the Rymill Collection (Cadzow 1926a, 1926b, 1926c, 1927). Informative as these sources are, they must be read with caution. As Jennifer Brown and Elizabeth Vibert (1998, xi) observe, "objectivity, like the historian's heaven, is an illusion," and we must be mindful of how we read documents, as "the voices of our documentary texts can be listened for, articulated, balanced with one another; but only through silencing or suppression can they be melded into a single voice or unquestioned truth." Brown and Vibert (ibid., xix) also remind us of the instability of the contexts in which documents were created and in which they are read today, a factor that they view as invigorating historical study, as well as complicating it. Their words apply to all the documents created by the Franklin Motor Expedition – but especially *Air-Cooled Adventure among the Aborigines* – as I discuss in more detail in the following chapter.

For Donald Cadzow, the expedition began in late June in Syracuse, New York, where he collected his new air-cooled automobile, a 1928 Series 12B four-door seven-seat sedan, from the H.H. Franklin Manufacturing Company.[36] Cadzow met the Rymill brothers in Winnipeg, and the expedition then followed the routes of his previous collecting trips. The first of these had concentrated on the Anishinaabe communities of Swan Lake and Long Plain in Manitoba and then visited twelve reserves in Southern Saskatchewan, including the four File Hills reserves of Little Black Bear, Okanese, Peepeekisis, and Star Blanket, where he collected from Plains Cree and Assiniboine people (Museum of the American Indian 1926, 5). The following year, with his colleague Kenneth Miller, he returned to the File Hills and then drove northwest to the predominantly Plains Cree reserves around the Battlefords. They then travelled farther north to Meadow Lake and the Western Woodlands Cree, before ending their trip at the Piikani Nation in Southern Alberta (Museum of the American Indian 1927, 6).[37] They made collections and took photographs at many of these reserves, and the documentation in the NMAI and with Cadzow's family provides important comparative data for the Franklin Motor Expedition.

The 1929 expedition combined the routes of Cadzow's two earlier field-trips, though the incompleteness of the documentation means that we cannot always be certain which communities were visited (Map 1). Furthermore, museum categorization systems often obscure the origin of some artifacts by glossing over the demographics of reserve communities. For example, the Anishinaabe items are listed simply as "Bungay" or "Bungi," a name that, as noted on page xiii, was historically used to refer to peoples who were also called western Ojibwe, Plains Ojibwe, or Saulteaux by outsiders. Similarly, some of the material labelled as "Cree" came from communities that were home to people with ancestral ties to many different nations, although the state systems in place for registering First Nations people did not take these complexities into account. In addition, given the number of reserves that the expedition could have visited as it crossed the prairies (especially in Saskatchewan), these provenances are vague, to say the least. However, the visual record, the expedition documentation, and the artifacts themselves show that much of the collecting activity took place at Swan Lake, the File Hills communities, and the Piikani Nation.

Driving conditions also influenced the choice of communities, and in turn shaped the collection itself. As Allan Pard of the Piikani Nation reminded me,

> You have to remember it was still pretty isolated ... Transportation was still a big factor here in Canada. It is such a big country, vast country, that it was hard to maintain the roads. So transportation only really improved in the sixties. That's when our people started seeing the value of buying vehicles. The roads we had on the reserves weren't good, so it was easier to drive a wagon. (Allan Pard, author interview, Fort Macleod, 6 August 1999)

Reserve roads continue to challenge those whose experience of driving on gravel is limited. Potholes are common, as are burst tires and chipped windshields. Flash floods can turn otherwise reasonable roads into muddy trails. There are good reasons why many residents of prairie reserves choose four-wheel-drive trucks, just as there were good reasons why transport by horse and buggy was more manageable (and affordable) in the 1920s than travelling by Ford or other vehicles less advanced than the Franklin. Moreover, the distance between reserves and major well-maintained highways also

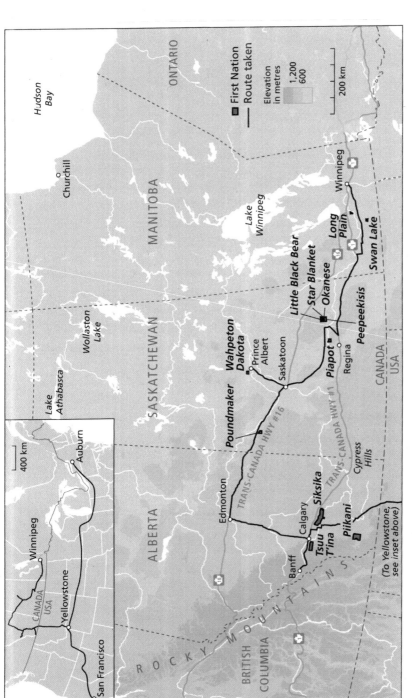

Map 1 The route taken by the Franklin Motor Expedition, showing the First Nations most likely to have been visited by the team. | Cartographer: Eric Leinberger

played a role. The four File Hills communities are relatively close to Fort Qu'Appelle, which lies near the Trans-Canada Highway, so the expedition reached the town with comparative ease and could take its time coping with the poor roads on the reserves. As Chapter 4 explains, Cadzow went to some effort in *Air-Cooled Adventure among the Aborigines* to show that the technological superiority of the car enabled the team to overcome such obstacles, although the expedition's visual record tells a different tale.

Beginnings: Southern Manitoba

From Winnipeg Cadzow and the Rymills headed southwest to the Anishinaabe community of Swan Lake. In 1999 Swan Lake elder Sam Cameron recalled Donald Cadzow's visits and said he had always wondered what happened to the things he took from the community: "They came about two times. They came one day and then went back, and then came back about a week later for some more meetings. I think they came back about two times" (Sam Cameron, author interview, Swan Lake Nation, 5 April 1999, quoted in Brown 2000, 94). Cameron remembered that during what was probably his 1925 visit, Cadzow spoke mostly with the older people, including two ceremonial leaders, Giigido Asin (John Talking Stone) and Gennahmodhi (Moose Bell/George Tanner).[38] Cadzow appears to have met several times with Gennahmodhi. In an article describing his Swan Lake fieldwork, he wrote that the cooperation of Giigido Asin and Gennahmodhi was prompted by the legislation forbidding ceremonial activity: "These sacred barks were given to the writer on condition they be kept in the Museum forever, and that duplicates of the more important ones be made on durable paper and sent to the society; for the two old *kichimotos*, or past-masters feared that the originals would become lost, as the Canadian Government has forbidden the performance of the midewin [sic] ceremony, and the fraternity is slowly becoming extinct" (Cadzow 1926a, 124; italics in original).[39] Whether Cadzow honoured this request is unknown, but archival evidence and oral histories do reveal that Swan Lake endured significant interference from the RCMP and missionaries during the mid-1920s; indeed, Gennahmodhi himself was jailed for two months in 1926 for participating in a giveaway and so had personal experience of the severity of the law and how it compromised spiritual expression.[40]

During his 1925 visit to Swan Lake, Cadzow also met with Ajidamoo (Squirrel), who was known as Dr. William due to his ability to heal (Rosie

Scott, author interview, Swan Lake Nation, 5 April 1999). United Church missionary-teacher James Donaghy referred to their meetings in his unpublished memoirs. Donaghy, who supported government initiatives to suppress First Nations spiritual practices, was irritated that Ajidamoo blocked the windows of his house with blankets whenever ceremonies took place. It seems that Ajidamoo did what he could to frustrate prying eyes but was willing to let sympathetic observers inside, as Donaghy explained:

> I have met one man who knows what goes on behind those quilts, but he was pledged not to mention it to anyone. He was Mr Cadzow of the Museum of the American Indian, New York. He visited the Mission to interview the old men on their ceremonies. He explained who he was, and that these things were to be put in books so that they would not be lost forever. So he had quite a long interview with them.[41]

When Cadzow returned to Swan Lake with the Franklin Motor Expedition, he visited Ajidamoo. On this occasion, Robert or John Rymill photographed the exterior of Ajidamoo's home, and Robert's identifying caption, written on the back of the print, was confirmed during my April 1999 visit to Swan Lake (Figure 8). There is no evidence either way to indicate whether Cadzow collected from Ajidamoo himself, but approaching respected spiritual leaders was an effective way for researchers to secure support from others in a community. Furthermore, these individuals had access to the knowledge, songs, and ceremonial artifacts that most interested anthropologists, and many were also concerned about the safety and future care of items. In 1925 Cadzow had also enjoyed a successful collecting experience at the neighbouring Anishinaabe community of Long Plain, so the Franklin Motor Expedition may have visited it as well. That said, the names that Robert Rymill recorded in his inventory and his photographic annotations are all of Swan Lake individuals. Nevertheless, the paucity of documentation is such that most statements about the provenance of Anishinaabe artifacts in the Rymill Collection should be made cautiously.

Sixty-six catalogue records relate to these artifacts. A small number are personal non-ceremonial items, such as a belt probably worn as dance clothing [1930.725], a hide scraper [1930.687], and a birch bark container [1930.658], identified by Rymill as a woman's item used for collecting and storing berries. Materials associated with the Midewiwin include an initiate's medicine bag made of mink skin [1930.709], Midé drums and beaters

Figure 8 Ajidamoo's house, Swan Lake Nation, June 1929 | Reproduced by permission of the Robert and John Rymill families

not well preserved

[1930.684A-B, 1930.685A-B], birch bark scrolls [1930.651, 1930.652, 1930.700], and healing equipment [1930.654A-B, 1930.711]. Five medicine bags made of mink or weasel skin, some of which contained medicines, were also collected by the team, but handwritten notes on the catalogue cards state that they were later destroyed by moths.[42]

Southern and Central Saskatchewan

Because they planned to cover such a great distance, Cadzow and the Rymills spent only a few days at each community, so after staying "several days with the Bungi Indians, studying their life and customs," they drove west to Regina (Cadzow n.d.). Cadzow reported that "the dirt roads of the province, together with the additional load, proved a real test for the car," but on reaching Regina, they were able to ship their first batch of specimens to Cambridge (ibid.). Cadzow then recorded that the team bought three weeks of food supplies in preparation for visiting the Qu'Appelle Valley, northeast of Regina. On arrival at the File Hills region, the expedition headed for the camp of *atim kâ-mihkwasit,* hereditary chief of the Star Blanket Nation whom Cadzow had met in 1925. Here, Cadzow (ibid.) wrote, he and the Rymills were warmly welcomed, and "the beautifully painted tepees of these people, together with their beaded skin clothing and the ancient ceremonies they held for us, made us wish we could stay among them all summer. Our three weeks were soon over and as we had only started our summer's work we had to tear ourselves away."

The records indicate that the team interacted with people from all four File Hills reserves (Little Black Bear, Okanese, Peepeekisis, and Star Blanket). Rymill's inventory lists the anglicized names of "Chief Red Dog" *(atim kâ-mihkwasit),* the healer "Keewist" *(kîwisk),* who was from the Star Blanket reserve, and "Pimotat" *(kâ-pimohtêt),* a younger brother of *acâhkosa k-ôtakohpit* (Chief Starblanket), who lived on the Okanese reserve. The team collected a selection of herbs [1930.757] from *kâ-pimohtêt,* which had belonged to his mother and which, it was recorded, he did not know how to use, and a further selection of medicines [1930.843] sold by *kîwisk.* The accompanying notes include a phonetic transcription of the Cree name for each plant, its intended use, and its application procedure.

The small clues provided by Rymill's inventory are amplified by a series of photos in which *kâ-mostoswahcâpêw* (Buffalo Bow, but identified by Rymill as Buffalo Bull) and Robert Rymill sit by a ceremonial altar (Figure 17). He was originally from the Okanese band, though he transferred to the Peepeekisis Nation in 1887 (Indian Claims Commission 2004, 165). Cadzow had met him in 1926 when he collected equipment *kâ-mostoswahcâpêw* had used in a healing ceremony for his son-in-law, who had been wounded in France during the First World War. The photographs replicate those used in Cadzow's (1927) article about the ceremony he witnessed in 1926, and he probably asked *kâ-mostoswahcâpêw* to show the Rymill brothers what he himself had experienced three years earlier. During the File Hills visit, John Rymill also shot several minutes of film footage. This and the photographs taken by the team, which the following chapter discusses in more depth, provided an important access point for File Hills people to identify those who interacted with the expedition, including *piskwatapiw* (Sits in Mound/ Heap), *k-owîkit* (One Who Dwells), and *mîkwanis* (Little Feather).

The success of Cadzow's previous meetings with File Hills political and ceremonial leaders undoubtedly eased the way for the Franklin Motor Expedition as it searched for materials and information. File Hills residents were accustomed to visits from outsiders professing an interest in their heritage. Anthropologists, artists, and writers had been attracted to the File Hills for some years, in part because the reserves were relatively easily accessible by car, but also because the File Hills Colony, on the Peepeekisis reserve, had made the area well known. The colony was established in 1898 by William Graham (who was then the Indian agent) with the aim of assimilating the Plains Cree into the Euro-Canadian way of life, and it was actively promoted as an Indian Affairs success story.[43] Industrial school graduates were selected with the assistance of school principals and were allotted farm land on the reserve. They lived in wooden houses, attended church, and were expected to advance toward civilization away from regressive influences on their reserves, which might hold them back (Carter 1991; Graham 1991; Bednasek 2009). Many of the colonists, whom Bednasek (2009, 1) describes as "placements," borrowing the term currently used by Peepeekisis band members, were not from the area, but officials brushed aside the tensions between original Peepeekisis band members and the newcomers.[44] The perceived progress of the colony, as well as the regular participation of File Hills leaders in fairs and agricultural exhibitions, contributed to the high profile of these nations in Southern Saskatchewan and beyond.

The women of the Qu'Appelle Valley were especially famed for their beadwork, and by the early 1930s, the File Hills were considered to be "the best single place for museum articles" in the province.[45] In a letter to his doctoral supervisor, Clark Wissler, David Mandelbaum listed the kinds of artifacts available and stated that

> at the File Hills Agency there are several complete costumes, shirt, leggings, moccasins, headdresses, gauntlets, neckpiece, all of which are profusely beaded. The Farm Instructor there told me that one of the Indians asked $125.00 for the complete outfit, but I think that one could be secured for less though I have not made any inquiries as to the price myself.[46]

According to Rymill's inventory, the Franklin Expedition bought such an outfit from *atim kâ-mihkwasit* [1930.834A-J]; in a rare instance of detailed accounting, it added that *atim kâ-mihkwasit* had given most of the payment to his daughter, who had made the outfit for him. I discuss contemporary responses to this outfit in Chapter 5.

Other pieces, such as the many ceremonial items collected by the expedition, may have been sold because their keepers desperately needed money or could not find persons seeking to have sacred items transferred to them. Anthropologist Edmund Carpenter discusses this point in an essay concerning repatriation and the collection assembled by George Heye, Cadzow's former employer. Carpenter (1991, 16) argues that "when traditionalists handed sacred treasures to ethnologists, they knew exactly what they were doing ... They believed that powers within those objects ... could survive anything except neglect ... Often ethnologists were their only listeners." It is unclear whether the ceremonial artifacts amassed by Cadzow and the Rymills were ceremonially transferred to them, though anthropologists did sometimes receive objects in this way. Mandelbaum, for example, wrote to Clark Wissler about the possibility of having bundles transferred to him during his fieldwork at the Poundmaker, File Hills, and Sweet Grass First Nations:

> Next week-end I am giving a feast for the Indians on the reserve as part of the transfer ceremony of the medicine bundle I wrote about. At the same time yet another bundle is to be given to me. It is a bear-skin worn by a noted chief in the old days – Big Bear. The man who has the latter bundle came up to me one day and asked if I would take the bundle and swear to keep it well. He has many children and "there is no place for the bundle." I shall have to give a gift in return but his main concern is finding a safe place for this medicine.[47]

The AMNH list of artifacts acquired during Mandelbaum's "Museum Expedition" includes one bundle and its constituent parts [AM3739 a-l]. The name of the individual associated with it is not recorded, but the bundle is identified as having come from the Poundmaker reserve.[48]

Mandelbaum's records at the AMNH illustrate the conventions used in some museums during the interwar years for recording ethnographic information. Robert Rymill's surviving records are not nearly as comprehensive as those of more experienced anthropologists. In his inventory and the catalogue cards he wrote on his return to Cambridge, he created 122 records for items identified as "Plains Cree," but only 7 of these can be linked to specific individuals, using his other written records. Nevertheless, analysis of the expedition's visual imagery and of other photographs of File Hills people has enabled the identification of several additional pieces (Figures 9 and 10). One example is the headdress [1930.728] worn by *mostāhtik* (Simply Wood) in Figure 9.[49] The museum documentation lists this simply as "Old style Cree warrior's headdress. True Plains Cree type," which reflects the practice of excising people's names in catalogue records as part of categorizing indigenous artifacts as type specimens. Regrettably, few other items labelled as Plains Cree can be linked to specific individuals.

Leaving the Qu'Appelle Valley, the expedition set off for Prince Albert in north-central Saskatchewan – a day and a half's drive away. With typical emphasis on the performance of the Franklin, Cadzow (n.d.) noted that they caused some excitement as they drove through the small towns dotting the prairies, with crowds gathering whenever they stopped for gas. Their arrival and goals were reported by the *Prince Albert Daily Herald* (Anon. 1929b, 1), which described the zoological work that the Rymill brothers were supposedly carrying out for the British Museum and their plans to spend "a few days among the Indians ... collect[ing] any relics that they might come into contact with." During the next two weeks, the *Herald* published two more articles to update readers on the expedition's progress.

During this period, the team split up to pursue separate interests. The Rymill brothers went hunting in the Pasqua Hills, and Cadzow moved to the Duck Lake area in pursuit of artifacts. According to a newspaper report published after the expedition ended, he met with some resistance. The article refers to an incident during which Cadzow encountered First Nations people who "evinced such hatred for white men" that he was glad to leave "with only one plate in [his] camera exposed" (Anon. 1929a, 14). In *Air-Cooled Adventure among the Aborigines,* Cadzow (n.d.) added another layer to the story, though he did not elaborate on the disagreement. He noted that the Duck Lake Saulteaux had "persistently spurned all dealings with the Canadian government" and were "the least approachable of all the Northwest tribes"; thus, "with the rest of my party in the hills and bitter hostility smouldering just beneath the surface on all sides, I was forced to put my trust in the instant availability and reliability of the car, and to work always with the possibility of flight uppermost in my plans."

Air-Cooled Adventure was written as promotional material for the H.H. Franklin Manufacturing Company, so its emphasis on the reliability of the car is unsurprising, but its reference to Cadzow's risky encounter with the Saulteaux would also have invoked the familiar stereotype of the savage. His narrative is an example of what Henrika Kuklick (2011, 14) deems the

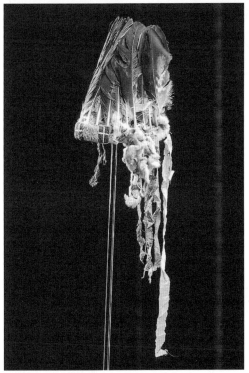

Figure 9 Three generations from File Hills with Indian Commissioner William Graham, c. 1914. *mostȧhtik* is seated in the second row, far left. | Library and Archives Canada, Miscellaneous collection, PA-066815

Figure 10 Headdress owned by *mostȧhtik* | Reproduced by permission of University of Cambridge Museum of Archaeology and Anthropology, 1930.728

"heroic ideal" of fieldwork. In her view, "field scientists have built formidable reputations with research conducted in safe places, but evidence of having endured danger and discomfort for the sake of one's work still testifies to authentic witnessing for many species of fieldworkers and may be especially important for those who – for whatever reason – aspire to public attention." Five collection records list items as Saulteaux: two pairs of beaded moccasins, a shell neck ornament, a pair of ear ornaments, and a drum and beater identified as "of Cree origin, but obtained from the Soto" [1930.888A-B to 1930.892A-B]. There is no further information about these pieces, so it is impossible to determine which Saulteaux band Cadzow encountered.

Having apparently narrowly escaped the wrath of the Saulteaux, Cadzow returned to Prince Albert, where things continued to go badly: two cans of special high-grade oil were stolen from his car while it was parked outside the Empress Hotel (Anon. 1929e, 1). Undeterred, he changed his plans and spent several days at the reserves of the Wahpeton Dakota, on the outskirts of Prince Albert, awaiting the return of his colleagues. At the reserve named Wahpeton 94B, he took several photographs of residents and collected thirty-eight items that, according to a newspaper report, included an "Indian pipe, headdress, leggings and beaded shoulder straps" (Anon. 1929c, 1). These objects also appear in Robert Rymill's inventory and so were catalogued once the team reassembled. Unfortunately, though Cadzow was an experienced collector and had taken comparatively detailed notes for the MAI, the MAA archives provide no further information on the Wahpeton Dakota items, and his private papers offer no clues.

On 16 August 1929, the expedition left Prince Albert and drove to Edmonton, probably stopping at the Plains Cree communities of Little Pine, Moosomin, Poundmaker, and Red Pheasant. No photographic or written records refer to these communities, but the collection does contain artifacts, such as moosehide bags, that were commonly made in this area. Moreover, Cadzow had visited these reserves while employed by the MAI and had every reason to return. Reverend Stan Cuthand, a Little Pine Nation elder who has clear memories of Cadzow, spoke to me about his family's encounter with him (Stan Cuthand, author interview, Saskatoon, 24 May 1999). Cadzow came to the Cuthand home to buy a bundle that was cared for by Cuthand's father, Josie. As Cadzow looked on, Josie Cuthand made a smudge and unwrapped the bundle before telling its story. This bundle was war apparel and was protected by the spirits. It was extremely powerful.

After hearing the story, Cadzow said that he wished to buy the bundle and asked how much it would cost. Stan Cuthand recalled that although his father needed the money, he didn't really want to sell the bundle, but he *did* want Cadzow to understand that it was very valuable. So he named a price that he thought would be too high: fifty dollars. Cadzow replied, "Maybe you should keep it. I don't want to take it. Maybe it will help your family." Josie Cuthand thought that after hearing the bundle's story, Cadzow realized it had a history and meaning, and that it should not be removed. He told his son that "maybe Cadzow had a little bit of knowledge of Indian religion and maybe that was why he didn't take the bundle." Cuthand also recalled that Cadzow "would buy anything" and that because many people badly needed money, they sometimes invented stories to secure a sale. They knew that anthropologists such as Cadzow and David Mandelbaum, who also briefly visited Little Pine, valued older items, but they thought it strange that they also bought easily available objects. Stan Cuthand gave an example of this practice:

> Mrs. *sāpostahikan* was having a sweat lodge, and Cadzow was in there and saw the rocks. He wanted to know what they meant, so Mrs. *sāpostahikan* explained how they were used. There was a little whisk made from grass that is used to splash the water onto the rocks to make the steam. Cadzow asked if he could look at it. He took it and asked if he could take it. Mrs. *sāpostahikan* was surprised. He gave her twenty-five cents for it. People laughed. They thought he could have gone and picked the grass and tied it together himself. They thought it was odd that it meant something to him.[50]

Of course, Cadzow could have made a whisk himself, but it is hard to imagine him doing so. Like most collectors, whether of the 1920s or today, he focused on acquiring the "real thing." Authenticity was essential, and so was age; artifacts that failed to meet these criteria were viewed as less important and less deserving of a place in an ethnographic collection. Cadzow's own collecting style was heavily influenced by George Heye. As Phillips (1998, 59) observes, Heye exemplified the "rare art collector," who not only avoided materials deemed to be "modern" but expected his staff to do likewise. Indeed, Cadzow's own field notebooks from his early days at the MAI repeat Heye's "Golden Rule" that "material *must* be old" and that *"no tourist material"* should be bought.[51] Cadzow clearly believed that the Franklin Motor Expedition had done well to acquire the items that properly belonged in a museum, and he told Louis Clarke that he was "especially proud of the old costumes and birchbark records," for such things could "never be obtained again from the northwest."[52]

Following Cadzow's lead, the Franklin team sought older First Nations items, which were thought to show few signs of European influence. The old and authentic were reified, and evidence of cultural exchange and adaptation in the older pieces was ignored; hence, Rymill made no remarks about a bone-handled hide scraper whose blade was fashioned from a piece of Massey-Harris machinery. Likewise, his inventory dismissed one of two beaded neckties bought at the File Hills [1930.765]: "This type is clearly copied from the white man's collar and tie, and is not part of the 'real' Indian clothing. Junk. Modern neck ornament."[53] Discussing a 1910 photograph of Dan Minde from Maskwacis (Hobbema), Alberta, Sherry Farrell Racette (2010, 79) suggests that beaded neckties may have been a stylistic innovation that moved east from Alberta to Saskatchewan and were worn on formal occasions around 1925 to 1940. They appear in all the photographs taken by John Rymill and Cadzow of File Hills men in their formal clothing. Like so many of their contemporaries, Cadzow and the Rymills viewed First Nations people through specific cultural lenses, identifying them first and foremost by tribal group rather than as creative individuals with the skill, resourcefulness, and imagination to absorb and adapt designs, materials, and ideas from the world around them. Accordingly, they attempted to fit collected artifacts into cultural categories, which were replicated at the museum throughout the following decades, a process I examine in Chapter 6.

Onward to Alberta

Travelling south from Edmonton, the expedition enjoyed a few days of sightseeing at Banff, the premier tourist resort in the Rocky Mountains. During the 1920s and 1930s, Banff was a haven for well-to-do tourists, and local businesses capitalized on its pristine image. In her study of the relationships between tourists and First Nations people in Banff, Laurie Meijer-Drees (1991, 46-47) discusses the motives of Banff visitors who were eager to acquire First Nations handicrafts as souvenirs:

Tourists were buying Indian curios not only in an attempt to authenticate their Banff experience, but through their purchase of Indian crafts were attempting to bridge the perceived distance between the culture they experienced during their visit to Banff. By taking a piece of Indian culture home, and displaying it on the mantle or wearing it, they were becoming one with Indian culture.

The town's main souvenir venues were the annual Banff Indian Days and the Sign of the Goat Trading Post, which specialized in taxidermy and Native "curios." Both were run by Norman Luxton, known locally as "Mr. Banff," whose close business connections with local Nakoda people ensured a steady supply of bags, belts, gauntlets, and moccasins for tourists to buy. His papers in the Glenbow Archives indicate how he and First Nations people negotiated their relationships. Luxton supplied Nakoda seamstresses and artists with rations and commissions, and in turn, they provided him with beadwork and other handicrafts for sale, thus increasing his profits. Although the Franklin Motor Expedition was too late to attend the Banff Indian Days, Cadzow and the Rymills probably went to the Sign of the Goat, just as most visitors do today. Buying artifacts from a trading post was not typical of their methodology, but the two items in the collection that Rymill identified as Stoney – a feather headdress [1930.894] and a pair of moccasins [1930.893A-B] – are entirely consistent with the kinds of souvenir goods available at Luxton's emporium.

From this point, Cadzow's description of the expedition route is not borne out by what the collection actually contains, which illustrates the need to question the reliability of *Air-Cooled Adventure among the Aborigines*. Cadzow (n.d.) wrote that after sightseeing at Lake Louise and Banff, the expedition "dropped down into British Columbia, over the Kootenai trail. Worked among the Kootenai Indians and then moved south and east through the Crow's Nest Pass to Southern Alberta." The content of the collection, however, does not relate to the geography, and it is more likely that after leaving Banff, the team drove to Calgary. Having missed the Calgary Stampede, held that year from 8 to 13 July, their first stop would have been the Tsuu T'ina (Sarcee/Sarsi) reserve, on the outskirts of the city. This community had suffered considerable hardship in the previous decades, and by the mid-1920s had a population of approximately 160.[54] Cadzow mentioned the expedition's encounter at the Tsuu T'ina reserve some thirty years later, when he was negotiating with the director of the MAI to find a secure location for First Nations artifacts he had kept in his own home. He wrote, "The Sarsi material was purchased when I was with Cambridge. I made the first contact with them when I was with Mr Heye. They would not deal with me on this trip but, later let me have some things. Objects from these people are very rare."[55] The expedition collected seventeen items from the Tsuu T'ina for the MAA, mostly footwear and clothing accessories, such as armbands or belts, all of which had been used. Only one, a cougar hide painted with the war deeds of its owner, would have been regarded as a prized find, though frustratingly, the name of the artist is not given in the surviving documentation (Figure 11).[56]

Though the expedition acquired relatively few items at this community, its visit inadvertently resulted in many more artifacts leaving the reserve the following year, destined for the Rochester Museum and Science Center (RMSC) in Rochester, New York. The author of a 1930 newspaper article, who lamented their removal, implied that the Franklin Expedition's abortive attempt to gather "Sarcee relics" prompted "a member of the tribe living in Calgary" to make a more comprehensive collection. The article stated, "It was only when the Calgary man, with his greater knowledge of the situation, took a hand in the search that a satisfactory collection was secured. Cambridge did not get it, however, and as things worked out it was an institution neither Canadian nor English that captured the prize" (Anon. 1930b, 4). Although the author did not name names, records in the RMSC reveal that the "member of the tribe" was Arnold Lupson, an Englishman also known as Eagle Tail, who had married Maggie Big Belly, the widow of Chief Big Belly in 1921 (Taylor and Dempsey 1999). Lupson was known and trusted on many Southern Alberta reserves, and he used his early training as a photographer to take portraits of his Tsuu T'ina, Siksika, and Nakoda friends.[57] Lupson's family relationships gave him access to Tsuu T'ina people who had traditional rights to ceremonial items – information that was not as readily available to outsiders such as Cadzow and the Rymills – and he had worked with collectors and dealers in the past. Correspondence between Cadzow and RMSC curator Arthur Parker shows that Lupson had accumulated at least some of his collection before the Franklin Motor Expedition arrived in Calgary and that Cadzow had examined it with a view to purchasing it for a museum. The asking price was $1,600, though Cadzow valued the part he saw at over $2,000. As the Franklin Expedition could not afford this sum, Cadzow probably directed Lupson to the RMSC. He encouraged

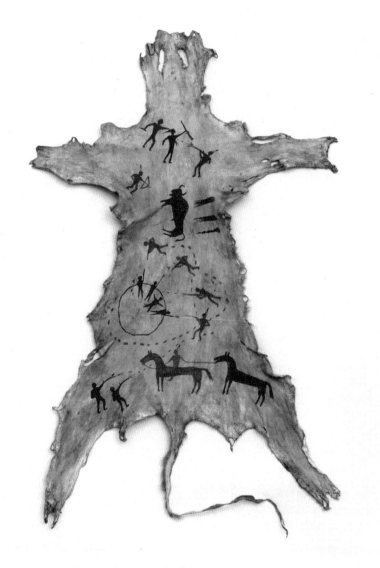

Figure 11 Cougar hide painted with war deeds | Reproduced by permission of University of Cambridge Museum of Archaeology and Anthropology, 1930.916

Arthur Parker to raise the funds, telling him that "there is a story with every piece. Do your darndest to land it as it is a bargain. And it would be nice to make them come to you to study Sarsi ethnology."[58]

Following the visit to the Tsuu T'ina reserve, the expedition turned its attention to the Blackfoot communities of Southern Alberta and went first to the Siksika reserve near Gleichen, some eighty kilometres east of Calgary. Again, the team failed to collect extensively, and only nine pieces were acquired for the museum. Most are small, easily transportable items of clothing, though a beaded buckskin shirt and leggings [1930.901 and 1930.902A-B] and an eagle feather headdress [1930.896] were also secured. The Franklin Motor Expedition was the not the only museum-sponsored collecting venture to pass through the Siksika reserve in a matter of weeks, so it is hardly surprising that comments such as "we have been so studied" are nowadays frequently made by local people to researchers.[59] As noted on page 74, Harlan Smith of the National Museum of Canada spent part of his 1928 fieldwork at Siksika and returned there the following year, shortly after the Franklin Expedition. His 1929 fieldwork instructions indicate that "a sum of $1,200" had been earmarked for the purchase of Blackfoot specimens. By the autumn, Smith notified Diamond Jenness that he had been collecting "fast and furious for 3 days" and had run out of film, which prevented him from filming more of a pipe ceremony. In a postscript he asked whether Jenness would "like Buffalo Skull &c from Sun Dance lodge – at what cost?"[60]

Although the Franklin team was unable to acquire many pieces at Siksika, once again Cadzow appears to have collected independently of the MAA. In 1957 he contacted the MAI to ask if it might be interested in purchasing some of his "collection of ethnology" that he had kept in storage since 1929. In a series of letters to MAI director Edwin K. Burnett, written during the months that followed, Cadzow expressed his concern about hazards such as "fire, storm and theft," and explained that he wanted them to be placed in a secure facility.[61] The items included materials from Siksika, as well as from the Piikani Nation and Swan Lake, such as clothing, two tipi flags, and a Beaver Bundle that he claimed to have secured where others, including Walter McClintock, author of *The Old North Trail* (1999), had failed. In his correspondence, Cadzow explained that he had heard about this bundle when working for George Heye but had been unable to buy it. Following the death of its last keeper, who was from Siksika, a relative hid it and sold it to Cadzow for $250 when he returned to the area in 1929. Cadzow told Burnett that he had never opened it and had stored it "in a tight trunk with naphthalene for 30 years."[62] It could be that Cadzow bought this and other items he sold to the MAI in the 1950s with the intention of selling them to a museum or private collector once the expedition concluded, though he told Burnett that "most of the objects were more or less contracted for [the MAI] when I was with the Museum." He continued, "I picked them up when I was in the field for Louis Clarke."[63] These pieces may well have been "more or less contracted" to the MAI, but in the event, Cadzow stored them in a safe place at home and forbade his children to touch them (Nannette Buhrman, author interview, Harrisburg, Pennsylvania, 4 April 1998). Not until he was nearing retirement and knew he needed to find a secure home for the Beaver Bundle did he approach the MAI. This important piece – which Cadzow claimed was "probably the only one in existence from the Northern Blackfoot" – was purchased by the MAI in 1958.

For the final leg of the journey, the team decided to forgo visiting the Kainai Nation as originally planned and instead headed southwest to Brocket, the agency town at the Piikani Nation, which Cadzow had visited in 1926.[64] This was to be one of the expedition's most successful collecting encounters, as Cadzow explained to Clarke: "We could have spent more money among the Piegans, as a matter of fact, I did spend a little too much among them as it was."[65] Cadzow and the Rymills would have arrived on the reserve toward the end of August, after the main Sun Dance ceremonies had ended. The Department of Indian Affairs did allow these ceremonies to go ahead at the Blackfoot nations at this time, although RCMP officers were present and restrictions on some elements of the ceremonies were enforced. According to a report by Sergeant Webb of the Fort Macleod RCMP detachment, approximately five hundred people had attended a Sun Dance at the Piikani reserve in mid-July, including Blackfeet, Kainai, and Siksika who had travelled from their own reserves. Webb added that "the only thing to put a damper on the Dance was the death of old 'Running Eagle,' who died on Friday morning 19th instant." He added that Running Eagle had "put on the dance" and that after his burial on the Friday afternoon, "everything went on as usual."[66]

At 199 accessioned items, the collection made at the Piikani reserve is one of the largest known to Piikani ceremonial leaders today. It features numerous everyday items, some of which were becoming less frequently used with the transition to a settled lifestyle. These comprise utensils such as hide scrapers [1930.924], pemmican pounders [1930.1096], and fire steels [1930.985]; sewing materials, including porcupine quills [1930.951] and awls [1930.955A-B]; and saddle bags [1930.1069] and a dog travois [1930.1110]. The collection also contains examples of women's and men's clothing: a dress [1930.1077] and a ceremonial weasel tail shirt and leggings [1930.1074

Figure 12 *Immoyiikimii* at the wheel of the Franklin, August 1929 | Glenbow Archives, NA-2908-4

and 1930.1073A-B], along with a few pairs of moccasins. Most striking is the number of items associated with Blackfoot ceremonial societies, such as the Brave Dogs, and transferable bundles, such as Thunder Medicine Pipes and Beaver Bundles.

Given the size of this part of the collection, the meagreness of the written documentation seems extraordinary. Cadzow's *Air-Cooled Adventure among the Aborigines* (n.d.) contains just one sentence about the Piikani leg of the trip – the expedition spent "several days among the Peigan Indians and hunting Mountain sheep" – and Robert Rymill's inventory lists the artifacts but gives no names. Despite the paucity of written data, the expedition photos facilitate a detailed examination of the team's methodology and help identify one First Nations person whom it met. The front page of *Air-Cooled Adventure* features a Piikani woman in a buckskin dress and a man wearing the weasel tail shirt now in the MAA who stand in front of the Franklin (Figure 16).[67] A copy of a second shot of the same man, now seated at the wheel of the Franklin, is in the Glenbow Archives (Figure 12). The Glenbow documentation identifies him as "Grassy Water" *(Immoyiikimii)*, describes him as "South Piegan," and dates the photograph to 1930.[68] Dressed in his weasel tail shirt, *Immoyiikimii* also appears in the footage shot by the Franklin team at the Piikani reserve, where he can be seen standing next to lodge poles before walking away from the camera's gaze.

The images taken at the Piikani reserve are some of the final visual records of the expedition. After Cadzow and the Rymills had exhausted their collecting budget at Piikani, they drove across the international border into Montana and headed to Yellowstone Park, where they recorded several minutes of footage of geysers, including the famous Old Faithful, as well as encounters with black bears. They then drove through Crowheart, Wyoming, and on to Cheyenne, at which point the expedition officially ended (Cadzow n.d.). Robert and John Rymill caught a train to San Francisco, where they boarded a ship for Australia, and Cadzow drove back to Syracuse alone. Although their journey was over, that of the collected artifacts continued. Shipped in crates across the Atlantic, they arrived in Cambridge during the autumn of 1929.[69]

THIS OVERVIEW OF THE Franklin Motor Expedition allows us to reflect on the tensions and opposing worldviews that are inherent in expeditions, especially in colonial contexts (see also M.L. Pratt 1992). First, the expedition was framed as an adventure, a point reinforced by the documentation. Given this, it could easily be characterized as somewhat frivolous in comparison with other anthropological ventures of the same period. Certainly, its methods were not as rigorous as those employed by lone ethnographers who based themselves in a single field site for a lengthy period, but this was survey ethnography supported by the ideology of ethnographic salvage. It may well have been an adventure, but it had a serious purpose as well, and there is no indication that its members saw their work as anything other than scientifically significant. As Ira Jacknis (1996a, 193) points out, it is difficult today to appreciate the urgency of ethnographic research in its early years, and though he focuses on salvage ethnography in the later nineteenth century, his comment is equally pertinent to the interwar years, during which time the effects of assimilation policies were indisputable.

Second, though Cadzow and the Rymills sincerely believed that their actions were justified and that the transactions in which they participated were legitimate, the unequal circumstances in which they operated must have been apparent to them, just as they are today, yet they never referred to this factor. Responding to the economic and social crises in their communities, First Nations people participated in the gradual commodification of materials that they would previously have treated very differently. This commodification – and the resultant exchange of artifacts for cash – has enabled museums to assert that the actions of collectors in the past were legal and valid, and that people who sold artifacts did so of their own free will (see Lokensgard 2010). By contrast, First Nations critics of this argument point to the harsh realities of life for their ancestors and the combination of economic conditions and challenges to traditional belief systems that made it difficult to resist the approaches of collectors. They claim that this view has been glossed over in debates regarding ownership and that it must be acknowledged.

A third tension arises from the team's presentation of the landscape through which it travelled as untamed and beyond the limits of civilized society. This description, shaped by the intersection of heroism, masculinity, and danger, was applied to many expeditions during the so-called golden age of exploration (see, for example, Bloom 1993; and Robinson 2006). Such "wild" landscapes provided the necessary setting for masculine activities; they were beautiful and threatening at the same time, and encounters with the people who inhabited them were all part of the package. This reimagining of remote spaces as pristine but dangerous was especially common in polar exploration narratives of the later nineteenth and early twentieth centuries. Given Cadzow's own lengthy experience of Subarctic living and his participation in Arctic expeditions, its appearance in his account of the Franklin Motor Expedition should come as no surprise. Technology played a role, too, as venturing into such a challenging environment required access to state-of-the-art machinery – in this case, the Franklin air-cooled automobile. Thus, stirring adventure, an untamed landscape, and technological innovation were integrated in a set of narratives that may seem simple on the surface but were produced through complex processes of negotiation. Taken together, the tensions outlined here highlight the vastly different perceptions of the individuals who engaged with the Franklin Motor Expedition as it traversed the prairies in the summer of 1929. In the following chapters, these and other tensions will be explored in more depth as I turn to the collecting exchanges that punctuated the journey and the nature of their representation.

4
Representing Collecting
Images and Narratives

Bob Rymill left Cambridge today. I told him not to collect too large specimens as we have no where to put them. I fear a tipi would be a white elephant.

> – Louis C.G. Clarke to Donald A. Cadzow,
> 11 June 1929[1]

See, a lot of these old guys, what they had they didn't show them. Special things, sacred things.

> – Donald Bigknife, author interview

THESE TWO STATEMENTS, the first from the curator of the Museum of Archaeology and Anthropology at Cambridge University (MAA), the second from a Plains Cree elder after studying photographs of artifacts collected by the Franklin Motor Expedition team, exemplify the tensions of ethnographic collecting. Clarke assumes that the expedition had free rein to choose, whereas Bigknife notes that such was not the case. Collections are assembled through a filtering process that begins with those who decide to sell or exchange items (Schindlbeck 1993; see also Thomas 1991; and Newell 2010). Accordingly, though Cadzow and the Rymill brothers had certain collecting goals in mind, they never entirely controlled the content of what they amassed. In this chapter I look at their representations of the expedition, drawing principally on film and photographs. Since the 1990s, as Marcus Banks and Richard Vokes (2010, 337) note, visual anthropology has increasingly read photographs in ways that go "beyond or behind the photographers' (presumed) intentions" to gain "access to historical traces of the peoples depicted." They continue: "No matter how staged or seemingly artificial, these images recorded points in individual and collective lives in which the subjects were sutured into the anthropological project." Hoping to "recover the details of the relationships" (ibid., 338) between photographer and subject, I also demonstrate how the Franklin Motor Expedition images can be read "against the grain" (Sekula 1984) so as to better understand First Nations participation in collecting exchanges.

In some respects, involvement in collecting transactions resembled other exchange relationships based on the circulation of goods. First Nations had traded inter-tribally for millennia and had sold furs to Europeans – directly or indirectly – for hundreds of years. The Piikani, for example, who had barred Europeans and Americans from their territory for the longest period of any First Nation visited by the Franklin Motor Expedition, had over 150 years of direct trading relationships with non-indigenous people by 1929. The negotiation skills of individuals in these communities were finely honed and were undoubtedly used to best advantage in many collecting transactions. Broadly speaking, selling or exchanging artifacts to collectors and anthropologists was an extension of trading practices. The difference lay in the conceptualization of the relationship between the parties. Collectors viewed the exchanges almost exclusively in economic terms, whereas for First Nations people, this was not always the case. On the surface, exchanges may have been about economics, but they also created alliances that could be drawn upon in future; sometimes they were expressions of hospitality and generosity, values that were (and are) highly regarded in First Nations communities (Noel Starblanket, e-mail to author, 14 December 2011). Indeed, collectors' field notes rarely refer to the importance of "gifting," though many participated in gift giving themselves. This included Cadzow and the Rymills, though they probably did not understand that engaging in such exchanges meant they were entering into a relationship with expectations, or that in indigenous cultural contexts, some "gifts" had "inherent, living qualities" that could not in themselves be commoditized (Lokensgard 2010).

That collections were shaped by First Nations people seems evident today, but in the past most anthropologists and field collectors did not fully acknowledge their contributions, at least not in their publications.[2] By the time of the Franklin Motor Expedition, when salvage ethnography was at its peak, museum field collectors viewed their activities not just as a race against time, but as a competition with each other. This point is supported by studies of collecting that emphasize the determination of collectors to acquire the desirable, the rare, and the singular, whatever the price. Accounts of the collecting exploits of professional field collectors seldom include those rather uncomfortable occasions where "they had been had" (Cole 1991, 49); instead, the language of salvage ethnography is replete with success stories, often relating to the procurement of a highly regarded piece that another museum had sought. The 1925-26 Museum of the American Indian (MAI) annual report, for example, boasts of a "Peace-pipe bundle" said to be the last in existence and bought by Cadzow at the Gordon First Nation, a predominantly Plains Cree community in the Touchwood Hills region of Southern Saskatchewan. According to the report (Museum of the American Indian 1926, 6), "This bundle has been mentioned in scientific articles published by other museums, but it was the privilege of our Museum to obtain the actual specimen."[3] Key to this account is not that Cadzow managed to acquire the bundle, but that he succeeded where other museums failed. Cadzow (1926b, 82) himself provided more detail: he had bought the bundle from "Makistukwam, wife of Atos who had been its keeper and who had recently died." He explained that

> it was a fortunate circumstance that the writer chanced to be in the region, as arrangements had been made by the old woman, who feared the calumet bundle, to "return" it to Manito and the powers responsible for its creation. This would have been done by carrying the pipe-stem bundle far into the bush and saying the appropriate prayer for the transfer, after which it would have been left on the ground to decay.

In his report, Cadzow (ibid., 83) wrote that Makistukwam *(mahkistikwân,* or Big Head) needed to consult with "four old men of a certain secret society" before proceeding and was travelling between reserves to consult with them when he arrived in the region.[4] Cadzow's diary of this MAI expedition, which is kept by his family, occasionally reveals how he learned who wished to sell artifacts. He was probably told of *mahkistikwân's* intent to return the bundle to the earth and decided to find her first. His persistence eventually paid off, as "after following Makistukwam for days, she was ultimately found on the Gordon reserve ... and was persuaded to place the precious *askushshi,* or 'pipe-stem of peace,' in the custody of the Museum" (Cadzow 1926b, 83). Although this account privileges the museum's caretaking role, it is difficult to read its description of pursuing an elderly woman throughout Southern Saskatchewan without wondering whether *she* were not only trying to consult with the elders but also doing her best to avoid Cadzow.

Clearly, some field collectors revelled in the competitive – and adventurous – aspects of their work. Cadzow's correspondence with the MAI, cited in the previous chapter, shows that he was no exception. Furthermore, his account of securing the pipe bundle from *mahkistikwân* is reminiscent of descriptions of stalking game, and hunting metaphors were commonly used at this time to describe collecting (see also Griffiths 1996). Indeed, Cadzow's diary mentions "specimen hunting," and there were undeniable links between the romance of the big-game-hunting lifestyle and participation in ethnographic expeditions.[5] In Western Canada, this connection was most explicit at the Sign of the Goat Trading Post in Banff, referred to in Chapter 3, which combined selling Nakoda souvenirs with a thriving taxidermy business. Here, customers could acquire hunting trophies (whether artifacts or animals) without actually expending any labour or putting themselves at risk from wildlife or potentially threatening Natives.[6] Such a sanitized and mediated form of acquisition would not have appealed to Cadzow and the Rymills, who wanted to experience the thrill of the chase for themselves.

Cadzow's contemporary Alanson B. Skinner also used the metaphor of collector as hunter. In an article on his relationship with the Menominee of the Great Lakes region, Skinner (1921, 53-54) emphasized his own collecting skills. From his descriptions of his activities, the name he was given, Sek ó'sa (Little Weasel), seems highly appropriate. He claimed that "the Menomini, owing to my success in ferreting out the abiding places of sacred objects, and my good fortune in obtaining them, had early fancied that I resembled the weasel, 'who never returns empty from the hunt,' so 'Little Weasel' I was forthwith dubbed." Published reports like this contrast markedly with many private descriptions, which demonstrate the more honest, but undoubtedly less heroic, aspects of collecting, and in which "First Contact" narratives and bravado are replaced by accounts of tedium, loneliness, and frustration. Cadzow's diary for his 1926 expedition, for example, often refers to the difficulties he faced: uncooperative First Nations people, poor driving conditions, uncomfortable weather, and relentless mosquitoes. Published accounts of the early to mid-twentieth century and beyond rarely mentioned the frustrations of collecting, and only with the more reflexive ethnographies of recent years have anthropologists departed from this convention (McCormack 1991; Price and Price 1992; O'Hanlon 1993; Geismar 2009; Bonshek 2010).

Visualizing the Expedition

Written descriptions help illuminate collecting processes of the past, but visual records offer additional insights that are rarely recorded in diaries and other accounts. Archives contain a mass of visual material related to the commodification and circulation of ethnographic artifacts that reveals how these items have been used in the construction of knowledge over time. Illustrated catalogues, such as those distributed by W.D. Webster, the London-based dealer of ethnographica, are excellent resources for tracing artifacts that became part of museum collections. Some museum archives contain images of artifacts in situ, often with their original users. Many also have photos of collectors posed with parts of their collections, which are similar in genre to shots of hunting expeditions where game animals are displayed "in decorative heaps, the artifice enhancing the prestige of the hunter" (MacDougall 1997, 278). Such images support theories about how collectors controlled their collections (through ordering and display) and speak to themes of competitiveness and expressed masculinity that seemingly characterized collecting in the later Victorian and early Edwardian periods. In the MAA, for example, there is an intentionally humorous photograph of Baron Anatole von Hügel (who became the museum's first curator); taken in 1875 with his collector friends in Fiji, it is captioned "The Rival Collectors."[7] However, as photos of collectors were frequently taken after artifacts were acquired, they represent a step away from the point of transaction and a later stage in the process of accumulation.

In contrast, the images created by the Franklin Motor Expedition record the collecting process itself. This makes them extremely rare and offers intriguing possibilities for thinking about collecting encounters. All three men were experienced photographers, and they used still and motion picture cameras during their trip. Cadzow's uncle had taught him how to use a camera, and he honed his photographic skills while employed by the MAI (N.B. Martinez 1998, 49-50).[8] His later use of film and photography in public archaeology programming is regarded as "innovative for the time"

(Custer 1996, 63). Robert and John Rymill had taken a 16mm motion picture camera with them on their 1928 hunting trip to Canada, and as John appears in none of the expedition's film footage, he seems to have been responsible for the film sequences. Twelve minutes of footage as well as approximately fifty photos have survived, though six exist only in the pages of Cadzow's *Air-Cooled Adventure among the Aborigines,* and the location of the negatives and any prints is unknown. There is some duplication in the images now cared for by the Cadzow and Rymill families, which suggests that copies were exchanged after the expedition ended as part of the networks that Elizabeth Edwards (2001, 27-50) notes were key to the creation of photo archives.

The film and photos enable the expedition to be understood as a series of encounters shaped as much by First Nations individuals as by Cadzow and the Rymills. Differing themes emerge from each set of visual images. For example, the principles of ethnographic salvage that initially motivated the team are apparent in many images as they are in the collection's content. That said, though several shots seem to fit the conventions of photographing First Nations people at this time (for instance, many File Hills people posed for the camera in beaded outfits), others express less populist imaginaries, and the framing seems ad hoc. Fifty photographs and twelve minutes of film footage seem a rather limited output for an expedition that lasted almost three months, but several factors would have accounted for this. In some communities, the brevity of visits and the nature of the business may have precluded extensive use of the camera. At Swan Lake, for example, the expedition's first stop, John Rymill took one landscape photo, two portraits of Giigido Asin, and two pictures in which his brother and young men inspect the Franklin's special cooling mechanism (Figure 13).

These two images of Giigido Asin aside, all the Swan Lake photographs seem to have been taken hastily, without much consideration given to framing. Rymill may have been uncomfortable with the camera, or perhaps with his subjects. Or perhaps many Swan Lake people were mistrustful of him. The photo of Ajidamoo's house (Figure 8), for example, gives the impression of a snapshot rather than a carefully composed image. Taken from the rear, it crops part of the house, and its angle suggests that Rymill did not attempt to plant his tripod on level ground. A few people stand with their backs to the camera, and one man sits on the ground and leans against the wall. Most look into the distance, but three appear to be distracted by the photographer and have turned their heads to watch what he is doing. Swan Lake people

Figure 13 Robert Rymill and Swan Lake men examine the Franklin, June 1929 |
Reproduced by permission of the Robert and John Rymill families

had good reason to be suspicious of outsiders, and like other leaders from Swan Lake, traditional healer Ajidamoo was subject to DIA scrutiny around this time. The shot seemingly records something occurring near his home, but its framing suggests that the photographer (at least) was not able to observe at closer range.

In contrast, the people photographed at the File Hills, where the expedition spent much more time, seem more at ease and perhaps found the team and its cameras less intrusive. This was Cadzow's third visit to the community, and his 1926 diary reveals that its photography session was a repetition of earlier interactions: "Visit the old men on the Star Blanket Reserve. They have a dance for us and dress up in their costumes. Both K [Kenneth Miller] and I dance with the Indians ... Take many photos."[9] Noel Starblanket, a direct descendent of some individuals photographed at the File Hills, suggests that Cadzow and the Rymills must have presented themselves in such a way that they were trusted; otherwise, they could not have taken some of the photographs they did and would not have been shown some of the materials they captured on film (Noel Starblanket, author interview, Fort Qu'Appelle, 8 June 1999). Indeed, the "warm relationship between photographer and subject," which Natasha Martinez (1998, 40) regards as characteristic of Cadzow's work, is apparent in many File Hills shots, regardless of who stood behind the camera. People in the File Hills film footage appear to be especially relaxed and seem to be enjoying the occasion. They were used to dressing formally for officially sanctioned occasions, such as the Regina Fair and Exhibition, and the 1925 Lebret Historical Pageant mentioned in Chapter 1; thus, their positive response to the expedition cameras is not surprising.

The first encounter recorded at the File Hills was undoubtedly pre-arranged and was filmed with still and motion picture cameras. In the opening sequence of the film, four men and a young boy, all wearing beaded buckskin outfits and eagle feather headdresses, stand in a line beside a painted tipi. They stand expectantly, with their arms by their sides, as if they are more familiar with posing for still cameras. Occasionally, they straighten their clothing, which is being blown about by the strong breeze. They are joined by *atim kâ-mihkwasit,* who strides toward them while adjusting his headdress. The men exchange a few words, and the camera pans slowly along their faces before switching to a profile view of each man. The photographs of this encounter show an expanded group, though the emphasis on posing for the camera remains the same (Figure 14). After the men had been

Figure 14   Posing for the camera at the Star Blanket Nation, July 1929 | Reproduced by permission of the Robert and John Rymill families

Figure 15 Profile view of *atim kâ-mihkwasit,* July 1929 | Reproduced by permission of the Robert and John Rymill families

filmed as a group, *atim kâ-mihkwasit* posed alone (Figure 15). The camera zoomed out to encompass a wider frame, which included the Franklin and a still camera and tripod operated by Cadzow.

Cadzow had an eye for the kinds of imaginaries that appealed to the Euro-American public, and the film shows him directing his subjects, perhaps with a view to the publicity uses of the footage. He invites *atim kâ-mihkwasit* to stand closer to a tipi, while guiding his teenaged daughter, Hortence, away from the gaze of the still camera. He then encourages a few curious bystanders to look through the camera's viewfinder. A profile portrait taken during this session subsequently appeared in *Air-Cooled Adventure among the Aborigines* (Figure 16). Two further encounters filmed with the movie camera at *atim kâ-mihkwasit'*s camp show everyday tasks and appear to have been recorded spontaneously, unlike the scenes just described. The first is a profile view of a man who sits on the ground and sands a lodge pole; the second shows an elderly woman tending a fire with the assistance of Hortence and another young girl. Only a few seconds of footage have survived for each activity, and the performative elements so transparent in

Air-cooled Adventure Among the Aborigines

Joint expedition of the Cambridge University Museum and British Museum of London, England into the Canadian Northwest wilderness.

Transported by a Franklin air-cooled car

Figure 16   Front page of *Air-Cooled Adventure among the Aborigines*

FACING PAGE ▶
Figure 17   Robert Rymill with *kā-mostoswahcāpēw*, File Hills, July 1929 | Reproduced by permission of the Robert and John Rymill families

the shots of the File Hills leaders are not replicated; indeed, the subjects display little interest in the filmmaker and his camera.

In *Air-Cooled Adventure among the Aborigines,* Cadzow (n.d.) wrote that the File Hills people held "ancient ceremonies" for the team. One of these – or what was probably a reconstruction – was recorded with a still camera. Cadzow had witnessed *kā-mostoswahcāpēw's* smoking tipi ceremony in 1926, and he published an ethnographic description of it in *Indian Notes* the following year (Cadzow 1927). During his 1926 trip, he collected material associated with the ceremony from *kā-mostoswahcāpēw,* and the Franklin team acquired additional items, described by Rymill as "Smoke lodge outfit. About 30 pieces and in two parcels."[10] Three images of *kā-mostoswahcāpēw*

with ceremonial artifacts have survived. Two show him kneeling on the ground beside what Cadzow described in his 1927 article as a "shrine." He holds a pipestem (which has no bowl) in front of him, and his attention is focused on the shrine. In the third picture, he and Robert Rymill flank the shrine, and Rymill sits cross-legged on the ground with his arms folded across his chest. Now the pipestem is placed on the altar, between the two men (Figure 17). Rymill looks into the distance, whereas *kā-mostoswahcāpēw*'s eyes are closed.

Figure 17 allows for speculation on the openness – and indeed the motives – of some persons who showed ceremonial materials to the expedition team and allowed them to be recorded. At a time when ceremonies were under threat, the interest and sympathy of visiting researchers may have prompted individuals to share ceremonial knowledge with them, albeit in modified form. The fact that neither Cadzow nor the Rymills could speak Cree and had little experience of Cree culture would have limited their understanding of what they were seeing. Perhaps they simply glossed as "ceremony" their exposure to materials and places associated with spiritual ways. Some clues do suggest that what they witnessed at the File Hills was not a "full" ceremony as understood by anthropologists who undertook more sustained study on First Nations reserves. For example, in his ethnographic account of the Plains Cree, which was based on mid-1930s fieldwork, David Mandelbaum (1996, 203) remarked that Cadzow's (1927) description of the smoking tipi ceremony was "quite different" from his own and that of Alanson B. Skinner, who had witnessed it in 1913, though he acknowledged that Cadzow's consultant came from a band with links to the Assiniboine, which may have accounted for discrepancies. Furthermore, the images themselves provide clues. First, only Robert Rymill and *kā-mostoswahcāpēw* appear in the shots, and it seems unlikely that the latter would have agreed to stage a ceremony on demand, though he may well have been amenable to showing the team where it had occurred in the past. Second, the pipestem is not connected to a pipe bowl, as it would be in ceremony. Regardless of how "real" their presentation is, the photos resemble shots of anthropologists and travellers with indigenous people that were taken throughout the world during this period. They are visual confirmation that Rymill spent some time in the company of a prominent ceremonial leader; thus, the capacity of the image to serve as a personal souvenir of the expedition is amplified.

Between leaving the File Hills and arriving at their final stop, the Piikani Nation, Cadzow and the Rymill brothers seem to have used their cameras sparingly, and when they did bring them out, it was to record the experience of travel. A few seconds of film show the poor condition of a prairie road, and several still shots of scenery often include the car as a motif. Collectively, the images illustrate rather more mundane aspects of the team's work and provide visual clues to the daily activities and divisions of labour that are rarely mentioned in expedition reports and field notes of this era. There is also a series of quite alarming photos and footage of encounters with black bears (Figure 18), taken at Yellowstone Park during the final days of the trip. All these images speak to how the team used their cameras to preserve what being part of an expedition entailed, as well as to record rather more conventional anthropological fieldwork. These two ways of thinking about the images collide in the film and photographs that survive from the final encounter at the Piikani Nation.

The footage from the Piikani Nation differs strikingly from that of the File Hills and adds weight to the narrative of ethnographic salvage that permeates the expedition's written documentation. With its concentration on familiar symbols of Indianness, such as tipis, feather headdresses, and beaded clothing, the File Hills film privileged the popular trope of the "vanishing Indian" (Dippie 1982). In contrast, the Piikani footage depicts ethnographic salvage in action, as Piikani people were filmed in the process of negotiating transactions with Cadzow and Robert Rymill. These images, which display examples of Piikani material culture that were no longer in

Figure 18 Encountering bears, August 1929 | Reproduced by permission of the Robert and John Rymill families

daily use, lent credence to the claims of anthropologists that "traditional" artifacts would soon be hard to find. Though deals like those seen in the footage were sometimes described after the event, recording them on film was highly unusual.

The two scenes of collecting last for less than a minute each and were probably recorded on different days. Both are set at the expedition camp, which was located in a wooded area near the Oldman River. In the first scene, three horse-drawn carts sit beside the Franklin, which indicates that Piikani people with things to sell approached the team directly. Cadzow appears to lead the discussion, while Robert Rymill looks on. Several men and women encircle the individuals participating in the negotiations, and young children amuse themselves by climbing onto the car or sitting on the ground beside the adults. Everyone ignores the dogs sniffing around. The artifacts brought for Cadzow's inspection are difficult to see clearly, due to the position of the people involved and the placement of the camera, and there is no evidence that Rymill or Cadzow took notes.

Figure 19   Robert Rymill collecting at the Piikani Nation, August 1929 |
Reproduced by permission of the Robert and John Rymill families

The second scene shows Robert Rymill on a camp stool outside the team tent, with a group of Piikani men seated on the ground opposite him (Figure 19). Items for his perusal, such as a dew claw rattle [1930.1063] and a powder horn [1930.1103], lie on the ground between the men and are discussed as the encounter unfolds. One man, who appears to be both interpreter and negotiator, picks up and shows off a painted and fringed rawhide bag. Rymill looks closely at each piece, counts out some banknotes, and hands them to an elderly man before pocketing his wallet. As the man puts the cash away, Rymill leans back on the stool and folds his arms to signify that the transaction has ended. Again, there is no evidence that notes were taken at the point of sale.

John Rymill's use of the movie camera to record transactions between team members and Piikani people offers insights into the expedition that would be difficult to replicate in other media. These few minutes of footage are crucial for understanding the acquisition process and the role of Piikani people in shaping the collection. As most transactions were made at or near the expedition camp, with people choosing to approach the team, the items they were prepared to sell must have been pre-selected. Furthermore, in the absence of field notes, the footage offers clues to the kind of

Figure 20 Dog modelling a travois, Piikani Nation, August 1929 |
Reproduced by permission of the Robert and John Rymill families

supplementary information that the team sought and how it was provided. Indeed, the team may have seen filming as a substitute for taking notes, since recording an object on film was far quicker than writing a detailed description. As David MacDougall (1997, 282) argues, during the early years of its use as an ethnographic recording tool, film emphasized "showing over telling." The evidential qualities of images were key. Discussing the well-known fire-making scenes recorded on the 1898 Cambridge Anthropological Expedition to the Torres Strait, MacDougall suggests that footage was regarded as akin to "a template for the process, allowing it to be reproduced, rather like following an instruction manual." Furthermore, "visual recordings 'saved' the event in some reified sense ... Interpretation could be provided later; the crucial thing was to salvage the data."

In an instance that illustrates MacDougall's point, the Franklin team filmed a dog strapped into a travois [1930.1110] (Figure 20). Blackfoot people had transported goods via dog-drawn travois for centuries, but these eventually fell from favour with the late-eighteenth-century flourishing of horse culture, which allowed them to carry more for lengthier distances. Once people were confined to reserves, they had less use for this technology. In the film, the dog sits low on the ground and is then encouraged to pull the travois by means of a kick to its rear. Rymill concluded his Piikani film with a scene showing the practicalities of preparing a field collection for shipment. Donald Cadzow constructs a packing crate, and Robert Rymill sits at a table, writing notes or perhaps labels for the crates. With them is a First

Nations man, presumably from the Piikani reserve, who may have been hired to assist with the packing. He holds a lance [1930.1111], one of the last items listed in Rymill's inventory.

Initially, Cadzow and the Rymills may have intended to undertake anthropological observational filmmaking, influenced as they were by the Edwardian view that the camera was "an indispensable piece of anthropological apparatus" (A.C. Haddon, quoted in MacDougall 1997, 282), but just as artifacts have complex meanings that are contextually driven and are part of their "social lives," so too does film footage; meanings can and do shift, and are multilayered. Indeed, as Banks and Vokes (2010, 339) state, given the performative qualities of images, we can see them as "essentially labile and fluid artefacts, at once 'at home' in any context, while at the same time in transit (albeit sometimes glacially slowly)." The purpose of the expedition was to collect artifacts, so imagery of its practice and the evidential qualities of having "been there" are foregrounded, but we should remember that the footage was created at a time when attitudes were changing regarding the potential of images to contribute to knowledge production. Elizabeth Edwards (2001, 46-47), for instance, observes that by the First World War, a gradual shift was under way in how British anthropologists valued photographic material acquired during fieldwork. Image making moved from "a process to a product of fieldwork" and thus "from a 'public' sphere to a private one." Banks and Vokes (2010, 340) write that "the transit of an image between the public and private (and vice versa) has the potential to rework the meanings which attach to it. Yet more than this, it may do so in ways which obscure, even erase, the prior 'social biography' of that image."

This point is supported by the reworkings of the Franklin Motor Expedition's images and their exploration during the photo-elicitation sessions that informed my own fieldwork. The images slip between the domains of public and private, in that their content is related to process, whereas their physical location – in a family archive – is very much tied to the private sphere. Cadzow and the Rymills blatantly inserted themselves into the photos and film in a way that placed them at the centre of events. As a result, the imagery accentuates narratives of encounter between the team and First Nations people, and supports its use as souvenirs for personal consumption rather than as public documents. Banks and Vokes (ibid., 345) refer to photos produced in this mode as "vernacular" in that they were created primarily for private reasons. As they note, such images are extremely useful for studying ethnographic practice, a point that applies to many

Franklin Motor Expedition photos as well. The team members' inclusion of themselves in the visual documentation thus reveals far more about the encounter and the role of First Nations people in it than if the sole emphasis had been on "exotic" others as was the norm for "ethnographic" images. There is, however, no neat distinction between "scientific" and populist forms of representation, and indeed it is now recognized that "these modes of expression are not ... as far apart as might be assumed since they both emanate from and shared common ideological ground" (Geary 1998, 150). Furthermore, as Edwards (1992, 13) observes, "photographs which were not created with anthropological intent or informed by ethnographic understanding may nevertheless be appropriated to anthropological ends." Thus, the film of the second Piikani transaction reveals indigenous agency in terms of direct collecting but also renders the File Hills images, with their performance of culture, even more jarring. Indeed, the Piikani footage (and the still photo of Robert Rymill with *kā-mostoswahcāpēw*) is reminiscent of what today are regarded as classic visual constructions of anthropological encounters.

Thinking through the Representations

Banks and Vokes (2010, 346) argue that though vernacular photographs "may not always be especially interesting from a strictly representational point of view, their study is invariably revealing of the wider social realities within and through which they are circulated." This is certainly true of the Franklin Motor Expedition shots, which offer multiple insights into the production and consumption of images of First Nations people. Every member of the team contributed to its visual record, but each one used the images for quite different narrative purposes. Cadzow included a selection in *Air-Cooled Adventure among the Aborigines,* consciously choosing pictures that reinforced stereotypes of First Nations people. Conversely, the Rymill brothers seem to have treated the images principally as travel souvenirs. Interestingly, all three men kept the film or photos throughout their lives and passed them on to their children.

Cadzow's use of expedition imagery in *Air-Cooled Adventure,* a narrative of modernization, is especially fascinating and was consistent with contemporary advertising, which used product placement in "exotic" settings (Lindstrom 2013). The pamphlet – which is about a thousand words in length – contains eleven expedition photographs, most accompanied by captions relating to the people they are said to depict or to the Franklin. With its emphasis on adventure and exploration, the title immediately grabs attention, but it is the interplay between captions and photos that romanticizes the people encountered by the team. This is especially explicit in instances of misidentification. A shot of *mihkostikwān* (Red Head), eldest daughter of *atim kâ-mihkwasit,* is captioned, "Dawn Star, daughter of Chief Red Dog, and Princess of the Crees, File Hills, Saskatchewan."[11] Perpetuating the myth of the Indian princess (Mithlo 2009) entailed changing *mihkostikwān*'s name and transforming her into Cree royalty.

At least *mihkostikwān*'s community was correctly identified. The caption accompanying the photo of *kā-mostoswahcāpēw* (Buffalo Bow) at his ceremonial altar misidentified his name, his community, and his activity:

> Buffalo Bull, Bungi Indian medicine man, praying at a shrine to Manitou for rain, which the white men secretly prayed would never come until they were well out of the Swan Lake district. From all the deep mud and snow that was encountered, the car was able to extricate itself under its own power and without the use of snow chains. (Cadzow n.d.)

Once again we are reminded of the need to approach *Air-Cooled Adventure* with caution. It was not a scholarly report, and we cannot determine whether it was edited by someone other than Cadzow. Moreover, the point of the caption was not to explain ethnographically what *kā-mostoswahcāpēw* was doing, but to link his activity with the car's ability to withstand difficult driving conditions. The caption tells one story, but the expedition film tells another – in one shot of a mountain road, Robert Rymill applies chains to the Franklin's tires.

Names were carelessly scattered throughout *Air-Cooled Adventure,* but not because Cadzow accidentally misidentified people. He knew the English translations of the names of many individuals whose images were reproduced, though he may have been unaware of their nuances and that some translations were truncated versions of names. Nevertheless, he sometimes replaced them with names that satisfied Euro-American expectations. In some instances, he simply used the name of another individual whom he had met on the trip; others were given names that better suited his tale of adventure. Occasionally, he got it right. For example, *kâ-pimohtêt* is correctly identified in a photo of Plains Cree men, who wear beaded outfits and stand by a tipi (although Cadzow used "Pimotat," an anglicized version of his name). The other men in the image are not: one is called "Talking Stone" (a mistranslation of Giigido Asin, who was from Swan Lake); another is misidentified as "Little Black Bear" (after a leader for whom one of the File Hills reserves is named). Perhaps it is unsurprising that people were misidentified; after all, the point of the text was to promote the car, not to provide a detailed (or even accurate) account of the expedition. Nonetheless, with its cavalier disregard for accuracy, it fit with the conventions of advertising, where the new, the exciting, and the "modern" were juxtaposed with the "traditional" and supposedly disappearing ways of indigenous people. The superiority of the product and the culture that produced it were made explicit, and indigenous people were represented as naive and backward. The romanticization of the text, in which the First Nations were granted a colourful past but had no future, simply reinforced the message.

The symbolism of the car played a crucial role in this narrative, both visually and in the written text. The choice of a Franklin was explained early in *Air-Cooled Adventure among the Aborigines* (Cadzow n.d.):

> A flexible, powerful car that could stand abuse would be necessary. It would also have to be "fool proof" as none of the members of the expedition had ever taken a degree as a mechanical engineer. To make a long story short – a general survey of automobiles pointed to one car, and one car only as being the most practical for our purpose – that car was the Franklin.

Further demonstrations of its suitability appeared as the story unfolded. In some areas, the expedition followed wagon trails, which were commonly high-centred and difficult to navigate: "Often, to avoid rocks and stumps, we had to ride the sides, one wheel up and the other down, with the flexible under-carriage managing in some way (which we could clearly see was pre-determined) in keeping the car from either overturning or losing traction" (ibid.). Such circumstances were undoubtedly difficult, but if Cadzow's narrative is to be believed, they were no match for the Franklin.

The car appears in over half the photos of *Air-Cooled Adventure among the Aborigines*. In three of them, First Nations people pose with it: at the wheel, standing before it, or sitting by the fender (Figure 12). In two of these shots, the men are dressed in formal clothes: *Immoyiikimii* wears his weasel tail shirt, and an elderly man, identified as Chief Four Stars "of the Wahpeton Sioux," is dressed in a suit of chief's clothing of the kind issued to band leaders by government officials as part of treaty agreements. Cadzow's early recognition that pictures of the car "in action" might have advertising potential may explain its frequent appearance in the visual record. Indeed, the recurrence of the Franklin is one of the most remarkable themes of the expedition imagery, whether in the foreground of the shot or as a ghostly presence in the background. Its inclusion in many of the still photographs served to amplify the team members' awareness of the social and economic gaps between themselves and their subjects, and was a visual metaphor for the rapid advancement of technology. According to Cadzow (n.d.), crowds of people gathered around it whenever the expedition paused in small Prairie towns to pick up supplies or ship specimens. It was the latest thing: the future of automobile transportation.[12] The rather brutish juxtaposition of the modern technologies represented by the Franklin with supposedly unsophisticated pre-modern First Nations people points to one of the many ironies in the expedition's representation. For instance, the interest of Swan Lake men in the car's cooling mechanism was simply not mentioned (Figure 13); instead, the staged image of *Immoyiikimii* was selected to illustrate First Nations' encounters with advancing technology. This example is one of the clearest indicators of the tangled relationship between expeditions, technologies, the performance of modernity, and the ideology of ethnographic salvage.

Cadzow may have intended to use his photographs commercially, but it is unlikely that the Rymill brothers shared this goal. Participating in an expedition for the first time, they created images to encapsulate their experience for themselves and to share it visually with family and friends back home. Souvenirs of individual experience are connected to biography, and as Susan Stewart (1993, 138) suggests, photographs preserve "an instant in time through a reduction of physical dimensions and a corresponding increase in significance supplied by means of a narrative." In this case, the photography was intended to become part of a conversation, illustrating the Rymills' narrative of their adventure.

Robert Rymill's organization of photographs into a captioned album supports this point. With the exception of John Rymill's shot in which a bear attempts to enter the car (Figure 18), all the prints in the album came from the File Hills, where most of the photography took place. The brief descriptive captions – such as "Red Dog at teepee door. Bob emerging from teepee" (Figure 21) and "Keevisk's shelter. File Hills. July 1929" – identify

Figure 21 "Red Dog at teepee door. Bob emerging from teepee" | Reproduced by permission of the Robert and John Rymill families

where and when the pictures were taken. Several loose images, captioned on the back with similar brevity, were taken at other reserves. In later life, Robert Rymill shared these photographs and the film with his wife and family, and the associated anecdotes became part of family history. In one such tale, Rymill was offered several horses in exchange for the red flannel shirts that had been made for him in Cambridge as part of his expedition kit (Susan Pender, author interview, Penola, South Australia, 5 March 1999). Collecting was seemingly turned on its head in an attempt to arrange a trade. Rymill, whose sole reason for being in Canada was to collect, was asked to make a trade of a different kind and to exchange for horses – themselves a measure of wealth – something that both he and the other man valued. Having little need for horses, but plenty of use for his shirts, Rymill declined the generous offer. At first glance, this incident underscores differing perceptions of value, but it is also possible that the man who initiated the trade was teasing Rymill by constructing an elaborate irony around the collecting process.

Anecdotes like this, reserved for friends and family, are more than simple adventure stories. They foreground the strategies adopted by some First Nations people to address the difficult economic circumstances outlined in Chapter 1 as well as the cultural misunderstandings that could arise during collecting encounters. As such, they are helpful for teasing out responses to the team and its activities that are not addressed in the published accounts. Similarly, the visual images take on more complex meanings when read against the grain. These relate to their potential to illuminate the dynamics of collecting practices, as shown above, but also to their meanings for First Nations communities who are now repatriating ceremonial artifacts in museum collections. Accordingly, though the footage has much to offer historians of film, anthropology, and museums, it holds negative connotations for some First Nations people, who point out that they deal with the repercussions of colonialism on a daily basis. Of course, the removal of cultural materials from First Nations communities (regardless of whether they were sold willingly) was a significant part of the colonial experience. Given this, we must ask about the value of films that reveal the identity of individuals who sold ceremonial artifacts. I address this point in Chapter 5 in my exploration of contemporary responses to the Franklin Motor Expedition and the collection it assembled.

THE DISCUSSION ABOVE has underscored the tensions between the narratives that emerge from and surround the Franklin Motor Expedition. The team used images to create stories about technology and its inevitable progress, with the Franklin automobile symbolizing this process. These stories were then paired with other tales that emphasized the decline of "traditional" First Nations ways. According to these narratives, as the expedition crossed the prairie, going "beyond the end of steel" (Cadzow n.d.), past and future came briefly together, but there was no doubt that the expedition was witness to a landscape and people in transition, and that "civilization" would prevail. Many of the accounts created by the team (and Cadzow in particular) deliberately foregrounded tropes of primitivism, heroism, the frontier, the clash of cultures, and the transcendence of new technologies. As such, they were in keeping with the spirit of the age in which science (and even pseudo-science) and exploration were immensely popular topics, framed within wider expansionist rhetoric. Other tales were more intimate and concerned personal experience of encounters, but the images fed into these as well. For instance, though the Rymill brothers eschewed an ongoing interest in the collection, they had good memories of their adventure and the meetings across cultures upon which it depended, as signified by their retention of their photographs and film.

Close scrutiny of the images themselves and the purposes to which they were put enables us to better understand how all these narratives were constructed. Visual analysis serves another important purpose, however; reading the images against the grain destabilizes the dominant narratives of heroism and adventure, and offers counter-interpretations to those provided in the public record of the expedition (such as *Air-Cooled Adventure among the Aborigines* and related newspaper articles). My analysis of the incorporation of visual sources into expeditionary narratives unpacks the complex processes involved in these cultural encounters, but the reflections of First Nations people are also crucial to understanding the legacies of these interactions. I turn to these in the following chapter.

5
Reflecting on the Franklin Motor Expedition
First Nations Perspectives

Nothing was really lost. The artifacts themselves are relevant to some individuals; they are relevant to a way of life that was suppressed by government legislation at the early part of this century. But to say that from the spiritual aspect rather than the cultural aspect, to say that it's lost, it's *not* really lost. Even the ceremonies that are no longer practised are not lost. We just need the right time and the right individual to seek that knowledge. And we seek knowledge not in terms of research in some archive; we seek it directly from the spirits. We ask them for that. So, it's still there with the people. It's just not practised.

– Lorne Carrier, author interview

IN THIS CHAPTER I examine First Nations responses to the Rymill Collection in order to highlight the potential of material heritage to support cultural revitalization. In essence, the chapter is an account of fieldwork undertaken in Western Canada from 1998 to 1999. Over thirteen months, I visited Swan Lake First Nation, Star Blanket Cree Nation, the Piikani Nation, and several other First Nations who encountered the Franklin Motor Expedition, to speak with people about the collection and about their views on the responsibilities of museums who hold items from their communities but are located at considerable distance away.[1] It is important to note that although these discussions date from over a decade ago, I have stayed in touch with most individuals whom I quote here; we have continued our conversations in person, by telephone, and by e-mail, and they have commented on drafts of this book. In addition, they remain committed to repatriating, where appropriate, artifacts from their communities, and to sharing their own cultural and historical knowledge with younger generations. They are also involved in cross-cultural education, and they see museums as playing a significant role in this area, with the proviso that First Nations people participate fully in the interpretation of their histories and contemporary lives.

Beginning the Dialogue

For over seventy years the Rymill Collection contributed to narratives about First Nations that were moulded by curatorial agendas and theoretical approaches affording little room for indigenous perspectives. My aim, when I began the project that informs this book, was to look beyond these dominant narratives to find those that were missing. I hoped that the descendants of people who had encountered the Franklin Motor Expedition would offer insights into the collecting process, but I also wanted to learn whether museums and First Nations could overcome cultural and geographical distances to incorporate historic collections into community agendas of cultural healing and knowledge dissemination. Though my research focused on the Rymill Collection and the Cambridge Museum of Archaeology and Anthropology (MAA), it highlighted challenges particular to many British (and other European) museums that hold important heritage materials but have little or no history of community engagement, other than as the agents of the colonialism that originally facilitated their acquisition. Furthermore, the research raised issues for *all* museums, regardless of their location, concerning the access of indigenous people to collections that are crucial for supporting cultural revitalization and pride, and to cross-cultural education.

My first methodological challenge was to find a way of mediating between the MAA and the communities visited by the expedition.[2] For this I used film and photographs, including the Franklin Motor Expedition photography, as well as the "Catalogue of the Rymill Collection in the University of Cambridge Museum of Archaeology and Anthropology" (Brown 1998), a compilation of the museum documentation on the artifacts. These sources were the focus of informal discussions and formal interviews, either with an individual or a couple, or sometimes with small groups. This approach is not novel; what has become known as photo-elicitation has a lengthy history as an anthropological research method (Collier and Collier 1986, 99-116; G. Rose 2007, 237-56). Franz Boas and John R. Swanton both used photographs of museum artifacts during their Northwest Coast fieldwork (Brown, Coote, and Gosden 2000, 267), and William Fenton (1966, 75-76) described his use of photographs of masks during fieldwork with Haudenosaunee (Iroquois) carvers. In his experience, "such photographs of tribal antiquities now in museums arouse enormous interest and stimulate comments on the artist, on the changing style, and they elicit new information on ceremonies, on older techniques and on activities now almost obsolete and nearly forgotten." There are numerous more recent examples of photo-elicitation projects that draw on diverse strategies and image genres, including interviewing with archival images (Binney and Chaplin 1991; J.A. Bell 2003; Halvaksz 2010) and family photographs (Geffroy 1990; Drazin and Frohlich 2007) as well as asking research participants to create photo-diaries (Latham 2004), all of which enable researchers to collate key data.

Gillian Rose (2007, 240) states that "while ordinary interview talk can explore many issues, discussing a photograph with an interviewee can prompt much more talk about different things" and can "prompt talk in different registers." It is worth reiterating that I used images of artifacts, not the objects themselves. Accordingly, though pictures can evoke "information, affect and reflection" (ibid., 238), the responses to the Rymill Collection would undoubtedly have been quite different had they involved direct engagement with the artifacts, rather than two-dimensional representations of them. I began most interviews by explaining who I was and why I was visiting the community. Interviewees then looked at the catalogue, to read about the collection and examine the photographs. We also looked at the expedition's still shots and film, although some people chose not to watch the latter as they were ambivalent about what, or whom, they might see. At the File Hills, for instance, many people asked to view it, and some fifty individuals attended a community meeting arranged for this purpose. In contrast, at the Piikani Nation, where the footage shows the sale of artifacts associated with ceremony, some people explained that they had no desire to see it in case they recognized the persons concerned. This point is a sharp reminder that the meanings of archival images are fluid and that assessments differ regarding their worth. As Elizabeth Edwards and Christopher Morton (2009, 11) note, "If history is textured by archival patterns, the contestation of those histories also constitutes a contestation of the archive." Though images of collecting have value from a collections history perspective, the identification of the individuals involved could have had negative repercussions in a small community such as Piikani, where the suppression of Blackfoot culture and the separation of people from ceremonial objects has left a legacy of tension.

In most cases, people browsed the artifact images slowly, commenting spontaneously on various pictures. I rarely asked about ceremonial items, because knowledge about them is restricted to certain persons. If, however, someone raised the topic first, such as by making a general statement that pertained to public knowledge, it was permissible to ask more detailed questions. Cultural restrictions on access to knowledge informed the questions that I, as an outsider, could acceptably ask and, by implication, what the MAA could know about the artifacts. Being aware of the cultural protocols for asking ceremonial leaders about the collection, which vary from community to community, was also crucial, though the extent to which these bind external researchers varies as well.[3] Quite often, people simply read out the information from Robert Rymill's catalogue cards, which I had transcribed in the catalogue as "collector's detail." Any glaring errors in his comments were usually remarked upon and corrected where appropriate.[4]

Collier and Collier (1986, 105) suggest that during photo-elicitation interviews, images perform as "a third party" and as visual probes by inviting "open expression while maintaining concrete and explicit reference points." My research bore out this point, and indeed, looking at three quite different forms of image – expedition photographs, film footage, and artifact photographs – may have enhanced the collective experience. I did not pre-select images – everything I had located was available for people to look at, think about, and discuss. Film and photographs evoke quite different responses due to their differing material qualities. As Edwards (1999, 226) notes, "Stillness [of photographs] invites evocation, contemplation and a certain formation of affective memory in a way that film and video, with their temporal naturalism and realistic narrative sequence, cannot." Nevertheless, the overarching theme of the interviews concerned people's contemporary experiences of museums, rather than detailed reflections on the content of the film and photos. This is an important point: though the research was very much dependent on historical materials, it was not a history project as such; instead, the images were used to encourage reflection on aspects of life and experience rather than as a means to record data regarding the images per se (see G. Rose 2007, 238). As I became more familiar with the visual cues in the pictures, I was able to ask more pointed questions about how history is constructed in First Nations communities; history is not confined to the past, but reaches forward into the future.

As the interviews progressed, four overlapping themes related to this point became apparent. First, certain questions arose for community members when confronted with the news that an overseas museum held artifacts of which they were entirely unaware. Second, they reflected on how the response of their ancestors to the Franklin Motor Expedition was related to the social and economic shifts of the 1920s. A third theme addressed how historic collections have the potential to contribute to the reclamation of knowledge that has become fragmented, particularly that which pertains to cultural practices or creative techniques. Finally, as many people wanted to know what the MAA was actually doing with the Rymill Collection and what its future might be, all of these themes were related to commentary about the roles of museums and how they could respond to First Nations concerns. In short, how might the Rymill Collection be used to benefit First Nations, who were not its intended audience when it was assembled but whose current need for access could no longer be overlooked? These themes shaped the research, this book, and my subsequent work, which has aimed to bridge the disconnections between indigenous communities and historic collections, particularly those in Britain (see Brown, Peers, and members of the Kainai Nation 2006; Brown, Massan, and Grant 2011; and Brown and Peers 2013). Each theme was explored to varying degrees and in slightly different ways in the many discussions I have had about the Rymill Collection during the initial research and since. As reactions to the collection are extremely complex, what follows is neither comprehensive nor intended to imply any unified community response. I am mindful of Gerald T. Conaty and Robert Janes's (1997, 35) observation, made in relation to Blackfoot understandings of sacredness, that opinions differ within and across communities and generations; museums may never understand these divisions, but they can remain open to the debates and learn more in the process.

Swan Lake First Nation

I began Chapter 1 with the words of the late elder Sam Cameron, who was in his eighties when I first visited Swan Lake. He remembered Donald Cadzow and "his big car," and though he was not certain which dates were involved, he knew that Cadzow came more than once. As we sat at his kitchen table, browsing the photographs, he explained that he had not been party to the discussions between Cadzow and spiritual leaders Ajidamoo and Giigido Asin, being in his teens at the time, but he knew the meetings were serious business and had often wondered about the fate of the ceremonial artifacts that left Swan Lake. Some of them, he knew, had gone to New York, but he was astonished to learn that others had been taken as far away as the United Kingdom (Sam Cameron, author interview, Swan Lake Nation, 5 April 1999, see Brown 2000, 124). The collection was also news to others in his community. A delegation from Swan Lake First Nation had visited the stores of the Museum of the American Indian (MAI) to see the items acquired by Cadzow in 1925, but no one with whom I spoke had any idea that he had made another collection four years later.

With a few exceptions, most Swan Lake items in the Rymill Collection are connected with ceremony; these include eagle bone whistles and rattles used in Sun Dances, as well as articles used by Midewiwin practitioners, such as birch bark scrolls, Midé bags associated with different degrees of Midewiwin membership, and *miigus* shells, which could cause or cure illness.[5] As mentioned in Chapter 1, Swan Lake had experienced sustained interference in its ceremonies from government, church officials, and the RCMP. Anyone who used or kept ceremonial artifacts could face repercussions; as a result, ceremonies went underground and the transfer of knowledge was interrupted though not completely halted. By the time the Franklin Motor Expedition came to Swan Lake, missionary activity, either on the reserve or in residential school, had obscured many people's understanding of ceremonial matters. Having been told that the Midewiwin and other Anishinaabe teachings were "Devil worship," but also knowing that ceremonial artifacts could be used for good or to cause harm, they were very frightened of them. One Swan Lake elder explained that in some instances when a person died, the family members who dealt with his or her belongings were so afraid of any ceremonial things that they wished only to be rid of them. Any collector who would relieve them of such items resolved the dilemma of keeping potentially dangerous objects that were also illegal. This comment echoes Susanne Küchler's (1997, 39) discussion of "riddance" in the Pacific during the colonial period, when visiting anthropologists or other collectors were sometimes viewed as appropriate recipients of artifacts that would otherwise have been left to rot in the bush.

The transmission of traditional teachings at Swan Lake was undoubtedly disrupted during the first half of the twentieth century, yet there was considerable resistance to colonial policies of assimilation. Some people retained their beliefs and passed on their knowledge when they could. As a result, many at Swan Lake continue to follow traditional teachings, and younger people are increasingly turning to them as part of their own healing process. That a museum holds ceremonial artifacts connected to the teachings of the Midewiwin and the Sun Dance was understandably troubling. Many people initially expressed bemusement that these sacred things had left the reserve in the first place. Some wondered how those who sold them could live with themselves and explained that, in their understanding, personal ceremonial artifacts should be buried with their owners on their death (see also Densmore 1979, 93). Their discomfort was compounded by a moral sense regarding the inappropriateness of questioning decisions made by elders decades earlier.

discomfort

Most Swan Lake items in the Rymill Collection are personal belongings; although individuals did have the right to pass on or sell their own ceremonial equipment, the sale of such items was controversial both at the time and now. Voicing his own ambivalence on this matter, community historian and elder Wayne Scott cautioned that whatever people might think was right or wrong, judging the actions of ancestors should be avoided as the specific circumstances of the transactions are unknown and would have varied from person to person:

> To me, anyway, I'd like to think that those old boys back then were thinking way ahead. One of the things that I don't like personally is, I will not sit here and defend the sale of those things. Whoever sold them, for whatever reason, personally, I would not do it. As an individual I would not sell my grandfather's things. Neither would I sell anybody else's water drum, or even a drum. I would not sell it. But that's me as an individual. That's got nothing to do with the fact that these things were sold in 1929, by so-called elders. By elders. By old people. And whatever caused those sales to go ahead I don't know. It's not important. To me it's not important, because I think maybe the circumstances were different from person to person. One person might have sold his water drum out of greed. The next might have had a big family with sick children and he'd sell the same thing. Two different reasons, and we're not in a position to pass judgment on those kinds of things. The fact that they're in a museum now is maybe that's where they belong. I don't know.

He added that, for Swan Lake, the issue was not the process through which the artifacts became part of the MAA collection:

> I'm not overly interested in how they came in someone else's possession, or the tactics they used, or whatever the heck it was – whether it was just an open sale. The question to me is, are we in any position to do anything about it, and if so, what are we willing to do? Are we in a position to bring these things home? If so, how do we do it? Are we even willing to? Are we prepared to tackle the responsibility? (Wayne Scott, comment made during a public meeting, Swan Lake Nation, 6 April 1999)

REPATRIATION

Scott made this comment during a public meeting at the Swan Lake Health Centre that he had arranged to discuss the Rymill Collection, which was attended by ten community members. The meeting emphasized that caring for ceremonial artifacts is a grave responsibility; keepers are subject to strict rules of behaviour, and they assume financial and social obligations that are constant and permanent. Even if a repatriation claim were to succeed, the story would not end there. The relationship between Swan Lake and the ceremonial artifacts had undoubtedly been disrupted, but as most were personal possessions, repercussions might arise if they were given to the wrong persons. Was it even possible for anyone in the community now, or in the future, to shoulder their care? Where would they be kept and who would look after them? Given their potential power, would it be safe for them to return to Swan Lake?

Swan Lake First Nation has considered building a cultural centre to publicly tell its history in its own way, but there has always been concern that ceremonial things should not be kept in such a place. Indeed, as band council member Don Daniels explained during one of our first meetings, from his perspective, such items were not made for display, and putting them in a museum at Swan Lake would be no better than keeping them in a museum anywhere else. This is not the Anishinaabe way of doing things. Cultural materials are not hoarded (Don Daniels, author interview, Swan Lake Nation, 25 February 1999). Ceremonial things must be cared for properly, in the appropriate manner, and must not be exploited or treated harshly. Some communities in the region are concerned that ceremonial artifacts and knowledge might be abused, albeit unintentionally, particularly by younger people who seek guidance through Anishinaabe knowledge systems but who, it was suggested, sometimes try to run before they can walk. This implied that younger people do not always undertake proper ceremonial training before they attempt to access powerful items, including those in museums, and that their desire to learn about their culture and heritage has sometimes prompted them to dabble with things for which they are unprepared and do not understand. The point was repeatedly made that this should not be allowed to happen at Swan Lake. In fact, it was suggested that the personal ceremonial artifacts of deceased community members should not be brought home and reinvigorated, and that their most appropriate future was to follow their rightful course – to be put in a clean place in the bush, where they would lie undisturbed and could return to the earth.

That the MAA holds personal ceremonial belongings was contentious enough, but the case of some ceremonial artifacts, which, in Anishinaabe belief, cannot be owned by an individual, was particularly sensitive. According to cultural protocols, they should be cared for by someone who has undergone the necessary training and has achieved a sufficient level of knowledge to do so. Swan Lake people were troubled by many ceremonial artifacts in the Rymill Collection, particularly two Midé drums (sometimes referred to in English as water drums) and drumsticks. The Midé drum – mitigwakik – is the most holy of objects, given to the Anishinaabeg by Gichi-manidoo (Sam Cameron, author interview, Swan Lake Nation, 5 April 1999, see Brown 2000, 175).[6] The drumstick was also a gift from the Creator and, according to some sources, is more sacred than the Midé drum (Hoffman 1891, 190, 223, cited in Angel 2002, 94; Densmore 1979, 96). Both must be treated with respect. The MAA was likened to a prison, with the drums being locked in, unhappy to be there (Wayne Scott, author interview, Swan Lake Nation, 5 April 1999; Vina Swain, author interview, Swan Lake Nation, 5 April 1999). It was acknowledged that museums certainly have the capacity to protect and care for these drums and artifacts physically, but their spiritual well-being was a very different matter.

In Anishinaabe ways of thought, all living beings, whether human or not, exhibit varying amounts of what Mary Black-Rogers (1977) calls "power-control" (see also Hallowell 1960). Levels of power-control differ between beings, though everyone has some, and it would be inappropriate and careless for an individual to advertise how much power he or she has. Hence, to avoid unpleasant outcomes by offending a being more powerful than oneself, it is important to be respectful to all creatures at all times. Moreover, as certain items associated with ceremony are used to mediate relations with other-than-human beings, it is wise to be watchful of how one behaves when around them. Most curators are not party to the appropriate knowledge systems and therefore cannot appreciate the power-control capabilities of the beings, such as the Midé drums, in their care, a fact that generates concern among First Nations people. Curators may be ignorant of the consequences of treating ceremonial artifacts in a way that does not attend to their spiritual as well as their physical needs. I was asked where the drums were kept and how they were looked after, and had to admit that they were not spoken to or fed with tobacco as they would be if a Midé leader cared for them (or indeed, if they were in a museum that was visited by people with the authority to carry out traditional care). In response, several individuals commented that the drums would be sad to be so far from Swan Lake; they were not treated with appropriate respect and care in the museum, and had not heard their own language in over seventy years. Most importantly, they were being prevented from fulfilling their ceremonial and teaching function.

The discussions at Swan Lake underscore some of the challenges First Nations people face when confronted with museum collections. Responses to images of artifacts may differ from those to the objects themselves, but this does not prevent fundamental and difficult questions from being asked. The discomfort of Swan Lake people upon learning of the collection's existence and their uncertainty regarding how to proceed constitute a tangible reminder that the collection was amassed when cultural ways of knowing were threatened but have nevertheless persisted despite enormous pressures upon the community to assimilate. The collection is also tangled within individual responses to those pressures and their longer-term impact. This is partly why histories of collecting, which are of such great interest to museum professionals, can be of limited value for communities, except in cases where they contribute to settling repatriation claims. What benefits are there to knowing who sold (or otherwise parted with) certain items – especially those used for the good of the community – if the circumstances informing their decision are not known? Whose interests does this serve?

As Wayne Scott made clear throughout our discussions, for Swan Lake First Nation, the issue is not what happened in the past, but what – if anything – should happen in the future. There is no clear-cut answer to this question. The MAA requires that requests for special access be initiated by the community, and I was told that although people were glad to know the collection existed, their feelings on the matter were mixed, and they were not ready to reach consensus on what to do about it. As Wayne Scott explained, the next steps required much careful consideration, which would take time. He also suggested that if the community does decide to establish a cultural centre, that might be the time to contact the MAA:

> We need to store all our history some place. Not only for ourselves, but for the kids that are going to school now, you know, for all them little babies that were born yesterday and the ones that are going to be born. We need to preserve that history. But we also need to teach those kids how to continue to preserve them. We need to do that. So maybe at that point in time, when we create ourselves an appropriate environment to be able to preserve these kinds of things, maybe at that point in time we may put in a proposal to that museum. Maybe. That's one thing we can think about (Wayne Scott, comment made during a public meeting, Swan Lake Nation, 6 April 1999).

With this eventuality in mind, the MAA's contact details and copies of the collection documentation are now in the band archive, ready for when, or if, the artifacts and the people reconnect physically.[7]

The File Hills

It is impossible to establish specific provenance for many of the items collected by the Franklin Motor Expedition in Southern and Central Saskatchewan. Robert Rymill did not identify reserves with sufficient precision, and his inventory describes many artifacts simply as "Plains Cree," a label that fails to take into account the complex demographics and migration histories of this region. As I discussed in Chapter 3, persons from the four File Hills reserves of Little Black Bear, Okanese, Peepeekisis, and Star Blanket have been identified as the source of some artifacts. As there was no doubt that the expedition had gone to the File Hills, I talked mostly with people from these nations, though I also met with many individuals from other Treaty 4 reserves who had professional and personal interests in museums and community histories. Just as at Swan Lake, our discussions involved formal interviews and less formal conversations, as well as both group and individual meetings, some of which were facilitated by community members who had considerable experience of liaising with Canadian museums.

The File Hills materials encompass artifacts, film, and photographs, and these articulated in such a way that discussions about the collection were rather more focused on the biographies of individuals than was possible elsewhere. For instance, *atim kâ-mihkwasit,* who was the hereditary chief at Star Blanket First Nation, was often referred to as a strong and considerate leader. Noel Starblanket described him as "one of the most significant leaders in that era. He was a very powerful man. He was a very religious, spiritual man. He was revered by both the Indian community and the white community for his strength and his statesmanship" (Noel Starblanket, author interview, Fort Qu'Appelle, 8 June 1999).[8] Elder Charlie Bigknife spoke about him in similar terms: "He was a good spokesman, a good leader, and he helped a lot of people out. He did good to other people, especially those that were sick. He'd look after them the best he knew how" (Charlie Bigknife, author interview, Star Blanket Nation, 8 July 1999). To illustrate these qualities of diplomacy and generosity, several people talked about *atim kâ-mihkwasit*'s friendship with Mr. McLaughlin, the director of the Regina branch of General Motors. He had given McLaughlin the name Strong Arm at the opening of the General Motors salesroom, and in recognition of the value of this gift, he received twenty five-dollar gold coins. His companions were each given a further ten dollars, also in gold. They spent the money on food and Christmas gifts for children from the Star Blanket Nation, and for many years afterward, McLaughlin donated to the band's Christmas fund, sending special gifts for *atim kâ-mihkwasit* and his wife (Noel Starblanket, author interview, Fort Qu'Appelle, 8 June 1999).

File Hills elders and other community members also spoke frequently of how *atim kâ-mihkwasit, kâ-pimohtêt,* and their contemporaries fought external pressures to assimilate and consistently stood up to the RCMP officers and government officials who tried to interfere in ceremonies. The resistance of ceremonial leaders to these pressures was commonly mentioned at all the reserves, often after an individual had examined the catalogue images of ceremonial materials. In one such example, Minnie Daniels, from Star Blanket Nation, recalled an instance when the Indian agent discovered that a thirst dance was under way and telephoned the RCMP, who tore down the lodge. Daniels remarked that "if the RCMP and agent had just asked the people not to do it, they would have stopped, but they shouldn't have torn down the lodge" (Minnie Daniels, author interview, Star Blanket Nation, 2 July 1999, quoted in Brown 2000, 196). A more extensive account of the desecration of the lodge appears in Danette Starr-Spaeth's

[Starblanket's] (1994, 64) study of Chief Star Blanket and his band. This narrative was taught to her by the late Hortence Watcheston, the younger of *atim kâ-mihkwasit's* two daughters, who said,

> As soon as this agent heard that they were gonna have a rain dance he went over and already the people were in the camp and they already had a lodge built up and when he got there he seen everything and he made the Indians break everything, they had to cut down the tree and everything and send all the people out of there.

The account then relates how all the leaders present were arrested but were subsequently defended by Mr. Mark, a lawyer from the nearby town of Melville:

> They phoned and he (the lawyer) came right away, they waited for him, he was prepared for it, so when he got there now he was the one who was talking and he told them, "It wasn't very nice for this man who was making that rain dance, he made a big promise that he was gonna make that rain dance because one of his kids was dying and he asked the Great Spirit, he wanted his boy to be alive, he didn't care what was gonna happen to him, he promised he was gonna make a rain dance if his boy lived. How come he had to try and do that and they (Indian Agent) broke everything," then he said, "How would you like it if these Indians burned down the Church?" (ibid., 64-65)

In her study of the repression of Prairie ceremonial beliefs, Katherine Pettipas (1994) examines archival materials that offer further insight into the harsh treatment of Plains Cree leaders at this time. She cites documents concerning a 1932 thirst dance at the Okanese reserve, which may well be the same one recalled by Minnie Daniels and Hortence Watcheston, and which resulted in the arrests of *atim kâ-mihkwasit, kā-mostoswahcāpēw, kā-otāsiw, kihiw,* and *kîsikâw-kêhkêhk* (ibid., 176).[9] Except for *kā-mostoswahcāpēw,* those arrested were members of the Star Blanket Nation, so they had contravened the Indian Act by attending a ceremony away from their own reserve without permission. Although, as Pettipas observes, the documentation does not reveal whether the men were actually convicted, Neal McLeod (2010, 64), who discusses these arrests in a recent essay, points out that *atim kâ-mihkwasit* was simply doing what he could to protect his people, and that his actions were an example of his "tenacity and future thinking."

In this same essay, which is based on research to support an exhibition of the works of James Henderson, a Scots artist who immigrated to Canada in 1910 and who painted portraits of many First Nations people in Southern Saskatchewan and Alberta, McLeod points to the legacy of portraiture of indigenous people for their descendants. Many individuals whom the Franklin Motor Expedition filmed and photographed also posed for artists such as Henderson, Nicholas de Grandmaison, Edmund Morris, and Mildred Valley Thornton during the 1920s and 1930s. McLeod (ibid., 63, 65) observes that such works "provide us with iconic memories through which we can gather an anti-colonial memory of the *kâ-têpwêwi-sîpiy* [Qu'Appelle River]." He argues that the meaning of these paintings "lies with the oral history and the narratives that mediate our understanding of these works," and that the stories of the people they depict continue to be held in the memory of their descendants. This point resonates with the responses of File Hills people to the images of Rymill Collection artifacts from their communities. With McLeod's remarks in mind, I focus here on how people from Star Blanket Nation but also from the other File Hills reserves reacted to the news that items associated with *atim kâ-mihkwasit* are in an overseas museum.

Figure 22 shows one of these, a beaded buckskin outfit, which incorporates a headdress, shirt, cuffs, belt, leggings, moccasins, pipe bag, and ceremonial club.[10] Unusually, Robert Rymill's record for this ensemble offers some context regarding its acquisition. His inventory describes it as "Complete chief's outfit. All of these items were obtained from Chief Red Dog. Most of the work was done by his daughter, to whom he handed on most of the purchase money."[11] Given *atim kâ-mihkwasit*'s reputation for generosity referred to above, the Star Blanket community was not surprised that his daughter *mihkostikwân* had received this money. In contrast, that the clothes were in an overseas museum was perplexing. Several people said they had understood that *atim kâ-mihkwasit* had been buried according to Cree cultural protocol in his beaded outfit when he died in 1940. It was described by the artist and writer Mildred Valley Thornton (2000, 27):

Red Dog's outfit was the most beautiful I have ever seen. His headdress with its magnificent eagle feathers and ermine skins reached to the ground.

Figure 22 *atim kâ-mihkwasit* and his daughters, *mihkostikwān (left)* and Hortence *(right),* Star Blanket Nation, July 1929 | Reproduced by permission of the Donald Cadzow family

It was said that such feathers had become increasingly difficult to procure and that sometimes the Indians paid as much as a dollar, or more, each for them. Add to that the fine workmanship and great quantities of beads and buckskin that made up an Indian's costume and one can readily understand why such articles were costly. The foundation of Red Dog's suit was deerskin. Almost every part of it was heavily embroidered with beads of many colours and it must have been exceedingly heavy to carry about.

The mounted policeman in charge of the camp told me that this costume aroused much interest among visitors, and had overheard a wealthy American offer Red Dog two hundred dollars in cash for his outfit, but Red Dog would not think of parting with it for so paltry a sum.[12]

The practice of burying the dead in their finest clothing was so well known that no one suspected that *atim kâ-mihkwasit* had another beaded outfit that still survived, even though community researchers had located File Hills clothing in Western Canadian museums.

The existence of this outfit raises questions regarding its potential impact on File Hills people, should they have the chance to see it for themselves. Mike Pinay, the Treaty 4 elders liaison officer, who is from Peepeekisis First Nation and is related to *atim kâ-mihkwasit,* noted its significance during our first meeting. He suggested that the social issues and dysfunction in First Nations communities have much to do with the continued separation of people from their material heritage and that the reconnection of younger people, in particular, with heritage items could be tremendously healing:

> There's a couple of pipes in there that I would like to see come back, from the File Hills, and I guess more than ever [what I'd like to see come home] is Chief Red Dog's outfit. Chief Red Dog was a very influential chief of his time, and so to bring those back to the people ... today, I think that's the reason why some of our people aren't getting along or aren't being together. It is because we don't have these items to bring us together, and to me that's very special. So if we can bring them back, I think once we start bringing them back, our people will start getting together, start getting along, start working together. (Mike Pinay, author interview, Calgary, 26 July 1999)

He added that if people who were "lost" in some way could see the possessions of past leaders who had fought for them, perhaps this would help them think about their own responsibilities as individuals and as First Nations people. It might also foster pride and a sense of community.

In his capacity as Treaty 4 elders liaison officer, Mike Pinay has been involved in discussions with Canadian museums regarding the loan and repatriation of ceremonial artifacts, and his comments were contextualized by having witnessed how people from Little Black Bear Nation responded when a rattle belonging to Chief Little Black Bear had been returned to the community. On long-term loan since 1991 from the Glenbow Museum, the rattle is brought out from time to time so that people can be close to it (Gerald Conaty, Glenbow Museum, e-mail to author, 1 June 2011). Pinay said,

> It's really emotional. I was there last year when they opened it, and hopefully, I'll be there again this year when they open it and bring that rattle out for the people. You even see tears, you know? That's how much it means to the people. Some of them are praying and it is just unbelievable.

You don't realize the feelings and what it does for the people, and that's why we want these things back. For the people. So they can have something. (Mike Pinay, author interview, Calgary, 26 July 1999)

Pinay's view is that access to heritage items has such an impact in First Nations communities that museums holding such materials need to cooperate more with them. This is especially so for museums far from Canada, where the curatorial staff have neither the cultural expertise to care for ceremonial artifacts nor an understanding of their place in First Nations communities. He also emphasized that people are very selective about what they need and take their time to do things properly. He explained that

we are not asking for everything back. We are just looking for a few items that our people can use ... But we still want to make sure that people get what they really want. There's a lot of items out there, and we are not asking for everything back. I think maybe the curators should have a look at that. (Mike Pinay, author interview, Calgary, 26 July 1999)

Another item connected to *atim kâ-mihkwasit* invoked the issue of repatriation, although its link to him was not established until Star Blanket individuals examined the photographs in the catalogue. As mentioned above, *atim kâ-mihkwasit* is known for his leadership qualities, but he is also remembered as a powerful singer who received many of his songs in dreams; indeed, his name is honoured by the Red Dog Singers drum group from the File Hills area, which was formed in 1998 (Willard Starblanket, author interview, Star Blanket Nation, 2 July 1999). His singing abilities were mentioned most frequently in relation to a drum in the Rymill Collection [1930.844], which men would have used to drum and sing for the people. The drum stands about thirty centimetres tall and has a diameter of sixty-five centimetres. Its hide surface is painted a rich bright blue, and a yellow circular central panel contains a symbol indicating the four directions, also in blue paint. The drum is one of the final items listed in the Plains Cree section of Robert Rymill's inventory, and although no contextual information was recorded, it was probably one of the last artifacts acquired at the File Hills. Indeed, its place in the inventory hints at its significance.

Ceremonial artifacts, including drums, can be used to ask for spiritual support and guidance. Some are personal property; others can circulate throughout the community and are cared for by a keeper on behalf of the people. The drum illustrated in the catalogue was recognized immediately because a drum with the same design and painted in the same colours is used today at Star Blanket Nation. When I visited the community, Elder Gilbert Starr was its keeper, and I was encouraged to talk to him about the drum in Cambridge. Since its 1929 arrival in the MAA, the drum has been kept quietly in storage except between 1994 and 1996, when it was part of a temporary exhibition, Living Tradition: Continuity and Change, Past and Present, that included a section on the powwow. Starr explained that the drum he cared for had a very different history of use. It regularly participated in ceremonies and funerals, and if Starr was approached according to the correct protocol and had given his consent, it sometimes was used at powwows (Gilbert Starr, author interview, Star Blanket Nation, 17 June 1999). Starr was told that its design had been given in a vision to his uncle *k-owīkit*, who was *atim kâ-mihkwasit*'s brother and who became its keeper. It was used in ceremonies at which *atim kâ-mihkwasit* sang, and if he were unable to attend, *k-owīkit* would go in his place. It seems that after the Franklin team took the drum, *k-owīkit* made another of the same design, which has since been transferred to Star Blanket Nation drum keepers, along with the songs and knowledge associated with it.

Like many ceremonial artifacts, the drum that was cared for by Gilbert Starr has a known genealogy, but the photographs I showed him of the Cambridge drum raised some perplexing questions. He had thought that the drum at Star Blanket was made by *k-owīkit,* and though he knew that parts of it had been replaced when they wore out, he had no idea that it was not the original. He could not comment on why the first drum left, or why no one had mentioned that another had replaced it. He speculated that *k-owīkit* had been guided to release the first drum and to make the second one in the knowledge that threatened ceremonial artifacts could safely return home at some later point. Furthermore, as *atim kâ-mihkwasit* could see into the future, this may have played a part in his decision. Starr said, "Maybe he was told they could try and bring it back, but to make another one to keep that ... not to forget ... how it was painted" (Gilbert Starr, author interview, Star Blanket Nation, 17 June 1999). He added that the spirit of the drum is in two places at once and that, in essence, the two drums are one and the same, even though physically they are different things. The drum in Cambridge is making itself known to people at Star Blanket Nation who can talk with it, care for it, and use it in the way for which it was made. Several community members, including Starr, asked whether it could be

Figure 23 Storage bag, used for food | Reproduced by permission of University of Cambridge Museum of Archaeology and Anthropology, 1930.827

repatriated. Because I had no authority to speak to this issue, I recommended that they contact the museum for guidance.

Artifacts associated with leaders clearly have great significance, not only for their direct descendants, but for communities as a whole. Most items in the Rymill Collection, however, cannot be associated with an individual; they were gathered as "type specimens" intended to fit into particular frameworks of scientific knowledge rather than because they were connected to specific people. Nonetheless, these "anonymous" artifacts have tremendous potential to contribute to narratives about the past, as well as to verify cultural information. Most items that the Franklin Motor Expedition described as "Plains Cree" would fall into this category, yet their anonymity does not lessen their capacity to generate knowledge and participate in processes of memory making. While looking at the catalogue photographs of hide scrapers, berry bags, beaded moccasins, and other such items, interviewees often mentioned similar examples owned and used by relatives. Thus, the catalogue images functioned as triggers to elicit recollections of specific individuals. Sometimes these biographical reflections took the form of short vignettes, laden with sensory experiences of childhood. Photographs of bags, such as that illustrated in Figure 23, evoked for some elders the taste of the saskatoon berries that their grandmothers would store in them.

Such responses are unsurprising, given the capacity of artifacts (and, it would seem, of their images) to participate in memory making. Indeed, as Elizabeth Edwards (1999, 222) reminds us, "Photographs belong to that class of objects formed specifically to remember, rather than being objects around which remembrance accrues through contextual association (although they become this as well)." Although the photos of artifacts used in this research were produced with a specific purpose in mind, one that differed sharply from that of the Franklin Motor Expedition, both forms of image had the capacity to participate in discussions about the past, but crucially about the role of the past in the present. Marius Kwint (1999, 2, 3) summarizes three key ways in which artifacts – including photographs – "serve memory." They "furnish recollection," allowing us to dig deep into our personal histories; they "stimulate remembering" and can "bring back experiences which otherwise would have remained dormant, repressed or forgotten"; and they "form records: analogues to living memory, storing information beyond individual experience." Likewise, Batchen (2004, 39-40) points to the metonymic memorial function of photographs and writes that

the photograph is certainly nothing if not humble, so ready is it to erase its own material presence in favour of the subject it represents. In most cases we are asked to look through the photograph as if it simply isn't there, penetrating its limpid, transparent surface with our eyes, and seeing only what lies within. Posing as pure sign, or even as no sign at all, the "good" photograph offers minimal resistance to this look. Invisible to the eye, it appears to provide a representation generated by the referent itself.

Much of the literature on photography refers to the indexicality of images (see Barthes 1980), but of course, indigenous ways of understanding visuality and thinking about memory are also essential to this discussion. Quoting Nicholas Thomas (1997, 45), Elizabeth Edwards (2001, 93) notes that

assumptions around photographs as historical sources have tended to be dominated by the Euro-American theoretical model, which has tended to "universalise an interest in certain modes of historical narrative ... A step taken in the name of democratising history ... curiously affirms the generalised authority in certain ways of establishing a command of the past." Such a position might thus obscure differently constituted relations between the photograph and the past.

Neal McLeod's (2010) analysis of how historic portraits of Cree people serve as mnemonic icons that articulate with Cree forms of narrative memory, to which I referred above, provides a helpful counterbalance to dominant modes of representing history and memory, and can be applied to other forms of material culture (see also N. McLeod 2009). These memory-making processes were apparent at the File Hills reserves (and at all the First Nations that I visited), and though some people were frustrated by the anonymity of museum artifacts and saw it as indicative of colonial processes of erasure, others looked beyond these silences to reclaim and reassert community history and knowledge.

This point is illustrated by the responses to the many Plains Cree items in the Rymill Collection that are associated with clothing production, such as awls, sewing kits, and sinew and hide scrapers. Few, if any, were obviously made for sale, yet they prompted considerable reflection on the production of saleable handicrafts and the role of women in supporting their families and maintaining traditional forms of education. Across Canada, making and selling handicrafts was more than just a livelihood; it was also a means of sustaining identity and, in some cases, preserving traditional art forms in the face of pressure to assimilate (Phillips 1998). By the 1920s, although wearing traditional clothing was largely discouraged, Department of Indian Affairs (DIA) officials conceded that the income generated by selling handicrafts was important to their creators and that it contributed to the ultimate goal of self-sufficiency. Summer celebrations, such as the Regina Fair and Exhibition, were opportunities to make some money, and several people with whom I spoke reflected upon their own family's interactions with collectors and tourists at these events. In some cases, their parents set up a stall outside the exhibition grounds, and the mother sold enough beaded bags, wall pockets, and picture frames to pay the family's entrance fee (Gilbert Starr, author interview, Star Blanket Nation, 17 June 1999).

As noted in Chapter 2, government officials sometimes promoted the work of skilled seamstresses and artists, and they liaised with museums and other organizations to assemble collections or acquire individual items. When looking at the images of beadwork and sewing equipment, elders whose mothers and grandmothers were involved in craft production during the 1920s and 1930s often mentioned, with pride, that First Nations and non-Native people alike had sought out their work. Florence Bigknife explained that her mother, Christina Buffalo, and her aunt, Mary Alice Kinequon, made beaded outfits for men from neighbouring reserves and that her mother beaded the communion cup and the altar cloth for the Anglican church on the Daystar reserve. Recognizing the beadwork style in the catalogue images and film footage, she was quite sure that her mother had made some of the outfits worn by the men in the film and possibly even two of the pieces in the collection itself (Florence Bigknife, author interview, Star Blanket Nation, 8 July 1999, cited in Brown 2000, 194).

Many people commented that making and selling beadwork was of tremendous economic importance during a time in which First Nations were under severe financial pressure; in this way women played a crucial role in working with their husbands to support their family. Robert Rymill's inventory note about a child's outfit (Figure 24) must be viewed in this context: "Part of the dress of a young girl. It should be noted that although the child who owned this suit was only about five years old, the money paid for the suit was regarded by her parents as being hers. Her father was unable to sell the suit until after he had consulted her mother."[13] In this instance, although the money from the sale belonged to the child, her mother, who had probably made the dress, had the final decision as to whether it would be sold. The outfit was probably for everyday wear, rather than for special occasions, and could have been replaced relatively easily. As Gilbert Starr observed, at a time when money was tight, there was no reason not to sell items that could be remade without much difficulty (Gilbert Starr, author interview, Star Blanket Nation, 17 June 1999).

The responses of File Hills people to the Franklin Motor Expedition materials demonstrate the possibilities for using heritage items to generate narratives of resistance and tenacity as well as for creating community cohesion and pride. People also spoke at length about the capacity of such objects to heal individuals who, for whatever reasons, had become disconnected from their community and identity. We can only speculate regarding what Cadzow and the Rymill brothers learned from the people they met at the File Hills, but seventy years after their visit, it was clear that though ceremonial artifacts and non-ceremonial items are valued in differing ways and according to their individual qualities and their spiritual and physical needs, they can all contribute to the strengthening of cultural knowledge and ways of being in First Nations communities.

Figure 24 Girl's outfit, identified by Robert Rymill as Plains Cree | Reproduced by permission of University of Cambridge Museum of Archaeology and Anthropology, 1930.784A-E

The Piikani Nation

The Piikani are one of three Blackfoot nations located in Canada, the other two being the Siksika and the Kainai. Following the creation of the international border between Canada and the United States, the Piikani were politically split between the *Amsskaapipiikani* (South Piegan or Blackfeet), whose reservation is in Northern Montana, and the *Apatohsipiikani* (North Peigan), whose reserve is in Southern Alberta, northwest of Fort Macleod.

It was this reserve that the Franklin Motor Expedition visited in August 1929. The Blackfoot nations were of particular interest to anthropologists during the late nineteenth and early twentieth centuries, in large part because their direct experience of colonialism came significantly later than that of First Nations farther east. Researchers were thus able to interview elderly people whose lives differed substantially from those of their children and grandchildren, and who could provide first-hand accounts of participating in buffalo hunts and periodic inter-tribal warfare, as well as about other topics of ethnological interest. Because their exposure to Christianity came relatively late, the Blackfoot retained their ceremonial traditions for longer than many First Nations who experienced missionary influence earlier. By the early twentieth century, as assimilation policies took their toll, anthropologists felt especially compelled to record information on ceremonies and the stories and artifacts associated with them.

By the 1920s the Piikani were experiencing extreme social and economic hardship and culture stress; at this time, anthropologists, museums, and other collectors began to acquire many of their ceremonial artifacts, including what in English are called "bundles." For the benefit of those who are unfamiliar with the Blackfoot worldview, Michael Ross and Piikani ceremonial leader Reg Crowshoe (1999, 248) liken the bundle to a museum – "an inspired assemblage of meaningful objects held together and presented for community benefit and education, and ritually cared for by its owners." William Farr's (1993, 9) explanation for the English term is also helpful:

> Once secured these revered, energizing powers exacted duties and obligations. They had to be guarded and protected, cared for daily like children; in fact, their owners are usually referred to as father and mother. Yet these same ritual wards were greatly feared. No one lived with them casually. Because they were housed in numerous skin or cloth wrappings, bundled up when they were not in actual use, and their privacy respected, they were referred to as bundles or, more properly because they frequently had therapeutic ability to heal and to deliver cosmic aid, "medicine bundles."

Finally, Maria Zedeño's (2008, 364) discussion of Thunder Medicine Pipes and concepts of agency and animacy provides the following explanation:

> A bundle is a complex object with a singular life history that begins in an individual's dream or vision. This vision, in turn, provides the instructions

for making the bundle, the liturgical order for using and transferring the bundle, and the means for assessing its authenticity. Bundles, therefore, are repositories of knowledge about specific rituals that are shared only among initiated individuals.

The centrality of bundles is perpetual and all-encompassing, and they are honoured, cherished, and respected by their keepers, who frequently speak of them as their children and remark upon their varying personalities. Many different kinds of bundles are associated with Blackfoot ceremonial societies, and each has its own protocols for its care, when it is opened, and how its owner must conduct him- or herself. Thunder Medicine Pipes, for instance, are usually opened in the spring, following the first sound of thunder. When they are not in ceremony, bundles are kept in a quiet place and are smudged with sweetgrass and prayed to daily. The transfer of bundles, with their stories and songs, creates a social network that links new and former owners and their families. The knowledge associated with them is not lost when they are transferred; rather, over time, as individuals care for and transfer more bundles, their understanding of Blackfoot cosmology increases as does their status in the community (Conaty 1995, 405-6; Conaty 2008, 248).[14] The frequency of bundle transfers varies; some ceremonial societies with multiple bundle holders transfer as a group every four to five years; in other instances a person may keep a bundle for much longer until approached by someone who is ready and able to take on the responsibility of its care.

The circulation of Blackfoot spiritual and cultural knowledge through the transfer of bundles became threatened as the twentieth century progressed. As recently as the 1970s, some elders, well aware of how residential schools were affecting younger generations, and perhaps having converted to Christianity themselves, believed that Blackfoot culture was a thing of the past, and they sold their bundles to museums and other collectors (Dempsey 2011, 176). Inter-generational differences were a key factor in the disruption of knowledge transmission and the circulation of Piikani bundles during this time, but there were others too, as Piikani ceremonial leader Allan Pard explained to me. He prefaced his comments by mentioning his community's mixed feelings toward traditional Blackfoot ways of knowing and the impact of collecting on the continuation of these knowledge systems:

Some people sold those artifacts because the younger people didn't care for them; they were getting too old to handle those materials, so they were, in a sense, sold for safekeeping to the museums. Some were just sold because of the social implications; some of those communities and some of those families resorted to alcohol abuse, and a lot of those items were sold for that reason. Again, some collectors – you're almost talking about the Dirty Thirties here – people were starving in this country. So a lot of that stuff was sold, I guess, because the elders or the old people were perhaps thinking, "I can replace this." They were sold just so they could buy groceries for their family. (Allan Pard, author interview, Fort Macleod, 6 August 1999)

At Piikani today, views regarding traditional Blackfoot knowledge remain diverse. People with transfer rights to bundles are in the minority, and on my first visit, I was informed that five different churches operated on the reserve. I was told, "They think they're helping us out, but they're not. Each church believes what they're doing is right and what everyone else is doing is wrong. With us, we're more open. We have a more open religious voice" (author's field notes, 18 November 1998). Christian denominations are active on the reserve, but there are also prominent Piikani families who are respected for their traditional ceremonial knowledge. During the past forty years, individuals from several of these families have worked to repatriate bundles from museums and to revitalize ceremonies and knowledge transfers that were interrupted during the first half of the twentieth century (Noble and Crowshoe 2002; Bell, Statt, and Mookaakin Cultural Society 2008; Conaty 2008; Noble, Crowshoe, and the Knut sum-atak Society 2008; Lokensgard 2010). Many have cultivated relationships of mutual respect with museum staff in Alberta and farther afield, and some were instrumental in developing the First Nations Sacred Ceremonial Objects Repatriation Act (Province of Alberta 2000) and the Blackfoot First Nations Sacred Ceremonial Objects Repatriation Regulation (Province of Alberta 2004), which permit the transfer of title to ceremonial artifacts in the Glenbow Museum and the Royal Alberta Museum to Alberta First Nations. Many years of trust building preceded this stage, but as a result, many more Piikani can now join the various age-grade societies that are active in the community, such as the Brave Dogs, Chickadees, and Bumblebees, and can participate in what Noble, Crowshoe, and the Knut sum-atak Society (2008, 302) refer to as "the larger collective ceremonials, such as the Thunder Medicine Pipes, the Sundance Headdresses, the Beaver Medicine Bundles, and Horse Medicine Bundles."

Negotiating a repatriation framework has been a pressing museum issue for the Blackfoot nations in recent years. It is a difficult endeavour and can be divisive, both in and between communities, and in museums. Nonetheless, as a result of successful repatriation claims, ceremonies that once were threatened due to the inaccessibility of bundles are now taking place again. For example, a revival in ceremonial transfers has occurred at Siksika since the mid-1990s, which ceremonial and elected leader Herman Yellow Old Woman believes has contributed to a renewed sense of cultural pride:

> In 1996 we started a whole new society that started bringing stuff back, repatriating ceremonial artifacts back into our community. Before 1996 our community was so distant, no identity ... People knew themselves, their identity was on books, on movies, anything but themselves living it ... And today, our people can honestly say that they belong to a Blackfoot culture, a Siksika culture, that they follow and that they believe in. They are born into that way ... Especially in the last twelve years, there's been so many transfers here, going on in Siksika. So many ceremonies that happen. Every month there's a ceremony: sweat lodge; a Medicine Pipe; a Beaver; sun dance; Prairie Chicken; Brave Dogs; Big Smokes. All these ceremonies used to take place in the past; they're all back (Herman Yellow Old Woman, author interview, Siksika Nation, 25 August 2010).[15]

At the Kainai Nation, many of the ceremonies held at the *akóka'tssin* (circle camp) each summer and at other times never completely ended, despite the loss of many bundles and pressure from government and church officials. Since the 1970s more ceremonial artifacts have "come home," and as with the other Blackfoot nations, this has enabled more community members to become immersed in Kainai ways of knowing and being (Crop Eared Wolf 1997). At the neighbouring reserve of Piikani, a Sun Dance was held in 1977, the first in forty-five years. This development occurred after young Piikani men, including Allan Pard and Jerry Potts Jr., studied Edward Curtis photographs of their ancestors dating from the early twentieth century and worked with elders to learn the songs and bring the ceremonies home (Makepeace 2001, 195). The Blackfeet in Montana have also sought the repatriation of ceremonial bundles and are able to draw on the Native

American Graves Protection and Repatriation Act (NAGPRA) for the return of items housed in federally funded US museums. Through traditional transfer processes, these items can subsequently circulate throughout the Blackfoot nations on both sides of the international border. Sometimes groups from only one Blackfoot nation visit museums to identify collections prior to submitting a repatriation claim; at other times, people from the Blackfoot communities work together. Cumulatively, the efforts initiated by Blackfoot ceremonialists have transformed approaches to repatriation at the provincial level, and they continue to influence repatriation policy and practice in museums that are far from the nations themselves. My own institution, the University of Aberdeen, agreed in 2003 to repatriate a Kainai ceremonial headdress acquired during the 1930s (Curtis 2005). Although this is the only case to date in which a European museum has permanently returned a Blackfoot ceremonial artifact, opportunities have increased since the early 2000s (though they remain few and far between) for community members to meet with museum staff and for dialogue to begin regarding the future care of collections in European institutions. In recent examples of this, a Kainai staff member and two Kainai community curators attended the 2004 opening of the Glenbow's travelling version of its Blackfoot Gallery at the Manchester Museum of Science and Industry; Dutch researcher Lea Zuyderhoudt has worked on several museum projects in the Netherlands over the past decade that have included travel funds for Siksika colleagues (see Crane Bear and Zuyderhoudt 2010); in 2010 four Kainai individuals attended a University of Aberdeen workshop focusing on the impact of repatriation; most recently, as part of the Blackfoot Shirts Project, which I co-directed, a delegation of twelve Blackfoot people attended a conference at Oxford's Pitt Rivers Museum, where they met curatorial and conservation staff from several British museums.

Blackfoot people involved in repatriation have also challenged the exhibition by museums of their cultural heritage and have worked closely with curatorial staff to improve it. For example, many people whom I met in Southern Alberta in 1998 belonged to the team that created a new gallery – Nitsitapiisinni: Our Way of Life – at Calgary's Glenbow Museum, in which Blackfoot people told their own story in their own words (Blackfoot Gallery Committee 2001; Conaty 2003; Conaty and Carter 2005). This gallery, which has become a model for redefining how museums work with indigenous communities, opened in November 2001 after several years of planning. A core team of seventeen elders and ceremonial people from each of the Blackfoot communities developed the storyline, and Glenbow staff used their technical expertise to bring it to life. Over the years, the four Piikani members of the team and others from their community have contributed to a range of interpretive projects utilizing the Glenbow's Blackfoot collections and have advised on policy issues at the Glenbow and at other museums in the province. Some Piikani have also been involved in museum projects outside Alberta. For example, educator Shirlee Crowshoe, who formerly worked at the Fort Whoop Up National Historic Site in Lethbridge, and her Blackfeet colleague the late Darrell Kipp contributed to the development of Pikuni Blackfoot: Good Things Stay the Same, an exhibition that opened at the Southwest Museum in Los Angeles in 2002 (Shirlee Crowshoe, author interview, Piikani Nation, 11 August 2010). Closer to home, Head-Smashed-In Buffalo Jump, a UNESCO world heritage site, is located alongside the Piikani reserve, and many community members have interpreted Piikani culture and history to the largely non-Native audience who come to its visitor centre (Brink 2008; Onciul 2013).

Many Piikani are thus very familiar with heritage bodies, such as museums, and though the associated bureaucracy can sometimes be tiresome, they are hopeful that, due to their participation, collections will be used in a more informed and inclusive manner. For example, during an interview about the material from his community in the MAA, Allan Pard, who has been active in the repatriation movement since it began, was explicit about the potential for museums to contribute to cross-cultural education:

> I think museums should allow people to talk about themselves and to share that information from their own perspectives, not what is assumed, but is projected by our people ... There is so much to tell, so much information comes from collections, and I think for countries like England, understanding First Nations, indigenous people in North America, understanding the real story, that this real story can be shared to future generations and the world, it is important to tell people what was really going on. (Allan Pard, author interview, Fort Macleod, 6 August 1999)

Since the late 1970s and early 1980s, then, relations between museums and the Piikani (and other Blackfoot) have realigned, particularly in traditional Blackfoot territory. My discussions with local people about the Piikani items in the Rymill Collection were thus informed by this changing museological landscape of which Piikani ceremonial leaders have been very much a part. Once seen as excluding First Nations people while holding on to ceremonial artifacts that they did not understand but that were necessary for keeping indigenous communities strong, museums began to be viewed as offering possibilities for knowledge regeneration. Jerry Potts Jr., a Piikani ceremonial leader who has been at the forefront of this movement, explained that

> the museum's role, rather than it being a storage house with a glass window that you look in, a lot of museums, well, those with material from Blackfoot communities that has ceremonial significance, have learned that they have to gain understanding and treat the religious artifacts with the respect they deserve ... They are not a storage facility; they have almost become keepers of some of these artifacts. (Jerry Potts Jr., author interview, Fort Macleod, 18 August 1999)

With this statement in mind, we must address the question of how the MAA, located some six thousand kilometres from the Piikani Nation, might curate the Rymill Collection. People who looked at the catalogue invariably commented on the large number of artifacts. The Rymill Collection's Piikani portion contains 199 records, and Allan Pard and Jerry Potts Jr., both of whom have extensive experience of visiting North American museums to identify collections, remarked on this point. Potts noted that he had never seen "so many Peigan things together" (ibid.), and Allan Pard related the number of artifacts to the size of the Piikani population in the late 1920s. He said,

> There's a lot of material there for a small reserve, a small community. The Peigan community was almost annihilated through all the starvation, all the white man diseases that were brought over. We were almost decimated to the point where, at that time [1929], there were only maybe five hundred people remaining in our tribe. And there is a lot of material there. (Allan Pard, author interview, Fort Macleod, 6 August 1999)

Both men also commented on the quantity of ceremonial material. Blackfoot people use many different kinds of ceremonial artifacts, which embody varying levels of power. Some are communal and transferable; others are privately transferable; and others are privately owned and not transferable (see also Conaty and Janes 1997; and Lokensgard 2010). Although the

Rymill Collection encompasses examples of all three types, many of which are significant from a spiritual perspective, I was told that it contains nothing *really* major – there are no primary bundles such as Beaver Bundles or Thunder Medicine Pipes.[16] Rather, much of the material is *associated* with particular bundles or ceremonies and has significance in that regard. Personal items, such as bracelets worn by those with rights to Thunder Medicine Pipes, can be made by someone who has the appropriate transferred rights to do so, and thus were probably sold because they could be replaced. To the Piikani people with whom I spoke, this implied that Cadzow and the Rymills did not understand the circulation of Blackfoot transfer rights and ceremonial knowledge, and in fact, had no appreciation of what they were actually collecting. Allan Pard was scathing:

> I think they were just going out and having some kind of a free-for-all. But it was a well-paid expedition, and really they didn't care. Because a lot of the stuff I see in there, there's nothing major or really significant in there that they went out and purchased. And to go all-out on a cost-paid trip like that, I think the collection was secondary to the expedition ... Seeing the country was a big thing, but the collection was a real minor purpose. (Allan Pard, author interview, Fort Macleod, 6 August 1999)

Although everyone who looked at the catalogue agreed that the Rymill Collection contains no *major* ceremonial artifacts, it nonetheless has meaning for Piikani people. The items could be used in ceremony if the correct cultural protocols were followed and the timing were right. According to Allan Pard, some "could be repatriated, but repatriated only to a situation where they are recirculated back into the communities. What I'm saying is I wouldn't want artifacts to be coming back to this area just to go back to another museum" (Allan Pard, author interview, Fort Macleod, 6 August 1999). In the meantime, it was suggested that the museum could do something significant in terms of sharing information, but this would depend on how motivated it was to improve the existing data. It was pointed out that, like the Rymills and Cadzow, who failed to appreciate what they acquired from Piikani people in 1929, museum staff will never understand Piikani people and their lives if they remain ignorant of the meanings of the artifacts and their relationship to Blackfoot knowledge systems. Nor could they effectively interpret the material for wider audiences or make informed decisions should a repatriation case arise. As mentioned above, some Piikani are deeply involved in cross-cultural education and see museums as places where fallacies and stereotypes can be challenged. If this is to occur, they believe that museums need to present accurate information (whether in exhibitions, publications, online databases, or other media). As Jerry Potts Jr. explained,

> I think the museum has a certain responsibility, if they are going to be keepers of this stuff, to make sure that they've got the proper information on a lot of it. Because museums are supposed to be educating people, and we are no longer being interpreted by middle-aged white explorers. We are real people. That's always been my education philosophy, and that's why I work and do interviews like this, because I feel that I have a certain responsibility to educate the system as to who we are, what we are, and where we come from. And as a Blackfoot person from the Peigan tribe, I'm responsible to my people first, but I'm also responsible to my kids and my grandkids, so that they get the respect they deserve when they grow up. (Jerry Potts Jr., author interview, Fort Macleod, 18 August 1999)

As far as Piikani leaders were concerned, if the MAA was serious about caring for the collection, it needed to involve knowledgeable people who could advise on its contents. This might entail reuniting items that ought to be stored together, or separating those that should not; it would also involve correcting inaccurate statements in the MAA database, considering the implementation of traditional care, and identifying ceremonial artifacts that might be subject to further discussion. Moreover, it was made clear that engaging in such a dialogue is a serious matter, for both the community and the museum. As Jerry Potts Jr. put it,

> They sent people over here in 1929 to collect this stuff, but going through the descriptions here, it is pretty clear that they don't have an explanation of what they have ... Now, they have an ideal opportunity, maybe a hundred years down the road. Well, they've at least got the real people that this stuff came from to get real explanations of what they have. (ibid.)

Having a delegation visit the museum is a priority, but community members repeatedly explained that museum staff must also travel to Piikani territory, as only then could they begin to get a sense of the meanings of ceremonial artifacts to Blackfoot people today.

Blackfoot people who have worked to repatriate ceremonial artifacts from museums often make a point of inviting museum staff to their ceremonies so that they can see the impact of the return of these relatives to their communities and understand why keeping them in museum storage is problematic. Beth Carter, whose curatorial work at the Glenbow had spanned over a decade when we first met, explained that watching Blackfoot people interact with ceremonial artifacts made her acutely aware of the tension between knowledge systems that see artifacts as things and those that experience them as living beings:

> Somebody came to take a *Naatowas* [holy woman's sacred headdress] bundle from the Glenbow. And it was all in pieces and it had been separated to museum standards, and everything was labelled, and it was all lying out on this giant shelf. They took it down and they had the wrappers and one by one they started to wrap it. And they wrapped it and wrapped it until finally it was this large bundle. And then they picked it up as if it were a baby ... The look on this woman's face as she picked it up and kind of cradled it in her arms. It was kind of like, "Okay, you've been put back together again, and you're whole, and you are my baby, and I'm going to take you and I'm going to take care of you. I'm going to feed you, and honour you and speak to you, and do all of those things." And it was such a touching moment. You could almost see the animation returned to the bundle. (Beth Carter, author interview, Calgary, 20 August 1999)

For Carter, and for other museum staff and researchers who have been involved with Blackfoot cultural revitalization projects, myself included, participation in ceremonies has quite possibly done more to transform views on repatriation than anything else. She said, "I've gone to quite a few [ceremonies] now too. It's a really amazing community experience. After you have done that, you stop being worried about it" (ibid.).

The importance of helping museum staff to learn about Blackfoot culture through participation was also mentioned by Jenny Bruised Head, who is from Kainai but had lived at Piikani for many years when we first met and has family ties to that community. As we discussed the Rymill Collection, she insisted that MAA staff needed to experience how ceremonial artifacts figure in the lives and well-being of Blackfoot people:

You can go back and you can write up everything we're telling you, and they [the MAA staff] can read it, but it's going to have very little effect. That's why we're saying to invite them. Invite them down and they'll see what we're really about. We're not just like the stories and the pictures in the books. We're living people and if people want to know more about it, I'll say, "Come to our sun dance and our sweats, and you'll know." It's something that we really, really take serious and it really means a lot to us. (Jenny Bruised Head, author interview, Piikani Nation, 18 November 1998)

Bruised Head's comment points to a view shared by many Blackfoot regarding the frustrated efforts to regain ceremonial artifacts – that most non-Blackfoot neither perceive the need for ceremony nor understand its role in their lives and do not know how it connects with their worldview. This is regarded as especially problematic for curators who have not visited the communities, where they could speak to people about issues that are of importance to them, attend ceremonies, and see and feel the difference made by the return of museum-held items. Again, the point was eloquently expressed that Piikani meanings and understandings of collections differ vastly from those of museums. Pat Provost, for example, discussed this point in relation to several bags in the Rymill Collection that are used to hold rattles and other materials associated with ceremonial societies. He said, "When we see these things here, all these items, these are our life. All these are our teachings and our teachers. Like these bags here, they hold all our ceremonial stuff. So when you think of ceremonial stuff, you think of your life, of who you are, and it's all packed into this bag" (Pat Provost, author interview, Piikani Nation, 18 November 1998). This comment makes explicit the ways in which material things have the capacity for biographical association. Many transferable Blackfoot items have known genealogies in terms of who cared for them over the years, but personal items, such as those discussed by Provost, can also remind their owners of particular times in their lives when they received or used such materials and of the individuals linked to them through the experience of ceremony.

The statements quoted above emphasize the importance of reconfiguring relationships between museums and Blackfoot people, from Blackfoot perspectives. Although short-term projects have their merits, they do not facilitate a full development of mutual respect between museum staff and First Nations, and indigenous people who support them may sometimes feel used. Respecting people and respecting collections are indivisible, and all my conversations with Piikani individuals about the Rymill Collection, whether during formal interviews or informal discussions, indicate that both the Piikani Nation and the MAA would benefit should a meaningful relationship replace the lack of understanding that currently exists. During all my visits to Southern Alberta, people mentioned their lack of knowledge regarding what articles from their community might be held in European museums, and they speculated on their numbers and possible location. Indeed, in our first interview, Allan Pard suggested that my bringing the collection photographs to Alberta represented "the door opening" for First Nations and European museums, and he noted that his community hadn't "had experience with any other European museums making contact or even attempting to make contact with us" (Allan Pard, author interview, Fort Macleod, 6 August 1999).

Showing the photographs in the catalogue and talking to individuals about the Franklin Motor Expedition film footage of Piikani people was the start of what ceremonial leaders in the community anticipate will be a long process of relationship building, one that they hope will have positive outcomes. In the interim, the MAA has responded to their concerns (mediated through my discussions with community members) as well as possible. For example, during my first fieldwork I also showed people photographs of MAA displays and asked whether any items should be removed from public view. MAA staff reacted positively and quickly to requests that ceremonial materials be withdrawn, and in Chapter 6 I discuss how I worked with them to develop a new display, a project that was aided by some of the individuals whose perspectives are included in this book.

Until very recently, constraints on time and resources, as well as previous commitments have prevented MAA staff from discussing the future of the Rymill Collection with Piikani people, though since the early 2000s they have hosted several delegations and individual research visitors from other First Nations and Native American groups (as well as from indigenous communities from elsewhere). The museum is also involved in international projects that utilize digital technologies to make collections better accessible. These include the Great Lakes Research Alliance for the Study of Aboriginal Arts and Cultures (GRASAC), and the Reciprocal Research Network (RRN), an online facility that enables reciprocal and collaborative research about cultural heritage from the Northwest Coast of Canada (see page 249). Such projects highlight the benefits of establishing research networks that bring together community members, museums, and academics, and that can help fund people who must travel long distances to find and research their heritage items (see also Phillips 2011, 277-96). Blackfoot people are starting to participate in such international networks, and in 2010 and 2011 individuals from all the Blackfoot nations attended two conferences in the United Kingdom that addressed issues of cultural heritage, one at the University of Aberdeen and the other at the Pitt Rivers Museum in Oxford. MAA staff attended both events and began discussions with ceremonial leaders on how best to proceed with establishing a direct relationship. Subsequently, in March 2013, the Leverhulme Trust awarded funding to the University of Aberdeen to create an International Research Network. With myself as coordinator, this will bring together museum staff at the MAA and the Royal Albert Museum and Art Gallery, Exeter, with representatives from the Blackfoot nations. These two museums have the most extensive and historically significant Blackfoot collections of any British institution, though neither had hosted Blackfoot visitors at the time of writing. The project, which will run for two years, involves reciprocal research visits to Canada and Britain, with the goal of establishing working relationships and sharing expertise that will inform how the collections are curated. The reciprocal element of the network responds to Jenny Bruised Head's statement above about the need for museum staff to visit the communities if they wish to get a better sense of who Blackfoot people are, and to Jerry Potts's suggestion that the MAA must recognize its responsibility to the collection and draw upon the knowledge of ceremonial people. It is hoped that these visits may lead to future mutually beneficial projects, though access to funding will play a role in determining these. Nonetheless, it is clear that the MAA, the Piikani, and other Blackfoot people are now committed to taking the next steps.

THIS CHAPTER HAS EXPLORED the complexities of attempts to re-establish links with historic cultural and ceremonial materials that have been long separated from their homeland. In particular, I have aimed to show that decisions regarding the future of material heritage are not taken lightly and that this is especially so among First Nations. Many years of concerted effort will be required to counteract the negative experience of some First Nations people with museums and to build upon more recent positive collaborations. For museums located at great distances from indigenous groups, projects such as the one described in this book offer opportunities to learn about the meanings that historic collections hold for them and, more importantly, for the communities to locate cultural materials of which they are currently unaware. Bringing together people and collections – even if this initially occurs via photography and digital imaging – can be a precursor for future collaborations that involve direct engagement with artifacts.

First Nations people were never the intended audience for collections like those acquired by the Franklin Motor Expedition. Nevertheless, this does not mean that museums, whose traditional mandate has been to preserve heritage items for posterity, do not have a responsibility to think about what that means in a world where many indigenous groups face social and economic challenges that are the legacy of colonialism (Warry 2007). Many museum staff across Canada accept this and now work closely with First Nations, Métis, and Inuit to address their concerns regarding access and repatriation, and to develop projects that are mutually beneficial.[17] In contrast, European museums have far less experience of overcoming both the geographical and cultural distances between themselves and First Nations communities, though the discussions are starting, and some researchers based in North America have facilitated links between European museums and indigenous groups with very positive results. Ann Fienup-Riordan for instance, has worked closely with Alaska Native people on documentation and exhibition projects involving the collections in the Ethnologisches Museum, Berlin (Fienup-Riordan 1998; Fienup-Riordan and Meade 2005). Similarly, Aaron Glass, a New York–based anthropologist, has worked with Kwakwaka'wakw colleagues from the BC coast and the Ethnologisches Museum to create a digital database of nineteenth-century artifacts (Glass 2014). In another example, Amber Lincoln coordinated a visit of five Iñupiaq heritage advisors to study collections from Northwest Alaska in the British Museum as part of her doctoral research undertaken at the University of Aberdeen (Lincoln et al. 2010). The experiences of these individuals have made it plain that European museums are willing to support such projects, though they are less likely to initiate them without specialized staff who have the time and expertise to become deeply involved in collections research. Indeed, it is striking that the majority of such projects are developed by researchers who are based *outside* of Europe. Their British (and European) counterparts have been criticized for their lack of initiative in generating projects with originating communities and for what has sometimes been regarded as their naive understanding of the complexities entailed in such work. However, these criticisms frequently underplay the profound difficulties facing museums that are located at such tremendous distance – both physically and culturally – from the communities, and the limited opportunities available for staff to engage with them in a sustained manner (though see Morse, Macpherson, and Robinson 2013). I address this point in more depth in the concluding chapter of this book.

6
Curating the Rymill Collection
The Prairies on Display

Well the expedition is all over and I am home again. The boys sail for Australia from Frisco on the 2nd of October. We passed a mighty busy summer, and they were the two finest boys it has ever been my pleasure to be associated with in any way. We were able to work unusually fast this year because of the very dry weather in Canada. Eleven cases and two bales will reach the Museum as a result of our summers [sic] work.

– D.A. Cadzow to L.C.G. Clarke, September 1929

In a large show-case at the north end of the [Andrews] gallery, which formerly contained a series from the Andaman Islands, [the curator] has arranged part of the American Indian material collected by Mr Rymill in Canada last year. Other specimens from the same source have been placed near by in two hanging wall-cases made in the Museum.

– *Annual Report of the Faculty Board of Archaeology and Ethnology*, 1930

IN THE FINAL CHAPTER of this book, I describe how British museums that are geographically as well as culturally distant from First Nations are moving toward establishing working relationships where previously none existed, but to understand the radical nature of this shift, it is necessary first to explore how UK museums have utilized First Nations collections historically.

I do this by tracing the museum history of the artifacts collected by the Franklin Motor Expedition, from their 1929 arrival in the University of Cambridge Museum of Archaeology and Anthropology (MAA). My goal is to assess how the categorization of one collection influenced museum narratives and ways of thinking about First Nations people across time. Jeremy Coote and Christopher Morton (2000, 40) suggest that to look at display history is to address how museums might do things differently, rather than to criticize our predecessors for not seeing things as we do. The starting point for understanding the display history of the Rymill Collection is the museum's documentary archive. Although it contains little information about the Franklin Motor Expedition per se, a number of sources illuminate how the artifacts have been used; these include annual reports, curatorial correspondence, internal documents, and exhibition labels. In addition, the MAA photographic archive provides a visual record of gallery and display case arrangements, although few interior photographs predate the 1970s.[1] The intentions of former curators for their displays cannot be fully apprehended, and indeed all visitors would have brought their own preconceptions to the displays. Nevertheless, analysis of the documentary sources does permit broad statements to be made about the representation of First Nations peoples in the context of UK museology.

Processing the Collection

In October 1929 it was reported to the Museums Committee that "a large ethnographical collection from American Indians has partly arrived and part was on its way but the entering [into the accession records] could not be commenced till next year."[2] The following spring, Robert and John Rymill returned to Cambridge to process the collection and to discuss its display with curator Louis Clarke. Supervised by Clarke, Robert Rymill sorted and catalogued the artifacts according to what Richard Hill (2000, 42) describes as "the anthropologist's checklist for defining Indian culture: house; cradleboards; dress; bands (beaded, woven, metal); ornaments; transportation; tools for war, hunting, fire-making, smoking; ceremonial items; and the ever-present miscellaneous." Once Rymill had completed this task, his involvement with the collection ended, although both he and his brother maintained their connections with the museum for some years. In the summer of 1930, for instance, they visited the MAA to see the newly displayed collection, and in the early 1930s, John Rymill donated artifacts that he collected in East Greenland during the British Arctic Air Route Expedition.[3] MAA documentation also shows that Robert Rymill acted as a museum representative in Australia until at least 1933, although what this position entailed is not clear.[4] Perhaps unsurprisingly, once Clarke left to become director of the Fitzwilliam Museum in 1937, the brothers' interest in the MAA dwindled, though their personal friendship with their mentor continued (Béchervaise 1995, 34). Indeed, Robert Rymill's wife and daughter recalled that during visits to Cambridge in the 1950s, they could not persuade him to go to the museum. Intrigued by the expedition and the collection, Gladys Rymill suggested that they see the latter, but he refused and said, "'Oh, I don't think they'd have it there now' ... He was so sure it was all in the past" (Gladys Rymill, author interview, Penola, South Australia, 5 March 1999). One of the many ironies of this story is that though Rymill's collection was perceived as a resource for the future, when the opportunity arose to revisit it, he thought that even the museum would have lost interest in it.

Robert Rymill may have thought that his relationship with the collection ended once it was catalogued, but his data, such as they were, have been repeated in all MAA displays of the artifacts. Rymill prepared the catalogue cards and also carefully wrote accession numbers on every artifact, having previously attached to each one a small circular disc with a number and a letter that corresponded to those in his inventory. The catalogue cards themselves – each stamped in black ink with the identifier "Collected by R. Rymill, 1929" – show that he copied the information from his inventory onto the cards. Few sketches were made to illustrate the use of artifacts, although the film footage reveals that the team was shown the function of some pieces, such as the dog travois discussed above. Only one illustration was copied directly onto a catalogue card from the inventory: that for a dart and hoop game collected at the Piikani Nation [1930.1093], which was illustrated with a simple line drawing and a note referencing Stewart Culin's *Games of the North American Indian* (1907).

Curatorial processes that marginalize indigenous peoples through the imposition of group classifications can also be seen in the catalogue cards. Ruth Phillips (2011, 95) argues that "the named categories that structure the museum system are a residue of obsolete nineteenth century ideologies" and are thus powerful indicators of deeply ingrained racial, ethnic, and gender groupings. The excising of personal names as part of these categorization processes is related to the classificatory systems that Phillips critiques, and to the wider controlling strategies that are common in colonial archives. Rymill's inventory gives the names of some people with whom the expedition dealt, but these are rare and, except for a few instances, were not transcribed onto the public records. For example, a tipi [1930.845A] is listed in the inventory as item CR 129, and a field note gives "Pimotat's tepee."[5] The catalogue card reads, "A: tipi and B: door. Made according to the old pattern, but made from canvas instead of buffalo hide. Hide tipis are now unobtainable." By today's standards, omitting the names of known individuals from catalogue records would be considered careless practice, but it was common during the early twentieth century. As Elizabeth Edwards (2001, 35) notes in relation to photographs, archiving was intended to arrange knowledge according to taxonomic structures that made sense within the archive, though ultimately it contributed to the destruction of context (see also Edwards 2004). In the case of the Rymill Collection, the artifacts were acquired as type specimens intended to represent particular First Nations cultural groups, rather than because they were associated with any one person. Biographical details of their makers or former owners were therefore irrelevant and thus were rarely solicited.

The examples described above are typical of how Robert Rymill moved information from his private inventory to the public sphere of the museum catalogue. Intriguingly, whereas the descriptions in most of his records are brief, those for two birch bark scrolls associated with the Midewiwin collected at Swan Lake [1930.651, 1930.652] stand out as comparatively extensive, and they also include information that was not usually given to uninitiated persons. Perhaps it is coincidental that these items were also the first to be obtained and catalogued, and were thus gathered at a time when Rymill was most inexperienced but conceivably most enthusiastic about the task ahead. The inventory illustrates the scrolls with very basic sketches and a detailed key, and though the key appears on the catalogue cards, the sketches were augmented by imagery copied from the scrolls themselves rather than from the inventory.[6] Interestingly, Rymill also wrote a memo to himself to "send copy of barks to George Tanner, Indian Springs, Man[itoba]," perhaps because Tanner (Gennahmodhi) had asked him to do so. Thus, the possibility that Rymill copied the images to fulfill this request (rather than solely to enhance the catalogue records) cannot be discounted.[7] Further analysis of the documentation indicates that Rymill's descriptions and sketches were based on Gennahmodhi's verbal explanations for the scrolls, though he himself had owned only one of them and had provided the reading for the other on behalf of a friend who did not speak English and whose name Rymill did not record. A note on the catalogue card also indicates that instructions were given regarding the care of the scrolls. A small piece of "white man's tobacco – Par-Qua-Siganan" accompanied one of the scrolls and "is to be kept inside the scroll as an offering when it is rolled up."[8] This comment not only reveals Gennahmodhi's concern for the future of the scrolls, but it also encompasses what would now be referred to as "traditional care," some seventy years before museums began to adopt such practices as standard.

Robert Rymill's family describes him as a meticulous note-taker, and the codes he devised for his inventory seem to confirm this (Robert Rymill, Penola, South Australia, 5 March 1999). Although the card catalogue truncated some information due to the conventions of museum documentation, it is worth observing that Donald Cadzow's records for the MAI, such as his 1925 "Catalogue of Bungi Specimens from Long Plains and Swan Lake Reserves, Manitoba Canada," are only marginally more detailed.[9] It is likely that in the field the younger man took his lead from the more experienced Cadzow. Also relevant to the processing of collections at the MAA is that staff shortages and the sheer number of artifacts meant that items could remain unpacked and uncatalogued for years. Brief catalogue entries were not uncommon during the first few decades of the MAA's history, and they reflect the difficulties of managing such an extensive collection at a time of physical disruption (which included relocating to a new building and coping with the disturbances of two world wars) rather than a lack of care. The collections brought back by A.C. Haddon from the Torres Strait in 1898 were not fully catalogued and displayed by him until 1920 (Herle 1998, 100). That the MAA's record keeping had been less than rigorous was acknowledged in the 1935 *Annual Report,* in which Louis Clarke noted that

> the process of registration implies carefully investigating the provenance of objects, inquiring into their artistic and cultural connexions and putting them into satisfactory physical condition; if an object is deemed worthy to be exhibited it must also be set up suitably and an informative label prepared. In the past the work of registration was not always done as fully and exactly as present practice requires and a concurrent effort is being made to supply deficiencies in older entries. (Museum of Archaeology and Anthropology 1936)

We cannot know whether Clarke would have regarded the Rymill Collection as poorly documented, but in most cases the descriptive information on the cards is brief, consisting of just a few words, such as "1930.774A-B – A: pipe. B: pipe stem" or "1930.1008 – Horse tail fly swat." The staccato tone and dislocation of detail are typical of what David Jenkins (1994, 253) calls the "archival systemization" of museum artifacts. To categorize and catalogue new acquisitions was to impose control over them by slotting them into a system of knowledge that had little regard for indigenous ways of knowing. For Jenkins (ibid., 255), these processes are integral to the transformation from object to museum artifact, in which "each step – field collection, proper labelling, archival systematization, and museum display – was apparently linked to the prior step, ensuring the authenticity and stabilizing the meanings of ethnographic collections."

If cataloguing and categorizing artifacts are crucial to this shift, the act of publicly displaying them completes the transformation. There is a hierarchy in museum collections, which ensures that certain types of artifact remain relegated to the stores, whereas others are repeatedly exhibited. As Adrienne Kaeppler (1989, 84) states, pieces that are visually striking or associated with a notable individual are the "stars" that, through research, documentation, and dissemination, become familiar to those with professional interests, as well as to individuals researching their own cultural heritage. Some ethnographic materials were selected for display because they conformed to widespread stereotypes of "exotic" tribal peoples. Irrespective of whether these pieces were accurately documented, they were chosen to fit pre-determined narratives rather than to be incorporated into artifact-led displays based on the stories they could tell. As Edward Bruner (1986, 143) explains, such "master narratives" of "past glory, present disorganization, future assimilation" were dominant in the 1930s and were commonly found in anthropological literature, despite having little to do with the current experiences of indigenous North Americans. He writes, "Our anthropological stories about Indians are representations, not to be confused with concrete existence of 'real' facts. In other words, life experience is richer than discourse."

Bruner's critique could also be applied to museum representations of First Nations people created at this time. This is especially so for cultural materials believed by curatorial staff to relate to warfare and violence. Everyday items, such as hide scrapers, rawhide ropes, and berry containers were less likely to be displayed than "war bonnets," trophies, and tomahawks.

To an extent, the selection of artifacts and the stereotypical displays that emerged were self-perpetuating. The illusions of noble savage, wild Indian, the princess and the brave, and of course, the vanishing Indian, were firmly entrenched in the European popular imagination, and there were few alternative representations that foregrounded diversity (Dippie 1982; Ellingson 2001).[10] Not surprisingly, given this context, First Nations people were associated with weapons and headdresses, items that museum audiences expected to see in galleries.

The First Displays

Stephanie Moser (2010, 22) writes that museum displays are "active agents in the construction of knowledge" and "are increasingly being recognized as discrete interpretative documents of great significance to the history of scholarly disciplines and the evolution of ideas." Historically, the display of First Nations material in the MAA may have been influenced to some degree by popular representations. However, given the museum's association with academic anthropology and that the displays were assembled by individuals who were at the forefront of the discipline, it is more likely that they were shaped by current conventions used to communicate ideas and create knowledge about indigenous peoples. The MAA was established in 1884 as the Museum of General and Local Archaeology, and was originally housed in a building on Little St. Mary's Lane.[11] The founding collections consisted of artifacts of local historical and archaeological significance belonging to the Cambridge Antiquarian Society as well as some 1,500 items collected in Fiji by Baron Anatole von Hügel and his associates during the 1870s (Ebin and Swallow 1984; Elliott and Thomas 2011, 7). Von Hügel (1854-1928) was to become the MAA's first curator, and he worked tirelessly to develop the collections and raise the museum's profile during a time when anthropology was gaining ground as a scientific discipline. In 1913, following an energetic fundraising campaign, the museum – by this time known as the University Museum of Archaeology and Ethnology – moved to its present purpose-built home on Downing Street, although the displays were not fully installed until after the First World War.

During the museum's early years, the use of the building space differed from that of today. Annual reports from 1913 and 1914 reveal that the Keyser Gallery on the ground floor was used for archaeology. The floor above included two galleries: the Babington Hall and the Maudslay Hall, the latter of which housed Alfred P. Maudslay's collection of casts of Guatemalan sculpture. The Andrews Gallery and the Bevan Hall were above the Maudslay Hall and the Babington Hall, respectively.[12] They were intended to house displays of ethnological material and, for the most part, were arranged by region. The MAA has maintained the regional approach ever since, with the exception of the Andrews Gallery, which, since 1990, has featured temporary exhibitions drawn from the archaeology and anthropology collections.

In her study of research and teaching of prehistory at Cambridge, Pamela Jane Smith (2009, 33) describes the 1920s as a period of "excitement and efflorescence" at the MAA. A.C. Haddon was appointed reader in ethnology in 1909, and the undergraduate anthropology program was established four years later (Rouse 1998, 69). Most of the teaching was undertaken by Haddon and William Rivers, his colleague and fellow participant on the 1898 Cambridge Anthropological Expedition to the Torres Strait. After the First World War, von Hügel, Haddon (who became deputy curator in 1920), and several honorary curators and volunteers set to work installing the new displays. In 1920 the Antiquarian Committee and the Board of Anthropological Studies amalgamated to become the Board of Anthropological and Archaeological Studies, and the museum's collections were considered essential to teaching in both areas. Space was made in the Maudslay Hall to display specimens used for teaching prehistoric and early European archaeology; an attic room functioned as an Egyptology classroom; the south end of the Babington Hall, which housed displays of African ethnology, was used as a teaching room for topics related to Africa; and the Bevan Hall was set aside for ethnology collections from the Pacific. The annual reports of the next decade indicate that staff and volunteers spent much time arranging displays and incorporating new material to highlight the riches of the museum's expanding collections.

What is less clear from the documentation is the extent to which dominant forms of display filtered into the galleries. By the later nineteenth century, two main modes of display had become common in anthropology museums: the typological approach, exemplified by the Pitt Rivers Museum at Oxford (Chapman 1985); and the geographical, or culture area, approach developed by Adolph Bastian at the Berlin Museum and subsequently championed by Franz Boas at the American Museum of Natural History (Jacknis 1985). Typological displays grouped artifacts of similar function from around the world with the aim of suggesting a progression from simple to complex technological forms. The geographical mode involved displaying items from the same region in galleries organized by colony, culture area, or continent, and it "relied heavily on written exegesis – labelling, text panels – to reinforce the notion that races developed at different rates" (Tythacott 2011, 133). In discussing these two modes, Annie Coombes (1988, 60) quotes the eminent US museum director William H. Holmes (1902): ethnographic material was "broadly recognised as falling into the two categories of a biological unit and a cultural unit. Ideally, since 'Man's physical evolution and anatomical structure related directly with all his activities,' race and culture were assumed to be 'intimately connected.' The objective for the curator was to demonstrate the relationship between the two." Coombes (1988, 61), whose focus is the use of ethnographic materials in British museums, notes that items from British colonies functioned principally "as signifiers of British sovereignty" and that "in this search for the perfect classification system, there was the certainty that somewhere there existed a 'natural' grouping. Since culture was seen to vary according to geographical and regional factors, and since environmental factors created regional affinities within the same groups, the 'natural' choice was thought to rest with a geographical classification."

Haddon, who was a strong believer in Edwardian municipal socialism, had served as advisory curator to the Horniman Museum and Gardens in London from 1902 to 1915, and he oversaw the installation of its inaugural displays. Accordingly, he had extensive experience of developing displays of ethnographic material that followed evolutionary schema, which may have informed his approach to displays in Cambridge, though as Sarah Byrne (2011, 314) notes in relation to his work at the Horniman, "he was not a slave to the evolutionary system and was aware of the multiple ways in which artefacts could be successfully displayed." To support her point, she quotes from his 1904 *Report on Some of the Educational Advantages and Deficiencies of London Museums,* which he presented to the UK Museums Association:

> The main object of collections of this nature is to illustrate the past and present culture of man, in other words to show ... the things he makes or has made for utilitarian and non-utilitarian purposes. The objects themselves may be regarded from points of view of space and time. Specimens may be collected from all parts of the world and these may be arranged according to countries and peoples, as is the case with the collections in the Ethnographic Department of the British Museum, or they

may be classified according to subject in order to illustrate the geographical distribution and local varieties of that class of object; or they may be arranged to demonstrate their own evolution, as is well done at the Pitt Rivers Museum at Oxford. (Haddon 1904, 10, quoted in Byrne 2011, 314)

Haddon's displays at Cambridge would thus have been partially influenced by his theoretical interests in evolutionism (see, for example, Haddon 1895) but also by his deep commitment to public education. Herle (1998, 98) cites his familiarity with the educational programming of the American Museum of Natural History and his enthusiasm for the policies of American museums regarding fieldwork, the dissemination of research, and teaching (Haddon 1902). Ethel Fegan, honorary librarian of the MAA's Haddon Collection from 1920 to 1930, recalled that upon becoming deputy curator, Haddon immediately focused on arranging the collections he had assembled during the 1898 Cambridge Anthropological Expedition to the Torres Strait: "Boxes were unpacked, specimens sorted into their appropriate regions or subjects, cases arranged and labelled and students were at last introduced to the various objects illustrating the material culture of the races which they were studying" (quoted in Pickles 1988, 3).

When Louis Clarke was appointed as curator in 1922, he took on the task of organizing the North, Central, and South American collections. The displays he installed mixed recently acquired items with others that had been in the museum for some time: these included the Northwest Coast artifacts collected on Captain Cook's third voyage, which Clarke bought in 1927 at the sale of Widdicombe House in southwest England (Kaeppler 1978; Tanner 1999, 3), and the Owen Collection of Meskwakie beadwork and clothing that had been on loan from the Folklore Society since 1901 (Owen 1904). Artifacts acquired by Clarke in 1923 at Zuni, New Mexico, were exhibited in the Andrews Gallery two years later, as were archaeological specimens amassed during excavations at Kechiba:wa (Museum of Archaeology and Anthropology 1926). A newly acquired Haida totem pole and a Kwakwaka'wakw grizzly bear house-post were installed in the Maudslay Hall in 1927, and the following year a large case was constructed in the Andrews Gallery to hold basketry from the Americas (Museum of Archaeology and Anthropology 1929). New displays of the archaeological collections from South and Central America were also prepared at this time, as the following extract from the *Annual Report* for 1930 reveals:

In a show-case at the other end of the [Andrews] gallery the greater part of the collection made by the late Dr. Gadow in Southern Mexico, and presented to the Museum in memory of him by Lord Revelstoke, has been placed on temporary exhibition. In a small upright case in the same part of the gallery the Curator has placed a feather head-dress and poncho from Nasca, Peru; in a flat wall-case next to this he has arranged an interesting series of textiles from old Peruvian graves, and in a larger show-case adjoining a number of fine examples of feather work, head-dresses, etc., from South America and three dried human heads from the Jivaro Indians, Ecuador. (Museum of Archaeology and Anthropology 1931)

Without doubt, the Franklin Motor Expedition collection was an important and extensive addition to the museum's American holdings, and as soon as Robert Rymill finished cataloguing it, Clarke began to incorporate it into the displays. Although no photographs of these have survived, once again Rymill's inventory provides some clues. As explained in Chapter 3, this inventory is a loose-leaf carbon copy of notes Rymill made in Canada, which records each item alongside a brief description and an accompanying inventory number. Over twelve pages toward the back of the document is an additional list of seventy-seven artifacts with MAA accession numbers written in Rymill's hand, which must have been added after he returned to Cambridge (Table 2). This list probably comprises the first items selected for display. "Bungay" and "Piegan" material predominates (though some pages may be missing), and the artifacts are loosely grouped by function, such as food utensils, healing paraphernalia, smoking equipment, and personal adornment.

As Table 2 shows, some entries on Rymill's list referred the reader to the accession cards, where slightly more detail regarding the artifacts could be found. In addition, descriptions in the main inventory are occasionally cross-referenced to the display list. For example, the inventory entry for CR5 [1930.730] reads, "Headdress. Though this headdress was obtained from the Cree, it is not of Cree type, but is typical of the Assiniboine from whom it must originally have come."[13] In the corresponding display list entry, Rymill wrote, "True type Assiniboine head dress. Do *not* place in Cree case. Ermine skin."[14] This statement is intriguing. First, it highlights the limitations of classifying artifacts according to ethnicity. Second, it raises the possibility that Rymill understood that simplistic "cultural group" applications did not account for complex family backgrounds and the circulation of material

TABLE 2
Rymill Collection artifacts proposed for display by Robert Rymill

Function/category (author's designations)	Artifacts (Rymill's notations)
Clothing	Hair ornament. North Blackfoot [1930.899],
	Medicine Man's Shirt. Bungay [1930.686A]
	Headdress. Assiniboine [1930.730]
	Old style hat. Plains Cree [1930.783]
	Roach. Plains Cree [1930.814]
	Small roach. Plains Cree [1930.805]
	Woman's left legging, very typical Bungay design [1930.701]
	Moccasins. Piegan [1930.1079]
	True Piegan type moccasins [1930.984]
	Pair of Sioux pattern moccasins. Wahpeton Dakota [1930.871]
	Pair of medicine moccasins. Plains Cree [1930.768]
	Medicine moccasins. Saulteaux [1930.892]
Personal ornament	Bear claw necklace. Wahpeton Dakota [1930.887]
Narrative objects	Puma skin. Sarsi [1930.916]
Containers	Calf head bag. Wahpeton Dakota [1930.875]
	Birch bark basket, Sioux design. Wahpeton Dakota [1930.873]
	Small woven bag. Nez Perce make [1930.1083]
Ceremonial materials/ healing	Paint bag. Piegan [1930.1065]
	Muskrat skin. For applying paint [1930.960]
	Singing buffalo stone on bird claw necklace, Piegan [1930.1068]
	Switch for splashing on the hot stones in a sweat bath. Piegan [1930.1040]
	Charm bag. Plains Cree [1930.753]
	Midewiwin medicine shooter. Plains Cree [1930.837]
	Medicine mink, bag. Bungay [1930.709]
	Cupping horn and three knives. Bungay [1930.654]
	Bleeding lancet with protector. Bungay [1930.655]
	Cupping tubes, probably formerly used for sucking out devils. Bungay [1930.711]

▶

Function/category (author's designations)	Artifacts (Rymill's notations)
	Charm for curing sickness. Piegan [1930.1024]
	Sacred Midewiwin snake. Bungay [1930.712]
	War charm. Piegan [1930.1066]
	Midewiwin symbol. Bungay [1930.698]
	Midewiwin symbol. Bungay [1930.672]
	Necklace charm. Piegan [1930.966]
	Woman's Sun Dance necklace. Piegan [1930.933]
	Man's war charm. Bungay [1930.716]
	Charm to be worn as a medicine. Plains Cree [1930.819]
	Singing buffalo stone. Piegan [1930.974] and [1930.1042A]
	Megus. Bungay [1930.699]
	Hair ball. Bungay [1930.704]
	Midewiwin bear paw. Bungay [1930.714]
	Midewiwin bear paw. Plains Cree [1930.836]
	Thunder bird. Bungay [1930.659]
	Mortar. Bungay [1930.657]
Feasting	Buffalo horn spoon. Piegan [1930.1072]
	Wooden food bowl. Wahpeton Dakota [1930.852]
	Sheep horn spoon. Wahpeton Dakota [1930.854]
	Wooden food bowl. Piegan [1930.1104]
Tools	Hide scraper. Piegan [1930.982]
Smoking materials	Pipe cleaner. Plains Cree [1930.751]
	Man's pipe, wrapped with loon necks. Wahpeton Dakota [1930.855]
	Man's pipe. Wahpeton Dakota [1930.856]
	Man's pipe. Piegan [1930.1011]
	Pipe with quilled stem. Piegan Man's pipe [1930.1097]
	Man's pipe. Piegan [1930.995]
	Preparation of red willow bark as tobacco. Bungay [1930.653]
	Red willow bark tobacco. Bungay [1930.656]
	Woman's pipe with bag of swan's foot. Piegan [1930.1062]

►

Function/category (author's designations)	Artifacts (Rymill's notations)
	Woman's pipe. Piegan [1930.1026]
	Partly made pipe. Piegan [1930.928]
	Formerly a peace pipe. Piegan [1930.1105]
	Pipe bag. North Blackfoot [1930.900]
	Three pieces [Tobacco Society material]. Piegan [1930.1098]
	Pipe bag. Piegan [1930.1017]
	Pipe cleaner and tobacco sample. Piegan [1930.1001]
Ceremonial materials (music)	Beaver Society drum with stick. Piegan [1930.1055]
	Drum, probably Buffalo Society. Piegan [1930.1059]
	Medicine rattle. Bungay [1930.691]
	Medicine rattle. Wahpeton Dakota [1930.853]
	Sun Dance rattle. Bungay [1930.694]
	Sun Dance rattle. Bungay [1930.693]
	Midewiwin rattle. Bungay [1930.692]
	Dog Dancer's rattle. Piegan [1930.1013]
	Man's sun dance whistle. Bungay [1930.682]
	Sun dance whistle. Plains Cree [1930.750]
	Sun dance whistle. Piegan [1930.1029]
	Dance rattle. Plains Cree [1930.739]
	Man's Midewiwin water drum and stick. Bungay [1930.684]

culture. Third, the use of "true type" reinforces the concept of authenticity, which was so crucial to the salvage project. Finally, although the use of "Cree case" indicates that organizing the displays by tribal groups had been considered, the display list suggests that this strategy was not strictly applied.

Although we do not know how the objects were arranged in each case, as most were small, and assuming that all the artifacts on the list were used, quite dense displays would have resulted. The only comparatively large items were a painted cougar hide [1930.916] (Figure 11) and a hide shirt decorated with beadwork, feathers, and hair [1930.686A]. The list gives the impression that artifacts were grouped according to function, with "Plains" as an overarching category. Thus, their arrangement may have corresponded to Boasian ideals, in which an artifact was placed "in the setting of its generating culture, and, by extension, those of its neighbours ... [so that] its true 'meaning' could be understood" (Jacknis 1996a, 185). Clarke and Rymill may have drawn upon the approaches of the major metropolitan museums in North America and Europe, but they would also have been influenced by the stylistic approach employed relatively recently by Haddon in the Pacific sections of the MAA. Today Clarke is considered more of an antiquarian than a scientist, but there is no reason to suppose that he diverged greatly from the display conventions favoured by Haddon.

Curatorial Networking

While incorporating the Rymill Collection into the American displays at the MAA, Clarke sought information about some pieces from his colleagues at the MAI. His correspondence shows that he regularly sent photographs of new accessions to George Heye and his staff to ask for their opinions on provenance and quality. In 1931, for example, MAI assistant director Frederick Webb Hodge responded to Clarke's queries about new MAA acquisitions, including parts of the Rymill Collection. Clarke had sent Hodge a photograph of a backrest banner [1930.797A] (Figure 25) that had been collected at the File Hills or a neighbouring Plains Cree reserve, which clearly intrigued him. Hodge rejected Robert Rymill's identification of the object as a "back rest, for use when sitting in a tepee" and asserted that

> so far as can be determined from the photograph, it would appear that someone had found an old piece of red baize, or strouding, and had sewed hereon the odd pieces of beadwork for the purpose of selling it. The panel has the appearance of the front of a pouch; the four triangular pieces above and the two below seem to be parts of moccasins, while the discs may have come from a blanket strip.

Hodge contextualized this comment with the news that the MAI had recently received a collection of medicine bundles from a man in Calgary, "all made up of odd pieces and having elaborate labels with an endless amount of 'information' that could not have been gathered from Indians."[15]

Though curators were wise to watch for people who hoped to profit from the urgency generated by salvage ethnography, Clarke had correctly recognized that the backrest banner was unusual. In his study of Plains

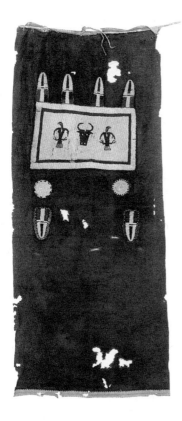

Figure 25 Trade cloth banner with beaded designs, used with backrest |
Reproduced by permission of University of Cambridge Museum of Archaeology and Anthropology, 1930.797A

Cree backrest banners, Ted Brasser (1984, 56) claims that the Rymill example is one of the nine complete backrests with banners in museum collections, though he has also located four other banners that probably belonged to backrests. The MAA specimen depicts a buffalo skull and two thunderbirds or eagles, which Brasser (ibid., 59) suggests represent the artist's visionary experiences. Brasser (ibid., 58) speculates that backrest banners were associated with the symbolism of buffalo hunting and that they were used in the southeastern part of Plains Cree territory until the late 1920s, well over a generation after the last buffalo hunts took place. The item's rarity may account for Hodge's conclusion that it was a one-off made for sale rather than an "authentic" piece.[16] Whether Clarke incorporated Hodge's opinion into the labels he developed for his display cannot be determined, though it is unlikely, given that most surviving labels from before the 1980s are descriptive rather than interpretive. Regardless, this exchange reveals that before exhibiting certain pieces, Clarke performed additional research to verify and expand upon Robert Rymill's information. The letters also illustrate

Clarke's concern about insufficient contextual information for the collections, as noted in the *Annual Report* for 1935 and discussed above. Finally, they demonstrate that curators in the 1930s (and for many decades since) were more likely to seek out the professional expertise of their colleagues than the cultural knowledge of indigenous people.

The surviving documentation suggests that the first displays of items from the Rymill Collection were intended to present an introductory overview of Plains culture. They were arranged first by nation/cultural group and, within that, by object type, as befitted the representational conventions of British museums during the 1920s and 1930s. The labels would have been largely descriptive, with the expectation that visitors would draw their own conclusions about the artifacts they viewed. As many scholars have observed, the use of the ethnographic present in museum displays had the effect of freezing indigenous cultures in a particular time period (for Plains collections, this was usually the mid-nineteenth century, before the reservation era) and reducing the lives of individuals to simplistic categories and bounded cultural areas (see, for example, Doxtator 1988; R.C. King 1998; Hill 2000; and Nason 2000). This strategy has been linked to wider processes of evolutionary thought and their resultant classification, which perpetuated the view that indigenous peoples, and the materials they produced, were unlikely to survive. In her discussion of the theoretical basis of British ethnographic exhibitions during the late Victorian and the Edwardian eras, Annie Coombes (1988, 62) notes that curators were

> well aware that "modern civilisation, has broken over all natural limits and by means of railroads and ships carries its generalised culture to the ends of the earth." But the resulting transformations brought about by this contact were not the designated domain of the ethnographic curator. For the material in these displays, then, and by implication the cultures they stood for, time stood still.[17]

The presentation of ethnographic materials as prehistoric "survivals" in the Tylorian sense, and of indigenous peoples as being farther down the evolutionary scale than Europeans, was retained well into the twentieth century in many British museums (see, for example, Coombes 1994b; Brown 2006; Alberti 2009; and Tythacott 2011). There is no evidence to suggest that the MAA diverged from this approach to any great extent.

The Rymill Collection in the Mid-Twentieth Century

Following the installation of the Rymill artifacts in the Andrews Gallery in 1930 and a 1935 loan to a temporary exhibition called The Art of Primitive Peoples, which is discussed below, the MAA archives did not explicitly mention the collection for some forty years. The staff made adjustments to all the displays during this period but were hampered by circumstances that they could not control. According to Peter Gathercole, curator from 1970 to 1981, the development of new displays between Clarke's curatorship and his own was impeded by spatial considerations and staff shortages (Peter Gathercole, pers. comm., 22 May 2000). At the beginning of the Second World War, the showcases were dismantled, for fear that Cambridge would be bombed, and many of the more valuable objects were sent to Stacpole Court in South Wales and a chalk cave in Balsham, Cambridgeshire.[18] At the same time, most staff and honorary keepers were absent on active service. In 1941, when it seemed less likely that the museum would be damaged, some displays were reinstalled, though with duplicate objects. At the end of the war, extensive reorganization began and displays that echoed those of Clarke and Haddon were returned to the cases: the Babington Hall housed the African collections; the Bevan Hall was used for the Pacific and Australian displays, which were largely returned to their pre-war arrangement; the Andrews Gallery exhibited art and material culture from New Guinea and Indonesia; and the Maudslay Hall was devoted to the anthropology and archaeology of the Americas.[19]

Throughout the 1950s and 1960s, the Americas displays were reorganized to create space for artifacts gathered on university-sponsored expeditions that had not previously been shown, particularly those of the Wordie Arctic Expedition (1934) and the Cambridge Calima Valley Expedition to Colombia (1962). Thomas Paterson and his successor, Geoffrey Bushnell (curator from 1948 to 1970), both had research interests in the Americas, so it is unsurprising that during the mid-twentieth century, a substantial part of the Maudslay Hall was devoted to displays of artifacts from the growing American collections (Figure 26) and that the MAA was known principally for its research expertise in the Americas.[20]

Photographs of the galleries that date from the 1970s but that show displays installed during the previous decade provide the most conclusive evidence for how the MAA utilized its Native American collections in the

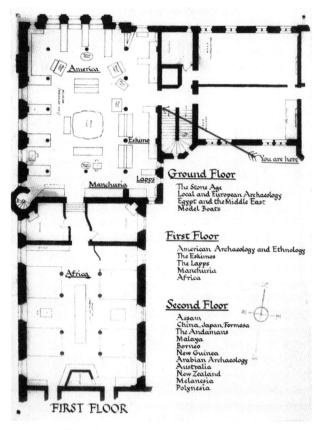

Figure 26   Floor plan showing the organization of space in the
Maudslay Hall, c. 1960 | Reproduced by permission of University of Cambridge
Museum of Archaeology and Anthropology

mid-twentieth century. The photos reveal that though the galleries' basic
organizational structure remained regional, interpretation had increased.
Five wall cases in the Americas section contained Plains and Prairie artifacts
(at the time of writing, there was only one), many of which were from the
Rymill Collection. These cases were arranged by anthropologically defined
cultural area: "Plains Indians, U.S.A," "Eastern Woodlands," and "The North-
West Coast of N. America." In some cases, specific nations were named:
the panel that introduced the Blackfoot Nation explained that this included
"tribes called Blackfoot, Piegan and Blood," who "live in reservations in
Montana and Alberta" (Figure 27). Although the panel's use of the present
tense acknowledged the continued presence of Blackfoot people in these

Figure 27 Display case with Blackfoot artifacts, c. 1960-70 | Reproduced by
permission of University of Cambridge Museum of Archaeology and Anthropology

areas, and the information that they lived on "reservations" hinted at their
political status, the minimalist captions and the objects chosen projected a
visual message that buckskin outfits and eagle feather headdresses were
everyday wear for the Blackfoot. The omission of any information that
would date or otherwise contextualize the pieces implied that the Blackfoot
had not changed since the artifacts were made. Items that stood for particular

aspects of life were laid out for the audience to consider, and then move on, oblivious to present-day realities.

John Osbourne, who worked as an MAA technician for some forty years, confirms that when he joined the museum in 1961, the displays were "object-dense" and that "the cases were plastered with labels" (John Osbourne, pers. comm., 8 June 2000). Ceremonial artifacts, which today would not be exhibited in deference to First Nations cultural protocols, were included in the cases. Although the numbers of text panels had increased, the contextual information remained superficial and was sometimes incorrect (for example, some items associated with the Midewiwin were labelled as "Sun Dance insignia"). Each showcase was a visual containment of a particular nation (occasionally two nations), with a range of materials chosen on the authority of the curator to summarize its whole existence. Because Robert Rymill's records did not always identify First Nations communities, the labelling tended to generalize: thus, it employed "Plains Cree" or "Plains Ojibwe," giving the impression that people confined their activities and habitation to one or another biome. Furthermore, few ethnological and no historical details were given, and photographs and maps, which would have enabled the audience to locate items in space and time, were absent. The sole exception was the display case for the "Crow Indians," which included a small photograph of a man who appears to be holding a ceremonial pipe, though no explanatory label linked the image to the artifacts. Interestingly, the panel introducing this case directed viewers to the scholarly literature rather than offering them detailed information about what was on show, a strategy possibly connected to the MAA's principal role as a university teaching museum, where students were expected to seek out information themselves rather than be given it directly.

The photographs highlight the extent to which museum representations of world cultures have changed over the past half-century. A display strategy that arranges historic artifacts according to cultural area is less problematic if the accompanying interpretation explains that those who made and used the artifacts were not isolated, bounded groups but were engaged in multiple relationships with other nations and settler societies. With its minimalist labelling that emphasized function but gave little contextual or temporal information, the mid-twentieth-century interpretation at the MAA was entirely in line with representational conventions of the day. We do not know how visitors read these displays, as visitor books from the period recorded only a person's name, hometown, and date of visit, but some speculation can nonetheless be attempted. In assessing viewer responses to displays of First Nations cultural material, Doering, DiGiacomo, and Pekarik (1999, 149) discovered that, if museums attempt to present the "traditional lives" of First Nations people, the pre-existing "entrance narrative" of viewers – "the internal storyline that visitors enter [the exhibition] with" – tends to be confirmed. The authors show that most visitors to First Nations/Native American exhibitions in North America have little experience of indigenous people. Perhaps as a result of this, their perceptions prior to visiting the museum are dominated by romantic stereotypes of social and spiritual freedom, harmony with nature, and peace between neighbouring tribes.[21] We must take care when projecting current critiques of historic displays onto audiences in the past and must remember that visitor experiences of museum displays are individualistic and highly personalized (Falk and Dierking 2000). Nevertheless, it is hard to imagine that mid-twentieth-century MAA visitors, most of whom would have been unfamiliar with social and political issues of concern to First Nations people, would have approached the North American displays any differently.

The Rymill Collection toward the End of the Twentieth Century

By the 1970s it was apparent that the MAA needed to address severe structural problems, so a building program was initiated that reduced the number and area of the galleries but increased staff workspace and collections storage. Due to the sheer numbers of artifacts and the few staff involved, this project took more than ten years to complete. The archaeology displays on the ground floor were completely redesigned to address emerging trends in museum practice, but given the demands on resources, the permanent ethnographic displays in the Maudslay Hall were not fully renovated until the 1980s.

During this time, though none of the staff had research expertise in North America, they were well aware of the public's continued fascination with Native American and First Nations peoples, especially those from the Plains, and they catered to this interest as best they could. For example, when Tom Stanier, the producer of *Watch,* a BBC television program aimed at children aged six to eight, wrote to Peter Gathercole in 1980 to inform him of a forthcoming series that would concentrate on "the Plains Indians and N. W. Coastal Indians," the museum altered its displays to coincide with the screening. Stanier anticipated that the program would be immensely popular and that school tours would visit museums with relevant collections. He wrote, "Next summer there are going to be an awful lot of children fired with enthusiasm for North American Indians and I am very anxious to channel this enthusiasm as constructively as possible."[22] With this in mind, Stanier asked if the MAA could complete a short survey about pertinent items in its collection and whether staff could offer support materials and a training day for teachers. Deborah Swallow, then the assistant curator for anthropology, responded that the museum's North American displays "are very old fashioned in style, and not very informative in themselves, but do *show* the material."[23] She added that the MAA was planning to improve the displays "radically" in the near future and that staff would be happy to liaise with the county museum teacher regarding educational resources.

A number of sources that survive from the 1981 Plains and Northwest Coast redisplay help clarify how the museum's interpretive style has transformed across time. The Plains material was installed in six cases in the Maudslay Hall, where it remained for five years, with some substitutions of artifacts made during that time. Sketches of the layouts, drawn when the cases were emptied, along with the labels and panel text, reveal that of the sixty-six artifacts in the new displays, thirty-seven were from the Rymill Collection. Organized thematically, the cases featured gender roles, clothing, warfare, and spiritual beliefs (Table 3).

The interpretive panels gave geographical, historical, and cultural context, and they addressed gender roles, environmental and social change, and the impact of trade goods.[24] Although the panels offered what was essentially an overview of the history and culture of "the High Plains," they nonetheless acknowledged diversity and the existence of many tribal traditions. They identified key periods of transition (e.g., "By the 18th century, with horses,

TABLE 3
Artifacts in the 1981 Plains display

Case theme[a]	Artifacts
Pipes	Medicine pipe with cleaner, corn-cob, and stick
	Pipe cleaner (Plains Cree) [1930.751]
	Pipe (Plains Cree) [1930.773A-B]
	Man's pipe (Wahpeton Dakota) [1930.855]
	Pipe bag and contents (Wahpeton Dakota) [1930.858A-C]

▶

Case theme[a]	Artifacts
War and religion (1)	Feather headdress used on horseback (Piikani) [1930.896] Skin dress and leggings decorated with quillwork (Blackfoot) Whistle (Piikani) Painted cougar skin (Tsuu T'ina) [1930.916] Stone club Stone club (Lakota) Tomahawk Gun War club (Piikani) Hand charm Quiver Medicine moccasins (Saulteaux) [1930.892A-B] Buffalo hide rattle (Piikani) [1930.749][b] Buffalo hide rattle (Piikani) [1930.976] Medicine pipe drum (Piikani) [1930.922] Medicine mink, bag (Anishinaabe) [1930.709] Lancet (Anishinaabe) [1930.655] Cupping horn and flints (Anishinaabe) [1930.654] Bag
War and religion (2)	Lance (Piikani) [1930.1111] Sun dance whistle (Plains Cree) [1930.750] Sun dance rattle (Anishinaabe) [1930.694] Sun dance rattle (Anishinaabe) [1930.693] Eagle wing fan (Wahpeton Dakota) [1930.880] Midewiwin material (Plains Cree) [1930.838A] Bear's foot (Plains Cree) [1930.836A] Midewiwin material (Anishinaabe)[1930.672] Midewiwin material (Anishinaabe) [1930.698] War medicine bundle War charm (Piikani) [1930.925B] Hoop war medicine (Crow)
Women's work	Painted bag (Wahpeton Dakota) [1930.882] Painted bag (Wahpeton Dakota) Painted buffalo hide worn under saddle Pipe bag (Cheyenne)

►

Case theme[a]	Artifacts
	Charm bag (Plains Cree) [1930.753]
	Saddle bag (Lakota)
	Baby carrier (Nez Perce)
	Parfleche (Wahpeton Dakota)
	Parfleche (Wahpeton Dakota) [1930.883]
	Hide scraper with iron blade (Crow)
	Hide scraper with notched edge (Crow)
	Hide scraper with iron blade (Piikani) [1930.982]
	Hide scraper made from antler (Piikani) [1930.1004]
	Birch bark basket and lid (Plains Cree) [1930.799A-B]
	Drinking cup of buffalo horn (Crow)
	Pemmican pounder (Piikani) [1930.1096]
	Knife and sheath (Piikani) [1930.810A-B]
	Stone berry pounder (Crow)
	Stone hammer (Lakota)
	Spoon of sheep horn (Wahpeton Dakota [1930.854]
Clothing	Man's costume (Gros Ventre)
	Headdress
	Child's costume (Plains Cree) [1930.784A-F]
	Woman's costume (Piikani) [1930.1077]
	Woman's leggings (Siksika) [1930.898A-B]
	Woman's costume (Crow)
Personal ornaments	Necklace of finger bones
	Silver necklace
	Necklace of beads and horse teeth (Plains Cree) [1930.806]
	Necklace of beads and bear's claws (Wahpeton Dakota) [1930.887]

a This table lists all the items in the display, including the nation, if known. Accession numbers have been provided for Rymill Collection pieces. Sketches made when the Plains display was dismantled in 1986 show that only a few pieces had been added to those listed here. Thus, it seems likely that the display remained largely unchanged between 1981 and 1986.

b The list in the MAA archives, which was used to compile this table, contains an error. Artifact 1930.749 is identified as a "Buffalo hide rattle, BLACKFOOT (Piegan)." In fact, this accession number refers to what Rymill described elsewhere as "Dog Dance rattle, PLAINS CREE." Notes, labels and correspondence referring to 1980s American Indian exhibition, FA1/1/7, MAA.

and with guns traded from the Europeans, a completely new way of life opened up for the Indian tribes"), though the narrative concluded at an unspecified point in time (presumably mid-nineteenth century), before the destruction of the bison, the devastation caused by disease, and the reduction of tribal lands through treaty and the establishment of reserves. No reference was made to the effect of colonial assimilation policies on Native American or First Nations peoples, or to contemporary issues they faced. Instead, the interpretation was purely historical and was illustrated by artifacts that, with few exceptions, dated from the late nineteenth and early twentieth centuries. The panel text was not alone in helping visitors contextualize the artifacts, however. Individual object labels were also provided, but, as with previous displays, they largely repeated information from the catalogue cards. Thus, even the most carefully researched Plains exhibition that the MAA had undertaken to that time recycled Robert Rymill's brief field notations and reinforced the authority of statements based on survey fieldwork.

As Deborah Swallow explained in her letter to the BBC, the Indians of North America exhibition was the precursor to a radical overhaul of the anthropology displays that began in 1986. The cases were emptied and a team of contract curators was brought in to transform the anthropology collections. The newly designed Maudslay Hall opened in 1990 to hold art and material culture from around the world, and the Andrews Gallery was set aside for temporary exhibitions that would be curated in-house. The new displays represented a significant thematic and interpretive shift for the MAA. They drew heavily upon the reflexive turn then current in anthropological theory in which scholars acknowledged that anthropological representations were the product of asymmetrical power relations (Clifford and Marcus 1986; Marcus and Fischer 1986). Calls were made to reject the realist and objectivist style that had long characterized conventional approaches to anthropology, and to work collaboratively with indigenous people to challenge traditional methods for constructing anthropological knowledge. In the museum world, a series of influential texts related these ideas to exhibition and other museum practices in order to subvert the established view of museums as sites of authority (see, for example, Karp and Lavine 1991; Ames 1992; and Karp, Kreamer, and Lavine 1992). The debates generated by these works fed into the approach developed by the curatorial and design team at the MAA. In an article describing the renovations, Paul Sant Cassia, assistant curator of anthropology during the reorganization, wrote about the difficulties of preserving the historical importance and character of the old displays while avoiding the problem of the museum becoming a stereotype of itself. As Sant Cassia (1992, 28) explained, the goals of the team were to

> present the historical development of anthropology as a discipline in the university as well as raise certain questions about the status of objects, the contemporary situation of the societies which produced them, and the relationship of those societies to their own cultural heritage, much of which is housed in museums overseas. Another aim was to stimulate new ways of looking at objects as aesthetically significant in their own right.

In addition to acknowledging changes in critical museology, which made explicit the responsibilities of museums to their audiences as well as to their collections, the team had to take into account the MAA's position as a teaching institution. Visitors to the new gallery were greeted by showcases that explored the development of anthropology as an academic disciple and that included a reconstruction of the Fijian displays of the first curator, Baron Anatole von Hügel, to emphasize the MAA's role in shaping anthropology in Cambridge. The remaining showcases were broadly arranged by cultural area and were augmented by a number of free-standing cases that allowed for the explication of themes and for a greater number of artifacts to be displayed. Some artifacts were not fully encased; many larger sculptural pieces, such as Malangan figures, the Haida totem pole, Solomon Islands feast dishes, and a Māori canoe prow, were placed on plinths or behind low barriers to enable closer viewing. The gallery interpretation included illustrated panels with extensive explanatory text to provide historical and ethnographic context, labels that went beyond the merely descriptive, and, occasionally, quotes from published ethnographies or relevant archival documents (ibid., 30). Many displays drew on the fieldwork of Cambridge-based anthropologists who were familiar with the regions represented, so though the panels undoubtedly projected an authoritative curatorial tone, they were consciously multi-authored, which would have been apparent to a careful reader.

Developed by Sant Cassia and contract designer Franca Vincent, the "Plains Indians" display was intended to provide an overview of the Plains region. Arranged in one wall case, it featured a number of pieces from the Rymill Collection, six of which had been included in the 1980s display, as

Figure 28 The "Plains Indians" case, following the 1990 redisplay | Reproduced by permission of University of Cambridge Museum of Archaeology and Anthropology

well as several items acquired through other sources (Figure 28 and Table 4). In keeping with the overall gallery design, the artifacts fit into the anthropological categories that were used as headings for the graphic panels, such as "History and Social Organisation" and "Ritual and Religion." Three large graphic panels fixed to the back wall provided introductory information on the display themes, and artifact identification labels, consisting of the accession number, a brief description, and the name of the nation were placed along the bottom of the case. Black-and-white archival as well as

TABLE 4

Rymill Collection artifacts in the 1990 Plains display

Artifacts (Rymill's description)	Nation
Sun Dance whip [1930.980]	Piikani
Medicine pouch, containing three charms [1930.1009A-D]	Piikani
Woven bag of Nez Perce origin, but obtained from the Piegan [1930.1086]	Nez Perce/Piikani
Woven bag of Nez Perce origin, but obtained from the Piegan [1930.1084]	Nez Perce/Piikani
Pair of moccasins [1930.1079A-B]	Piikani
Saddle bag [1930.1069]	Piikani
Woman's Sun Dance charm [1930.948]	Piikani
Headdress of a type which is only used on horseback [1930.896]	Siksika
Medicine moccasins. The design on A represents a Thunder Bird that on B a Bear. If a woman were to step on these she would die [1930.892A-B][a]	Saulteaux
Wooden bowl [1930.852]	Wahpeton Dakota
Pipe cleaner [1930.751][a]	Plains Cree
Sun Dance whistle [1930.750][a]	Plains Cree
Dog Dance rattle [1930.749][a]	Plains Cree
Medicine mink, bag [1930.709][a]	Bungi
Sun Dance rattle [1930.694][a]	Bungi

a These items were included in the 1980s redisplay of the Plains Collection.

contemporary colour photos were used as illustrations, an approach intended to alleviate, albeit in a limited fashion, the sense of timelessness that has characterized so many displays of world cultures. Another strategy used to address this issue was the incorporation of "proverbs and myths from each society ... to give some feel of the way other societies construct their worlds" (Sant Cassia 1992, 30). In addition, the text panels not only dealt with the "evolution of the society concerned" but also referred to relations between indigenous people and anthropologists to provide context for the artifacts, illustrations, and text. The desired result was to demonstrate the dynamism of indigenous communities, without ignoring the impact of relations with the West. Although the approach worked well for some of the new displays, it was less successful in the Plains case as the reliance on nineteenth-century artifacts reinforced the idea of people frozen in the past. Furthermore, though the display featured many nations (Crow, Meskwakie, Piikani, Plains Cree, and Wahpeton Dakota, to name a few) and attempted to identify them in the labelling, the generic text panels offset this, and the overall message was that "Plains Indians" were effectively all the same.[25]

The reliance on historic artifacts was by necessity and was not restricted to the Plains display, but until the accession of two powwow outfits collected in Saskatchewan in 1994 by Tim Raybould [1995.1-1995.19A-B] and forty items I acquired in 1998-99 [1999.194-1999.233A-B], the MAA had no recent pieces from the Plains. The information in the 1990s Plains Indians display was also based on collectors' notes rather than on primary scholarship as none of the staff involved had conducted fieldwork in this part of North America and were mostly unfamiliar with the changing approaches to representational strategies then emerging from Canada. This is made obvious by comparing the Plains case with the Arctic display, which benefited from the input of a researcher (Barbara Bodenhorn) who had done considerable fieldwork in that region (Anita Herle, MAA, pers. comm., 2 October 2000). The similarity in the layout and content of Plains displays over the preceding fifty years is less easy to explain. A comparison of Figures 27 and 28 shows that not only were the same artifacts displayed for decades (albeit in slightly different configurations), but that the very arrangement of items seemed to follow a pattern that was only partially dictated by the limited space.

Curatorial and Collaborative Challenges

In late 2000, hoping to better understand the constraints faced by the MAA with regard to the presentation of its Plains collection and also in response to First Nations concerns about the inappropriate exhibition of ceremonial artifacts, I applied for a grant from the MAA's Crowther-Beynon Fund to curate a new display of the Plains collection for the museum. In the application, I observed that the current display was more than ten years old and that the redisplay would consist of historic pieces and items acquired during the previous decade. The funding application was successful and research for the new display began in 2001, although due to my other commitments, it was not installed until the spring of 2004 (Brown 2005). It has remained largely unchanged since then, although the graphic panels were reprinted in early 2012 during the most recent renovation of the MAA to improve the colour of the images and slightly reduce the length of the text.

The display's storyline was principally informed by my discussions with First Nations people over the preceding years but was also shaped by institutional factors. First, it had to fit thematically with the other showcases in the Maudslay Hall, which had undergone various levels of upgrading since their installation in 1990. This meant providing a generalized overview of the region, while stressing its cultural diversity. It also required attention to continuity and change in the aesthetic form of the artifacts and demanded that I was mindful of disciplinary histories. Second, as the display was to be permanent, the interpretive text would have to be phrased in such a way that it would not rapidly become outdated. Finally, although the museum holds over 2,500 artifacts from the Plains, the physical fragility of certain pieces and the restrictions on displaying ceremonial artifacts immediately ruled out some items (including several that had been shown in previous years).

My prior knowledge of the MAA's approach to presenting Plains materials, combined with First Nations critiques about museum representation, contributed to the overall message. In particular, I was keen to address the issue of anonymity in museum displays, which many First Nations people see as problematic and a contributory factor in their marginalization. As is clear from my analysis of the Rymill Collection, museums and archives may be rich in holdings but are often poor in biographical knowledge of the artifacts themselves. As far as can be ascertained from the documentation, Donald Cadzow and Robert Rymill saw the people from whom they collected as "types"; their names were thus irrelevant. Likewise, most archival photographs of First Nations individuals (and other indigenous people) do not name their subjects. Collaborative community-based projects to identify the makers of artifacts and the people in archival photos are becoming commonplace, but it takes time for their findings to filter into museum displays.[26] For some indigenous people, projects that facilitate reconnection between artifacts, images, and individuals can help restore honour and dignity to their ancestors (Greenhorn 2005; Brown, Peers, and members of the Kainai Nation 2006, 111). Although I was working with only one showcase, it was crucial to keep this in mind, and after considerable discussion with Senior Curator for Anthropology Anita Herle, it was agreed that focusing on artifacts associated with known individuals would enable us to think through how museums have categorized and thus made anonymous – and powerless – the people they represent. We also hoped that the new display

Figure 29 The "Plains Indians" case, following the 2004 redisplay | Photograph by the author

would highlight the importance of kinship connections to museum collections, as frequently expressed by First Nations and Native American people.

Most artifacts in the showcase were associated with a named person (the maker, owner, or collector), whose image was also exhibited whenever possible (Figure 29). As the following extract from one of the two graphic panels shows, the text made explicit that this was a deliberate strategy and a reflection of changing practice:

Early anthropological thought was concerned with cultural "types" and collectors sought artefacts that they believed were representative of different groups of people. They rarely recorded the names of the individuals that made or used them. The Museum still supports collecting in the Plains, but today works with Aboriginal people to find out what they would like to say to visitors.

Many Aboriginal people regard artefacts as links with their ancestors. Sometimes it is possible to make connections between artefacts in museums and real people. In this display we show how important these connections can be for understanding the lives of Aboriginal people in the present as well as in the past.

To fit with the gallery's goal of incorporating MAA history into the displays, the text referred to the Franklin Motor Expedition. For example, the label for a painted tipi door [1930.731] read,

> In 1929 the Museum sponsored a collecting expedition to the Canadian Prairies. Over 500 artefacts were collected from several Nations, during a period when many museums felt that time was running out to collect "authentic" objects. Some of these relate to the important relationship between Plains people and horses. Robert Rymill, an anthropology graduate who participated in the expedition, recorded that the painting on this tipi door shows Walking Bear (*nêhiyaw* Plains Cree), stealing horses from the Blackfoot. This would have been one of Walking Bear's war deeds.

Similarly, the section that explored contemporary life named the creators of its artefacts, several of which I had collected myself. These included a woman's outfit [1999.229A-B] designed by Patricia Piché, which I had purchased in a gift shop at the Tsuu T'ina Nation, and a pendant [1999.218] and a beaded barrette [1999.219] made by Grace Stanley, whom I had met in Regina. The text for these items – which was illustrated by photographs of both women – was informed by their explanations of the role of sewing in their lives. The label for Grace Stanley's work read, "Grace Stanley (*nêhiyaw* Plains Cree) is from Nekaneet First Nation, Saskatchewan. Her sister taught her how to do beadwork and she has been beading as a hobby for several years. She often makes small items, including cigarette lighter cases and jewellery, for sale or as gifts for friends and family." The emphasis on the social and personal meanings of the artifacts rather than on their function and type was unlike any previous display of Plains material at the MAA and made explicit the biographies of the items in a way that had rarely been attempted elsewhere in its permanent displays.

First Nations people were also involved in the development of the 2004 Plains display. Since the late 1990s, and arguably more than any other UK museum, the MAA has taken sustained steps to involve indigenous communities, a point that is even more remarkable given how comparatively understaffed it was until the early 2000s. Much of this work has been driven by Anita Herle, who has been at the museum since the late 1980s. She is probably best known for her research in the Torres Strait (see Herle and Philp 1998; Herle and Rouse 1998; Herle 2000, 2003), but she has also been involved in collaborative projects with indigenous groups in other parts of the world. These have included collections management initiatives, such as the establishment of culturally appropriate storage for material collected by Nepalese Pachyu shaman Yarjung Kromchhain Tamu (Gurung) (Herle 1994), and supporting an Indigenous Artists in Residence program. The MAA has also developed several temporary exhibitions that have entailed varying degrees of co-management. These include Paired Brothers: Concealment and Revelation (Herle and Moutu 2004), and Pasifika Styles (Salmond and Raymond 2008). This work is not restricted to the anthropology collections. For example, Robin Boast, senior curator for world archaeology until 2012, participated in developing digital resources to assist communities located at a distance to access and comment on museum collections and, in turn, to rethink how digital information can be used and transformed by these engagements (Boast, Bravo, and Srinivasan 2007; Srinivasan et al. 2009; Srinivasan et al. 2010). It was against this evolving background of collaborative curatorial practice that the Plains redisplay was conceived.

The funding did not permit the MAA to ask First Nations visitors from the Rymill Collection communities to come to Cambridge, so alternative strategies were sought. By this time, I had spent several years developing research connections with Northern Plains communities, so I was able to draw upon these links as the themes were developed. For example, given the proposed goal of highlighting materials associated with named individuals, I hoped to include *atim kâ-mihkwasit*'s beaded outfit, discussed in Chapter 5, alongside a photograph of him with his daughters. In order to proceed, it was crucial that people at the Star Blanket Nation could deliberate this matter and, if they agreed to the inclusion of the outfit, could contribute to the interpretation. Through e-mail dialogues with Noel Starblanket, himself a relative of *atim kâ-mihkwasit,* I was able to take this process forward. Due to Starblanket's efforts, elders and other family members of *atim kâ-mihkwasit* met to discuss the proposal. He reported that the elders appreciated that the museum had shown sensitivity in the matter, and that although they felt that the outfit rightly belonged in their community where their own people could see it, they nonetheless agreed to its display in an educational context (Noel Starblanket, e-mail to author, 10 March 2004).

I also worked with Jenny Bruised Head, who provided guidance on the redisplay as a whole, as well as specifically on the Blackfoot artifacts proposed for inclusion. An educator from the Kainai First Nation in Southern Alberta, Bruised Head was part of the curatorial team that developed the Glenbow Museum's Blackfoot gallery. She also advised the Canadian Museum of Civilization team that developed Legends of Our Times, an exhibition about First Nations ranching and rodeo (Baillargeon and Tepper 1998), and had been involved in my Rymill Collection research. Moreover, as a ceremonial leader in her own community, with transfer rights to several Blackfoot knowledge disciplines, she has the authority to comment on associated materials. Images of the artifacts under consideration were e-mailed to Bruised Head, who suggested possible interpretations and identified those that, in her view, were not appropriate for display. She also made suggestions for the layout and text.

In no sense could the redisplay be described as "collaborative," as the term applies to museum projects that attempt to realign authority and control of indigenous collections (see, for example, Clifford 2004; Harrison 2005a; and Phillips and Coombes 2013). Its aims were far more modest, and "consultative as far as was practicable" would perhaps be a better gloss for its development. However, this did not mean that my discussions with First Nations colleagues were merely concessions; nor were they treated as such by those who supported the project. Because they were conducted via e-mail and telephone rather than direct engagement, they were considerably more limited than they would have been for a museum in Canada. Nonetheless, they exceeded British norms at the time (and arguably since). It was hoped that the display made explicit that historic (and contemporary) artifacts can be recast to emphasize their connections with individuals; though they are physically decontextualized in museums, their interpretation does not need to separate them from people, communities, and histories. Yet few British museums have the necessary funds or staff to develop more fully collaborative projects. I will return to this issue in the final chapter, as museums must address it if they are serious about developing positive, mutually respectful, relationships with First Nations people.

The Rymill Collection and Temporary Exhibitions

The discussion above has traced how the MAA used the Rymill Collection to contribute to a range of narratives about First Nations people. Although the interpretation was not extensive, especially in the early years, the regional and thematic approach highlighted connections between the artifacts and social life, as one might expect in a museum of anthropology. From 1935 Rymill pieces began to be loaned to other UK museums, with the result that they contributed to narratives about First Nations that address topics beyond the survey/reference display model. Temporary exhibitions have the advantage of allowing curators to raise questions and subjects that are less easy to address in permanent galleries (where "permanent" usually means between fifteen and twenty-five years). Furthermore, in a museum such as the MAA, where curatorial staff undertake grant-funded field research and can also draw upon the research of graduate students in a way that is rare for non-university museums, temporary exhibitions facilitate both the incorporation of recent research and greater consultation about display content.

Artifacts from the Rymill Collection were first loaned to an externally curated temporary exhibition during the summer of 1935, when two Wahpeton Dakota items were included in a larger loan to London's Burlington Fine Arts Club for The Art of Primitive Peoples. The club operated from 1866 to 1951 and was originally founded "to bring together collectors, amateurs, and persons variously interested in matters of art, and to provide a centre for the exhibition and comparison among its members of objects of interest in their possession" (Nicolson 1952, 97). On occasion, and under certain conditions, these exhibitions would be open to the public, and according to Nicolson (ibid., 98), they "did more to stimulate appreciation in London of the art of the past than any similar enterprises, at least until the first war." The Art of Primitive Peoples was something of a departure at a time when the fine and decorative arts were generally understood to be those of Europe, India, China, and Japan, but the exhibition fitted well with trends in modernism and primitivism that began to emerge before the

First World War (Rhodes 2004). A review of the show congratulated the Burlington Fine Arts Club for "giving its aesthetic patronage" to artifacts that, only twenty years earlier, "would have been regarded as of merely ethnological interest" (Anon. 1935a, 42). In fact, a reviewer for the journal *Nature* did opine that non-Western art was "of merely ethnological interest." Though he or she was impressed by the range of artifacts in the exhibition, concern was expressed that the emphasis on aesthetic qualities came at the expense of scientific knowledge. The reviewer argued that "while it is true that this collection contains some of the finest known examples of so-called primitive art – it is indeed a possible criticism of the exhibition that it includes so little that is crude, but at the same time scientifically instructive – the general level of execution is higher than might reasonably be expected" (Anon. 1935b, 927).

Louis Clarke was on the exhibition's sub-committee, and the MAA loaned eighty-two specimens from the ethnology collection for the show.[27] The two items from the Rymill Collection were a horn spoon whose handle was carved in the image of a duck's head and a shallow wooden food bowl with a carved head of a bear protruding from the rim (Figure 30). The Art of Primitive Peoples catalogue did not refer to the bowl, but the listing for the spoon (exhibition number 141) repeated the information that Robert Rymill had transferred to the catalogue card when he processed the artifacts in 1930: "Sheep horn spoon, with carved head in form of a duck. Length 9". Dakota (Wahpeton), Canada. Collected by R. Rymill 1929" (Burlington Fine Arts Club 1935, 37).[28] In the Burlington show, Native American pieces were outnumbered by artifacts from other world cultures, which may be related to Ruth Phillips's (1999, 97) assertion that the art gallery exhibition of the former began relatively late in the history of the appreciation of "primitive art" (around 1930), though one reviewer who picked up on this discrepancy noted that the Burlington Fine Arts Club had held an exhibition of indigenous American art as recently as 1925, which had included some Northwest Coast and Inuit sculpture (Anon. 1935b, 927).[29]

In his introduction to The Art of Primitive Peoples catalogue, Adrian Digby (1935, 10) defined primitive art as that which showed little or no extraneous influence from industrialized civilization and added that

> in some cases, indeed, the objects produced by [indigenous people] seem
> to have very little artistic merit, and the critic may be inclined to say that
> primitive peoples have no art. But a true understanding of primitive

Figure 30 Bowl and spoon collected at the Wahpeton Dakota Nation, August 1929 | Reproduced by permission of University of Cambridge Museum of Archaeology and Anthropology, 1930.852 and 1930.854

carvings, of primitive textiles, and, indeed, of all other forms of the products of primitive peoples can only be achieved by a study of the conditions governing the lives of these people.

Digby divided these factors into three groups – religious, economic or sociological, and technological – though it is not clear whether the show was arranged along these lines. The published reviews reveal that some visitors found it challenging, as they were sidetracked by "the rarity or ritual purpose of certain objects ... to the neglect of artistic merit" (Anon. 1935b, 927). The Burlington Fine Arts Club presentation of artifacts as art was in marked contrast to the MAA's own approach, which emphasized social context rather than form.

After The Art of Primitive Peoples, there is no evidence that other Rymill Collection items appeared in temporary exhibitions until the 1990s. Since then, several UK museums have borrowed artifacts on short-term loan to illustrate particular themes in temporary displays or, less frequently, to contribute to regionally focused exhibitions about North American indigenous peoples. These loans included the two Midewiwin birch bark scrolls acquired at Swan Lake, which were displayed in Image and Text, a 1991 show at the Fitzwilliam Museum, Cambridge, curated by Education Officer Frances Sword. Image and Text showcased "a selection of books and manuscripts ... chosen to demonstrate the relationship between text and illustration."[30] The scrolls, which would probably not be loaned for display purposes today due to cultural sensitivities, were selected purely for their visual qualities and because they broadened the geographic range of the exhibition rather than for their ceremonial associations. The following year, seven "Amerindian artefacts" were loaned to Glasgow Museums for the Home of the Brave exhibition, developed to coincide with the quincentennial of Christopher Columbus's arrival in the Americas (Museum of Archaeology and Anthropology 1992). The loan included one piece from the Rymill Collection, a bead and bird claw necklace with an *iniskim* (buffalo stone) attached [1930.1068], which came from the Piikani Nation (Patricia Allan, Glasgow Museums, e-mail to author, 17 November 2010). The show's main goals were to address the impact of colonialism on indigenous peoples and to draw attention to the contemporary social and political status of Native Americans. Despite this latter aim, most of the artifacts were historic pieces, which came from Glasgow Museums' own collections or were borrowed from other museums. One item – a crest pole carved by Coast Salish artists Doug and Aubrey LaFortune – was commissioned to represent contemporary artistic traditions and cultural strength in spite of colonization.[31]

More recently, a woman's strap dress from the File Hills was displayed at the Royal Albert Memorial Museum and Art Gallery, Exeter (2005), and then at Stroud's Museum in the Park (2005-06), in Wrapping the Globe: British South West Trade Cloth around the World, an exhibition curated by textile conservator Morwena Stephenson as part of a research project of the same name. The label for the dress focused on particular motifs used by the seamstress and included provenance information that went beyond Rymill's record:

> This dress is extremely rare and unusual. It incorporates Plains-style beadwork techniques and motifs (lazy-stitch horizontal stripes and circular medallions) in a Great Lakes-style of dress. Originally, it would have had

detachable sleeves. This garment clearly shows the decorative use of the selvedge or saved list. The dress was collected on a reserve in Saskatchewan, Canada in 1929, probably in the File Hills area. Most people on the four reserves that make up the File Hills are of Plains Cree heritage.[32]

Although the label's final sentence continues the museological tendency to link artifacts to a bounded ethnicity, the text does discuss the skills of the seamstress in such a way that it is possible to imagine her as a real person rather than a cultural type. Finally, the Science Museum in London borrowed a drum and beater [1930.891A-B] for inclusion in its Who Am I? gallery, which opened in 2010 to mark the tenth anniversary of the Human Genome Project's completion. Described by Rymill as "of Cree origin, but collected from the Soto [Saulteaux]," these items are displayed in a showcase titled "How did you get here?" alongside ethnographic artifacts from various parts of the world. Their accompanying interpretation reads, "Medicine man's drum and beater: By playing repetitive sounds using this drum and drumstick, a medicine man could alter his state of consciousness. These instruments are from North America." This language simplifies rather than distorts the indigenous meanings of the pieces, but glossing over their origins and using the term "medicine man" are rather more troubling; aside from the lack of awareness regarding the diversity of North American indigenous nations, the authoritative tone of the text gives no meaningful context for visitors to respond to these objects.

Except for Home of the Brave, these exhibitions addressed their themes cross-culturally rather than billing themselves as being *about* "Indians." Outside the MAA's permanent reference displays, the Rymill artifacts were not usually presented as type specimens; instead, they were used to illustrate broad topics (literacy, genetic connections, the consumption of a particular fabric), as has become standard in recent approaches to museum interpretation. Since the 1990s, following the renovation of the anthropology galleries and the installation of temporary exhibition space in the Andrews Gallery, the MAA has also used items from the Rymill Collection thematically, most notably in Living Traditions: Continuity and Change, Past and Present (1994-96), which looked at the dynamic role of tradition and the meanings of cultural symbols and beliefs in communities as diverse as Aboriginal Australia, the students and staff of Cambridge University, and the Swahili of the East African Coast (Herle and Phillipson 1994). One section of the exhibition traced the development of the powwow and pan-Indianism in

North America. It displayed a pair of quillwork armbands collected at the Wahpeton Dakota Nation [1930.877] and the drum from the Star Blanket Nation [1930.844] discussed on pages 172-74 in relation to the powers of the leader *atim kâ-mihkwasit* and his family. These appeared with contemporary powwow outfits commissioned by the museum and film footage shot in the early 1990s at Southern Saskatchewan powwows, which was provided by the Royal Saskatchewan Museum. In some respects, Living Traditions followed the convention established by Louis Clarke during the 1930s for showcasing new acquisitions and the research of current university staff and students, but it differed in that its many new items were commissioned specifically to highlight the ongoing creativity of indigenous people rather than as part of the tradition of ethnographic salvage. Most importantly, by emphasizing cultural continuity, the interpretive approach successfully acted as a foil to the ahistorical representation of indigenous peoples in the permanent displays.

THIS CHAPTER HAS CHARTED the museum history of the Rymill Collection since its 1929 arrival in Cambridge. Over time, the arrangement and interpretation of the Rymill artifacts remained strikingly consistent, not only in terms of the uncritical repetition of information provided by the collectors but also in the selection of display styles and indeed in the repeated use of the same items, although there were several hundred from which to choose. Temporary exhibitions that featured objects from the Rymill Collection adopted rather different approaches, using the artifacts to explore a greater diversity of themes than was possible for permanent displays. That said, the tendency to rely heavily on Rymill's own interpretation remains in place. The wider question that arises from this analysis, then, is why have museums persisted in using these materials so uncritically? Is it simply because the collection history was not well known? Had it been understood that the artifacts were acquired hastily, and taking into account changing curatorial paradigms, would the subsequent interpretation have accorded less authority to the collector? These questions indicate that whereas the histories of collecting may have ambivalent value for First Nations people, as indicated in Chapter 5, a better understanding of these processes should nevertheless inform how museums interpret collections. This, in turn, has ramifications for future working relationships.

These issues also highlight the difficulties for the curatorial teams who wish to discuss their proposals with First Nations people. For decades after the Rymill Collection arrived in Cambridge, initiating such a dialogue would have been unthinkable, but this is no longer the case. In my search for practical solutions to this challenge, I turn next to how British museums are taking steps to break down cultural and geographical distance in their attempts to curate First Nations collections. In the summer of 2012, the MAA reopened following a major refurbishment that improved visitor access and allowed for the development of new displays. As with the 1970s renovation, the archaeology displays were the focus of the reorganization, but the long-term plan is to secure funds to redisplay the anthropology collections. If this goes ahead, it is hoped that new technologies, including experimentation with film and sound, will allow for an interpretive approach that brings community and curatorial perspectives somewhat closer together than has been possible in the past and will facilitate representations of First Nations people that are at least partly generated by First Nations people themselves.

7
Building Relationships
British Museums and First Nations

This is a start between the museum over there in Britain and with the Peigan people. At least now we're aware that there's some artifacts in Britain, and we can go out and tell people what there is.

– Jenny Bruised Head, author interview

If you look back a few years, even today, most of the places that have things are far away, and the people can't get out there when they want to. And that's hard. That's why I think we should have more cooperation from the keepers. We are not asking for everything back. We are just looking for a few items that our people can use ... We're out to try and develop an understanding and to develop a good relationship with the people that are keeping these items.

– Mike Pinay, author interview

I BEGAN THE STUDY on which this book is based because the Rymill Collection intrigued me. I wanted to know how and why such a large collection of First Nations material had come to be in a museum thousands of kilometres from Canada and what that meant for the descendants of the people involved. What I found was a complex story shaped by the impact of colonial assimilation policies and reflections on how access to museum collections today, and specifically the cultural knowledge associated with them, can contribute to recovery from those policies. The focus on one case study allowed me to address how the historical trajectories of artifacts have informed popular imaginaries of First Nations peoples but also, and perhaps more importantly, how multiple biographies of collections have the potential to inform new relations between museums and indigenous communities that are grounded by a deeper, and more open, understanding of the histories that link them. Thus, I chose to write *around* the Franklin Motor Expedition artifacts, rather than *about* them, focusing on their cultural, rather than their material aspects. Highlighting the perspectives of three communities encountered by the expedition underscored the diversity of opinions within and between First Nations regarding experiences of museums, both historically and in the present.

In essence, the study underlines the range of opinions about museums and what they can offer First Nations today, as well as drawing attention to how the diversity of the latter was glossed over in the past. Artifacts like those in the Rymill Collection were employed to create "representative" bounded images of particular First Nations whose own perspectives were excluded as part of wider political processes of erasing indigenous peoples themselves. This point serves as an important reminder to museums that they must be cognisant of the diversity of historic contexts in which collections emerged. Indeed, many First Nations people welcome the opportunity to establish new relations with museums, *especially* those located at a distance, but they do expect them to be aware of the inequalities that produced their dislocation from their own historical artifacts and other manifestations of their culture. This book has demonstrated that bringing together multiple perspectives can greatly enrich collections-based research by fostering new questions about collections and the social relationships in which they have been *and can be* embedded. I hope that it will facilitate thinking more broadly about the questions that collections can inspire and how they can inform emerging, and more equitable, relations between museums and indigenous people.

Rethinking the History of Collecting

The study has taken two paths that have implications for how collections are conceptualized theoretically, but also for how they are dealt with museologically. First, I historicized the Rymill Collection by bringing together the extant documentation about the Franklin Motor Expedition and the context in which it was assembled. Oral history interviews with the Cadzow and Rymill families and with people from the communities visited by the expedition enabled me to put names to faces and to better understand who was involved and, in some cases, why they participated. Seeking out different voices highlights the value of looking beyond the written and visual sources that are most commonly utilized in collections research. Such work has merits not only for scholars aiming to better understand collections, but also for indigenous people who see them as part of their cultural heritage. It can also have merits for the families of collectors. As a result of discussing the expedition, the younger members of the Rymill and Cadzow families became interested in family stories. Certainly, not all descendants of collectors might be as invested in their family histories, but the response of the Rymill and Cadzow families to the research does suggest that descendants' perspectives have a place in dialogues about collections. Taking on board different voices in this way can offer significant challenges to collecting histories and can encourage re-evaluation of the questions that are most frequently asked of collections. As Julie Cruikshank observes, all oral accounts, including those of First Nations, are open to biases and cultural interpretations, as are other forms of historical reconstruction, and their meanings are related to how these accounts are used in practice. Drawing on the work of David Cohen (1989), Cruikshank (1994, 411) writes that "we must be careful not to reify oral tradition ... because to do so inevitably privileges particular classes or clans whose traditions most closely approximate our own definitions." Anthropologists now recognize that the purposes of oral histories may differ from those of other historical traditions and that the two forms should be used in tandem. I kept this point in mind as I wove together the recollections of First Nations people, the Rymill and Cadzow families, and the written and visual documents that survive from the expedition itself.

Museum collections were shaped by particular social dynamics. How these dynamics played out in colonial spaces has much to contribute to studies of cross-cultural encounters, but my own view of the value of collecting histories has shifted since I began the research. A turning point came when I asked a ceremonial leader if anyone in his community would remember stories about the Franklin Motor Expedition. His response was blunt: "That is not the kind of thing we remember" (author's field notes, 14 July 1999). These kinds of encounters can have limited relevance in communities that are dealing with the legacy of colonialism, which itself enabled collecting activity to occur, so collecting histories are valued very differently depending on who asks the questions and what they aim to achieve. Until I started speaking with First Nations people, my perceptions of the Rymill Collection were entirely shaped by its museum context and history, and so were my questions. I understood the artifacts in terms of how they related to each other as part of an ensemble and how they could be used to think about social relations in the past, but I had no solid framework for looking beyond that. I was reliant on rather patchy secondary literature and had no way of knowing how the artifacts might contribute to First Nations' own histories or goals for cultural revitalization. As it turned out, most of the First Nations people with whom I spoke fully supported research into collecting history, not because it contributes to a better understanding of knowledge production in the abstract sense, but because it can inform decisions about the future use and ownership of specific artifacts.

During the research, people often spoke of museum collections as representing, to varying degrees, the deliberate state-sponsored attempt to annihilate their culture. This is not a loose association, but many individuals also identified ways in which collections could teach aspects of community history, strengthen cultural knowledge, and help heal the damage caused by colonial policies. People also associated loss or theft with collections that were made when the First Nations experienced the greatest assault on their lives and ways of being, following the arrival of the military, the North-West Mounted Police, and missionaries. "Loss" and "theft" mean much more than the removal of artifacts from communities; they relate to the ability to learn about and practise culture. It is also important to note that a significant number of historic First Nations artifacts now in museums were given as gifts or were bought or traded entirely legitimately, and that many people do make this distinction. Such items can be used to reflect upon a time when relationships between First Nations and others were considerably more equal than in the period addressed in this book.

Museum collections have the potential to articulate with the processes of knowledge regeneration and cultural revitalization that First Nations people see as being of greatest importance. Collections do matter. This is not to say that collection studies that privilege the perspectives of collectors are irrelevant; indeed, biographical studies have much to contribute to the understanding of collecting as a social phenomenon. Furthermore, recent studies that treat ethnographic collecting within a relational framework, in which networks between collectors are mapped out (see Gosden and Larson

2007), are useful for highlighting the social processes involved in collecting and for thinking beyond the standard model of a single collector working alone. My argument is that we need to go significantly farther than this to involve a wider spectrum of voices and to think more critically about how collections history is used, what audiences the research targets, and how to address current challenges to historic collections that are informed by multi-perspectival histories.

Rethinking Curatorial Practice

The second path I followed in this book considers the implications of collections research for curatorial practice. There were historical dimensions here, too: the MAA used the Rymill Collection to raise issues regarding the representation of Plains and Prairie First Nations by British museums. As cultural institutions, museums are key players in constructing depictions of indigenous peoples, and as the historical connections shaped by trade, emigration, and colonization between the UK and Canada are so lengthy, British museums have been involved in this process for several centuries, almost entirely without input from First Nations people themselves. As I outlined above, the improved relations that many Canadian museums now enjoy with First Nations arose from a period of introspection during which museums were forced to address their reticence to involve indigenous people in the care and interpretation of their material heritage. As an extensive and easily accessible literature covers this topic, I have not explored it in depth here, but it nonetheless influenced my research into the Rymill Collection and my subsequent museum career.

When I began the research, most regional British museums, and many of their national and university counterparts, still exercised scholarly perspectives and a level of control that would no longer be tolerated in parts of the world where indigenous people have demanded an active role in curatorial affairs (see, for example, Tapsell 1998, 2005; Fforde, Hubert, and Turnbull 2002; and Cooper 2007). Clearly, the issue of geographical location has played a significant role here. In settler societies, indigenous people have consistently called for greater accountability from museums, and though these calls have been received in Europe, it is difficult to sustain pressure to implement them. Thus, there have been few attempts to develop guidelines or protocols for collaboration, such as those advocated in museum policy documents produced at the institutional, provincial, and national level in Australia, Canada, and New Zealand (see Hill and Nicks 1992; Museums Association of Saskatchewan 2001, 2009; and Dolan 2005). National guidelines *have* been developed in the United Kingdom for caring for ancestral remains (Museum Ethnographers' Group 1991; Department for Culture, Media and Sport 2005; Museums Galleries Scotland 2011), but such is not the case for ceremonial materials or other matters of concern to indigenous people. This is largely due to the difficulty of making generalizations, given the global spread of collections in British museums, but it is also because *written* policies generate their own issues and need regular revision. Instead, British museums that have developed strategies to care for ceremonial materials, which tend to be larger institutions with specialist staff and which generally have more indigenous research visitors, follow informal policies based on agreed good practice. For example, if the Pitt Rivers Museum is advised by community members to care for a particular item in a certain way, that information will be entered into the museum database but can only be read internally and cannot be accessed on the online version of the catalogue (Laura Peers, Pitt Rivers Museum, e-mail to author, 24 July 2012). Likewise, the MAA deals with such requests on a case-by-case basis and draws upon the knowledge of staff and new information gathered from visiting researchers and fieldwork (Anita Herle, MAA, e-mail to author, 24 July 2012). These approaches are positive steps forward, but museums continue to struggle with the issue of who has the authority to speak for communities, and this is especially so when they have limited familiarity with the groups concerned. Smaller regional institutions requiring guidance on this matter often turn to colleagues in larger museums or to the UK's Museum Ethnographers Group (MEG), a national organization that promotes research and good practice in museum ethnography. MEG has developed "Guidance Notes on Ethical Approaches in Museum Ethnography" (2003), though it does not specifically deal with issues of traditional care. As an example of MEG's active engagement with museums on these matters, it organized a series of workshops in 2013 for a project called Engaging Communities, which critiqued the concept of collaboration and discussed what collaboration means in practice for institutions who wish to establish ethically informed and sustainable relations with local and global users.[1]

There are clear signs that change is on the horizon. In July 2000, for example, the Australian and British prime ministers released a joint statement to work together to facilitate the repatriation of Aboriginal and Torres

Strait Islander ancestral remains held in British collections, and several repatriations have occurred since (Fforde 2004, 135-51; see also Turnbull and Pickering 2010). As yet no similar initiatives have been launched respecting First Nations artifacts or ancestral remains. The Royal Commission on Aboriginal Peoples (RCAP 1996, 593) suggested that Canadian museums could work with First Nations to locate and repatriate cultural materials held in overseas collections, and there has certainly been activity in this area, using digital technologies rather than full repatriation. However, Ottawa has made no formal moves comparable to the Australian government's support of Aboriginal and Torres Strait Islander repatriation, and the very few repatriations to First Nations from British museums have been negotiated entirely by the parties concerned. One could argue that this lack of activity is due in part to more pressing domestic concerns, but it also reflects relations between Aboriginal peoples and the Canadian state more broadly and the lack of support for Aboriginal rights, which tend to make the news only during moments of crisis. In two instances of this which occurred toward the later stages of writing this book, the media focused on the housing crisis at the Attawapiskat First Nation in 2011-12 and the rise of the Idle No More movement, which emerged following the October 2012 introduction of Bill C-45. Idle No More campaigns to raise awareness about legislation believed to threaten the sovereign rights of First Nations and to have a detrimental impact on resources.[2] The mainstream media eventually had a great deal to say about the flash mobs, Canada-wide demonstrations, and the National Day of Action, in the early days of Idle No More, but commentary was initially circulated through indigenous media and social networking. Some weeks passed before the national media ran stories associated with the protest. At that point, a flurry of editorials, opinion pieces, and reports examined the movement, which undoubtedly drew attention (not all of it positive) to its arguments, but in a world where news moves rapidly onward and the mainstream media play a key role in perpetuating fallacies about Aboriginal people, it is of no surprise that the press soon lost interest in the underlying issues. Its fleeting response to the protest – the most visible and significant coming together of First Nations and other Aboriginal people since the Oka crisis – is indicative of their challenges in raising awareness and resolving the complex issues and many social problems they face (see also Warry 2007, 69-84). Understandably, though many Aboriginal people attempt to counter the threats to their livelihoods, lands, and culture, and to emphasize their distinctiveness, keeping the pressure on federal and provincial officials to support cultural matters, such as to initiate bilateral discussion on repatriation issues, is tremendously difficult when there are other more immediate challenges.

Moving Forward

Though a nation-to-nation agreement supported by the Canadian and British governments on matters of First Nations cultural heritage may not presently be on the political agenda, there are clear signs that the British museum sector is becoming much more responsive to the needs of indigenous people. Some museums have made dedicated efforts to address the challenge of cultural and geographical distance, and to find ways of working with First Nations. These projects have drawn on the experiences of colleagues in Canada and have raised awareness among museum staff that indigenous groups are deeply invested in historic collections, and that important questions about the responsibilities of museums need to be asked. They have also demonstrated that collaborating with First Nations people in the interpretation and development of collections can create new relationships that are less extractive in character and have long-term possibilities for continuation beyond one-off ventures.

One such project was Tim Paul's residency at the Royal Albert Memorial Museum and Art Gallery (RAMM) in Exeter, southwest England. Paul is a master carver from the Hesquiaht band of the Nuu-chah-nulth Nation, British Columbia. In June 1998, he led a team of carvers to create a crest pole commissioned by the museum; named Ilchinik, the pole was intended to commemorate the relationship between Paul's ancestors and the sailors who travelled from Exeter to the Northwest Coast during the previous two centuries.[3] The project was initiated in the mid-1990s by Jane Burkinshaw, then a curator in the World Cultures department of the RAMM. Much of the funding was provided by Exeter City Council, though the initial discussions about the project began when Burkinshaw self-funded a three-week research visit in 1996 to Vancouver and Vancouver Island to meet with curatorial staff. Burkinshaw brought photographs of the RAMM artifacts to British Columbia, and as well as holding formal meetings about the collection with artists, archivists, and curators, she showed the photographs to many First Nations people. During this visit, Burkinshaw met Tim Paul at his Port Alberni home, where they discussed the possibility of producing a crest pole for the museum and the protocols surrounding such a project.

As Paul's ideas for the pole took shape, their discussions continued by phone and mail (Jane Burkinshaw, e-mail to author, 10 October 2011).

Paul and the other carvers brought their families with them to Exeter, and as they worked in the gallery, they talked to visitors about carving Ilchinik; they also got to know museum staff and volunteers far better than is usually the case with short-term community visits (Burkinshaw 1999; MacKeith 1999). Burkinshaw explains that Paul's

> emphasis has always been on doing things in the correct way by consulting with the Elders of the community at every stage and being true to the traditions of his community. That was the reason for the large support group who came over with him, as it was imperative that the correct songs were sung and the correct dances danced, and the appropriate ceremonies performed. Some of the ceremonies were open [and] some were held in private between the Na-yii-i family members. (Jane Burkinshaw, e-mail to author, 7 October 2011)

Such was the closeness of the relationship that developed between Paul and his colleagues at the RAMM that one of the museum volunteers, the late Graham Searle, was appointed Ilchinik's spiritual keeper, a title that has now passed to his daughters.[4] This particular example illustrates the point that individual curators are often intensely committed to increasing access to collections but can be limited by institutional policies and procedures (see also Harrison 2005a). In this instance, and in the absence of institutional support, Burkinshaw chose to pay for her research trip to British Columbia and was later successful in obtaining Leverhulme Trust funding to undertake additional archival and community-based research in the province. It is unusual for British museum staff to invest so much of their own resources in this kind of work, yet as the RAMM experience shows, the commitment of individual curators to increasing access can result in important new connections that benefit museums enormously.

Around the same time as the RAMM crest pole project was being developed, staff at the British Museum worked with several Native American and First Nations consultants to plan the Chase Manhattan Gallery of North America, though the gallery's interpretive panels did not mention these associations (Peers 1999a, 24). The Chase Manhattan Gallery, which opened in 1999, was designed as a permanent gallery aimed at highlighting the historical and regional breadth of the British Museum's extensive North American collections. To some degree, the curatorial team was constrained by the wider interpretive strategies of the British Museum and could not incorporate multiple perspectives in its labelling and graphic panels, as this would have diverged from the conventions of the museum. Accordingly, the curatorial voice is dominant. This is in contrast to the interpretive strategy used in the more recent permanent gallery, Living and Dying, which opened in 2003 and is situated next to the Chase Manhattan Gallery. It utilizes first-person quotations and curatorial perspectives to reveal how people throughout the world address the challenges of life and death, and it includes an extensive section on human-animal relations in the Canadian Subarctic (Bolton 2007). The interpretive requirements of permanent galleries differ markedly from those of temporary exhibitions, given that their lifespan is usually at least twenty years. This means that curatorial freedom to experiment with controversial topics is greater in temporary galleries, and there are often more opportunities for showcasing collaborations. Indeed, the British Museum has long been involved in projects with First Nations and Native Americans, though visitors to its permanent displays would find little evidence of this. For example, Jonathan King, who worked with the museum's North American collections for over three decades before taking a research position at the MAA, conducted repeat fieldwork in the Canadian Arctic for many years. One outcome of his research was the 2001 exhibition Annuraaq: Arctic Clothing from Igloolik and an associated conference and publication (King, Pauksztat, and Storrie 2005).[5] Noteworthy for its contemporary focus, the project was developed as a partnership between the British Museum; the Department of Culture, Language, Elders, and Youth of the Government of Nunavut; the Inullariit Elders' Society, Igloolik; and the Igloolik Research Centre of the Research Institute of Nunavut.

The temporary exhibition format clearly affords opportunities for exploring topics in more depth than is possible in permanent exhibitions, but venue is also significant. Prior to 1997, the institutional structure of the British Museum included a Department of Ethnography, whose collections were displayed in a separate building, the Museum of Mankind.[6] Departmental staff curated many innovative exhibitions that drew upon their fieldwork in various regions and involved differing levels of input from indigenous people.[7] According to Anthony Shelton (2006, 74), the 1970-97

Museum of Mankind exhibitions "breached and questioned conventional distinctions between ethnographic and contemporary art and contributed significantly to rethinking museum displays more generally." The museum's Living Arctic exhibition is illustrative here; it opened in 1988 and was developed in collaboration with Indigenous Survival International (ISI) (Brody 1987; J.C.H. King 1989). It sprang from discussions between George Erasmus, then ISI co-chairman and national chief of the Assembly of First Nations, John Bekale of the Dene Nation, Marc Leclair of the Métis National Council, anthropologist Hugh Brody, and Museum of Mankind staff. By showcasing the complex mix of tradition and modernism in northern life, Living Arctic aimed to undermine southern stereotypes that northern peoples remained largely untouched by industrialization. It addressed the continuing role of traditional subsistence activities in the North and included quotes from Inuit, First Nations, and Métis contributors. Given its emphasis on contemporary northern life, the show was deliberately "people – rather than art – or artefact-oriented" (J.C.H. King 1989, 65). The associated publications included children's books, wall charts, and films and interactive video games about hunting, conservation, and storytelling that used technologies new to museums (ibid., 66). Specialized school programming was delivered by an Inuk educator, David Serkoak, and lectures were presented to adult audiences by historians and anthropologists experienced in the North. Living Arctic and its associated events were hugely successful, attracting over 300,000 visitors, including some 10,000 children who participated in the educational activities (ibid., 66, 74). It did receive some negative criticism that, according to King (ibid., 74), "arose either from the perceived failure of the exhibition to emphasise certain aspects of northern life, or from the reaction of people to the challenges in the exhibition to popular stereotypes." Nonetheless, it is worth remembering that Living Arctic ran concurrently with The Spirit Sings and that press, public, and First Nations responses to both exhibitions differed significantly. Developed by Calgary's Glenbow Museum as part of the Arts Festival of the 1988 Winter Olympics, The Spirit Sings was intended to highlight the artistic traditions of indigenous people in Canada. As mentioned on pages 6-7, it was boycotted by supporters of the Lubicon Lake Cree Nation, including some European museums who withdrew loans, as well as the executive of the Canadian Ethnology Society. The exhibition was partly sponsored by Shell Canada, one of several resource extraction companies active on lands claimed by the Lubicon Cree. As Graburn and Lee (1988, 12-13) observe, whereas The Spirit Sings was funded by the establishment and did not draw on First Nations perspectives in its development, Living Arctic was initiated by indigenous people, and its motives were mutually beneficial:

> The British Museum wanted the money for the largest exhibition on northern peoples ever organized in Europe; ISI wanted the publicity to combat the increasingly stringent European regulations against trapping and the importation of furs, and the Canadian government was canny enough to realize that a sympathy-generating public exhibition about native people would promote the Canadian fur industry as a whole, even though native people generate less than 15 percent of the annual fur harvest.

More recently, in 2006, National Museums Scotland, which cares for the earliest surviving collection of Dene material heritage in a public museum, partnered with the Prince of Wales Northern Heritage Centre in Yellowknife, Northwest Territories, the Tłı̨chǫ government (formerly the Dogrib Treaty 11 Council), and the University of Dundee to loan forty Tłı̨chǫ artifacts from the National Museum of Scotland (NMS) for exhibition and handling workshops with Tłı̨chǫ people (Knowles 2007, 2011; Stable and Scott 2008). The NMS continues to host research visits from Tłı̨chǫ people to Edinburgh and has since mounted Extremes: Life in Subarctic Canada in its own temporary exhibition gallery (Wrightson 2012). Other efforts to link UK institutions with North American indigenous groups include the Haida Project, which involved re-engagements with Haida and cultural treasures in the Pitt Rivers Museum and the British Museum (Krmpotich and Peers 2013); my own work with the Kainai Nation on a photographic history project (Brown, Peers, and members of the Kainai Nation 2006); and a partnership between the Pitt Rivers Museum, the University of Aberdeen, the Glenbow Museum, Lethbridge's Galt Museum and Archives, and the Blackfoot nations in which five early-nineteenth-century shirts were loaned to the Glenbow and Galt for exhibition and for "visits" involving elders and ceremonial people, artists, schoolchildren, and college students (Brown and Peers 2013). Loan projects such as these, though welcomed by many people as an all too rare opportunity to engage with heritage materials, undoubtedly raise tensions regarding the unequal power relations between museums that hold such materials and people located at a distance who need to access them. Such projects are fleeting, and despite their good intentions, the museums involved are open to criticism that they are merely waving heritage items under the noses of community members before taking them back to the stores for another few decades, if not forever.

Access and cultural revitalization projects are not restricted solely to museums with ethnographic collections, though they have been the principal venues for collaborative exhibitions. Art historian Stephanie Pratt, a Crow Creek Dakota Sioux Nation member, has curated art shows that have entailed responsive consultation with First Nations and Native Americans. In 2007, for example, she co-curated the temporary exhibition Between Worlds: Voyagers to Britain, 1700-1850, held at the National Portrait Gallery, London, which featured the experiences of political delegations and distinguished individuals who came to London from Africa, the Indian subcontinent, North America, and the Pacific in the eighteenth and nineteenth centuries (Hackforth-Jones et al. 2007). Pratt worked with Six Nations historian Keith Jamieson to write text and select artifacts. More recently, she co-curated a second exhibition for the National Portrait Gallery about the display strategies used by the artist George Catlin in his "Indian Gallery," which he brought to Europe during the mid-nineteenth century. Titled George Catlin: American Indian Portraits, the show ran during the spring of 2013, and Pratt worked with tribal representatives from the Crow, Dakota, and Mandan Nations connected to the people whom Catlin painted to devise curatorial strategies that highlighted their perspectives. Their insights were incorporated into wall texts and catalogue entries. Subsequently, in the conference held to coincide with the exhibition's opening, Calvin Grinnell, historian of Mandan and Hidatsa peoples, talked about the ways that Mandan ceremonial leaders have used Catlin's portraits to re-create or reimagine their original O-Kee-Pa ceremony – a further example of how engagement with historic collections can contribute to cultural revitalization (Stephanie Pratt, e-mail to author, 30 May 2013).

Securing resources for such projects is always difficult, and I have no wish to minimize the challenge of locating funds, especially during a period of financial uncertainty in which museums have been key targets for budget cuts. Nonetheless, innovative solutions are being developed to improve access to collections digitally, if not physically. Some British museums are starting to experiment with teleconferencing to enable indigenous researchers to view artifacts in museum workspaces. For instance, the Ojibwe Cultural Foundation based on Manitoulin Island, Ontario, has collaborated with the Pitt Rivers Museum in Oxford on an access project (de Stecher and Loyer 2009, 145). In this project, an Odawa elder at the Ojibwe Cultural Foundation was able to control a webcam focused on artifacts laid out in the Pitt Rivers Museum research room. Other museums have developed web-based exhibitions or are participating in database projects with varying degrees of input from First Nations. Internet-based access to collections has been criticized by some as a poor substitute for physical access, but it can be seen as a temporary solution rather than an alternative and a means to begin working together to improve collections records with a view to developing physical access projects in future. As stated in Chapter 6, the MAA has been involved in this kind of work for some years; of particular note is the Recontextualizing Digital Objects project, a collaboration between the MAA, the Ashiwi Awan Museum and Heritage Center, representing the Zuni Tribe, New Mexico, and UCLA-based researcher Ramesh Srinivasan to develop cultural and ethnographic approaches for creating digital information systems (Srinivasan et al. 2009; Srinivasan et al. 2010). Other major database projects currently under way in British museums (and in Europe and North America) are the Great Lakes Research Alliance for the Study of Aboriginal Arts and Cultures (GRASAC), which aims to bring together dispersed heritage materials through digital repatriation in situations where physical repatriation is not currently possible, and the Reciprocal Research Network (RRN), based at the Museum of Anthropology, University of British Columbia, which has similar goals for collating information on Northwest Coast collections in museums at a distance from the region (Rowley et al. 2010; Phillips 2011, 227-96).[8] It should be noted that both projects, though international in composition, were initiated and are led by teams of First Nations researchers, museum professionals, and university-based academics, and are principally funded by Canadian research grants.

In recent years, the projects developed by British museums that have worked with First Nations have tended to be exhibition-focused. To date, there is far less emphasis on involving First Nations people in collections management and other aspects of curatorial and conservation work. This is partly because, as First Nations people and curators in Canada have explained, building up relationships of trust takes many years, and these links are often based on the commitment of individuals rather than institutions (Hanna 1999; Harrison 2005a; Conaty 2008). Moreover, just because a museum invites a First Nation to participate in a particular project with the hope of implementing policy change as a result, the timing may not be right for the community, or other internal issues may prevent a relationship from being nurtured. Laura Peers's (2003) discussion of her attempt to work with the Anishinaabe community of Red Lake, Minnesota, to curate hair samples in the Pitt Rivers Museum that a staff member collected from residential school pupils during the 1920s, is a case in point. Peers emphasizes the tensions of working with such emotive materials and notes that although the museum could use its other Red Lake artifacts to support community-centred education projects, this is unlikely to occur until it has resolved the issue of curating the hair samples to the community's satisfaction (ibid., 91).

What these examples make clear is that many First Nations people are extremely interested in learning what articles from their communities are held in British museums, so that appropriate ways can be found to work with them. As First Nations seek to heal from the colonial experience, many of these items may be far more important to them now than they were when they were collected, despite having been absent for decades. For instance, the revival of artistic skills that has flourished with increased access to historic collections is linked to the renewal of traditional social practices and ceremony, and to the strengthening of contemporary cultural identity (see also Farrell Racette 2009, 305-6). Clearly, more needs to be done to identify collections so that communities may more easily approach museums. Although some First Nations have collated informal inventories, and some museums have put full or partial database information online, more could certainly be done to establish accurate information about the location and extent of collections in European museums. Centralizing these resources is especially important, and there are a number of websites that use links to indicate the location of collections throughout the world. One instance is the Burke Museum of Natural History's digital imaging project, which includes 25,000 pictures of Northwest Coast artifacts from two hundred museums and private collections (including several in Britain) that were digitized from 35mm slides taken by Bill Holm and Robin K. Wright during the course of their careers.[9] Another is the Splendid Heritage website, which focuses on a limited number of private collections of Native North American art and includes interpretive notes written by art historians and other scholars.[10] Such sites are often assembled with minimal input from indigenous people themselves and are essentially databases of images; they are nevertheless extremely helpful for determining the whereabouts of particular artifacts and collections. In contrast, projects such as GRASAC and the RRN have demonstrated that the combination of community, museum, and scholarly expertise can contribute to community initiatives, including language revitalization projects and the regeneration and transmission of craft skills. Of course, these web-based projects are far more complex than those that simply post images on the Internet. As these two networks concern collections from the Great Lakes and Northwest Coast respectively, perhaps the next stage is to develop a similar project that collates information on Plains collections. A project of this nature would involve numerous communities in Canada and the United States, and would be an immense undertaking logistically, financially, culturally, and politically, but the network model developed by the RRN and GRASAC indicates that it is feasible, and it may be possible to join forces with the few database projects that do deal with collections from this region, such as the Kainai-maintained Blackfoot Digital Library.[11] There is certainly a need for clarity on the extent of First Nations collections held in public institutions. At present, this matter is uncertain, and published estimates about the number of artifacts in British museums can be misleading, based as they are on incomplete and often inaccurate museum records.[12] Although this book focuses on a collection that originated on the Prairies, many of the issues raised would resonate with First Nations in other parts of Canada, especially regarding the disconnection between knowing that artifacts are "out there" and having concrete evidence of where they are actually located.

Final Thoughts

My analysis of the Rymill Collection, the expedition that assembled it, its museum life, and the First Nations perspectives regarding it has indicated the richness of the narratives that can enfold museum collections, even those that, at first glance, seem disassociated from the people and histories that shaped them. Historic collections can contribute to cultural revitalization and healing of the damage caused by colonialism. They can also mediate new, more positive relationships between First Nations and others. It is the educational capacity of museums that is so crucial here; they have the potential to challenge misunderstandings about current Aboriginal issues and to explain their historical roots. Through exhibitions and associated activities, they can also offer support to navigate the many conflicting perspectives on Aboriginal issues. Although such steps may have more immediate relevance in Canada, British museums also have a role to play. They are entering a new stage in how they represent First Nations people, where emergent forms of collaboration are replacing more entrenched curatorial approaches that ignore First Nations views, hopes, and goals. Indeed, this new stage is very much focused on people, whereas those of the past privileged artifacts. It is my hope that this book will encourage museum staff to reflect upon institutional histories of representation and how these histories can be reconfigured to develop meaningful partnerships with tangible benefits for First Nations and museums alike.

Notes

Introduction

1 A founder of anthropology in Britain, Professor Alfred Cort Haddon (1855-1940) trained first as a natural scientist at the University of Cambridge and then moved to Dublin, where he taught at the College of Science. In 1888 he participated in a scientific expedition to the Torres Strait, where he witnessed the impact of European and Australian colonial influences on the lives of local people and became increasingly interested in the study of human life and culture. He returned to Cambridge in 1894, and in 1898 he led the Cambridge Anthropological Expedition to the Torres Strait, a seminal event in the history of anthropology due to the comprehensive nature of its fieldwork (Herle and Philp 1998; Herle and Rouse 1998). Haddon was instrumental in developing the teaching of anthropology at Cambridge University and was also directly involved in managing the Museum of Archaeology and Anthropology.

2 The Victoria Memorial Museum's name has changed several times since its foundation, and I use the names interchangeably according to the period to which I refer. It became the National Museum of Canada in 1927 and was subsequently titled the Canadian Museum of Civilization in 1986 when it relocated to Gatineau, Quebec. A 2012 announcement revealed that it would be renamed the Canadian Museum of History and would undergo a major renovation timed to be completed in 2017, the 150th anniversary of Confederation.

3 It is important to note that, though this book makes some broad statements using the collective "First Nations, Métis, and Inuit," it focuses on relations between museums and First Nations, and does not attempt to encompass museum relations with other indigenous peoples in Canada, though there may be parallel issues. In addition, I use the term "First Nations" in the knowledge that extremely diverse views exist within and between communities regarding museums, and that these can and do shift in relation to experiences of various institutions. It should also be remembered that the improved working relations between many Canadian museums and First Nations, Métis, and Inuit are not necessarily replicated in relations with indigenous peoples from other countries.

4 Perspectives on the controversy and its impact on Canadian museum practice can be found in, for example, Harrison (1988, 1993); Nicks (1992); McCloughlin (1993); and Devine (2010).

5　There is an extensive literature on how Canadian museums have responded to the suggestions of the two reports and on the unequal relations between museums and people of First Nations, Métis, and Inuit heritage that precipitated change within the sector. Examples of curatorial shifts in specific institutions can be found in Ames (1999, 2000); Hanna (1999); Jessup and Bagg (2002); Harrison (2005a, 2005b); Conaty (2006); and Phillips (2011). Clavir (2002) and Dignard et al. (2008) address changing practices in the conservation of First Nations collections.

6　The MAA was one of the first museums in the United Kingdom, and indeed the world, to make its entire collections database available online (Robin Boast, MAA, e-mail to author, 20 April 2011). The database is a work in progress, and only a minority of records have associated digital images. It can be accessed at http://maa.cam.ac.uk/maa/. Throughout this book, I have included the MAA artifact accession numbers so that readers may consult the online database should they require further information.

7　At the MAA, for example, about 25 percent of research visits to the Anthropology section between 2005 and 2011 were made by indigenous researchers (Anita Herle, MAA, e-mail to author, 26 December 2011).

8　For example, in 1990, a number of curators of British ethnographic collections participated in a conference held in Wellington in connection with the groundbreaking Te Māori exhibition that toured New Zealand and the United States between 1984 and 1987. The exhibition and conference are widely acknowledged as having transformed how curators (whether Pakeha or from overseas) understood the *taonga* Māori they cared for in their own institutions (M. Lindsay 1991; McCarthy 2007, 146).

9　Distinguishing between local audiences and those from originating communities does not reflect the rapidly changing demographic of many urban centres. Paul Basu (2011, 37) writes about the needs of diaspora communities in relation to accessing material heritage, with a focus on collections from Sierra Leone, many of whose citizens were displaced during the Civil War of 1991-2002 and now reside in urban centres in Europe and North America. He notes, however, that his approach is not applicable to all communities and does not alter the principles that underlie calls from some marginalized people for the repatriation of ancestral remains and material heritage. One might ask how far Basu's arguments can be extended to the experiences of First Nations, many of whom are born and raised in urban centres and do not often return to their reserve.

10　See, for example, Lynch (2013) as well as the other essays that appear in "Working through Conflict in Museums: Museums, Objects and Participatory Democracy," a special issue of *Museum Management and Curatorship*.

11　There is an extensive critical literature on these controversies. For accounts of Into the Heart of Africa and its repercussions, see Cannizzo (1991); Mackey (1995); and Butler (1999). For discussions of how the Smithsonian Institution handled the proposed display of the *Enola Gay*, see Linenthal and Engelhardt (1996); Gieryn (1998); and Dubin (2007).

12　Essays by Nicholson (1985); Durrans (1988); Pierson Jones (1992); Shelton (1992); and Hunt (1993), as well as articles published in the *Journal of Museum Ethnography*, indicate the ways in which UK-based museum ethnographers were critically challenging their discipline during the late 1980s and early 1990s.

13　One of these permanent posts was established only in 2012, though an Anthropology curator was also employed on a temporary contract during the early 2000s.

14　At the time of writing, three British museums employed curatorial staff dedicated to their American collections: the Pitt Rivers Museum at Oxford University; World Museum, which is part of National Museums Liverpool; and the British Museum. The post-holders in all three are responsible for collections from throughout the Americas.

15　Hamilton (2010, 98-106) does include a brief but useful discussion of the activities of several Aboriginal people who were collectors themselves.

16 For a critique of the contact zone concept as applied to museums, see Boast (2011). See also Onciul (2013, 83-85) for discussion of what she terms "engagement zones," a model that, she suggests, resolves some of the limitations of Clifford's model, particularly as they relate to the intercommunity engagements that are often part of cross-cultural collaborative museum work.

17 This became starkly apparent during a February 2010 workshop funded by the Royal Society of Edinburgh, which I organized at the University of Aberdeen, and which was attended by Kainai, Lakota, and Cherokee individuals who had worked on international repatriation, as well as by curators from Scottish museums. The curators had been asked to give presentations on the Native American and First Nations collections for which they were responsible. With each presentation it became increasingly clear that though museum staff can be very good at *describing* artifacts, their understanding of cultural meanings is often negligible. I intend this point not as a criticism of the individuals concerned, but to illustrate both the need for dialogue and the extent of the challenges faced by curators working with ethnographic collections that are often worldwide in scope.

18 In 1998 Peers became curator of the Americas Collections, Pitt Rivers Museum, and anthropology lecturer at Oxford University. She also supervised the final two years of my doctorate.

19 Although some contemporary newspaper reports state that the expedition was connected to the British Museum, there is no conclusive evidence that this was the case.

20 I made two additional month-long research visits to Calgary in 2000 and 2001, during which I gained a unique external perspective on how the relationship between the Glenbow staff and the Blackfoot communities had strengthened as the gallery's completion drew closer.

Chapter 1: Community Contexts

1 Sam Cameron was probably referring to Donald Cadzow's 1925 visit to Swan Lake to collect for the Museum of the American Indian (MAI) (Cadzow 1926a). Campbell Matoas was chief of the Swan Lake Nation from 1924 to 1934.

2 G. Gooderham, "Twenty-Five Years as an Indian Agent to the Blackfoot Band," 28 January 1972, George H. Gooderham fonds, M-4738-394, Glenbow-Alberta Institute, Calgary.

3 Ibid., 2.

4 Wherever possible, I use the names by which individuals were (and still are) known in their own communities. As I discuss in Chapter 4, the records of the Franklin Motor Expedition identified many of these people using English translations – or mistranslations – of their names.

5 B. Blackwood, "Notes on the Sarcees. Reserve Visited July 1925," 1925, 2, Beatrice Blackwood Papers, Related Documents File, BB.A3 19-43, Pitt Rivers Museum Manuscript Collections (PRM), University of Oxford, Oxford.

6 See, for example, Inspector W.J. Chisholm's report (Department of Indian Affairs 1905, 187) for the Battleford Inspectorate, in which he claimed that progress on the Beardy's and Okemasis reserve was due primarily to "the wise counsel and kindly supervision of the officials in charge."

7 J.A. Donaghy, "History of the Swan Lake Indian Reserve and Mission from 1875-1927," 1947, 5-6, Rev. James A. Donaghy Papers (ID 3120), 1920-27, United Church of Canada Archives, Conference of Manitoba and Northwestern Ontario, University of Winnipeg, Winnipeg (UCCA).

8 Dr. F.A. Corbett to W.M. Graham, "Report of Health Conditions at Old Sun, Crowfoot, Sarcee, Ermineskin and St. Albert Schools, 07 December 1920," Report on Boarding Schools in Alberta by Dr. F.A. Corbett, 1920-22, RG 10, vol. 4,092, file 546,898, Library and Archives Canada (LAC), Ottawa.

9 B. Blackwood, "Diary of North American Trip 1924-27," 3 August 1925, Beatrice Blackwood Papers, B.12.10, PRM.

10 D.G. Mandelbaum, Field notebook, vol. 2, 1935a, 16, David G. Mandelbaum fonds, R-875, file 5.i, Saskatchewan Archives Board, Regina (SAB).

11 Museums benefited directly from state-supported attacks on the Potlatch. The most promin-'ent case was the 1922 seizure of goods and the prosecution of participants in Dan Cranmer's Potlatch at 'Mimkwamlis (Village Island), Alert Bay, British Columbia. Most of the masks and regalia were divided between the Victoria Memorial Museum and the Royal Ontario Museum, Toronto. Some pieces were sold to George Heye for the MAI, and Deputy Superintendent General of Indian Affairs D.C. Scott kept others for his private collection. Most of the treasures in public museums have since been repatriated to the U'Mista Cultural Society, but the whereabouts of an undetermined number remain unclear (Loo 1992; Jacknis 1996b; Harkin 2005).

12 Peigan [Piikani] Nation members to the DIA, 11 February 1915 (copy), RG 10, vol. 3,826, file 60,511-3, LAC.

13 See Hallowell (1936) for discussion of the Midewiwin in the Lake Winnipeg region. Hallowell (ibid., 38) refers to Donald Cadzow's 1925 visit to the Long Plain and Swan Lake reserves, where he observed that the dominion government had banned the expression of Midewiwin beliefs and the use of associated ceremonial materials (Cadzow 1926a). For an overview of the role of the Midewiwin in Anishinaabe society, see Angel (2002).

14 Donaghy, "History of the Swan Lake Indian Reserve," 26, UCCA.

15 Collected missionaries to D.C. Scott, 23 July 1923, RG 10, vol. 3,827, file 60,511-4B, LAC.

16 T.A. Moore to J.W. McLean, 30 August 1912, RG 10, vol. 3,826, file 60,511-3, LAC, quoted in Dempsey (2008, 55).

17 *An Act to Amend the Indian Act,* SC 1914, c. 35, 4-5 Geo. V, quoted in Department of Indian and Northern Affairs (1981, 132).

18 D.G. Mandelbaum, Field notebook, vol. 4, 1935b, 54, R-875, file 5.i, SAB.

19 Chief Red Dog to D.C. Scott, February 1918, RG 10, vol. 3,826, file 60,511-4, pt. 1, LAC.

20 There are numerous archival references to the war effort contributions made by the four File Hills reserves. Though First Nations men were exempt from military service, most File Hills men who were of age enlisted, handicrafts were sold to raise funds for the Red Cross, and the loyalty of the File Hills people to the cause is said to have far outstripped that of nearby settler communities (Graham 1991, 97-101).

21 Mandelbaum, Field notebook, vol. 2, 36-37, SAB.

22 D.G. Mandelbaum, Field notebook, vol. 5, 1935c, 28, R-875, file 5.i, SAB.

23 Although this occurred several years after Cadzow had last visited Swan Lake, the community leaders seem to have viewed him as a potential ally.

24 Chief Matoose to D.A. Cadzow, 20 April 1932, RG 10, vol. 3,827, file 60,511-4B, LAC.

25 D.A. Cadzow to D.C. Scott, 3 May 1932, RG 10, vol. 3,827, file 60,511-4B, LAC. "Bungi," or "Bungee," was first used by fur traders in Southern Manitoba to describe the Western or Plains Ojibwe (Peers 1994, xvi). The ethnonym "Saulteaux" was also used to refer to these peoples. By the 1920s some commentators were noting that "Bungay" was a nickname (MacLean 1924, 397). The Swan Lake people today refer to themselves as Anishinaabe.

26 A.G. Hamilton to D.A. Cadzow, 23 May 1932, RG 10, vol. 3,827, file 60,511-4B, LAC.

27 Blackwood, "Diary of North American Trip," 16 August 1925, PRM. Harlan I. Smith (1872-1940) is best known for his research on the Northwest Coast, most particularly his participation in the Jesup North Pacific Expedition (1897-1902) and his involvement with the Totem Pole Preservation Committee, established in the 1920s following a public outcry about the removal of totem poles from Canada by overseas collectors (Cole 1985, 267-71; see also Dawn 2006).

28 See Brown, Peers, and members of the Kainai Nation (2006, 47-77) for discussion of this point as it relates to the fieldwork of anthropologist Beatrice Blackwood, who visited several Western Canadian reserves during the 1920s.

Chapter 2: Collecting on the Prairies

1 It should be noted that Boas distinguished between smaller institutions and large metropolitan museums organized by scientific principles. He also recognized that diverse audiences used museum services and that museums could provide a range of educational functions (Boas 1905, 1907).

2 D.A. Cadzow to L.C.G. Clarke, 27 December 1928, Cadzow Family Private Collection (CF); Untitled clipping, *Edmonton Journal,* 21 August 1928, RG 10, vol. 6,816, file 486-6-1, pt. 1, Library and Archives Canada, Ottawa (LAC); *Calgary Albertan,* 30 July 1930, Newspaper Clipping Files, Indians – Culture, Glenbow-Alberta Institute, Calgary (GAI). The *Albertan* article describes an expedition led by artist and writer Paul Coze "to study Indian civilization and take back relics for French museums." It included natural scientists, ethnographers, a filmmaker, and a journalist (Raymond Gid), who prepared its official reports and made sound recordings. Coze led four expeditions to Western Canada between 1928 and 1934 on behalf of the Musée d'Ethnographie (Trocadero) in Paris and the Heye Foundation in New York. In the 1990s, the Royal Alberta Museum in Edmonton acquired over a hundred artifacts from his personal collection, along with photographs and paintings.

3 For example, Edward Hopkins's collection in the Pitt Rivers Museum, Oxford University, which was assembled in the early 1840s when he accompanied the governor of the Hudson's Bay Company on a trip round the world, includes several artifacts from the Northern Plains (Peers 1999b). Other notable collections from this period are those of the Palliser Expedition, now at Kew Gardens, London, and that of James Carnegie, the Ninth Earl of Southesk, assembled during his 1859-60 hunting trip through Western Canada. This collection was kept in the family castle in Scotland until 2006, when much of the Métis and Northern Plains material was purchased by the Royal Alberta Museum (Berry 2011).

4 As noted in the Introduction, the museum will become the Canadian Museum of History to mark the 150th anniversary of Confederation. Some critics of this plan state that the revised name and mandate fail to acknowledge that Aboriginal people's presence predates the founding of Canada.

5 Dorsey acquired 136 artifacts during his visit to the Kainai reserve. These are described in VanStone (1992).

6 D. Jenness to H. Smith, 16 May 1928, Diamond Jenness Correspondence, Field Instructions, 1926-37, box 661, f. 41, Canadian Museum of Civilization, Gatineau (CMC).

7 E. Sapir to L.L. Bolton, 23 May 1925, Edward Sapir Correspondence, Wintemberg, W.J., 1911-25, box 637, f. 36, CMC.

8 Some families with Aboriginal ancestry chose to suppress this heritage, and though they sometimes retained artifacts connected to it, both they and the associated stories were often hidden (Brown, Massan, and Grant 2011). By contrast, some individuals wore identifiably Native clothing, such as mittens and moccasins, out of choice or necessity. Wearing such items is, of course, very different from creating formal and static displays of First Nations objects, but it is worth remembering that material expressions of First Nations culture have always been visible in many ways to those who choose to look.

9 Anon., "Natural History Museum Will Be Established in Calgary in Near Future," *Calgary Herald,* 25 January 1912, Newspaper Clipping Files, Museums – Alberta – Calgary, GAI.

10 J. Thurston, quoted in "Museum Idea Is for Education," *Calgary Herald,* 1 March 1929, Newspaper Clipping Files, Museums – Alberta – Calgary – Calgary Museum, GAI.

11 Mrs. E. Lavington to the Curator, 28 January 1931, Calgary Public Museum fonds, M-2111, file 17, GAI.

12 Alberta's other major museum of cultural history is the Glenbow Museum in Calgary, which houses significant artifact and archival collections relating to the people of Western Canada, as well as internationally important collections of art. The core of the collection was assembled

by Eric Harvie, a lawyer and businessman, who began acquiring artifacts connected to the history of Western Canada in the 1950s. Having established the Glenbow Foundation in 1954, he and his family donated the collection to the people of Alberta in 1966. As these collections were established after the period addressed in this chapter, I have omitted them from the discussion.

13 In Britain, as in other parts of Europe, popular imagery of First Nations people was largely informed by romanticized notions of Indianness – the noble (or ignoble) savage, the ecological Indian, the fearsome warrior, the Indian princess, and so on. These characterizations were exacerbated by the limited interaction between British and indigenous people, and by the images produced by Hollywood, advertising, and the Wild West shows. Such stereotypes are less firmly entrenched than they were even ten or twenty years ago. Nevertheless, although the public is rather better informed nowadays, lack of understanding about the realities of life for many First Nations and Native American people remains widespread.

14 D. Jenness to L.C.G. Clarke, 17 December 1928, Diamond Jenness Correspondence, Clarke, Louis C.G., 1928-37, box 642, f. 7, CMC.

15 D. Jenness to L.C.G. Clarke, 11 November 1937, Diamond Jenness Correspondence, Clarke, Louis C.G., 1928-37, box 642, f. 7, CMC.

16 L.C.G. Clarke to E. Sapir, 10 November 1923, Edward Sapir Correspondence, Clarke, Louis C.G., 1923, box 622, f. 13, CMC.

17 E. Sapir to L.C.G. Clarke, 23 November 1923, Edward Sapir Correspondence, Clarke, Louis C.G., 1923, box 622, f. 13, CMC.

18 D. Jenness to W.H. Collins, 22 April 1926, Diamond Jenness Correspondence, National Museum of Canada, Director (W.H. Collins), 1926-27, box 652, f. 1, CMC; W. Malcolm, Acting Director, to F.F. Cosgrove, Canadian Government Exhibition Commission, 18 November 1929, Diamond Jenness Correspondence, Imperial Institute, 1929, box 646, f. 23, CMC.

19 Examples include Haudenosaunee material in Liverpool's World Museum, which was donated in 1913 by an individual named "Chief Hiawatha" (Phillips 2005, 89-97), and Lakota artifacts in Glasgow Museums, acquired from interpreter George Crager during the 1891-92 visit of Buffalo Bill's Wild West Show to the city (Maddra 1996).

20 Following Clarke's departure to take up the directorship of Cambridge University's Fitzwilliam Museum, Paterson became the MAA curator in 1938 and was succeeded by Bushnell, who was curator from 1948 to 1970.

21 Clarke was also a generous benefactor to other institutions, including the British Museum and the Victoria and Albert Museum in London and the Fitzwilliam Museum, which received the bulk of his vast personal collection of pictorial and decorative arts (Anon. 1961, 454).

22 G. Dawson to E.B. Tylor, 15 March 1897, RG 45, no. 124, Director's Letter Books, LAC, quoted in Avrith (1986, 231).

23 C. Harrison to E.B. Tylor, 10 May 1900, Edward B. Tylor Papers, box 17, folder 1, Pitt Rivers Museum, Oxford (PRM).

24 These items, and the associated museum documentation, can be viewed on the AMNH collection database at http://anthro.amnh.org/anthro_coll.shtml.

25 D.C. Duvall to C. Wissler, 12 October 1904, David C. Duvall fonds, M-4376, 3, 741, GAI.

26 Phillip Godsell (1889-1961) found fame by writing adventure stories that were based on his experiences in the Canadian Arctic and Subarctic. This letter to Jenness was written shortly after he retired from the HBC.

27 D. Jenness to P.H. Godsell, 14 October 1929, Diamond Jenness Correspondence, Godsell, P.H., 1929-39, box 645, f. 8, CMC.

28 D. Jenness to W.H. Collins, 31 May 1926, Diamond Jenness Correspondence, National Museum of Canada. Director (W.H. Collins), 1926-27, box 652, f. 1, CMC. The "party" to whom Jenness referred was Donald A. Cadzow.

29 P.H. Godsell to Diamond Jenness, undated August 1929, Diamond Jenness Correspondence, Godsell, P.H., 1929-39, box 645, f. 8, CMC.

30 For discussions of the relationship between anthropology, the state, and indigenous peoples in Canada, see Kulchyski (1993); Harrison and Darnell (2006); and Peyton and Hancock (2008).

31 D.C. Scott to D. Jenness, 11 January 1927, RG 10, vol. 6,816, file 486-6-1, pt. 1, LAC.

32 David Martínez (2008, 80) also reminds us that by the early twentieth century, a number of Native Americans had become anthropologists and were collecting for museums; examples include Ella Deloria (Yankton Dakota), Francis LaFelsche (Omaha), James Murie (Delaware), and Arthur C. Parker (Seneca).

33 E. Sapir to D.C. Scott, 19 February 1915, Edward Sapir Correspondence, D.C. Scott, 1912-18, box 633, f. 15, CMC.

34 D.C. Scott to E. Sapir, 22 February 1915, Edward Sapir Correspondence, D.C. Scott, 1912-18, box 633, f. 15, CMC.

35 As recently as 2004, beadwork owned by Joseph T. Faunt, who worked as an Indian agent on several Alberta reserves in the 1920s, was donated to National Museums Scotland.

36 Robert N. Wilson (1863-1944) worked as a trader before becoming the Indian agent on the Piikani (1898-1903) and Kainai reserves (1904-11). Unlike some of his colleagues, he appears to have been sympathetic toward his charges and became increasingly concerned that government policies were deliberately forcing Blackfoot people (and the Kainai in particular) into poverty and increased dependency (Wilson 1921). Several Blackfoot items he collected are now in the Field Museum of Natural History, Chicago, and his notes and photographs are in the Glenbow Archives, Calgary.

37 R.N. Wilson to D.C. Scott, 3 December 1913, RG 10, vol. 8,619, file 1/1-15-6, pt. 1, LAC.

38 D.C. Scott to R.N. Wilson, 16 December 1913, RG 10, vol. 8,619, file 1/1-15-6, pt. 1, LAC.

39 R.W. Brock to D.C. Scott, 16 February 1914, RG 10, vol. 8,619, file 1/1-15-6, pt. 1, LAC. These items, which are now at the Canadian Museum of Civilization, have the following registration information: shield and cover [V-B-38 a-c] and shield [V-B-39] (Morgan Baillargeon, CMC, e-mail to author, 2 November 2005).

40 D.C. Scott to D. Jenness, 17 March 1927, Diamond Jenness Correspondence, Dept. of Indian Affairs D.C. Scott, 1926-29, box 643, f. 2, CMC.

41 D. Jenness to D.C. Scott, 25 March 1927, Diamond Jenness Correspondence, Dept. of Indian Affairs D.C. Scott, 1926-29, box 643, f. 2, CMC.

42 W. Graham to J.T. Faunt, 2 September 1920, Blood Indian Agency Papers, correspondence, 1923-24, M-1788/128, GAI.

43 Blackwood, "Diary of North American Trip," 29 July 1925, PRM.

44 The catalogue information for this piece [1935.32.13] can be found at the Pitt Rivers Museum website, http://www.prm.ox.ac.uk/databases.html.

45 D.C. Scott to S.H. Hooke, 12 January 1926, RG 10, vol. 6,816, file 486-6-1, pt. 1, LAC.

46 Samuel H. Hooke (1874-1968) was a Biblical scholar with interests in anthropology and archaeology. In 1927 he critiqued the analysis of the Sun Dance in Wissler's *Relation of Nature to Man in Aboriginal America* (1926) but made no specific reference to his own Canadian fieldwork (Hooke 1927). William J. Perry (1887-1949) was a cultural anthropologist who specialized in the history of religion. Although both men published extensively on comparative religion, no evidence has yet been located that they conducted research in Western Canada.

Chapter 3: Collecting in Action

1 Anthropologists paid comparatively high prices for their purchases, which did not escape the notice of First Nations individuals who carved a niche for themselves as middlemen and

maintained a business relationship with them from a distance. In 1930, for instance, Donald Cadzow received a number of pieces "on approval" from a Peigan man, which he offered to the University Museum at Philadelphia (D.A. Cadzow to J. Alden Mason, 10 October 1930, John Alden Mason Papers, B/M384, American Philosophical Society, Philadelphia).

2   For a related study, see May's (2010, 9) discussion of the 1948 Arnhem Land Expedition. Although the expedition was well publicized when it took place, the collections it assembled were, she writes, "acutely lacking in context."

3   Most of the expedition documentation used the ethnonym "Bungay" or "Bungi." The associated community is Swan Lake First Nation. "Sarsi" refers to the Tsuu T'ina Nation, and "North Blackfoot" applies to the Siksika Nation. It should be noted that "Northern Blackfoot" was also used in some contexts to refer to the Piikani in Canada, as their name in Blackfoot – *Apatohsipiikani* – translates as Northern Piikani. This distinguishes them from the Blackfeet in Montana, who in Blackfoot are called the *Amsskaapipiikani,* or Southern Piikani. Finally, although the documentation used the American-English spelling of Piegan, the Franklin Motor Expedition did not visit the Montana Blackfeet and collected only at the Peigan reserve in Southern Alberta. This community today is known as the Piikani Nation.

4   On the reverse of the collection inventory is a "Hotel Classification" key, devised by Robert Rymill to grade the facilities of the establishments in which he stayed on his travels throughout Europe, the South Pacific, and North America.

5   When I began the research, the MAA archives had no visual records of the expedition, but three photographs were subsequently donated by the Donald A. Cadzow family and have been accessioned as P.45592-P.45594. A copy of the film footage was donated to the MAA by Robert Rymill's family in 2010, and the section filmed at File Hills was included in the 2011 exhibition titled James Henderson: Wicite Owapi Wicasa, the Man Who Paints the Old Men, hosted by the Mendel Art Gallery, Saskatoon.

6   On the teaching of anthropology at Cambridge, see Rouse (1998).

7   D.A. Cadzow to E.K. Burnett, 23 July 1953, Museum of the American Indian/Heye Foundation Records, box 206, folder 25, National Museum of the American Indian Archive Center, Smithsonian Institution, Washington, DC (NMAI).

8   Memorandum of Expenses of Kechipauan Expedition, 1923, Notes and Correspondence Relating to the Museum of the American Indian, Heye Foundation, 1920s, W03/1/3, Museum of Archaeology and Anthropology, Cambridge (MAA). This excavation was part of the Hendricks-Hodge Expedition (1916-23), the first major expedition undertaken by the MAI (Martinez and Wyaco 1998, 97-106).

9   In 1927 Cadzow joined the Putnam Baffin Island Expedition, which undertook archaeological survey work in Labrador (Cadzow 1928).

10 D.A. Cadzow to L.C.G. Clarke, 23 October 1926, letters box 1926, MAA.

11 The written documentation and several photographs relating to the Franklin Motor Expedition are part of Donald A. Cadzow's personal papers and are cared for by his family. Robert Rymill's family also has photographs taken on the expedition, some of which Rymill organized into an album with captions. The film footage is jointly owned by the families of John Rymill and Robert Rymill.

12 T.W. Mitchell, "Midway Peak," n.d., 101, Mitchell Family Papers, ML MSS 2228, box 1, State Library of New South Wales, Sydney.

13 Due to Clarke's generosity, the MAA's Native American collection is the second-largest in the United Kingdom, outstripped only by that of the British Museum.

14 Many UK museums contain ethnographic material that can be traced to either Webster or Oldman. See Waterfield and King (2007, 54-77) for biographical information on these dealers.

15 According to his fellowship certificate, which is held in the Royal Geographical Society archives, Robert Rymill hoped to explore the interior of South America after his return from

Canada. Following the Wall Street crash, however, he returned home to Penola, South Australia, to assist with running the family estate (Béchervaise 1995, 104). Though his career led him in a different direction, he nonetheless maintained an interest in anthropology and museums for some time. In the 1930s he considered accepting an appointment as a curator in Singapore, though he eventually decided to remain in Australia (Gladys Rymill, author interview, Penola, South Australia, 5 March 1999).

16 Records relating to Donald Cadzow's career can be found in the Museum of the American Indian/Heye Foundation Records at the National Museum of the American Indian Archive Center, Smithsonian Institution; the State Museum of Pennsylvania; the Rochester Museum and Science Center; and the American Philosophical Society (see also Custer 1996, 61-63).

17 A. Skinner, "Biographical Sketch of D.A. Cadzow," n.d., box 229, folder 17, NMAI.

18 D.A. Cadzow to G.B. Gordon, 10 January 1917, Correspondence from the Director's Office, G.B. Gordon, box 3/14 C, University of Pennsylvania Museum, Philadelphia.

19 Skinner, "Biographical Sketch of D.A. Cadzow," NMAI.

20 D.A. Cadzow to L.C.G. Clarke, draft letter 1928, Cadzow Family, Private Collection (CF).

21 D.A. Cadzow to L.C.G. Clarke, 27 December 1928, CF.

22 Ibid.

23 Ibid. The name "Keevisk" appears in census data and treaty pay lists as "Keewist," "Keevisk," or "Keewisk." At my request, Noel Starblanket consulted his relatives about this name. They explained that the man was called *kīwisk,* but they were uncertain as to the translation of his name and whether it was an abbreviated version of a longer name (Noel Starblanket, e-mail to author, 20 December 2011). For a list of the medicines Cadzow acquired from *kīwisk* during his 1925 expedition, see D. Cadzow, "Catalogue of Specimens Collected from the Prairie Cree, on the Piapot, Muskepetin, Daystar, File Hills, Touchwood, Poorman, and Starblanket Reserves, Saskatchewan," 1925, box 198, folder 13, NMAI.

24 D.A. Cadzow to R. Rymill, 1 February 1929, CF.

25 R.R. Rymill to D.A. Cadzow, 18 January 1929, CF.

26 The Natural History Museum has no record of correspondence from the team members, and their families were not aware that zoological collecting was part of the expedition's agenda. The Rymill brothers certainly hunted during the trip but for their own amusement. They had neither the experience nor the resources to accommodate the requirements of a specialized natural history museum.

27 D.C. Scott to Officials, Department of Indian Affairs, 4 June 1929, CF.

28 L.C.G. Clarke and E. Minns to whom it may concern, 18 May 1929, CF.

29 Cadzow to Rymill, 1 February 1929, CF.

30 Rymill to Cadzow, 18 January 1929, CF.

31 G. Heye to L.C.G. Clarke, 25 February 1929, Notes and Correspondence Relating to the Museum of the American Indian, Heye Foundation, 1920s, W03/1/3, MAA.

32 Cadzow to Clarke, 27 December 1928, CF. According to archival staff at the Wellcome Trust, Wellcome's papers contain no record that he was contacted about the Franklin Motor Expedition (Annie Lindsay, e-mail to author, 18 January 1999). For the collections of Henry Wellcome, see Arnold and Olsen (2003) and Larson (2009).

33 D.A. Cadzow to L.C.G. Clarke, 3 April 1929, CF.

34 Cadzow to Clarke, draft letter 1928, CF.

35 Cadzow to Clarke, 27 December 1928, CF. Documentary evidence in Cadzow's papers and the Rochester Museum and Science Center archives suggests that Clarke, Cadzow, and the Rymills hoped to send an expedition to St. Lawrence Island, west of Alaska, after the Franklin Motor Expedition had ended. In addition, a 1930 biographical sketch of Cadzow reported that "the work being done by Cambridge University and the British Museum is designed to unveil the mystery of the origin of [the] first Americans" (Anon. 1930a, 24). The onset of

the Depression seems to have terminated these plans, although, as noted above, John Rymill undertook expeditions to both the Arctic and Antarctic during the 1930s.

36 Based in Syracuse, New York, the H.H. Franklin Manufacturing Company was in business from 1902 to 1934, during which time it produced the most successful luxury air-cooled cars in the United States (Powell 1999).

37 See also D. Cadzow, "Diary 1926. For specimens for Museum," CF.

38 Talking Stone is referred to as "Speaking Stone" in some documentation in the National Museum of the American Indian Archive Center, Smithsonian Institution. According to Anishinaabe linguist Roger Roulette, this is a more accurate translation of his name (Roger Roulette, e-mail to author, 26 April 2010). Wayne Scott, from Swan Lake First Nation, explained that Gennahmodhi means the "throat of a stork" and that it probably refers to the sac where the bird carries fish (Wayne Scott, e-mail to author, 28 July 2010).

39 Cadzow's use of kichimotos may refer to Gichi-manidoos (Roger Roulette, e-mail to author, 26 April 2010).

40 Sergt. R.H. Nicholson, Crime Report re George Tanner, Swan Lake Reserve, Man. Illegal Dancing, Indian Act, RCMP Brandon Detachment, 25 July 1926, RG 10, vol. 3,827, file 60,511-4B, Library and Archives Canada, Ottawa (LAC).

41 J.A. Donaghy, "History of the Swan Lake Indian Reserve and Mission from 1875-1927," 1947, 28-29, Rev. James A. Donaghy Papers (ID 3120), 1920-27, United Church of Canada Archives, Winnipeg (UCCA).

42 The handwriting for these notes is that of Curator Geoffrey Bushnell, which dates the loss of the items to 1948-70.

43 The Indian Claims Commission (2004, 175) reported that the Crown decision to implement a farming scheme on Peepeekisis reserve land without the knowledge and consent of the band was in breach of Treaty 4, the Indian Act, and the Crown's fiduciary obligation.

44 Bednasek notes that the term "original members" is contested in the Peepeekisis community, which disagrees regarding what constitutes "original." Following his lead, however, I have chosen to retain this division.

45 D. Mandelbaum to C. Wissler, 22 July 1934, David G. Mandelbaum Correspondence, Division of Anthropology, American Museum of Natural History, New York (AMNH).

46 Ibid.

47 D. Mandelbaum to C. Wissler, 6 September 1934, AMNH.

48 The AMNH has placed online extensive information about its holdings, including images of artifacts and scans of related manuscript records. The bundle is included in the online catalogue, but it should be noted that each constituent part has been separated out and photographed individually, which reflects curatorial practice that some may consider to be culturally disrespectful. AMNH, Division of Anthropology, North American Ethnographic Collection, http://anthro.amnh.org/north.

49 Arok Wolvengrey, Doreen Oakes, and Barry Ahenakew note that mostāhtik's name can be interpreted as "'Simply Wood' or 'Bare Wood' (i.e., without bark)" (Arok Wolvengrey, e-mail to author, 25 November 2011).

50 Arok Wolvengrey, Doreen Oakes, and Barry Ahenakew suggest the following interpretation for sāpostahikan: "'Needle; Awl' (cf. the verb stem sāpostah – 'pierce s.t. through with a needle'; the /ikan/ ending indicates that this is an item which is used in the accomplishment of the verbal action). It may refer to some other piercing instrument, such as an 'awl,' since the more usual word for 'needle' is sāponikan." Wolvengrey notes that as the name is in the form of a concrete noun, he and his colleagues have suggested "needle" or "awl" (Arok Wolvengrey, e-mail to author, 25 November 2011). David Mandelbaum (1996, 4) stated that one of his main informants was "Sapostahikan," whose name he translated as "Shooting-through."

51 D.A. Cadzow, "Field Notebook and Diary, 1917," box 193, folder 10, NMAI; see also Lenz (2004).

52 D.A. Cadzow to L.C.G. Clarke, 24 September 1929, CF.

53 Notes Referring to the Rymill Collection of Artefacts from Canadian Indians, 1929, FA5/1/2, MAA.

54 During her July 1925 visit to the Tsuu T'ina reserve, Beatrice Blackwood of the Pitt Rivers Museum commented, "There are 158 Indians on the Reserve – not all pure Sarcees. The numbers were decreasing up till four years ago when Dr. Murray [the Indian agent] went there – in 1921 the births and deaths balanced. Since then there has been a slight increase." B. Blackwood, "Diary of North American Trip 1924-27," 30 July 1925, Beatrice Blackwood Papers, B.12.10, Pitt Rivers Museum, Oxford.

55 D.A. Cadzow to E.K. Burnett, 25 May 1958, box 206, folder 25, NMAI. The NMAI has twelve items in its collection that Cadzow acquired at the Tsuu T'ina Nation.

56 For unknown reasons, the piece's original catalogue card no longer exists, and a label attached to its replacement offers a far more detailed interpretation than Rymill's brief notes normally provided. The label reads, "Puma skin, painted on the inner side with black and red ochre paint. The black figures represent the enemy, red figures the Sarsi. The man with the feathers in his hair is the owner of the skin. Reading the design from the head of the animal down: the owner shoots an enemy and the friend scalps him, the owner shoots at a buffalo with a bow and arrow, the owner takes part in a fight against some of the enemy who are behind cover, probably in a buffalo wallow, the owner steals a horse, two of the enemy shoot at him but miss him, the three scalps show that the men were killed by the raiding party." This item was illustrated by Colin Taylor (1975, 76), who may have provided the interpretation.

57 The photographs were subsequently bound into five volumes, with biographical details provided by George Gooderham, Indian agent at the Siksika Nation (Godsell and Gooderham 1955).

58 D.A. Cadzow to A.C. Parker, 10 November 1929, Primary files, ACC 1930.124, Rochester Museum and Science Center, Rochester, New York. The Lupson Collection is considerably better documented than the Rymill Collection, and most pieces are accompanied by the name of their owner or seller.

59 Siksika participants in an April 2010 Glenbow Museum workshop on Blackfoot collections in British museums made similar comments to the author.

60 H.I. Smith to D. Jenness, 23 October 1929, Diamond Jenness Correspondence, Harlan I. Smith, 1926-27, box 657, f. 50, Canadian Museum of Civilization, Gatineau.

61 D.A. Cadzow to E.K. Burnett, 5 June 1958, box 206, folder 25, NMAI.

62 D.A. Cadzow to E.K. Burnett, 19 March 1957 and 29 December 1958, box 206, folder 25, NMAI.

63 D.A. Cadzow to E.K. Burnett, 13 October 1958, box 206, folder 25, NMAI.

64 Cadzow, "Diary 1926. For Specimens for Museum," 12 August 1926, CF.

65 Cadzow to Clarke, 24 September 1929, CF.

66 Sergt. A. Webb, Report re Sun Dance Peigan Reserve 1929, RCMP Lethbridge Sub-District, Macleod Detachment, 22 July 1929, RG 10, vol. 3,827, file 60,511-4B, LAC.

67 The original photograph, which is now lost, was probably sent to the H.H. Franklin Manufacturing Company, who printed *Air-Cooled Adventure among the Aborigines*. The Rymill Collection does include a woman's buckskin dress [1930.1077], but the image in *Air-Cooled Adventure* is too poor to determine whether it is the same one.

68 This copy was made from a print in the personal collection of Adolf Hungry Wolf, who has published many books on Blackfoot history and culture. After receiving the print from a relative, he had a copy made for the Glenbow Archives (Adolf Hungry Wolf, pers. comm., 5 June 2004). Hungry Wolf did not know how his relative acquired the photograph, but it was probably sent to *Immoyiikimii* by Rymill or Cadzow, as there is no other logical explanation. As mentioned above, Cadzow maintained a business connection with at least one Piikani individual from whom he received a number of pieces in 1930, so the photograph

probably came from him. Cadzow to Mason, 10 October 1930, American Philosophical Society.

69 Meeting of the Museums Committee, October 1929, Museums Committee Minutes Book, 140, MM1/2/6, MAA.

Chapter 4: Representing Collecting

1 Choosing to ignore this advice, the expedition team acquired a tipi cover and door [1930.845A-B] at the File Hills from *kâ-pimohtêt*.

2 There are, of course, some exceptions. Clark Wissler, for instance, named David Duvall as co-author on one of the six volumes on the Blackfoot published by the American Museum of Natural History (reprinted in 1995 by the University of Nebraska Press), and Franz Boas and George Hunt (1905, 1906) co-authored two volumes of reports for the Jesup North Pacific Expedition.

3 The National Museum of the American Indian (NMAI) accession number for this bundle is 14/3170. Cadzow's notes in the NMAI archives show that he paid sixty dollars for it, which was the largest amount he spent on a single item during that summer's fieldwork (D.A. Cadzow, "Catalogue of Specimens Collected from the Prairie Cree, on the Piapot, Muskepetin, Daystar, File Hills, Touchwood, Poorman and Starblanket Reserves," 1925, MAI/Heye Foundation Records, box 198, folder 13, National Museum of the American Indian Archive Center, Smithsonian Institution, Washington, DC, NMAI).

4 Regarding the name "Makistukwam," Arok Wolvengrey suggests that it is "most likely to be *mahkistikwân* 'Big Head,' which is a fairly common name which has been recorded in Cree and in translation previously" (Arok Wolvengrey, e-mail to author, 2 January 2012).

5 D.A. Cadzow, "Diary 1926. For Specimens for Museum," 12 June 1926, Cadzow Family, Private Collection (CF); see also Bell, Brown, and Gordon (2013).

6 See Pauline Wakeham (2008) for a discussion of the intersection of romanticized notions of aboriginality, wildlife, and the frontier in Banff.

7 This image is reproduced in Boast, Guha, and Herle (2001, 2).

8 An independent trader at Rampart House in Gwich'in territory in the Yukon, Daniel Cadzow was a keen amateur photographer (see Vyvyan 1998, 280). A number of his photographs are part of the Donald A. Cadzow Photograph Collection, 1882-1919, at the National Museum of the American Indian, Smithsonian Institution; others are housed at the Glenbow Archives (Engelstad 2013, 22).

9 Cadzow, "Diary 1926. For Specimens for Museum," 10 June 1926, CF. Cadzow's colleague Kenneth Miller accompanied him on the 1926 trip.

10 The accession number of these items is 1930.726A-B. Given the similarity between the smoke lodge outfit collected by Cadzow from *kâ-mostoswahcâpêw* in 1926 and the visual evidence described here, it is probable that *kâ-mostoswahcâpêw* was the source of the smoke lodge outfit now in the MAA.

11 *mihkostikwân* was identified by Willard Starblanket, 2 July 1999.

12 The crowds were not to know that the H.H. Franklin Manufacturing Company would not survive the Depression years. Production ceased in 1934. Cadzow's Franklin did rather better and was used by his family until it was scrapped in 1943 (Nannette Burhman, author interview, Harrisburg, Pennsylvania, 4 August 1998).

Chapter 5: Reflecting on the Franklin Motor Expedition

1 As in earlier chapters, I draw most extensively on the perspectives of Swan Lake, File Hills, and Piikani people. The Rymill Collection contains material from other First Nations (such

as the Wahpeton Dakota, Tsuu T'ina, and Siksika), but as most came from Swan Lake, the File Hills (specifically the Star Blanket Nation), and the Piikani Nation, this shaped the direction of the research. Responses to the Rymill Collection from members of the other communities can be found in Brown (2000).

2 At this point, I was no longer an MAA employee, a fact that worked in my favour; I was ethically unable to answer questions concerning the museum's repatriation policy, but I could provide contact information for the appropriate staff. Had I still worked for the museum, progressing beyond the topic of repatriation might have been difficult. Furthermore, my intent was to learn, and this meant attending community events as well as formal meetings. I have since been told by several people who contributed to this book that, unlike some curators, who have tight schedules and can come across as in a rush to get what they want, I took the time to get to know people as people, rather than solely wanting to learn about their views on museums.

3 See Innes (2009) for a discussion of the politics of doing anthropological research with Prairie First Nations communities.

4 In this phase of the fieldwork, I conducted thirty-four formal interviews, and interviewees approved the transcripts; in other instances, I summarized the main points of conversation in handwritten notes that I created during or after a discussion.

5 For descriptions of how some of these materials were used, based on analysis of historical records, see Angel (2002).

6 Note that the plural form of Anishinaabe is Anishinaabeg (Alan Corbiere, e-mail to author, 2 January 2012).

7 Museums should never assume that First Nation communities will always want to reconnect physically with artifacts from the past, and this is especially so when sensitive materials are involved. See Peers (2003) for a case study on this issue that also concerns materials in a British museum.

8 Noel Starblanket himself is a prominent political leader, having been president of the National Indian Brotherhood (now the Assembly of First Nations) for two terms between 1976 and 1980.

9 In her discussion of this case, Pettipas retains the English translations of names that are in the archival documentation, though I have chosen to use the Cree names. Four of these men were sons of *acāhkosa k-ōtakohpit: atim kâ-mihkwasit, kihiw* (Eagle/Adelard Starblanket), *kisikâw-kêhkêhk* (Day Hawk/Allan Starblanket), and *kā-otāsiw*. In English records, *kā-otāsiw's* name is usually written as either Cotasso or Kohtaso. This name refers to leggings (Noel Starblanket, e-mail to author, 15 December 2011).

10 According to Robert Rymill's inventory, the outfit also originally included an "outer cape of calfskin," though a note written on the catalogue card states that it was destroyed by moths. Notes Referring to the Rymill Collection of Artefacts from Canadian Indians, 1929, FA5/1/2, MAA.

11 Ibid.

12 Thornton (2000, 29) also reported that although *atim kâ-mihkwasit* was buried in his outfit, he left his headdress to the same Mr. McLaughlin whom he had named Strong Arm many years previously.

13 Notes Referring to the Rymill Collection of Artefacts, MAA.

14 For more extensive discussions of the role of bundles in Blackfoot life, see Conaty and Janes (1997); Hernandez (1999); Bastien (2004); R. Heavy Head (2005); Zedeño (2008); and Lokensgard (2010).

15 This interview was undertaken as part of the Blackfoot Shirts Project, co-directed by myself and Laura Peers of the Pitt Rivers Museum (Brown and Peers 2013).

16 Though, as mentioned on page 103, Cadzow did collect at least one primary bundle during his 1929 visit to the Piikani reserve.

17 Many have described their experiences in a growing and extremely helpful literature. See, for example, Phillips and Johnson (2003); Marie and Thompson (2004); Conaty (2006); Dignard et al. (2008); Phillips (2011); and Andrews (2013).

Chapter 6: Curating the Rymill Collection

1 T.A.G. Strickland was the MAA's honorary photographer during the 1920s, but no professional photographer was affiliated with the museum until the mid-twentieth century. Len Morley became the first faculty photographer around 1947 and was succeeded in 1974 by Gwil Owen, who retired in 2007. Both men were affiliated with the Anthropology and Archaeology sections as well as with the museum (Gwil Owen, e-mails to author, 16 October 2011 and 1 March 2012).

2 Meeting of the Museums Committee, October 1929, Museums Committee Minutes Book, 140, MM1/2/6, box 22, Museum of Archaeology and Anthropology, Cambridge (MAA).

3 Visitors Book, May 1884-Jan. 1932, MM1/5/1, MAA.

4 See, for example, L.C.G. Clarke to A. Vogan, 8 August 1933, letters box 1933, MAA.

5 Notes Referring to the Rymill Collection of Artefacts from Canadian Indians, 1929, FA5/1/2, MAA.

6 Archived exhibition labels, which are believed to date from the 1950s, recycled the catalogue card information and reproduced Rymill's sketches so that visitors could more clearly see the imagery on the scrolls.

7 Notes Referring to the Rymill Collection, MAA. George Tanner was the English name used by Gennahmodhi (Wayne Scott, e-mail to author, 28 July 2010). Cadzow (1926a) identifies "Kennamodhi" as the source of birch bark records he acquired for the Museum of the American Indian (MAI) in 1925. As mentioned in Chapter 3, Cadzow was also asked to send copies of birch bark scrolls to their former keepers at Swan Lake in 1925.

8 Par-Qua-Siganan is a phonetic spelling of the Anishinaabe word *apaakozigan,* which translates as "mixed tobacco" (Alan Corbiere, e-mail to author, 15 June 2011).

9 "Catalogue of Bungi Specimens from Long Plains and Swan Lake Reserves, Manitoba Canada," 1925, Museum of the American Indian/Heye Foundation Records, box 198, folder 1, National Museum of the American Indian Archive Center, Smithsonian Institution, Washington, DC (NMAI). Cadzow's records often include the prices paid for artefacts, whereas Rymill's do not.

10 There is a growing literature on European representations of Native people: for art history, see S. Pratt (2005); for anthropology, consult Harkin (2006); and for history and cultural studies, see Feest (1999); Maddra (2006); and Wernitznig (2007). In addition, an important body of literature addresses the accumulation and display of North and Central American indigenous material in European cabinets of curiosities, prior to the development of public museums (see Feest 1993; Mason 1994; Yaya 2008). These works add considerable depth to our knowledge of how indigenous Americans have been represented in Europe, but as my focus is on collections acquired within the paradigm of ethnographic salvage, and few of these works concern items acquired in what are now the Prairie provinces, I have chosen not to address early UK displays of First Nations material.

11 The MAA's name has changed several times since its foundation. Between 1884 and 1906, it was the Museum of General and Local Archaeology; from 1906 to 1913, it was the Museum of General and Local Archaeology and Ethnology in recognition of its growing world cultures collection; from 1913 to 1978, it was the University Museum of Archaeology and Ethnology; and in 1979 it became the University of Cambridge Museum of Archaeology and Anthropology. The acronym was simplified to MAA in 2007.

12 The Keyser Gallery is named after Charles E. Keyser, president of the British Archaeological Association and fellow of Trinity College; Babington Hall commemorates Charles Cardale Babington, past president of the Cambridge Antiquarian Society; the Andrews Gallery was named after benefactor James Bruyn Andrews; and the Bevan Hall honours Biblical scholar Anthony Ashley Bevan.

13 As this headdress is yet to be located in the MAA, it cannot be described or illustrated here.

14 Notes Referring to the Rymill Collection, MAA.

15 F.W. Hodge to L.C.G. Clarke, 3 April 1931, Notes and Correspondence Relating to the Museum of the American Indian, Heye Foundation, 1920s, W03/1/3, MAA.

16 Hodge couldn't possibly have been familiar with everything in the MAI's vast holdings and was seemingly unaware of a similar banner acquired at the File Hills by Cadzow during his 1926 collecting expedition for the MAI. Cadzow paid ten dollars for this banner [14-7960], described simply in his field notes as "Back rest, beaded" (D.A. Cadzow, "Catalogue of Specimens Collected from the Prairie Cree, on the Piapot, Muskepetin, Daystar, File Hills, Touchwood, Poorman and Starblanket Reserves," 1925, Saskatchewan, November 1925, Museum of the American Indian/Heye Foundation Records, box 198, folder 13, NMAI). His expedition diary does not refer to the backrest, simply grouping all the File Hills objects together: "See Red Dog and a number of others on the Star Blanket Reserve. Gather a few specimens and have a long talk with the old men" (D.A. Cadzow, "Diary 1926. For Specimens for Museum," 9 June 1926, Cadzow Family, Private Collection).

17 In this extract Coombes is quoting W.H. Holmes's (1902, 355) influential article on classification systems for anthropological collections.

18 List of Specimens Sent Away for Safe Keeping with the Fitzwilliam Museum Specimens, MM1/7/11, MAA.

19 Extract from CUMAE Museum Reports 1939-1945, MM1/3/13, MAA.

20 Paterson had undertaken fieldwork in the Eastern Arctic, and Bushnell was a specialist in pre-Columbian archaeology. Currently, the MAA is best known as a centre for the study of Pacific peoples and cultures.

21 Furthermore, as Krmpotich and Anderson (2005, 399) argue in their evaluation of visitor responses to the Glenbow Museum's Blackfoot Gallery, even when a museum has taken extraordinary steps to incorporate First Nations voices into displays, visitors do not always recognize the extent of collaborative curatorship and can fail to notice the intended messages of self-representation.

22 T. Stanier to Gathercole, 15 October 1980, Notes, labels and correspondence referring to 1980s American Indian exhibition, FA1/1/7, MAA.

23 D. Swallow to T. Stanier, 12 November 1980, Notes, labels and correspondence referring to 1980s American Indian exhibition, FA1/1/7, MAA.

24 Notes, labels and correspondence referring to 1980s American Indian exhibition, FA1/1/7, MAA.

25 Indeed, the mannequin in the display wore clothing from at least two different nations (Anita Herle, MAA, e-mail to author, 26 December 2011).

26 Projects to reattach names to First Nations people photographed in the early twentieth century include the Kainai-Oxford Photographic Histories Project (Brown, Peers, and members of the Kainai Nation 2006) and a travelling exhibition developed by Alberta Community Development (Historic Sites Service, Head-Smashed-In Buffalo Jump and the Provincial Archives of Alberta) and Museums Alberta, which focused on archival photos of First Nations people from the Treaty 7 area. Lost Identities: A Journey of Rediscovery is now on permanent display at the Head-Smashed-In Buffalo Jump interpretive centre in Southern Alberta.

27 List of Loans and Transfers, Including Various Museums in Canada, MMA/7/11, MAA. Other sub-committee members were Adrian Digby of the Department of Oriental Antiquities and Ethnography at the British Museum, Henry Balfour of the Pitt Rivers Museum, Finnish art historian Tancred Borenius, and art historian and collector Archibald G.B. Russell.

28 Whether Rymill had anything additional to say about these items can only be guessed at, as the relevant page of his inventory is missing. The catalogue card entries read, "Sheep horn spoon. The carved head represents a duck" and "Wooden bowl for food."

29 The reviewer was referring to a 1920 show titled Indigenous American Art, which focused principally on pre-Columbian art from Central America and Peru held in private collections (Bunt 1920).

30 Events leaflet 1991, Exhibition files, Fitzwilliam Museum, Cambridge.

31 Home of the Brave is most celebrated as the catalyst for the first repatriation of a Native American artifact from a British museum. The exhibition included a ghost dance shirt, reputedly acquired at the site of the Battle at Wounded Knee, which had been in Glasgow Museums' collection since 1891, following the visit of Buffalo Bill's Wild West Show to Glasgow. Following a public meeting, the shirt was repatriated in 1999 and is currently in the care of the South Dakota Historical Society (Maddra 1996; O'Neill 2006).

32 For an image of this dress and the label text, see Digital Stroud, "Wrapping the Globe: Stroud's Best Kept Secret!" 2013, http://www.digitalstroud.co.uk/.

Chapter 7: Building Relationships

1 From 2014, MEG will be disseminating a series of case studies and guidance documents emerging from the Engaging Communities project on its website, www.museum ethnographersgroup.org.uk/en/.

2 Bill C-45, which received royal assent in December 2012, is better known as the second omnibus budget bill. It concerns legislation related to some sixty acts and regulations including the Indian Act, the Navigation Protection Act, and the Environmental Assessment Act. Supporters of the Idle No More movement argue that the bill was passed without sufficient discussion with indigenous peoples.

3 This project was not the first in Britain to involve a crest pole, but it was one of the first initiated by a regional museum. Several poles were raised in British cities during the 1980s (Jonathan King, MAA, e-mail to author, 22 July 2012). For example, in 1984 the Canadian High Commission invited Kwakwaka'wakw artist Richard Hunt to carve a pole to commemorate the 1984 Liverpool Garden Festival. The following year, Tlingit artist Nathan Jackson carved and raised a pole at the Horniman Museum and Gardens in London. Jackson also joined several other Native American artists who gave demonstrations of their practice at the British Museum during the 1985 Festival of Native American Artists (Simpson 2001, 59).

4 See Royal Albert Memorial Museum and Art Gallery, "Totem Pole Protected," 22 January 2008, http://www.rammuseum.org.uk/.

5 For details regarding the exhibition, see British Museum, "Annuraaq: Clothing in the Arctic," http://www.britishmuseum.org/.

6 Now called the Department of Africa, Oceania and the Americas, the Department of Ethnography returned to the main British Museum site in 1997.

7 Some instances of early collaborations include Shelagh Weir's (1970, 1989) work with Yemeni, Palestinian, and Bedouin craftspeople, and Malcolm McLeod's (1984) involvement with the royal Asante house. More recently, British Museum staff have undertaken fieldwork and have partnered with other UK museums and indigenous cultural centres, mostly in the Pacific, as part of projects aimed at increasing access to the extensive Oceania collections

(see, for example, O'Hanlon 1993; and Adams et al. 2012). I am grateful to Jonathan King for providing details of the museum's work with originating communities (Jonathan King, MAA, e-mail to author, 22 July 2012).

8 For information regarding the RRN, visit "Reciprocal Research Network: First Nations Items from the Northwest Coast," http://www.rrnpilot.org/.

9 To access this resource, visit Burke Museum of Natural History and Culture, "Ethnology Objects Search," http://collections.burkemuseum.org/.

10 See "Splendid Heritage: Treasures of Native American Art," http://www.splendidheritage.com/.

11 The Blackfoot Digital Library (BDL) (http://blackfootdigitallibrary.org/) aims to collate information on scattered Blackfoot collections, including artifacts, sound recordings, and archival photographs. It also includes video footage and interviews recorded by the co-ordinator, Adrienne Heavy Head, and her colleagues that relate to cultural projects. The BDL is supported by the University of Lethbridge and Red Crow Community College, Kainai First Nation. As yet, few similar initiatives associated with First Nations exist in other parts of the prairies, or with tribal groups from the Plains region of the United States.

12 One such example is a newspaper article written by a Canadian journalist, based in Scotland, who claimed that British museums held 16,500 indigenous Canadian artifacts (Stewart-Robinson 2006). Though the article was largely sympathetic to the challenges facing curators who have inherited poorly documented collections, and included perspectives from curators and First Nations people involved in research and repatriation with UK museums, un-substantiated information in museum catalogue records led to some inaccuracies.

References

Archival Sources

American Philosophical Society, Philadelphia (APS)
John Alden Mason Papers. Donald A. Cadzow Correspondence

Archives Section, Ethnology Division, Canadian Museum of Civilization, Gatineau, Quebec (CMC)
Diamond Jenness Correspondence
  Clarke, Louis C.G., 1928-37, box 642, f. 7
  Dept. of Indian Affairs D.C. Scott, 1926-29, box 643, f. 2
  Field Instructions, 1926-37, box 661, f. 41
  Godsell, P.H., 1929-39, box 645, f. 8
  Imperial Institute, 1929, box 646, f. 23
  National Museum of Canada. Director (W.H. Collins), 1926-27, box 652, f. 1
  Smith, Harlan I., 1926-27, box 657, f. 50
Edward Sapir Correspondence
  Clarke, Louis C.G., 1923, box 622, f. 13
  Scott, D.C., 1912-18, box 633, f. 15
  Wintemberg, W.J., 1911-25, box 637, f. 36

Cadzow Family, Private Collection (CF)
Donald A. Cadzow Papers
Donald A. Cadzow Photograph Collection

Division of Anthropology, American Museum of Natural History, New York
David G. Mandelbaum Correspondence

Fitzwilliam Museum, University of Cambridge, Cambridge
Exhibition files

Glenbow-Alberta Institute, Calgary, Alberta (GAI)
Calgary Public Museum fonds, 1911-36
    Correspondence, 1929-35. Regarding arms permit, museum artifacts, thefts from museum, taxidermy, accounts, exhibitions of Clare Leighton, school tours, and slide presentations. M-2111, file 17.
David C. Duvall fonds, 1904-12 (Originals in American Museum of Natural History, Division of Anthropology Archives)
    David C. Duvall's Blackfoot research – Letters to Clark Wissler. M-4376
Department of Indian Affairs. Blood Indian Agency Papers, 1885-1944
    Correspondence re supplies, accounts, nurse, cattle, machinery, Regina Exhibition, Indian artifacts, Calgary Exhibition. 1923-24. M-1788/128.
George H. Gooderham fonds, 1886-1976
    "Twenty-Five Years as an Indian Agent to the Blackfoot Band," 28 January 1972. M-4738-394.
Newspaper Clipping Files

Library and Archives Canada, Ottawa (LAC)
RG 10, Department of Indian Affairs
    Vol. 3,826, file 60,511-3. Microfilm reel C-10144. Manitoba and Northwest Territories – Correspondence Regarding Indian Dances More Particularly the Sun Dance, 1909-15.
    Vol. 3,826, file 60,511-4, pt. 1. Microfilm reel C-10145. Manitoba and Northwest Territories – Correspondence Regarding Indian Dances More Particularly the Sun Dance, 1915-18.
    Vol. 3,827, file 60,511-4B. Microfilm reel C-10145. Manitoba and Northwest Territories – Correspondence regarding Indian Dances More Particularly the Sun Dance, 1922-33.
    Vol. 4,092, file 546,898. Microfilm reel C-10186. Report on Boarding Schools in Alberta by Dr. F.A. Corbett, 1920-22.
    Vol. 6,816, file 486-6-1, pt. 1. Microfilm reel C-8538. Correspondence, memoranda and reports of archaeologists, anthropologists and ethnological research at the Department of Mines and various universities and museums (Publications), 1890-1929.
    Vol. 8,619, file 1/1-15-6, pt. 1. Microfilm reel C-14237. Ethnological, anthropological and historical research – Indian Museums and Historical Indian Objects, 1893-1964.

Mitchell Library, State Library of New South Wales, Sydney, Australia
Mitchell, T.W. n.d. "Midway Peak," Mitchell Family Papers, 1400-1983, ML MSS 2228, box 1.

Museum of Archaeology and Anthropology, University of Cambridge, Cambridge (MAA)
Extract from CUMAE Museum Reports 1939-45. MM1/3/13.
Letters boxes, 1920-35.
List of Loans and Transfers, Including Various Museums in Canada. MMA/7/11.
List of Specimens Sent Away for Safe Keeping with the Fitzwilliam Museum Specimens. MM1/7/11.
Museums Committee Minutes Book. MM1/2/6.
Notes and Correspondence Relating to the Museum of the American Indian, Heye Foundation, 1920s. W03/1/3.
Notes, labels and correspondence referring to 1980s American Indian exhibition. FA1/1/7.

Notes Referring to the Rymill Collection of Artefacts from Canadian Indians, 1929. FA5/1/2.
Visitors Book, May 1884-Jan. 1932. MM1/5/1.

National Museum of the American Indian Archive Center, Smithsonian Institution,
Washington, DC (NMAI)
Museum of the American Indian/Heye Foundation Records
  Cadzow, D.A. 1917. "Field Notebook and Diary, 1917." MAI/Heye Foundation Records,
    box 193, folder 10.
  —. 1925. Catalogue of Specimens Collected from the Prairie Cree, on the Piapot,
    Muskepetin, Daystar, File Hills, Touchwood, Poorman and Starblanket Reserves,
    Saskatchewan. November 1925. MAI/Heye Foundation Records, box 198, folder 13.
  Catalogue of Bungi Specimens from Long Plains and Swan Lake Reserves, Manitoba
    Canada, 1925. MAI/Heye Foundation Records, box 198, folder 1.
  Correspondence between D.A. Cadzow, D.A. and E.K. Burnett. MAI/Heye Foundation
    Records, box 206, folder 25.
  Skinner, A. n.d. "Biographical Sketch of D.A. Cadzow." MAI/Heye Foundation Records,
    box 229, folder 17.

Pitt Rivers Museum Manuscript Collections, University of Oxford, Oxford (PRM)
Blackwood, B. 1924-27. "Diary of North American Trip 1924-27." Beatrice Blackwood Papers,
  B.12.10.
—. 1925. "Notes on the Sarcees. Reserve Visited July 1925." Beatrice Blackwood Papers, Related
  Documents File, BB.A3 19-43.
Edward B. Tylor Papers, box 17, folder 1. Correspondence and papers relating to Charles
  Harrison and the Haida.

Rochester Museum and Science Center, Rochester, New York
Primary files, ACC 1930.124. Collection of Sarci Buffalo record, painting and ceremonial
  articles

Royal Saskatchewan Museum, Regina, Saskatchewan
F. Bradshaw Correspondence. File 229/1830

Rymill Family, Private Collection
John R. Rymill Photograph and Film Collection
Robert R. Rymill Photograph and Film Collection

Saskatchewan Archives Board, Regina, Saskatchewan (SAB)
David G. Mandelbaum fonds, F 15 (Property of the University of Regina)
  Mandelbaum, D.G. 1935a. Field notebook, vol. 2, 28 June-2 July 1935, Sweet Grass, Little
    Pine Sun Dance, R-875, file 5.i.
  Mandelbaum, D.G. 1935b. Field notebook, vol. 4, 10-16 July 1935, Sweet Grass Reserve,
    R-875, file 5.i.
  Mandelbaum, D.G. 1935c. Field notebook, vol. 5, 16-23 July 1935, Sweet Grass Reserve,
    R-875, file 5.i.

United Church of Canada Archives. Conference of Manitoba and Northwestern Ontario,
University of Winnipeg, Winnipeg (UCCA)
Rev. James A. Donaghy Papers, 1920-27
  Donaghy, J.A. 1947. "History of the Swan Lake Indian Reserve and Mission from
    1875-1927."

University of Pennsylvania Museum Archives, Philadelphia
Correspondence from the Director's Office, G.B. Gordon Papers, box 3/14 C.

Secondary Sources

Adams, J., L. Bolton, E. Bonshek, and N. Thomas. 2012. *Melanesia: Art and Encounter.* London: British Museum Press.
Adams, M. 2009. "Both Sides of the Collecting Encounter: The George W. Harley Collection at the Peabody Museum of Archaeology and Ethnology, Harvard University." *Museum Anthropology* 32, 1: 17-32.
Ahenakew, E. 1995. *Voices of the Plains Cree.* Ed. R. Buck. Regina: Canadian Plains Research Center, University of Regina.
Alberti, S.J.M.M. 2009. *Nature and Culture: Objects, Disciplines and the Manchester Museum.* Manchester: Manchester University Press.
Alsop, J. 1982. *The Rare Art Traditions.* London: Thames and Hudson.
Ames, M.M. 1992. *Cannibal Tours and Glass Boxes: The Anthropology of Museums.* Vancouver: UBC Press.
–. 1999. "How to Decorate a House: The Re-Negotiation of Cultural Representations at the University of British Columbia Museum of Anthropology." *Museum Anthropology* 22, 3: 41-51.
–. 2000. "Are Changing Representations of First Peoples in Canadian Museums and Galleries Challenging the Curatorial Prerogative?" In *The Changing Presentation of the American Indian: Museums and Native Cultures,* ed. W.R. West, 73-88. Washington, DC, and Seattle: National Museum of the American Indian in association with the University of Washington Press.
Andrews, T. 2013. "Mobile Architecture, Improvisation, and Museum Practice: Revitalizing the Tłı̨chǫ Caribou Skin Lodge." In *About the Hearth: Perspectives on the Home, Hearth and Household in the Circumpolar North,* ed. D.G. Anderson, R. Wishart, and V. Vaté, 29-53. New York: Berghahn Books.
Angel, M. 2002. *Preserving the Sacred: Historical Perspectives on the Ojibwa Midewiwin.* Winnipeg: University of Manitoba Press.
Anon. 1897. "American versus Canadian Enterprise." *Fort MacLeod Gazette,* 28 May, 1.
–. 1929a. "Auburn Man Averaged 450 Miles Per Day." *Syracuse American,* clipping in Donald Cadzow Papers, Cadzow Family, Private Collection.
–. 1929b. "British Museum Expedition Here to Study Indians." *Prince Albert Daily Herald,* 29 July, 1.
–. 1929c. "British Museum Men Finish Work." *Prince Albert Daily Herald,* 16 August, 1.
–. 1929d. "Encampment of Indians Very Beautiful." *Gleichin Call,* 26 June, 1.
–. 1929e. "Visitor Reports Theft of Special Oil from Car While Parked Here." *Prince Albert Daily Herald,* 5 August, 1.
–. 1930a. "Auburn Scientist Returns to North Soon to Study Origin of Early Races in Alaska." *Syracuse Post Standard,* 12 January, s. 2, 1, 24.
–. (A.F.) 1930b. "The Third Column: Alberta Loses More of Its Own Oldtime Specimens." *Edmonton Journal,* 21 June, 4.
–. (H.R.) 1935a. "The Art of Primitive Peoples." *Burlington Magazine for Connoisseurs* 135 (July): 42.
–. 1935b. "The Art of Primitive Peoples." *Nature* 135, 3422: 927.
–. 1960. "Obituary: Donald Cadzow." *Pennsylvania Archaeologist* 30, 1: 35.
–. (G.A.) 1961. "Obituary. L.C.G. Clarke." *Cambridge Review,* 29 April, 454.
–. 1970. "Doctors Prominent in Museum Development." *Manitoba Medical Review* 50, 6: 18-19.

Appadurai, A., ed. 1986. *The Social Life of Things: Commodities in Cultural Perspective.* Cambridge: Cambridge University Press.

Arnold, K., and D. Olsen, eds. 2003. *Medicine Man: The Forgotten Museum of Henry Wellcome.* London: British Museum Press.

Avrith, G. 1986. "Science at the Margins: The British Association and the Foundations of Canadian Anthropology, 1884-1910." PhD diss., University of Pennsylvania.

BAAS (British Association for the Advancement of Science). 1887. *Third Report of the Committee for Investigating and Publishing Reports on the Physical Characters, Languages, and Industrial and Social Conditions of the North-Western Tribes of the Dominion of Canada.* London. https://archive.org/details/cihm_14335.

Baillargeon, M., and L. Tepper. 1998. *Legends of Our Times: Native Ranching and Rodeo Life on the Plains and Plateau.* Vancouver: UBC Press in association with University of Washington Press, Seattle, and Canadian Museum of Civilization, Hull.

Banks, M., and R. Vokes. 2010. "Introduction: Anthropology, Photography and the Archive." *History and Anthropology* 21, 4: 337-49.

Barbeau, M. 1924. *Indian Days in the Canadian Rockies.* Toronto: Macmillan.

Barringer, T., and T. Flynn. 1998. *Colonialism and the Object.* London: Routledge.

Barron, F.L. 1988. "The Indian Pass System in the Canadian West, 1882-1935." *Prairie Forum* 13, 1: 25-42.

Barthes, R. 1980. *Camera Lucida: Reflections on Photography.* Trans. R. Howard. New York: Hill and Wang.

Bastien, B. 2004. *Blackfoot Ways of Knowing: The Worldview of the Siksikaitsitapi.* Calgary: University of Calgary Press.

Basu, P. 2011. "Object Diasporas, Resourcing Communities: Sierra Leonean Collections in the Global Museumscape." *Museum Anthropology* 34: 28-42.

Batchen, G. 2004. "Ere the Substance Fade: Photography and Hair Jewellery." In *Photographs Objects Histories: On the Materiality of Images,* ed. E. Edwards and J. Hart, 32-46. London: Routledge.

Battiste, M., ed. 2000. *Reclaiming Indigenous Voice and Vision.* Vancouver: UBC Press.

Beaulieu, D.L. 1984. "Curly Hair and Big Feet: Physical Anthropology and the Implementation of Land Allotment on the White Earth Chippewa Reservation." *American Indian Quarterly* 8, 4: 281-314.

Béchervaise, J. 1995. *Arctic and Antarctic: The Will and the Way of John Riddoch Rymill.* Huntingdon: Bluntisham Books.

Beck, D.R. 2010. "Collecting among the Menomini: Cultural Assault in Twentieth Century Wisconsin." *American Indian Quarterly* 34, 2: 157-93.

Bednasek, C.D. 2009. "Aboriginal and Colonial Geographies of the File Hills Farm Colony." PhD diss., Queen's University.

Belk, R. 2001. *Collecting in a Consumer Society.* London: Routledge.

Bell, C. 2009. "Repatriation of Cultural Material to First Nations in Canada: Legal and Ethical Obligations." In *Cultural Heritage Issues: The Legacy of Conquest, Colonization and Commerce,* ed. J.A. Nafziger, 81-106. Leiden: Martinus Nijhoff.

Bell, C., G. Statt, and the Mookaakin Cultural Society. 2008. "Repatriation and Heritage Protection: Reflections on the Kainai Experience." In *First Nations Cultural Heritage and Law: Case Studies, Voices and Perspectives,* ed. C. Bell and V. Napoleon, 203-57. Vancouver: UBC Press.

Bell, J.A. 2003. "Looking to See: Reflections on Visual Repatriation in the Purari Delta, Gulf Province, Papua New Guinea." In *Museums and Source Communities: A Routledge Reader,* ed. L. Peers and A.K. Brown, 111-21. London: Routledge.

Bell, J.A., A.K. Brown, and R.J. Gordon, eds. 2013. *Reinventing First Contact: Expeditions, Anthropology and Popular Culture.* Washington, DC: Smithsonian Institution Scholarly Press.

Bernstein, B. 2004. "The National Museum of the American Indian Collections." *American Indian Art Magazine* 29, 4: 52-55.

Berry, S. 2011. "Recovered Identities: Four Métis Artists in 19th-Century Rupert's Land." In *Recollecting: Lives of Aboriginal Women of the Canadian Northwest and the U.S. Borderlands,* ed. S. Carter and P.A. McCormack, 29-59. Edmonton: Athabasca University Press.

Bieder, R.E. 1986. *Science Encounters the Indian, 1820-1880: The Early Years of American Ethnology.* Norman: University of Oklahoma Press.

Binney, J., and G. Chaplin. 1991. "Taking the Photographs Home: The Recovery of a Maori History." *Visual Anthropology* 4, 3-4: 431-42.

Blackfoot Gallery Committee. 2001. *Nitsitapiisinni: The Story of the Blackfoot People.* Toronto: Key Porter Books.

Black-Rogers, M. 1977. "Ojibwa Power Belief System." In *The Anthropology of Power,* ed. R. Fogelson and R. Adams, 141-51. New York: Academic Press.

Bloom, L. 1993. *Gender on Ice: American Ideologies of Polar Expeditions.* Minneapolis: University of Minnesota Press.

Boas, F. 1905. "The Educational Functions of Anthropological Museums." In *The Shaping of American Anthropology, 1883-1911: A Franz Boas Reader,* ed. G.W. Stocking Jr., 297-300. New York: Basic Books.

–. 1907. "Some Principles of Museum Administration." *Science* 25: 921-33.

Boas, F., and G. Hunt. 1905. *Kwakiutl Texts.* Vol. 3 of *Publications of the Jesup North Pacific Expedition.* Leiden: E.J. Brill.

–. 1906. *Kwakiutl Texts, Second Series.* Vol. 10, pt. 1 of *Publications of the Jesup North Pacific Expedition.* Leiden: E.J. Brill.

Boast, R. 2011. "Neocolonial Collaboration: Museum as Contact Zone Revisited." *Museum Anthropology* 34, 1: 56-70.

Boast, R., M. Bravo, and R. Srinivasan. 2007. "Return to Babel: Emergent Diversity, Digital Resources, and Local Knowledge." *Information Society* 23, 5: 395-403.

Boast, R., S. Guha, and A. Herle. 2001. *Collected Sights: Photographic Collections of the Museum of Archaeology and Anthropology, 1860s-1930s.* Cambridge: University of Cambridge Museum of Archaeology and Anthropology.

Bolton, L. 2007. "Living and Dying: Ethnography, Class and Aesthetics in the British Museum." In *Museums and Difference,* ed. D. Sherman, 330-53. Bloomington: Indiana University Press.

Bonshek, E. 2010. "Collecting Relations in Melanesia: Making a Contemporary Collection in the Western Highlands of Papua New Guinea." *Journal of Museum Ethnography* 23: 7-20.

Borden, R. 1986. "An Institution That Matters." *Liaison* 3, 1: 5-9.

Brass, E. 1987. *I Walk in Two Worlds.* Calgary: Glenbow Museum.

Brasser, T. 1984. "Backrest Banners among the Plains Cree and Plains Ojibwa." *American Indian Art Magazine* 10, 1: 56-63.

Brink, J. 2008. *Imagining Head-Smashed-In: Aboriginal Buffalo Hunting on the Northern Plains.* Edmonton: Athabasca University Press.

British and Foreign Aborigines Protection Society. 1837. *Reprint of the Report of the Parliamentary Select Committee on Aboriginal Tribes (British Settlements).* London: William Ball.

–. 1856. *Canada West and the Hudson's-Bay Company. A Political and Humane Question of Vital Importance to the Honour of Great Britain, to the Prosperity of Canada and to the Existence of the Native Tribes: Being an Address to the Right Honourable Henry Labouchere, Her Majesty's Principal Secretary of State for the Colonies.* London: William Tweedie.

Brock, R.W. 1911. *Summary Report of the Geological Survey Branch of the Department of Mines for the Calendar Year 1910.* Ottawa: Department of Mines, F.A. Acland.

Brody, H. 1987. *Living Arctic: Hunters of the Canadian North.* London: Faber and Faber.

Bronner, S.J. 1989. "Object Lessons: The Work of Ethnological Museums and Collections." In *Consuming Visions: Accumulation and Display of Goods in America, 1880-1920*, ed. S.J. Bronner, 217-54. New York: W.W. Norton.

Brown, A.K. 1998. "Catalogue of the Rymill Collection in the University of Cambridge Museum of Archaeology and Anthropology." Cambridge, University of Cambridge Museum of Archaeology and Anthropology.

—. 2000. "Object Encounters: Perspectives on Collecting Expeditions to Canada." PhD. diss., University of Oxford.

—. 2005. "The Plains Redisplay at the University of Cambridge Museum of Archaeology and Anthropology." *Journal of Museum Ethnography* 17: 232-40.

—. 2006. "The Kelvingrove 'New Century Project': Changing Approaches to Displaying World Cultures in Glasgow." *Journal of Museum Ethnography* 18: 37-47.

—. 2009. "'Mokisins,' 'Cloaks' and 'a Belt of a Peculiar Fabrik': Recovering the History of the Thomas Whyte Collection of North American Clothing, Formerly in the Grierson Museum, Thornhill." *Transactions of the Dumfries and Galloway Natural History Society* 83: 131-49.

Brown, A.K., J. Coote, and C. Gosden. 2000. "Tylor's Tongue: Material Culture, Evidence, and Social Networks." *Journal of the Anthropological Society of Oxford* 31, 3: 257-76.

Brown, A.K., with C. Massan and A. Grant. 2011. "Christina Massan's Beadwork and the Recovery of a Fur Trade Family History." In *Recollecting: Lives of Aboriginal Women of the Canadian Northwest and Borderlands,* ed. S. Carter and P.A. McCormack, 89-111. Edmonton: Athabasca University Press.

Brown, A.K., and L. Peers. 2013. "The Blackfoot Shirts Project: 'Our Ancestors Have Come to Visit.'" In *Museum Transformations: Art, Culture, History,* ed. R.B. Phillips and A.E. Coombes. The International Handbook of Museum Studies. Oxford: Wiley. http://onlinelibrary.wiley.com/doi/10.1002/9781118829059.wbihms993/full.

Brown, A.K., and L. Peers, with members of the Kainai Nation. 2006. *"Pictures Bring Us Messages" / Sinaakssiiksi aohtsimaahpihkookiyaawa: Photographs and Histories from the Kainai Nation.* Toronto: University of Toronto Press.

Brown, J.S.H., and E. Vibert. 1998. "Introduction." In *Reading beyond Words: Contexts for Native History,* ed. J.S.H. Brown and E. Vibert, ix-xxvii. Peterborough: Broadview Press.

Brownstone, A. 2002. "Ancestors: The Deane-Freeman Collections from the Bloods." *American Indian Art Magazine* 27, 3: 38-49, 73-77.

—. 2008. "Reverend John Maclean and the Bloods." *American Indian Art Magazine* 33, 3: 44-57.

Bruhac, J. 1994. "The Heye Centre Opens in Manhattan with Three Exhibitions of Native Arts." *Smithsonian* 25, 7: 40-48.

Bruner, E.M. 1986. "Ethnography as Narrative." In *The Anthropology of Experience,* ed. V. Turner and E.M. Bruner, 139-55. Urbana: University of Illinois Press.

Buckley, H. 1993. *From Wooden Ploughs to Welfare: Why Indian Policy Failed in the Prairie Provinces.* Montreal and Kingston: McGill-Queen's University Press.

Bunt, C. 1920. "American Art at the Burlington Fine Arts Club." *Burlington Magazine for Connoisseurs* 37, 208: 40-41, 44-46.

Burkinshaw, J. 1999. *Klaya-ho-alth: Collections from the Northwest Coast of North America in the Royal Albert Memorial Museum.* Exeter: Exeter City Museums.

Burlington Fine Arts Club. 1935. *Catalogue of an Exhibition of the Art of Primitive Peoples.* London: Burlington Fine Arts Club.

Burnett, K. 2010. *Taking Medicine: Women's Healing Work and Colonial Contact in Southern Alberta, 1880-1930.* Vancouver: UBC Press.

Bushnell, G. 1961. "Obituary – Louis Colville Gray Clarke: 1881-1960." *Man* 61, 220: 191-92.

Butler, S.R. 1999. *Contested Representations: Revisiting "Into the Heart of Africa."* London: Routledge.

Byrne, S. 2011. "Trials and Traces: A.C. Haddon's Agency as a Museum Collector." In *Unpacking the Collection: Networks of Material and Social Agency in the Museum.* One World Archaeology, ed. S. Byrne, A. Clarke, R. Harrison, and R. Torrence, 307-25. New York: Springer.

Byrne, S., A. Clarke, R. Harrison, and R. Torrence. 2011. "Networks, Agents and Objects: Frameworks for Unpacking Museum Collections." In *Unpacking the Collection: Networks of Material and Social Agency in the Museum.* One World Archaeology, ed. S. Byrne, A. Clarke, R. Harrison, and R. Torrence, 3-26. New York: Springer.

Cadzow, D.A. n.d. *Air-Cooled Adventure among the Aborigines.* Syracuse, NY: H.H. Franklin Manufacturing Company.

–. 1920. *Native Copper Objects of the Copper Eskimo.* Indian Notes and Monographs. New York: Museum of the American Indian, Heye Foundation.

–. 1926a. "Bark Record of the Bungi Medewin Society." *Indian Notes* 3, 2: 123-34.

–. 1926b. "Peace-Pipe of the Prairie Cree." *Indian Notes* 3, 2: 82-89.

–. 1926c. "The Prairie Cree Tipi." *Indian Notes* 3, 1: 19-27.

–. 1927. "Smoking Tipi of Buffalo-Bull the Cree." *Indian Notes* 4, 3: 271-80.

–. 1928. "Archaeological Work with the Putnam Baffin Island Expedition. *Indian Notes* 5, 1: 98-106.

Cannizzo, J. 1991. "Exhibiting Cultures: 'Into the Heart of Africa.'" *Visual Anthropology Review* 7, 1: 150-60.

Carpenter, E. 1991. "Repatriation Policy and the Heye Collection." *Museum Anthropology* 15, 3: 15-18.

–. 2005. *Two Essays: Chief and Greed.* North Andover, MA: Persimmon Press.

Carter, S. 1990. *Lost Harvests: Prairie Indian Reserve Farmers and Government Policy.* Montreal and Kingston: McGill-Queen's University Press.

–. 1991. "Demonstrating Success: The File Hills Farm Colony." *Prairie Forum* 16, 2: 157-83.

Chambers, C.M., and N.J. Blood. 2009. "Love Thy Neighbour: Repatriating Precarious Blackfoot Sites." *International Journal of Canadian Studies* 39-40: 253-79.

Chapman, W.R. 1985. "Arranging Ethnology: A.H.L.F Pitt Rivers and the Typological Tradition." In *Objects and Others: Essays on Museums and Material Culture,* ed. G.W. Stocking Jr., 15-48. Madison: University of Wisconsin Press.

Christen, K.A. 2006. "Ara Irititja: Protecting the Past, Accessing the Future – Indigenous Memories in a Digital Age. A Digital Project of the Pitantjatjara Council." *Museum Anthropology* 29, 1: 56-60.

–. 2011. "Opening Archives: Respectful Repatriation." *American Archivist* 74 (Spring-Summer): 185-210.

Clavir, M. 2002. *Preserving What Is Valued: Museums, Conservation and First Nations.* Vancouver: UBC Press.

Clifford, J. 1997. "Museums as Contact Zones." In J. Clifford, *Routes: Travel and Translation in the Late Twentieth Century,* 188-219. Cambridge, MA: Harvard University Press.

–. 2004. "Looking Several Ways: Anthropology and Native Heritage in Alaska." *Current Anthropology* 45, 1: 5-30.

Clifford, J., and G. Marcus. 1986. *Writing Culture: The Poetics and Politics of Ethnography.* Berkeley: University of California Press.

Cohen, D.W. 1989. "The Undefining of Oral Tradition." *Ethnohistory* 36, 1: 9-18.

Cole, D. 1985. *Captured Heritage: The Scramble for Northwest Coast Artifacts.* Norman: University of Oklahoma Press.

–. 1991. "Tricks of the Trade: Some Reflections on Anthropological Collecting." *Arctic Anthropology* 28, 1: 48-52.

Cole, D., and I. Chaikin. 1990. *An Iron Hand upon the People: The Law against the Potlatch on the Northwest Coast.* Vancouver: Douglas and McIntyre in association with the University of Washington Press.

Collier, J., and M. Collier. 1986. *Visual Anthropology: Photography as Research Method.* Albuquerque: University of New Mexico Press.

Colwell-Chanthaphonh, C., and T.J. Ferguson, eds. 2008. *Collaboration in Archaeological Practice: Engaging Descendent Communities.* Lanham, MD: AltaMira Press.

Conaty, G.T. 1995. "Economic Models and Blackfoot Ideology." *American Ethnologist* 22, 2: 403-12.

–. 2003. "Glenbow's Blackfoot Gallery: Working towards Coexistence." In *Museums and Source Communities: A Routledge Reader,* ed. L. Peers and A.K. Brown, 227-41. London: Routledge.

–. 2006. "Glenbow Museum and First Nations: Fifteen Years of Negotiating Change." *Museum Management and Curatorship* 21, 3: 254-56.

–. 2008. "The Effects of Repatriation on the Relationship between the Glenbow Museum and the Blackfoot People." *Museum Management and Curatorship* 23, 3: 245-59.

Conaty, G.T., and B. Carter. 2005. "'Our Story in Our Words': Diversity and Equality in the Glenbow Museum." In *Looking Reality in the Eye: Museums and Social Responsibility,* ed. R.R. Janes and G.T. Conaty, 43-58. Calgary: University of Calgary Press.

Conaty, G.T., and H. Dumka. 1996. "Care of First Nations Sacred Material – Glenbow Museum." *ICOM Ethnographic Conservation Newsletter* 13: 4-5.

Conaty, G.T., and R.R. Janes. 1997. "Issues of Repatriation: A Canadian View." *European Review of Native American Studies* 11, 2: 31-37.

Cook, I., and D.P. Tolia-Kelly. 2010. "Material Geographies." In *The Oxford Handbook of Material Culture Studies,* ed. D. Hicks and M. Beaudry, 99-122. Oxford: Oxford University Press.

Coombes, A.E. 1988. "Museums and the Formation of National and Cultural Identities." *Oxford Art Journal* 11, 2: 57-68.

–. 1994a. "Blinded by 'Science': Ethnography at the British Museum." In *Art Apart: Art Institutions and Ideology across England and North America,* ed. M. Pointon, 102-19. Manchester: Manchester University Press.

–. 1994b. *Reinventing Africa: Museums, Material Culture, and Popular Imagination in Late Victorian and Edwardian England.* New Haven and London: Yale University Press.

Cooper, K.C. 2007. *Spirited Encounters: American Indians Protest Museum Policies and Practices.* Lanham, MD: AltaMira Press.

Coote, J., and C. Morton. 2000. "A Glimpse of the Guinea Coast: Regarding an African Exhibition at the Pitt Rivers Museum." *Journal of Museum Ethnography* 12: 39-56.

Coutts, R., and K. Pettipas. 1994. "The HBC Museum Collection: 'Mere Curiosities Are Not Required.'" *The Beaver* 74, 3: 13-19.

Crane Bear, C., and L.M. Zuyderhoudt. 2010. "A Place for Things to Be Alive: Best Practices for Cooperation That Respects Indigenous Knowledge." In *Sharing Knowledge and Cultural Heritage: First Nations of the Americas. Studies in Collaboration with Indigenous Peoples from Greenland, North and South America,* ed. L. van Broekhoven, C. Buijs, and P. Hoven, 133-39. Leiden: National Museum of Ethnology and Sidestone Press.

Cronin, M. 2013. "Technological Heroes: Images of the Arctic in the Age of Polar Aviation." In *Northscapes: History, Technology, and the Making of Northern Environments,* ed. D. Jørgensen and S. Sörlin, 57-81. Vancouver: UBC Press.

Crop Eared Wolf, A. 1997. "Protecting Religious Rights and Freedoms: Blood Tribe/Kainai Efforts through Cultural and Intellectual Properties Policy and Repatriation." *Alberta Museums Review* 23, 3: 38-40.

Crowther, G.M. 1993. *Catalogue of the Northwest Coast Collection.* Cambridge: Cambridge University Museum of Archaeology and Anthropology.

Cruikshank, J. 1994. "Oral Tradition and Oral History: Reviewing Some Issues." *Canadian Historical Review* 75, 3: 403-18.

–. 2000. *The Social Life of Stories: Narrative and Knowledge in the Yukon Territory.* Lincoln and London: University of Nebraska Press.

Culin, S. 1907. *24th Annual Report of the Bureau of American Ethnology: Games of the North American Indians.* Washington, DC: US Government Printing Office.

Curtis, N. 2005. "Going Home: From Aberdeen to Standoff." *British Archaeology* 82 (May-June): 40-43.

Custer, J.F. 1996. *Prehistoric Cultures of Eastern Pennsylvania.* Anthropological Series 7. Harrisburg: Pennsylvania Historical and Museum Commission.

Cuthand, S. 1991. "The Native Peoples of the Prairie Provinces in the 1920s and 1930s." In *Sweet Promises: A Reader on Indian-White Relations in Canada,* ed. J.R. Miller, 381-92. Toronto: University of Toronto Press.

Daniels, D. 1981. "Swan Lake Indian Reserve." In *Memories of Lorne, 1880-1980,* ed. Y. Brandt, 250-65. Somerset, MB: Municipality of Lorne.

Darnell, R. 1984. "The Sapir Years in the Canadian National Museum, Ottawa." In *Edward Sapir: Appraisals of His Life and Work,* ed. K. Koerner, 159-86. Philadelphia: John Benjamins.

–. 1998. "Toward a History of Canadian Departments of Anthropology: Retrospect, Prospect and Common Cause." *Anthropologica* 40 (2): 153-68.

Dawn, L. 2006. *National Visions, National Blindness: Canadian Art and Identities in the 1920s.* Vancouver: UBC Press.

de Stecher, A., and S. Loyer. 2009. "Practising Collaborative Research: The Great Lakes Research Alliance Visits to the Pitt Rivers Museum and British Museum." *Journal of Museum Ethnography* 22: 145-54.

Dempsey, H.A. 2008. "The Indians and the Stampede." In *Icon, Brand, Myth: The Calgary Stampede,* ed. M. Foran, 47-72. Edmonton: Athabasca University Press.

–. 2011. *Always an Adventure: An Autobiography.* Calgary: University of Calgary Press.

Densmore, F. 1979. *Chippewa Customs.* St. Paul: Minnesota Historical Society Press. (Orig. pub. 1929.)

Department for Culture, Media and Sport. 2005. *Guidance for the Care of Human Remains in Museums.* London: Department for Culture, Media and Sport.

Department of Indian Affairs. 1905. *Annual Report of the Department of Indian Affairs for the Year Ended June 30, 1904.* Ottawa: S.E. Dawson.

–. 1930. *Annual Report of the Department of Indian Affairs for the Year Ended March 31, 1929.* Ottawa: F.A. Acland.

Department of Indian and Northern Affairs. 1981. *Indian Acts and Amendments, 1868-1950.* Ottawa: Department of Indian and Northern Affairs Canada.

DeSilvey, C. 2006. "Observed Decay: Telling Stories with Mutable Things." *Journal of Material Culture* 11, 3: 318-38.

Devine, H. 2010. "After the Spirit Sang: Aboriginal Canadians and Museum Policy in the New Millennium." In *How Canadians Communicate III: Contexts of Canadian Popular Culture,* ed. B. Beaty, D. Briton, G. Filax, and R. Sullivan, 217-39. Edmonton: University of Athabasca Press.

Digby, A. 1935. "Introduction." In *Burlington Fine Arts Club Catalogue of an Exhibition of the Art of Primitive Peoples,* 9-14. London: Burlington Fine Arts Club.

Dignard, C., K. Helwig, J. Mason, K. Nanowin, and T. Stone, eds. 2008. *Preserving Aboriginal Heritage: Technical and Traditional Approaches. Proceedings of Symposium 2007.* Ottawa: Canadian Conservation Institute.

Dippie, B. 1982. *The Vanishing American: White Attitudes and U.S. Indian Policy.* Middletown, CT: Wesleyan University Press.

Doering, Z.D., K.R. DiGiacomo, and A.J. Pekarik. 1999. "Images of Native Americans." *Curator* 42, 2: 130-51.

Dolan, J. 2005. *Continuous Cultures, Ongoing Responsibilities: Principles and Guidelines for Australian Museums Working with Aboriginal and Torres Strait Islander Cultural Heritage.* Canberra: Museums Australia.

Dominion Bureau of Statistics. 1930. *The Canada Yearbook.* Ottawa: F.A. Acland.

Doxtator, D. 1988. "The Home of Indian Culture and Other Stories in the Museum." *Muse* 4, 3: 26-28.

Drazin, A., and D.M. Frohlich. 2007. "Good Intentions: Remembering through Framing Photographs in English Homes." *Ethnos* 72, 1: 51-76.

Dubin, S.C. 2007. "The Postmodern Exhibition: Cut on the Bias, or Is *Enola Gay* a Verb?" In *Museums and Their Communities,* ed. S. Watson, 213-27. London: Routledge.

Dubois, J. 1991. "The Manitoba Museum of Man and Nature: A Museum with an Environmental Mission." *Muse* 8, 4: 51-55.

Dudley, S. 2012. "Museums and Things." In *The Thing about Museums: Objects and Experience, Representations and Contestation,* ed. S. Dudley, A.J. Barnes, J. Binnie, J. Petrov, and J. Walklate, 1-11. London: Routledge.

Duncan, K.C. 2000. *1001 Curious Things: Ye Olde Curiosity Shop and Native American Art.* Seattle: University of Washington Press.

Durrans, B. 1988. "The Future of the Other: Changing Cultures on Display in Ethnographic Museums." In *The Museum Time Machine,* ed. R. Lumley, 144-69. London: Routledge.

Ebin, V., and D. Swallow. 1984. *"The Proper Study of Mankind ...": Great Anthropological Collections in Cambridge.* Cambridge: Cambridge University Museum of Archaeology and Anthropology.

Edwards, E. 1992. "Introduction." In *Anthropology and Photography, 1860-1920,* ed. E. Edwards, 3-17. New Haven and London: Yale University Press in association with the Royal Anthropological Institute.

–. 1999. "Photographs as Objects of Memory." In *Material Memories: Design and Evocation,* ed. M. Kwint, C. Breward, and J. Aynsley, 221-36. Oxford: Berg.

–. 2001. *Raw Histories: Photographs, Anthropology and Museums.* Oxford: Berg.

–. 2004. "Mixed Box: The 'Cultural Biography' of a Box of 'Ethnographic' Photographs." In *Photographs Objects Histories: On the Materiality of Images,* ed. E. Edwards and J. Hart, 47-61. London: Routledge.

Edwards, E., and C. Morton. 2009. "Introduction." In *Photography, Anthropology, and History: Expanding the Frame,* ed. C. Morton and E. Edwards, 1-26. Farnham, UK: Ashgate.

Ellingson, T.J. 2001. *The Myth of the Noble Savage.* Berkeley: University of California Press.

Elliott, M., and N. Thomas. 2011. *Gifts and Discoveries: The Museum of Archaeology and Anthropology, Cambridge.* London: Scala.

Elsner, J., and R. Cardinal, eds. 1994. *The Cultures of Collecting.* London: Reaktion Books.

Engelstad, B.D. 2013. "Donald Cadzow – Arctic Ethnographer." *Arctic Studies Center Newsletter,* National Museum of Natural History, Smithsonian Institution 20: 21-22.

Falk, J., and L. Dierking. 2000. *Learning from Museums: Visitor Experiences and the Making of Museums.* New York: AltaMira Press.

Farr, W.E. 1993. "Troubled Bundles, Troubled Blackfeet: The Travail of Cultural and Religious Renewal." *Montana: The Magazine of Western History* 43, 4: 2-17.

Farrell Racette, S. 2008. "Confessions and Reflections of an Indigenous Research Warrior." In *Material Histories: Proceedings of a Workshop Held at Marischal Museum, University of Aberdeen, 26-27 April 2007,* ed. A.K. Brown, 57-68. Aberdeen: Marischal Museum, University of Aberdeen.

–. 2009. "Looking for Stories and Unbroken Threads: Museum Artifacts as Women's History and Cultural Legacy." In *Restoring the Balance: First Nations Women, Community, and Culture*, ed. E. Guimond, G.G. Valaskakis, and M.D. Stout, 283-312. Winnipeg: University of Manitoba Press.

–. 2010. "Plains Cree Men's Clothing (1895-1926)." In *James Henderson: Wicite Owapi Wicasa: The Man Who Paints the Old Men*, ed. D. Ring and N. McLeod, 79-81. Saskatoon: Mendel Art Gallery.

Feest, C. 1993. "European Collecting of American Indian Artefacts and Art." *Journal of the History of Collections* 5, 1: 1-11.

–, ed. 1999. *Indians and Europe: An Interdisciplinary Collection of Essays*. Lincoln: University of Nebraska Press.

Fenn, C. 1996. "Life History of a Collection: The Tahltan Materials Collected by James A. Teit." *Museum Anthropology* 20, 3: 72-91.

Fenton, W.N. 1966. "Field Work, Museum Studies, and Ethnohistorical Research." *Ethnohistory* 13, 1-2: 71-85.

Fforde, C. 2004. *Collecting the Dead: Archaeology and the Reburial Issue*. London: Gerald Duckworth.

Fienup-Riordan, A. 1998. "Yup'ik Elders in Museums: Fieldwork Turned on Its Head." *Arctic Anthropology* 35, 2: 49-58.

Fienup-Riordan, A., and M. Meade, eds. 2005. *Ciuliamta Akluit/Things of Our Ancestors: Yup'ik Elders Explore the Jacobsen Collection at the Ethnologisches Museum Berlin*. Seattle: University of Washington Press in association with Calista Elders Council, Bethel, Alaska.

Fortes, M. 1953. *Social Anthropology at Cambridge since 1900: An Inaugural Lecture*. Cambridge: Cambridge University Press.

Freed, S.A., and R.S. Freed. 1983. "Clark Wissler and the Development of Anthropology in the United States." *American Anthropologist* 85, 4: 800-25.

Gabriel, M., and J. Dahl, eds. 2008. *Utimut: Past Heritage, Future Partnerships*. Copenhagen: International Work Group for Indigenous Affairs and the Greenland National Museum.

Gathercole, P., and A. Clarke. 1979. *Survey of Oceanian Collections in Museums in the United Kingdom and the Irish Republic*. Paris: UNESCO.

Geary, C. 1998. "Different Visions? Postcards from Africa by European and African Photographers and Sponsors." In *Delivering Views: Distant Cultures in Early Postcards*, ed. C. Geary and V.-L. Webb, 147-77. Washington, DC: Smithsonian Institution Press.

Geffroy, Y. 1990. "Family Photographs: A Visual Heritage." *Visual Anthropology* 3: 367-409.

Geismar, H. 2009. "Contemporary Traditions: Museum Collecting and Creativity in Vanuatu." In *Re-Presenting Pacific Arts*, ed. K. Stevenson and V.-L. Webb, 70-89. Bathurst: Crawford House.

–. 2011. "'Material Culture Studies' and Other Ways to Theorize Objects: A Primer to a Regional Debate." *Comparative Studies in Society and History* 53, 1: 210-18.

Geismar, H., and W. Mohns. 2011. "Social Relationships and Digital Relationships: Rethinking the Database at the Vanuatu Cultural Centre." *Journal of the Royal Anthropological Institute* 17: S133-55.

Gell, A. 1998. *Art and Agency: An Anthropological Theory*. Oxford: Clarendon Press.

Geller, P. 1996. "Hudson's Bay Company Indians: Images of Native People and the Red River Pageant, 1920." In *Dressing in Feathers: The Construction of the Indian in American Popular Culture*, ed. E.S. Bird, 65-77. Boulder, CO: Westview Press.

Gieryn, T.F. 1998. "Balancing Acts: Science, *Enola Gay* and History Wars at the Smithsonian." In *The Politics of Display: Museums, Science, Culture*, ed. S. Macdonald, 197-228. London: Routledge.

Glass, A. 2014. "Indigenous Ontologies, Digital Futures: Plural Provenances and the Kwakwa̱ka'wakw Collection in Berlin and Beyond." In *Translating Knowledge: Global Perspectives on Museum and Community,* ed. R. Silverman. London: Routledge.

Godsell, P.H., ed., with G.H. Gooderham. 1955. *Northern Plains Tribes.* Calgary: Glenbow Foundation.

Gosden, C., and C. Knowles. 2001. *Collecting Colonialism: Material Culture and Colonial Change.* Oxford: Berg.

Gosden, C., and F. Larson. 2007. *Knowing Things: Exploring the Collections at the Pitt Rivers Museum, 1884-1945.* Oxford: Oxford University Press.

Gosden, C., and Y. Marshall. 1999. "The Cultural Biography of Objects." World Archaeology 31, 2: 169-78.

Gosden, C., R.B. Phillips, and E. Edwards, eds. 2006. *Sensible Objects: Colonialism, Museums and Material Culture.* Oxford: Berg.

Graburn, N., and M. Lee. 1988. "'The Living Arctic': Doing What 'The Spirit Sings' Didn't." *Inuit Art Quarterly* 3, 4: 10-13.

Graham, W.M. 1991. *Treaty Days: Reflections of an Indian Commissioner.* Calgary: Glenbow Museum.

Greenhorn, B. 2005. "Project Naming: Always on Our Minds." In *Museums and the Web 2005: Proceedings,* ed. J. Trant and D. Bearman. Toronto: Archives and Museum Informatics. http://www.archimuse.com/.

Gresko, J. 1975. "White 'Rites' and Indian 'Rites': Indian Education and Native Responses in the West, 1870-1910." In *Western Canada Past and Present,* ed. A.W. Rasporich, 163-81. Calgary: University of Calgary and McClelland and Stewart West.

Griffiths, T. 1996. *Hunters and Collectors: The Antiquarian Imagination in Australia.* Cambridge: Cambridge University Press.

Gruber, J.W. 1970. "Ethnographic Salvage and the Shaping of Anthropology." *American Anthropologist* 72, 6: 1289-99.

Hackforth-Jones, J., D. Bindman, S. Pratt, and R. Ray. 2007. *Between Worlds: Voyagers to Britain, 1700-1850.* London: National Portrait Gallery.

Haddon, A.C. 1895. *Evolution in Art: As Illustrated by the Life-Histories of Designs.* London: Walter Scott.

–. 1902. "What the United States of America Is Doing for Anthropology." *Journal of the Anthropological Institute of Great Britain and Ireland* 32: 8-24.

–. 1904. "Report on Some of the Educational Advantages and Deficiencies of London Museums." Paper presented to the Museums Association, London Metropolitan Archives, London.

–. 1912. "The Anthropological Survey of Canada." *Nature* 88, 2209: 597-98.

Hail, B.A., and K.C. Duncan. 1989. *Out of the North: The Subarctic Collection of the Haffenreffer Museum of Anthropology.* Bristol, RI: Haffenreffer Museum of Anthropology.

Hall, J. 1983. "Canadian Ethnology Service: National Museum of Man, National Museums of Canada." *American Indian Art Magazine* 9, 1: 50-59.

Hallowell, A.I. 1936. "The Passing of the Midewiwin in the Lake Winnipeg Region." *American Anthropologist* n.s. 38: 32-51.

–. 1960. "Ojibwa Ontology, Behaviour and World View." In *Culture and History: Essays in Honor of Paul Radin,* ed. S. Diamond, 19-52. New York: Columbia University Press.

Halvaksz, J. 2010. "The Photographic Assemblage: Duration, History and Photography in Papua New Guinea." *Anthropology and History* 21, 4: 411-29.

Hamilton, M. 2010. *Collections and Objections: Aboriginal Material Culture in Southern Ontario.* Montreal and Kingston: McGill-Queen's University Press.

Handler, R. 1985. "On Having a Culture: Nationalism and the Preservation of Quebec's *Patrimoine*." In *Objects and Others: Essays on Museums and Material Culture*, ed. G.W. Stocking Jr., 192-217. Madison: University of Wisconsin Press.

Hanks, L.M., and J.R. Hanks. 1950. *Tribe under Trust: A Study of the Blackfoot Reserve of Alberta.* Toronto: University of Toronto Press.

Hanna, M.G. 1999. "A Time to Choose: 'Us' versus 'Them' or 'All of Us Together.'" *Plains Anthropologist* 44, 170: 43-52.

Harkin, M.E. 2005. "Object Lessons: The Question of Cultural Property in the Age of Repatriation." *Journal de la Société des Américanistes* 91, 2: 9-29.

—. 2006. "'I'm an Old Cow Hand on the Banks of the Seine': Representations of Indians and Le Far West in Parisian Commercial Culture." In *New Perspectives on Native North America: Cultures, Histories and Representations*, ed. S. Kan and P. Turner Strong, 815-46. Lincoln and London: University of Nebraska Press.

Harrison, J.D. 1988. "'The Spirit Sings' and the Future of Anthropology." *Anthropology Today* 4, 6: 6-10.

—. 1993. "Completing a Circle: *The Spirit Sings*." In *Anthropology, Public Policy and Native People in Canada*, ed. N. Dyck and J.B. Waldram, 334-57. Montreal and Kingston: McGill-Queen's University Press.

—. 2005a. "Shaping Collaboration: Considering Institutional Culture." *Museum Management and Curatorship* 20: 195-212.

—. 2005b. "What Matters: Seeing the Museum Differently." *Museum Anthropology* 28, 2: 31-42.

Harrison, J.D., and R. Darnell, eds. 2006. *Historicizing Canadian Anthropology.* Vancouver: UBC Press.

Harrison, J.D., R. Whitehead, R.B. Phillips, T. Brasser, B. Driscoll, and M. Reid. 1987. *The Spirit Sings: Artistic Traditions of Canada's First Peoples.* Toronto: McClelland and Stewart.

Hawker, R.W. 2003. *Tales of Ghosts: First Nations Art in British Columbia, 1922-1961.* Vancouver: UBC Press.

Heavy Head, R. 2005. "Feeding Sublimity: Embodiment in Blackfoot Experience." Master's diss., University of Lethbridge.

Henare, A. 2005. *Museums, Anthropology and Imperial Exchange.* Cambridge: Cambridge University Press.

Henare, A., M. Holbraad, and S. Wastell, eds. 2006. *Thinking through Things: Theorising Artefacts Ethnographically.* London: Routledge.

Herle, A. 1994. "Museums and Shamans: A Cross-Cultural Collaboration." *Anthropology Today* 10, 1: 2-5.

—. 1998. "The Life-Histories of Objects: Collections of the Cambridge Anthropological Expedition to the Torres Strait." In *Cambridge and the Torres Strait: Centenary Essays on the 1898 Anthropological Expedition*, ed. A. Herle and S. Rouse, 77-105. Cambridge: Cambridge University Press.

—. 2000. "Torres Strait Islanders: Stories from an Exhibition." *Ethnos* 65, 2: 253-74.

—. 2003. "Objects, Agency and Museums: Continuing Dialogues between the Torres Strait and Cambridge." In *Museums and Source Communities: A Routledge Reader*, ed. L. Peers and A. Brown, 194-207. Routledge: London.

Herle, A., and A. Moutu. 2004. *Paired Brothers: Concealment and Revelation. Iatmul Ritual Art from the Sepik, Papua New Guinea.* Cambridge: University of Cambridge Museum of Archaeology and Anthropology.

Herle, A., and D. Phillipson, eds. 1994. "Living Traditions: Continuity and Change, Past and Present." Special issue, *Cambridge Anthropology* 17, 2.

Herle, A., with J. Philp. 1998. *Torres Strait Islanders: An Exhibition Marking the Centenary of the 1898 Cambridge Anthropological Expedition.* Cambridge: University of Cambridge Museum of Archaeology and Anthropology.

Herle, A., and S. Rouse, eds. 1998. *Cambridge and the Torres Strait: Centenary Essays on the 1898 Anthropological Expedition.* Cambridge: Cambridge University Press.

Hernandez, N. 1999. "Mokakssini: A Blackfoot Theory of Knowledge." PhD diss., Harvard University.

Hill, R.W. 2000. "The Museum Indian: Still Frozen in Time and Mind." *Museum News* 79, 3: 40-74.

Hill, T., and T. Nicks. 1992. *Turning the Page: Forging New Partnerships between Museums and First Peoples.* Report of the Task Force on Museums and First Peoples. Ottawa: Assembly of First Nations and Canadian Museums Association.

Hinsley, C. 1981. *Savages and Scientists: The Smithsonian Institution and the Development of American Anthropology, 1846-1910.* Washington, DC: Smithsonian Institution Press.

Hirsch, M., and A. Pickworth, eds. 2005. *The Native Universe and Museums in the Twenty-First Century: The Significance of the National Museum of the American Indian.* Washington, DC: NMAI, Smithsonian Institution.

Hodder, I., ed. 1987. *The Archaeology of Contextual Meanings.* Cambridge: Cambridge University Press.

–. 1989. *The Meanings of Things: Material Culture and Symbolic Expression.* London: Unwin Hyman.

–. 2012. *Entangled: An Archaeology of the Relationships between Humans and Things.* Chichester: John Wiley and Sons.

Hoffman, W.J. 1891. "The Midewiwin or 'Grand Medicine Society' of the Ojibwa." *Annual Reports of the Bureau of American Ethnology* 7: 143-300.

Holm, M., and D. Pokotylo. 1997. "From Policy to Practice: A Case Study in Collaborative Exhibits with First Nations." *Canadian Journal of Archaeology* 21, 1: 33-43.

Holmes, W.H. 1902. "Classification and Arrangement of the Exhibits of an Anthropological Museum." *Journal of the Anthropological Institute of Great Britain and Ireland* 32: 353-72.

Hooke, S.H. 1927. "Diffusionism with a Difference." *American Anthropologist* 29, 4: 615-24.

Hooper-Greenhill, E. 1992. *Museums and the Shaping of Knowledge.* London: Routledge.

Hoskins, J. 1998. *Biographical Objects: How Things Tell the Stories of People's Lives.* London: Routledge.

Houghton, D. 2010. "What Is Virtual Repatriation?" In *Museums and the Web Forum* (30 April). http://www.museumsandtheweb.com/.

Hudson's Bay Company. 1923. *Catalogue of the Hudson's Bay Company's Historical Exhibit at Winnipeg,* 3rd ed. Winnipeg: Hudson's Bay Company.

Humphreys, A. 2012. "Alberta Aboriginal Rock Etchings Defaced with Drill, Power Washer, Acid." *National Post* (Toronto), 18 September. http://news.nationalpost.com/.

Hunt, C. 1993. "The Museum: A Sacred Arena." *Zeitschrift für Ethnologie* 118, 1: 115-23.

Indian Claims Commission. 2004. *Peepeekisis First Nation File Hills Colony Inquiry Report.* Ottawa. http://dsp-psd.pwgsc.gc.ca/Collection/RC31-21-2004E.pdf.

Ingold, T. 2007. "Materials against Materiality." *Archaeological Dialogues* 14, 1: 1-16.

Innes, R.A. 2009. "'Wait a Second: Who Are You Anyways?': The Insider/Outsider Debate and American Indian Studies." *American Indian Quarterly* 33, 4: 440-61.

Jacknis, I. 1985. "Franz Boas and Exhibits: On the Limitations of the Museum Method of Anthropology." In *Objects and Others: Essays on Museums and Material Culture,* ed. G.W. Stocking Jr., 75-111. Madison: University of Wisconsin Press.

–. 1996a. "The Ethnographic Object and the Object of Ethnology in the Early Career of Franz Boas." In *Volksgeist as Method and Ethic: Essays on Boasian Ethnography and the*

German Anthropological Tradition, ed. G.W. Stocking Jr., 185-214. Madison: University of Wisconsin Press.

–. 1996b. "Repatriation as Social Drama: The Kwakiutl Indians of British Columbia, 1922-1980." *American Indian Quarterly* 20, 2: 274-86.

–. 2002. *The Storage Box of Tradition: Kwakiutl Art, Anthropologists and Museums, 1881-1981.* Washington, DC: Smithsonian Institution Press.

–. 2006. "A New Thing? The NMAI in Historical and Institutional Perspective." *American Indian Quarterly* 30, 3-4: 511-41.

Jackson, P. 2000. "Rematerializing Social and Cultural Geography." *Social and Cultural Geography* 1: 9-14.

Janes, R., and G.T. Conaty, eds. 2005. *Looking Reality in the Eye: Museums and Social Responsibility.* Calgary: University of Calgary Press.

Jenkins, D. 1994. "Object Lessons and Ethnographic Displays: Museum Exhibitions and the Making of American Anthropology." *Comparative Studies in Society and History* 36, 2: 242-70.

Jenness, D. 1937. *The Indian Background of Canadian History.* Ottawa: King's Printer.

–. 1938. *The Sarcee Indians of Alberta.* Bulletin No. 23, Anthropology Series. Ottawa: National Museum of Canada.

–. 1996. *The Indians of Canada.* Toronto: University of Toronto Press in association with the National Museum of Man, National Museums of Canada, Ottawa. (Orig. pub. 1932.)

Jenness, S.E., ed. 1991. *Arctic Odyssey: The Diary of Diamond Jenness, 1913-1916.* Hull, QC: Canadian Museum of Civilization.

Jessup, L., and S. Bagg, eds. 2002. *On Aboriginal Representation in the Gallery.* Canadian Ethnology Service Mercury Series 135. Hull, QC: Canadian Museum of Civilization.

Joyce, R.A. 2012. "Life with Things: Archaeology and Materiality." In *Archaeology and Anthropology: Past, Present and Future,* ed. D. Shankland, 119-32. London: Berg.

Judd, N.M. 1967. *The Bureau of American Ethnology: A Partial History.* Norman: University of Oklahoma Press.

Kaeppler, A.L. 1978. *"Artificial Curiosities": An Exposition of Native Manufactures Collected on the Three Pacific Voyages of Captain James Cook, R.N.* Bernice P. Bishop Museum, Special Publication 65. Honolulu: Bishop Museum Press.

–. 1989. "Museums of the World: Stages for the Study of Ethnohistory." In *Museum Studies in Material Culture,* ed. S. Pearce, 83-96. Leicester: Leicester University Press.

Karp, I., C.M. Kreamer, and S.D. Lavine, eds. 1992. *Museums and Communities: The Politics of Public Culture.* Washington, DC, and London: Smithsonian Institution Press.

Karp, I., and S.D. Lavine, eds. 1991. *Exhibiting Cultures.* Washington, DC, and London: Smithsonian Institution Press.

Kasprycki, S. 2007. "A Devout Collector: Johann Georg Schwarz and Early Nineteenth-Century Menominee Art." In *Three Centuries of Woodlands Indian Art: A Collection of Essays.* European Review of Native American Studies Monographs 3, ed. J.C.H. King and C.F. Feest, 113-22. Altenstadt: ZKF.

Kidwell, C.S. 1999. "Every Last Dishcloth: The Prodigious Collecting of George Gustav Heye." In *Collecting Native America, 1870-1960,* ed. S. Krech III and B.A. Hail, 232-58. Washington, DC: Smithsonian Institution Press.

King, J.C.H. 1981. *Artificial Curiosities from the Northwest Coast of North America.* London: British Museum Publications.

–. 1989. *Living Arctic: Hunters of the Canadian North: An Exhibition at the Museum of Mankind Sponsored by Indigenous Survival International (Canada).* London: Trustees of the British Museum [and] Indigenous Survival International (Canada).

–. 1991a. "A Century of Indian Shows: Canadian and United States Exhibition in London, 1825-1925." *European Review of Native American Studies* 5, 1: 35-42.

—. 1991b. "Collecting in the Subarctic Today: The Entrenchment of Some 19th and 20th Century Prejudices." *Arctic Anthropology* 28, 1: 138-44.

—. 1994. "Vancouver's Ethnography: A Preliminary Description of Five Inventories from the Voyage of 1791-95." *Journal of the History of Collections* 6, 1: 53-54.

King, J.C.H., B. Pauksztat, and R. Storrie. 2005. *Arctic Clothing*. London: British Museum Press.

King, R.C. 1998. *Colonial Discourses, Collective Memories, and the Exhibition of Native American Cultures and Histories in the Contemporary United States*. Lincoln: University of Nebraska-Lincoln Press.

Knappett, C. 2005. *Thinking through Material Culture: An Interdisciplinary Perspective*. Philadelphia: University of Pennsylvania Press.

Knowles, C. 2007. "Object Journeys: Outreach Work between National Museums Scotland and the Tłįchǫ." In *Material Histories Proceedings of a Workshop Held at Marischal Museum, University of Aberdeen, 26-27 April 2007*, ed. A.K. Brown, 37-56. Aberdeen: Marischal Museum, University of Aberdeen.

—. 2011. "Objects as Ambassadors: Representing Nation through Museum Exhibitions." In *Unpacking the Collection: Networks of Material and Social Agency in the Museum*. One World Archaeology, ed. S. Byrne, A. Clarke, R. Harrison, and R. Torrence, 231-47. New York: Springer.

Kopytoff, I. 1986. "The Cultural Biography of Things: Commoditization as Process." In *The Social Life of Things: Commodities in Cultural Perspective*, ed. A. Appadurai, 64-91. Cambridge: Cambridge University Press.

Krech, S., III. 1989. *A Victorian Earl in the Arctic*. London: British Museum Publications.

Krech, S., III, and B.A. Hail, eds. 1999. *Collecting Native America, 1870-1960*. Washington, DC: Smithsonian Institution Press.

Kreps, C.F. 2003. *Liberating Culture: Cross-Cultural Perspectives on Museums, Curation and Heritage Preservation*. London: Routledge.

Krmpotich, C., and D. Anderson. 2005. "Collaborative Exhibitions and Visitor Reactions: The Case of *Nitsitapiisinni: Our Way of Life*." *Curator* 48, 4: 377-405.

Krmpotich, C., and L. Peers. 2013. *This Is Our Life: Haida Material Heritage and Changing Museum Practice*. Vancouver: UBC Press.

Krupnik, I., and W. Fitzhugh, eds. 2001. *Gateways: Exploring the Legacy of the Jesup North Pacific Expedition, 1897-1902*. Contributions to Circumpolar Anthropology 1. Washington, DC: Arctic Studies Center, National Museum of Natural History, Smithsonian Institution.

Küchler, S. 1997. "Sacrificial Economy and Its Objects: Rethinking Colonial Collecting in Oceania." *Journal of Material Culture* 2, 1: 39-60.

Kuklick, H. 2007. "The British Tradition." In *A New History of Anthropology*, ed. H. Kuklick, 52-78. Oxford: Wiley-Blackwell.

—. 2011. "Personal Equations: Reflections on the History of Fieldwork, with Special Reference to Sociocultural Anthropology." *Isis* 102, 1: 1-33.

Kulchyski, P. 1993. "Anthropology in the Service of the State: Diamond Jenness and Canadian Indian Policy." *Journal of Canadian Studies* 28, 2: 21-50.

Kwasnik, E.I. 1993. *A Wider World: Collections of Foreign Ethnography in Scotland*. Edinburgh: National Museums of Scotland in association with the Scottish Museums Council.

Kwint, M. 1999. "Introduction." In *Material Memories: Design and Evocation*, ed. M. Kwint, C. Breward, and J. Aynsley, 1-16. Oxford: Berg.

Laforet, A. 2006. "Narratives of the Treaty Table: Cultural Property and the Negotiation of Tradition." In *Questions of Traditions*, ed. M. Salber Phillips and G. Schochet, 33-55. Toronto: University of Toronto Press.

Larson, F. 2009. *An Infinity of Things: How Sir Henry Wellcome Collected the World.* Oxford: Oxford University Press.

Lassiter, L.E. 2005. "Collaborative Ethnography and Public Anthropology." *Current Anthropology* 46, 1: 83-106.

Latham, A. 2004. "Research and Writing Everyday Accounts of the City: An Introduction to the Photo-Diary-Interview Method." In *Picturing the Social Landscape: Visual Methods and the Sociological Imagination,* ed. C. Knowles and J. Sweetman, 117-31. London: Routledge.

Legacy of Hope Foundation. 2003. *Where Are the Children? Healing the Legacy of the Residential Schools.* Ottawa: Legacy of Hope Foundation in association with the Aboriginal Healing Foundation.

Lenz, M.J. 2004. "No Tourist Material: George Heye and His Golden Rule." *American Indian Art Magazine* 29, 4: 86-95, 105.

Lincoln, A., with J. Goodwin, P. Goodwin, F. Ongtowasruk, R. Senungetuk, and B. Weyiouanna. 2010. *Living with Old Things: Inupiaq Stories, Bering Strait Histories.* Anchorage: US National Park Service.

Lindsay, D. 1993. *Science in the Subarctic: Trappers, Traders and the Smithsonian Institution.* Washington, DC: Smithsonian Institution Press.

Lindsay, M., ed. 1991. *Taonga Māori Conference: New Zealand, 18-27 November 1991.* Wellington: Department of Internal Affairs Te Tari Taiwhenua.

Lindstrom, L. 2013. "On Safari with Martin and Osa Johnson." In *Reinventing First Contact: Expeditions, Anthropology and Popular Culture,* ed. J.A. Bell, A.K. Brown, and R. Gordon, 147-61. Washington, DC: Smithsonian Institution Scholarly Press.

Linenthal, E., and T. Engelhardt, eds. 1996. *History Wars: The Enola Gay and Other Battles for the American Past.* New York: Holt Paperbacks.

Livesay, J.F.B. 1929. "Faith in West Is Not Shaken by Poor Crops." *Ottawa Journal,* 3 August, 10.

Lokensgard, K. 2010. *Blackfoot Religion and the Consequences of Cultural Commoditization.* Farnham, UK: Ashgate.

Lonetree, A., and A. Cobb-Greetham, eds. 2008. *The National Museum of the American Indian: Critical Conversations.* Lincoln: University of Nebraska Press.

Loo, T. 1992. "Dan Cranmer's Potlatch: Law as Coercion, Symbol and Rhetoric in British Columbia, 1884-1951." *Canadian Historical Review* 72, 2: 124-65.

Lothrop, S.K. 1957. "George Gustav Heye, 1874-1956." *American Antiquity* 23: 66-67.

Lynch, B. 2013. "Reflective Debate, Radical Transparency and Trust in the Museum." In "Working through Conflict in Museums: Museums, Objects and Participatory Democracy," special issue, *Museum Management and Curatorship* 28, 1: 1-13.

Macdonald, S. 2006. "Collecting Practices." In *A Companion to Museum Studies,* ed. S. Macdonald, 81-97. Oxford: Wiley-Blackwell.

MacDougall, D. 1997. "The Visual in Anthropology." In *Rethinking Visual Anthropology,* ed. M. Banks and H. Morphy, 276-95. New Haven, CT, and London: Yale University Press.

MacGregor, A. 2007. *Curiosity and Enlightenment: Collectors and Collections from the Sixteenth to the Nineteenth Century.* New Haven, CT: Yale University Press.

MacKeith, L. 1999. *A Report on the Totem Pole Project at the Royal Albert Memorial Museum with Special Reference to the Potential for Teaching about Northwest Coast People in the World Cultures Gallery.* Exeter: Royal Albert Memorial Museum.

MacKenzie, J.M. 2009. *Museums and Empire: Natural History, Human Cultures and Colonial Identities.* Manchester: Manchester University Press.

Mackey, E. 1995. "Postmodernism and Cultural Politics in a Multicultural Nation: Contests over Truth in the *Into the Heart of Africa* Controversy." *Public Culture* 7, 2: 403-32.

MacLean, J. 1924. "Bungay and Others." *The Beaver* 4, 11: 397-99.

Maddra, S. 1996. "The Wounded Knee Ghost Dance Shirt." *Journal of Museum Ethnography* 8: 41-58.

—. 2006. *Hostiles? The Lakota Ghost Dance and Buffalo Bill's Wild West.* Norman: University of Oklahoma Press.

Makepeace, A. 2001. *Edward S. Curtis: Coming to Light.* Washington, DC: National Geographic.

Mandelbaum, D.G. 1940. "The Plains Cree." *Anthropological Papers of the American Museum of Natural History* 37: 163-316.

—. 1996. *The Plains Cree: An Ethnographic, Historical and Comparative Study.* Regina: Canadian Plains Research Center, University of Regina. (Orig. pub. 1979.)

Marcus, G.E., and M.M. Fischer. 1986. *Anthropology as Cultural Critique: An Experimental Moment in the Human Sciences.* Chicago: Chicago University Press.

Marie, S., and J. Thompson. 2004. *Whadoo Tehmi: Long-Ago People's Packsack: Dene Babiche Bags: Tradition and Revival.* Canadian Ethnology Service, Mercury Series 141. Gatineau, QC: Canadian Museum of Civilization.

Martin, L. 2002. "Negotiating Space for Aboriginal Art." In *On Aboriginal Representation in the Gallery.* Canadian Ethnology Service Mercury Series 135, ed. L. Jessup and S. Bagg, 239-46. Hull, QC: Canadian Museum of Civilization.

Martínez, D. 2008. "Out of the Woods and into the Museum: Charles A. Eastman's 1910 Collecting Expedition across Ojibwe Country." *American Indian Culture and Research Journal* 32, 4: 67-84.

Martinez, N.B. 1998. "An Indian Americas: NMAI Photographic Archive Documents Indian Peoples of Western Hemisphere." In *Spirit Capture: Photographs from the National Museum of the American Indian,* ed. T. Johnson, 29-57. Washington, DC: Smithsonian Institution Press in association with the National Museum of the American Indian.

Martinez, N.B., with R. Wyaco. 1998. "Camera Shots: Photographers, Expeditions and Collections." In *Spirit Capture: Photographs from the National Museum of the American Indian,* ed. T. Johnson, 77-106. Washington, DC: Smithsonian Institution Press in association with the National Museum of the American Indian.

Mason, P. 1994. "From Presentation to Representation: *Americana* in Europe." *Journal of the History of Collections* 6, 1: 1-20.

May, S.K. 2010. *Collecting Cultures: Myth, Politics, and Collaboration in the 1948 Arnhem Land Expedition.* Lanham, MD: AltaMira Press.

McCaffrey, M. 2002. "Crossing New Borders to Exhibit Iroquois Tourist Art." In *On Aboriginal Representation in the Gallery.* Canadian Ethnology Service Mercury Series 135, ed. L. Jessup and S. Bagg, 73-92. Hull, QC: Canadian Museum of Civilization.

McCarthy, C. 2007. *Exhibiting Māori: A History of Colonial Cultures of Display.* Berg: Oxford and New York.

McClintock, W. 1999. *The Old North Trail: Life, Legends and Religion of the Blackfeet Indians.* Lincoln: University of Nebraska Press. (Orig. pub. 1910.)

McCloughlin, M. 1993. "Of Boundaries and Borders: First Nations' History in Museums." *Canadian Journal of Communication* 18, 3: 365-85.

McCormack, P.A. 1991. "'That's a Piece of Junk': Issues in Contemporary Subarctic Collecting." *Arctic Anthropology* 28, 1: 124-37.

McIlwraith, T.F. 1930. "The Progress of Anthropology in Canada." *Canadian Historical Review* 11, 2: 132-50.

McLeod, M.D. 1984. *The Asante.* London: British Museum Press.

McLeod, N. 2009. *Cree Narrative Memory: From Treaties to Contemporary Times.* Saskatoon: Purich.

–. 2010. "Rethinking Indigenous History: James Henderson's Paintings as Mnemonic Icons." In *James Henderson: Wicite Owapi Wicasa: The Man Who Paints the Old Men*, ed. D. Ring and N. McLeod, 55-67. Saskatoon: Mendel Art Gallery.

Meijer-Drees, L. 1991. "Making Banff a Wild West: Norman Luxton, Indians and Banff Tourism." Master's diss., University of Calgary.

Miller, D. 1987. *Material Culture and Mass Consumption*. Oxford: Blackwell.

–, ed. 2005. *Materiality*. Durham: Duke University Press.

–. 2007. "Artefacts and the Meaning of Things." In *Museums in the Material World*, ed. S. Knell, 166-86. London: Routledge.

–. 2009. *Stuff*. Cambridge: Polity.

Miller, J.R. 1991. *Skyscrapers Hide the Heavens: A History of Indian-White Relations in Canada*. Toronto: University of Toronto Press.

Milloy, J.S. 1999. *A National Crime: The Canadian Government and the Residential School System, 1879 to 1986*. Winnipeg: University of Manitoba Press.

Mills, D. 2003. "Professionalizing or Popularising Anthropology? A Brief History of Anthropology's Scholarly Associations in the UK." *Anthropology Today* 19, 5: 8-13.

–. 2008. *Difficult Folk: A Political History of Social Anthropology*. Oxford: Berghahn.

Mithlo, N.M. 2009. *Our Indian Princess: Subverting the Stereotype*. Santa Fe: School for Advanced Research Press.

Morse, N., M. Macpherson, and S. Robinson. 2013. "Developing Dialogue in Co-Produced Exhibitions: Between Rhetoric, Intentions and Realities." In "Working through Conflict in Museums: Museums, Objects and Participatory Democracy," special issue, *Museum Management and Curatorship* 28, 1: 91-106.

Moser, S. 2010. "The Devil Is in the Detail: Museum Displays and the Creation of Knowledge." *Museum Anthropology* 33, 1: 22-32.

Museum Ethnographers Group. 1991. "Guidelines on the Management of Human Remains." *Journal of Museum Ethnography* 6: 22-24.

–. 2003. "Guidance Notes on Ethical Approaches in Museum Ethnography." *Journal of Museum Ethnography* 15: 157-69.

Museum of Archaeology and Anthropology (MAA). 1926. *Report of the Board of Archaeological and Anthropological Studies, 1924-25*. Cambridge: University of Cambridge Board of Archaeological and Anthropological Studies.

–. 1929. *Annual Report of the Faculty Board of Archaeology and Anthropology, 1928*. Cambridge: University of Cambridge Faculty Board of Archaeology and Anthropology.

–. 1930. *Annual Report of the Faculty Board of Archaeology and Anthropology, 1929*. Cambridge: University of Cambridge Faculty Board of Archaeology and Anthropology.

–. 1931. *Annual Report of the Faculty Board of Archaeology and Ethnology, 1930*. Cambridge: University of Cambridge Faculty Board of Archaeology and Anthropology.

–. 1936. *Annual Report of the Faculty Board of Archaeology and Ethnology, 1935*. Cambridge: University of Cambridge Faculty Board of Archaeology and Anthropology.

–. 1992. *Annual Report for 1991-92*. Cambridge: University Museum of Archaeology and Anthropology.

Museum of the American Indian. 1926. *Annual Report, 1925-1926*. New York: Museum of the American Indian, Heye Foundation.

–. 1927. *Annual Report, 1926-1927*. New York: Museum of the American Indian, Heye Foundation.

Museums Association of Saskatchewan. 2001. *Standards for the Care of First Nations/Métis Collections*. Regina: Museums Association of Saskatchewan.

–. 2009. *First People's and Saskatchewan Museums Committee Elders Protocol*. Regina: Museums Association of Saskatchewan.

Museums Galleries Scotland. 2011. *Guidelines for the Care of Human Remains in Scottish Museum Collections.* Edinburgh: Museums Galleries Scotland.

Nason, J.D. 2000. "'Our' Indians: The Unidimensional Indian in the Disembodied Local Past." In *The Changing Presentation of the American Indian: Museums and Native Cultures,* ed. W.R. West, 29-46. Washington, DC, and Seattle: National Museum of the American Indian in association with the University of Washington Press.

Newell, J. 2005. "Exotic Possessions: Polynesians and Their Eighteenth-Century Collecting." *Journal of Museum Ethnography* 17: 75-88.

–. 2010. *Trading Nature: Tahitians, Europeans and Ecological Exchange.* Honolulu: University of Hawai'i Press.

Nicholson, J. 1985. "The Museum and the Indian Community: Findings and Orientation of Leicestershire Museums Service." *Museum Ethnographers Group Newsletter* 19 (September): 3-14.

Nicks, T. 1992. "Partnerships in Developing Cultural Resources: Lessons from the Task Force on Museums and First Peoples." *Culture* 12, 1: 87-93.

Nicolson, B. 1952. "Editorial: The Burlington Fine Arts Club." *Burlington Magazine* 94, 589: 97-99.

Noble, B., and R. Crowshoe. 2002. "'Nitooii – The Same That Is Real': Parallel Practice, Museums, and the Repatriation of Piikani Customary Authority." *Anthropologica* 44, 1: 113-30.

Noble, B., in consultation with Reg Crowshoe and in discussion with the Knut sum-atak Society. 2008. "Poomaksin: Skinnipiikani-Nitsiitapii Law, Transfers, and Making Relatives: Practices and Principles for Cultural Protection, Repatriation, Redress, and Heritage Law Making with Canada." In *First Nations Cultural Heritage and Law: Case Studies, Voices and Perspectives,* ed. C. Bell and V. Napoleon, 258-311. Vancouver: UBC Press.

Nurse, A. 2006. "Marius Barbeau and the Methodology of Salvage Ethnography in Canada, 1911-51." In *Historicizing Canadian Anthropology,* ed. J.D. Harrison and R. Darnell, 52-64. Vancouver: UBC Press.

–. 2008. "'Their Ancient Customs Are Gone': Anthropology as Cultural Process." In *Around and about Marius Barbeau: Modelling Twentieth-Century Culture,* ed. L. Jessup, A. Nurse, and G.E. Smith, 13-26. Canadian Ethnology Service Mercury Series 83. Gatineau, QC: Canadian Museum of Civilization.

Nyce, A. 2008. "Transforming Knowledge: The Nisga'a and the Marius Barbeau Collection." In *Around and about Marius Barbeau: Modelling Twentieth-Century Culture.* ed. L. Jessup, A. Nurse and G.E. Smith, 257-68. Canadian Ethnology Service Mercury Series 83, Gatineau, QC: Canadian Museum of Civilization.

Oberholtzer, C. 1996. "'This Isn't Ours': Implications of Fieldwork on Material Culture Studies." *Journal of Museum Ethnography* 8: 59-74.

–. 2002. "Six Degrees of Separation: Connecting Dr John Rae to James Bay Cree Objects in the Royal Ontario Museum." In *Selected Papers of the Rupert's Land Colloquium 2002, Oxford, England,* comp. D.G. Malaher, 211-25. Winnipeg: Centre for Rupert's Land Studies.

–. 2008. "Trading amongst Themselves in Nineteenth Century Canada: John Henry Lefroy and His Contacts and Connections." *Journal of Museum Ethnography* 20: 33-48.

Ogden, S., ed. 2004. *Caring for American Indian Objects: A Practical and Cultural Guide.* St. Paul: Minnesota Historical Society Press.

O'Hanlon, M. 1993. *Paradise: Portraying the New Guinea Highlands.* London: British Museum Press.

O'Hanlon, M., and R.L. Welsch, eds. 2000. *Hunting the Gatherers: Ethnographic Collectors, Agents and Agency in Melanesia, 1870s-1930s.* Oxford and New York: Berghahn Press.

Onciul, B. 2013. "Community Engagement, Curatorial Practice, and Museum Ethos in Alberta, Canada." In *Museums and Communities: Curators, Collections and Collaboration,* ed. V. Golding and W. Modest, 79-97. London: Bloomsbury.

O'Neill, M. 2006. "Repatriation and Its Discontents: The Glasgow Experience." In *Who Owns Objects? The Ethics and Politics of Collecting Cultural Artefacts,* ed. E. Robson, L. Treadwell, and C. Gosden, 105-28. Oxford: Oxbow Books.

Owen, M.A. 1904. *Folklore of the Musquakie Indians of North America and Catalogue of Musquakie Beadwork and Other Objects in the Collection of the Folk-Lore Society.* London: D. Nutt.

Pearce, S. 1992. *Museums, Objects and Collections.* Leicester: Leicester University Press.

–. 1995. *On Collecting: An Investigation into Collecting in the European Tradition.* London: Routledge.

–. 1998. *Collecting in Contemporary Practice.* London: Sage.

Pearce, S., and P. Martin, eds. 2002. *The Collector's Voice: Critical Readings in the Practice of Collecting.* Aldershot, UK: Ashgate.

Peers, L. 1994. *The Ojibwa of Western Canada, 1780 to 1870.* Winnipeg: University of Manitoba Press.

–. 1999a. "Curating Native American Art: The North American Perspective." *British Museum Magazine* 34 (Summer): 24-27.

–. 1999b. "'Many Tender Ties': The Shifting Contexts and Meanings of the S BLACK Bag." *World Archaeology* 31, 2: 288-302.

–. 2003. "Strands Which Refuse to Be Braided: Hair Samples from Beatrice Blackwood's Ojibwe Collection at the Pitt Rivers Museum." *Journal of Material Culture* 8, 1: 75-96.

–. 2009. "On the Treatment of Dead Enemies: Indigenous Human Remains in Britain in the Early Twenty-First Century." In *Social Bodies,* ed. H. Lambert and M. McDonald, 77-99. Oxford: Berghahn Books.

Peers, L., and K. Pettipas. 1996. "Reverend John West's Collection, Red River, 1820-1823." *American Indian Art Magazine* 21, 3: 62-73.

Penny, H.G. 2002. *Objects of Culture: Ethnology and Ethnographic Museums in Imperial Germany.* Chapel Hill: University of North Carolina Press.

Pettipas, K. 1993. "'Turning the Page' – Museums and First Nations: A Manitoba Case Study." *Manitoba Archaeological Journal* 3, 1-2: 86-97.

–. 1994. *Severing the Ties That Bind: Government Repression of Indigenous Religious Ceremonies on the Prairies.* Winnipeg: University of Manitoba Press.

–. 2009. "The Hudson's Bay Company Collection in the Manitoba Museum." *American Indian Art Magazine* 35, 1: 56-67.

Peyton, J., and R.L.A. Hancock. 2008. "Anthropology, State Formation, and Hegemonic Representations of Indigenous People in Canada, 1910-1939." *Native Studies Review* 17, 1: 45-69.

Phillips, R.B. 1984. *Patterns of Power: The Jasper Grant Collection and Great Lakes Indian Art of the Early Nineteenth Century.* Kleinburg: McMichael Canadian Collection.

–. 1998. *Trading Identities: The Souvenir in Native North American Art from the Northeast, 1700-1900.* Seattle: University of Washington Press.

–. 1999. "Art History and the Native-Made Object: New Discourses, Old Differences?" In *Native American Art in the Twentieth Century,* ed. W.J. Rushing III, 97-112. London and New York: Routledge.

–. 2005. "Re-Placing Objects: Historical Practices for the Second Museum Age." *Canadian Historical Review* 86, 1: 83-110.

–. 2011. *Museum Pieces: Towards the Indigenization of Canadian Museums.* Montreal and Kingston: McGill-Queen's University Press.

Phillips, R.B., and A.E. Coombes, eds. 2013. *Museum Transformations: Art, Culture, History.* Oxford: Blackwell.

Phillips, R.B., and E. Johnson. 2003. "Negotiating New Relationships: Canadian Museums, First Nations, and Cultural Property." In *Politics and the Past: On Repairing Historical Injustices,* ed. J. Torpey, 149-67. Lanham, MD: Rowman and Littlefield.

Pickles, J.D. 1988. "The Haddon Library, Cambridge." *Library History* 8, 1: 2-9.

Pierson Jones, J. 1992. "The Colonial Legacy and the Community: The Gallery 33 Project." In *Museums and Communities: The Politics of Public Culture,* ed. I. Karp, C. Mullen Kreamer, and S.D. Lavine, 221-41. Washington, DC, and London: Smithsonian Institution Press.

Pole, L. 2000. *World Connections: World Cultures Collections in the South West of England.* Taunton: South West Museums Council.

Powell, S. 1999. *The Franklin Automobile Company: The History of the Innovative Firm, Its Founders, the Vehicles It Produced (1902-1934), and the People Who Built Them.* Warrendale, PA: Society of Automotive Engineers.

Pratt, M.L. 1992. *Imperial Eyes: Travel Writing and Transculturation.* London: Routledge.

Pratt, S. 2005. *American Indians in British Art, 1700-1840.* Norman: University of Oklahoma Press.

–. 2006. "Blackfoot Culture and World Culture: Contexts for the Collection and Display of the Decorated Shirt of Issapoomahsika (or Crowfoot) in the Royal Albert Memorial Museum and Art Gallery, Exeter." *Journal of the History of Collections* 18, 2: 237-47.

Price, R., and S. Price. 1992. *Equatoria.* New York: Routledge.

Price, R.T. 1999. *The Spirit of the Alberta Indian Treaties.* 3rd ed. Edmonton: University of Alberta Press.

Proctor, A. 1994. *Cultures of the World: The Ethnographic Collections of Dundee Art Galleries and Museums.* Dundee: Dundee Art Galleries and Museums.

Province of Alberta. 2000. *First Nations Sacred Ceremonial Objects Repatriation Act.* C. F-14. Edmonton: Alberta Queen's Printer.

–. 2004. *Blackfoot First Nations Sacred Ceremonial Objects Repatriation Regulation.* Alberta Regulation 96/2004. Edmonton: Alberta Queen's Printer.

Qureshi, S. 2011. *Peoples on Parade: Exhibitions, Empire, and Anthropology in Nineteenth-Century Britain.* Chicago: University of Chicago Press.

Racine, D. 2009. "Indigenous Knowledge and Collecting in the North American Northwest: An Analysis of the Hudson's Bay Company." PhD diss., University of Oxford.

Rainger, R. 1980. "Philanthropy and Science in the 1830's: The British and Foreign Aborigines' Protection Society." *Man* 15, 4: 702-17.

Ray, A.J., J. Miller, and F. Tough. 2000. *Bounty and Benevolence: A History of Saskatchewan Treaties.* Montreal and Kingston: McGill-Queen's University Press.

RCAP (Royal Commission on Aboriginal Peoples). 1996. *Report of the Royal Commission on Aboriginal Peoples.* Vol. 3, *Gathering Strength.* Ottawa: Canada Communications Group.

Regular, W.K. 2008. *Neighbours and Networks: The Blood Tribe in the Southern Alberta Economy, 1884-1939.* Calgary: University of Calgary Press.

Rhodes, C. 2004. "Non-European Art in the *Burlington Magazine* before 1930." *Burlington Magazine* 146, 1211: 98-104.

Richling, B. 1990. "Political Contexts of Early Twentieth Century Indian Research: A Manitoba Dakota Example." Unpublished paper cited with permission of the author.

–. 1995. "Politics, Bureaucracy, and Arctic Archaeology in Canada, 1910-1939." *Arctic* 48, 2: 109-17.

Ridington, A., and K. Hennessy. 2008. "Building Indigenous Agency through Web-Based Exhibition: Dane-Wajich – Dane-zaa Stories and Songs: Dreamers and the Land." In *Museums and the Web 2008: Proceedings,* ed. J. Trant and D. Bearman. Toronto: Archives and Museum Informatics. http://www.archimuse.com/.

Robinson, M.F. 2006. *The Coldest Crucible: Arctic Exploration and American Culture.* Chicago: University of Chicago Press.

Rose, A. 2000. *Bringing Our Ancestors Home: The Repatriation of Nisga'a Artifacts.* New Aiyansh: Nisga'a Tribal Council.

Rose, G. 2007. *Visual Methodologies: An Introduction to the Interpretation of Visual Materials.* London: Sage.

Ross, M., and R. Crowshoe. 1999. "Shadows and Sacred Geography: First Nations History-Making from an Alberta Perspective." In *Making Histories in Museums,* ed. G. Kavanagh, 240-56. London: Leicester University Press.

Ross, W.G. 1984. "George Comer, Franz Boas, and the American Museum of Natural History." *Études Inuit Studies* 8, 1: 145-64.

Rouse, S. 1996. "Ethnology, Ethnobiography, and Institution: A.C. Haddon and Anthropology at Cambridge, 1880-1926." PhD diss., University of Cambridge.

—. 1998. "Expedition and Institution: A.C. Haddon and Anthropology at Cambridge." In *Cambridge and the Torres Strait: Centenary Essays on the 1898 Anthropological Expedition,* ed. A. Herle and S. Rouse, 50-76. Cambridge: Cambridge University Press.

Rowley, S., D. Schaepe, L. Sparrow, A. Sanborn, U. Radermacher, R. Wallace, N. Jakobsen, H. Turner, S. Sadofsky, and T. Goffman. 2010. "Building an On-Line Research Community: The Reciprocal Research Network." In *Museums and the Web 2010: Proceedings,* ed. J. Trant and D. Bearman. Toronto: Archives and Museum Informatics. http://www.archimuse.com/.

Rymill, J.R. 1938. *Southern Lights: The Official Account of the British Graham Land Expedition, 1934-1937.* London: Chatto and Windus.

Salmond, A. 2012. "Digital Subjects, Cultural Objects: Special Issue Introduction." *Journal of Material Culture* 17, 3: 211-28.

Salmond, A., and R. Raymond, eds. 2008. *Pasifika Styles: Artists inside the Museum.* Dunedin: Otago University Press.

Sant Cassia, P. 1992. "Ways of Displaying." *Museums Journal* 92, 1: 28-31.

Sapir, E. 1911. "An Anthropological Survey of Canada." *Science* 34, 884: 789-93.

Schildkrout, E., and C.A. Keim, eds. 1998. *The Scramble for Art in Central Africa.* Cambridge: University of Cambridge Press.

Schindlbeck, M. 1993. "The Art of Collecting: Interactions between Collectors and the People They Visit." *Zeitschrift für Ethnologie* 118: 57-67.

Scott, D.C. 1931. *The Administration of Indian Affairs in Canada.* Ottawa: Canadian Institute of International Affairs.

Sekula, A. 1984. *Photography against the Grain: Essays and Photo Works, 1973-1983.* Halifax: Press of the Nova Scotia College of Art and Design.

Shelton, A.A. 1992. "The Recontextualization of Culture in UK Museums." *Anthropology Today* 8, 5: 11-16.

—, ed. 2001a. *Collectors: Expressions of Self and Other.* London/Coimbra: Horniman Museum and Gardens/Museu Antropológico da Universidade de Coimbra.

—. 2001b. *Collectors, Individuals and Institutions.* London/Coimbra: Horniman Museum and Gardens/Museu Antropológico da Universidade de Coimbra.

—. 2006. "Museums and Anthropologies: Practices and Narratives." In *A Companion to Museum Studies,* ed. S. Macdonald, 64-80. Oxford: Wiley-Blackwell.

Shewell, H. 2004. *"Enough to Keep Them Alive": Indian Welfare in Canada, 1873-1965.* Toronto: University of Toronto Press.

Sillar, B., and C. Fforde, eds. 2005. *Conservation, Identity and Ownership in Indigenous Archaeology.* London: Earthscan/James and James.

Sillitoe, P. 2004. "Making Links, Opening Out: Anthropology and the British Association for the Advancement of Science." *Anthropology Today* 20, 6: 10-15.

Simpson, M. 2001. *Making Representations: Museums in the Post-Colonial Era*. London and New York: Routledge. (Orig. pub. 1996.)

Skinner, A.B. 1914a. "Notes on the Plains Cree." *American Anthropologist* 16, 1: 86-87.

—. 1914b. "Political and Ceremonial Organization of the Plains-Ojibway." *Anthropological Papers of the American Museum of Natural History* 2, 6: 475-512.

—. 1914c. "Political Organization, Cults and Ceremonies of the Plains Cree." *Anthropological Papers of the American Museum of Natural History* 2, 6: 515-42.

—. 1921. "Recollections of an Ethnologist among the Menomini Indians." *Wisconsin Archaeologist* 20: 41-74.

Sleeper-Smith, S., ed. 2009. *Contesting Knowledge: Museums and Indigenous Perspectives*. Lincoln: University of Nebraska Press.

Smith, C., and H.M. Wobst, eds. 2005. *Indigenous Archaeologies: Decolonizing Theory and Practice*. London: Routledge.

Smith, D.G. 2001. "The 'Policy of Aggressive Civilization' and Projects of Governance in Roman Catholic Industrial Schools for Native Peoples in Canada, 1870-95." *Anthropologica* 43, 2: 253-71.

Smith, K.D. 2009. *Liberalism, Surveillance, and Resistance: Indigenous Communities in Western Canada*. Edmonton: Athabasca University Press.

Smith, L.T. 1999. *Decolonizing Methodologies: Research and Indigenous Peoples*. London and New York: Zed Books.

Smith, P.J. 2009. *A Splendid Idiosyncrasy: Prehistory at Cambridge, 1915-1950*. British Archaeological Reports, No. 485. Oxford: Archaeopress.

Srinivasan, R., K.M. Becvar, R. Boast, and J. Enote. 2010. "Diverse Knowledges and Contact Zones within the Digital Museum." *Science, Technology and Human Values* 35, 5: 735-68.

Srinivasan, R., J. Enote, K.M. Becvar, and R. Boast. 2009. "Critical and Reflective Uses of New Media Technologies in Tribal Museums." *Museum Management and Curatorship* 24, 2: 161-81.

Stable, C., and R. Scott. 2008. "Object Journeys: International Lending and Increasing Access Opportunities for Tłįchǫ Cultural Artifacts from the National Museums of Scotland." In *Preserving Aboriginal Heritage: Technical and Traditional Approaches. Proceedings of Symposium 2007*, ed. C. Dignard, K. Helwig, J. Mason, K. Nanowin, and T. Stone, 61-66. Ottawa: Canadian Conservation Institute.

Starkey, J. 1998. *Myths and Mirrors: A Report on Ethnographic Collections in the North-East of England*. Newcastle-upon-Tyne: North East Museums.

Starn, O. 2011. "Here Come the Anthros (Again): The Strange Marriage of Anthropology and Native America." *Cultural Anthropology* 26, 2: 179-204.

Starr-Spaeth [Starblanket], D. 1994. "Chief Star Blanket and His Band: A Brief History." Bachelor's thesis, Department of Indian Studies, Saskatchewan Indian Federated College, University of Regina.

Stewart, S. 1993. *On Longing: Narratives of the Miniature, the Gigantic, the Souvenir, the Collection*. Durham, NC: Duke University Press.

Stewart-Robinson, T. 2006. "Hidden Treasures: That's How Many Indian and Inuit Artifacts and Human Remains Are Housed in Museums across Britain. Native Communities Would Like Them Back." *Toronto Star*, 7 October, F1.

Stocking, G.W., Jr. 1983. "The Ethnographer's Magic: Fieldwork in British Anthropology from Tylor to Malinowski." In *Observers Observed: Essays on Ethnographic Fieldwork*, ed. G.W. Stocking Jr., 70-120. Madison: University of Wisconsin Press.

—. 1985. "Philanthropoids and Vanishing Cultures: Rockefeller Funding and the End of the Museum Era in Anglo-American Anthropology." In *Objects and Others: Essays on Museums and Material Culture*, ed. G.W. Stocking Jr., 112-45. Madison: University of Wisconsin Press.

–. 1987. *Victorian Anthropology.* New York: Free Press.

–. 1992. *The Ethnographer's Magic and Other Essays in the History of Anthropology.* Madison: University of Wisconsin Press.

–. 1999. *After Tylor: British Social Anthropology, 1888-1951.* Madison: University of Wisconsin Press. (Orig. pub. 1995.)

Stonechild, B. 2010. "Tales of Two Valleys: Pageants and Portraits." http://www.mendel.ca/.

Syms, E.L. 1997. "Increasing Awareness and Involvement of Aboriginal People in Heritage Preservation: Recent Developments at the Manitoba Museum of Man and Nature." In *At a Crossroads: Archaeology and First Peoples in Canada,* ed. G.P. Nicholas and T.D. Andrews, 224-34. Burnaby, BC: Simon Fraser University Archaeology Press.

Tamarapa, A. 1996. "Museum *Kaitiaki:* Māori Perspectives on the Presentation and Management of Māori Treasures and Relationships with Museums." In *Curatorship: Indigenous Perspectives in Post-Colonial Societies: Proceedings,* 160-69. Ottawa: Canadian Museum of Civilization with the Commonwealth Association of Museums and the University of Victoria.

Tanner, J. 1999. *From Pacific Shores: Eighteenth Century Ethnographic Collections at Cambridge. The Voyages of Cook, Vancouver and the First Fleet.* Cambridge: University of Cambridge Museum of Archaeology and Anthropology.

Tapsell, P. 1998. "Taonga: A Tribal Response to Museums." PhD diss., University of Oxford.

–. 2005. "Out of Sight, Out of Mind: Human Remains at the Auckland Museum-Te Papa Whakahiku." In *Looking Reality in the Eye: Museums and Social Responsibility,* ed. R.R. Janes and G.T. Conaty, 153-74. Calgary: University of Calgary Press.

Taylor, C. 1975. *The Warriors of the Plains.* London: Hamlyn.

Taylor, C., and H.A. Dempsey. 1999. *With Eagle Tail.* London: Vega.

Taylor, J. 1984. *Canadian Indian Policy during the Interwar Years, 1918-1939.* Ottawa: Indian and Northern Affairs Canada.

Thomas, N. 1991. *Entangled Objects: Exchange, Material Culture and Colonialism in the Pacific.* Cambridge, MA: Harvard University Press.

–. 1997. *In Oceania: Visions, Artifacts, Histories.* Durham, NC, and London: Duke University Press.

–. 1999. "The Case of the Misplaced Ponchos." *Journal of Material Culture* 4, 1: 5-20.

–. 2010. "The Museum as Method." *Museum Anthropology* 33, 1: 6-10.

–. 2011. "Introduction." In *Gifts and Discoveries: The Museum of Archaeology and Anthropology, Cambridge,* ed. M. Elliott and N. Thomas, 4-15. London: Scala.

Thompson, J., and I. Kritsch. 2005. *Yeenoo Dài' K'ètr'ijilkai' Ganagwaandaii: Long Ago Sewing We Will Remember: The Story of the Gwich'in Traditional Caribou Skin Clothing Project.* Canadian Ethnology Service Mercury Series 143. Gatineau, QC: Canadian Museum of Civilization.

Thornton, M.V. 2000. *Buffalo People: Portraits of a Vanishing Nation.* Surrey, BC: Hancock House.

Titley, E.B. 1995. *A Narrow Vision: Duncan Campbell Scott and the Administration of Indian Affairs in Canada.* Vancouver: UBC Press. (Orig. pub. 1986.)

Tobias, J.L. 1976. "Protection, Civilization, Assimilation: An Outline History of Canada's Indian Policy." *Western Canadian Journal of Anthropology* 4, 2: 13-30.

Tracy, W. 1991. "Collecting Contemporary Native Arts in the Boreal Forest of Western Canada." *Arctic Anthropology* 28, 1: 101-9.

Treaty 7 Elders and Tribal Council, with W. Hildebrandt, D. First Rider, and S. Carter. 1996. *The True Spirit and Original Intent of Treaty 7.* Montreal and Kingston: McGill-Queen's University Press.

Turnbull, P., and M. Pickering, eds. 2010. *The Long Way Home: The Meaning and Values of Repatriation.* New York: Berghahn Books.

Tythacott, L. 2011. "Race on Display: The 'Melanesian,' 'Mongolian' and 'Caucasian' Galleries at Liverpool Museum (1896-1929)." *Journal of Early Popular Visual Culture* 9, 2: 131-42.

University of Cambridge. 1929. *Cambridge University Reporter.* Cambridge: University of Cambridge.

Urry, J. 1984. "Englishmen, Celts and Iberians: The Ethnographic Survey of the United Kingdom, 1892-99." In *Functionalism Historicized: Essays on British Social Anthropology,* ed. G.W. Stocking Jr., 83-105. Madison: University of Wisconsin Press.

van Broekhoven, L., C. Buijs, and P. Hovens, eds. 2010. *Sharing Knowledge and Cultural Heritage: First Nations of the Americas. Studies in Collaboration with Indigenous Peoples from Greenland, North and South America.* Leiden: National Museum of Ethnology and Sidestone Press.

VanStone, J.W. 1983. *The Simms Collection of Plains Cree Material Culture from Southeastern Saskatchewan.* Fieldiana Anthropology New Series 6. Chicago: Field Museum of Natural History.

–. 1992. *Material Culture of the Blackfoot (Blood) Indians of Southern Alberta.* Fieldiana Anthropology New Series 19. Chicago: Field Museum of Natural History.

Venbrux, E. 2001. "On the Pre-Museum History of Baldwin Spencer's Collection of Tiwi Artefacts." In *Academic Anthropology and the Museum: Back to the Future,* ed. M. Bouquet, 55-74. Oxford: Berghahn.

Venne, S. 1997. "Understanding Treaty 6: An Indigenous Perspective." In *Aboriginal and Treaty Rights in Canada: Essays on Law, Equity, and Respect for Difference,* ed. M. Asch, 173-207. Vancouver: UBC Press.

Vergo, P., ed. 1988. *The New Museology.* London: Reaktion Books.

Vyvyan, C.C. 1998. *The Ladies, the Gwich'in, and the Rat: Travels on the Athabasca, Mackenzie, Rat, Porcupine and Yukon Rivers, 1926.* Ed. I.S. MacLaren and L.N. LaFramboise. Edmonton: University of Alberta Press.

Wakeham, P. 2008. *Taxidermic Signs: Reconstructing Aboriginality.* Minneapolis: University of Minnesota Press.

Wallace, K. 1960. "A Reporter at Large: Slim-shin's Monument." *New Yorker* 36, 104-46.

Waller, N. 2004. "The Spirits of Things: Understanding Crow Religious Experience and Museum Custodial Practices." Master's diss., Göteborg University.

Warry, W. 2007. *Ending Denial: Understanding Aboriginal Issues.* Peterborough: Broadview Press.

Waterfield, H., and J.C.H. King. 2007. *Provenance: Twelve Collectors of Ethnographic Art in England, 1760-1990.* Paris: Somogy Art Publishers in association with Barbier-Mueller Museum, Geneva.

Weir, S. 1970. *Spinning and Weaving in Palestine.* London: British Museum Press.

–. 1989. *Palestinian Costume.* London: British Museum Press.

Wernitznig, D. 2007. *Europe's Indians: Indians in Europe.* Lanham, MD: University Press of America.

Wickwire, W. 2005. "'They Wanted ... Me to Help Them': James A. Teit and the Challenge of Ethnography in the Boasian Era." In *With Good Intentions: Euro-Canadian and Aboriginal Relations in Colonial Canada,* ed. C. Haig-Brown and D.A. Nock, 297-320. Vancouver: UBC Press.

Willmott, C. 2006. "The Historical Praxis of Museum Anthropology: A Canada-US Comparison." In *Historicizing Canadian Anthropology,* ed. J.D. Harrison and R. Darnell, 212-25. Vancouver: UBC Press.

Wilson, R.N. 1921. *Our Betrayed Wards: A Story of Chicanery, Infidelity and the Prostitution of Trust.* Ottawa: Privately published.

Wissler, C. 1910. *Material Culture of the Blackfoot Indians.* Anthropological Papers 5, Part 1. New York: American Museum of Natural History.

—. 1911. *The Social Life of the Blackfoot Indians.* Anthropological Papers 7, Part 1. New York: American Museum of Natural History.

—. 1912. *Ceremonial Bundles of the Blackfoot Indians.* Anthropological Papers 7, Part 2. New York: American Museum of Natural History.

—. 1913. *Societies and Dance Associations of the Blackfoot Indians.* Anthropological Papers 11, Part 4. New York: American Museum of Natural History.

—. 1918. *The Sun Dance of the Blackfoot Indians.* Anthropological Papers 16, Part 3. New York: American Museum of Natural History.

—. 1926. *The Relation of Nature to Man in Aboriginal America.* New York: Oxford University Press.

Wissler, C., and D.C. Duvall. 1995. *Mythology of the Blackfoot Indians.* Lincoln: University of Nebraska Press. (Orig. pub. 1908.)

Wissler, C., and A.B. Kehoe. 2012. *Amskapi Pikuni: The Blackfeet People.* Albany, NY: SUNY Press.

Wrightson, K. 2012. "(Mis/Dis/Re)Articulation: Audience Perception and Misperception at *Extremes* Exhibition at the National Museums Scotland." Paper presented at Museum Ethnographers Group Annual Conference, National Museums Scotland, Edinburgh, 16 April.

Yaya, I. 2008. "Wonders of America: The Curiosity Cabinet as a Site of Representation and Knowledge." *Journal of the History of Collections* 20, 2: 173-88.

Yellowhorn, E. 1999. "Heritage Protection on Indian Reserve Lands in Canada." *Plains Anthropologist* 44, 170: 107-16.

Zaslow, M. 1975. *Reading the Rocks: The Story of the Geological Survey of Canada, 1842-1972.* Toronto: Macmillan.

Zedeño, M.N. 2008. "Bundled Worlds: The Roles and Interactions of Complex Objects from the North American Plains." *Journal of Archaeological Method and Theory* 15: 362-78.

Index

Note: "(f)" after a page number indicates a figure; "MAA" stands for Museum of Archaeology and Anthropology.

Aborigines Protection Society, 66
access: and cultural revitalization projects, 247-48, 250-51; and digitization, 8, 29, 248-49; and healing, 9, 16, 171; impact of, 172. *See also* database projects
agency: and animacy, 27; in collecting, 21, 133, 146, 149
agriculture: Department of Indian Affairs control of, 43; and self-sufficiency, 41
Air-Cooled Adventure among the Aborigines, 142(f); illustrations in, 130, 141, 152; limitations of, 111, 151; misrepresentations in, 151; as promotional material, 114, 120, 149-51
Ajidamoo (Squirrel), 114-15, 138-39, 161
American Museum of Natural History: catalogue records of, 119, 262n48; collecting activities of, 85-86; influence of, 203
ancestral remains, 241-42
anonymity: of artifacts/photographs, 224; in museum exhibits, 224-25
anthropologists: as advocates, 22, 57-58, 93, 94, 119; and artifact collection, 18, 119; as authorities, 75; and fieldwork, 74; indigenous people as, 259n32;

professional links between, 73, 79, 83. *See also individual anthropologists*
anthropology: as academic discipline, 3-4; Boasian, 3, 72; in Britain, 19, 73, 79; in Canada, 63, 70-71, 85; collaborative practice, 27; colonialist model of, 23, 66, 71; criticism of, 15, 59; decolonization of, 15-16, 28; and "disappearing Indian," 64; epistemological constraints of, 27; and ethnographic museums, 3, 19, 201; and filmmaking, 147-48; histories of, 19; methodologies, 73, 131; nationalist tradition in, 23, 71; reflexive turn in, 15, 219; and salvage, 63-65, 75, 83, 131; and social evolutionism, 70; in the United States, 84-85. *See also* ethnography; visual anthropology
Applebaum-Hébert Report, 71
archaeological sites: destruction of, 60; protection of, 60
archives: and taxonomic structures, 197
artifacts: artistic engagement with, 24; and authenticity, 123-24; classification of, 196, 199, 201-3, 204; commodification of, 131; as "curios," 125; display of, 199, 201-3; as documents of culture, 19; as

ethnographic representation, 199, 210; First Nations relations with, 15, 189; and healing, 9, 16, 171, 177; and knowledge, 186; and knowledge production, 24, 239; market for, 94; rights of ownership of, 6; as souvenirs, 125; as type specimens, 120, 124, 174, 197, 207

assimilation: effects of, 49, 57; legacy of, 59; legislation, 39

atim kâ-mihkwasit (Red Dog), 41, 56, 117, 141(f), 265*n*12; arrest of, 168; beaded outfit of, 118, 169-71, 170(f), 227; film and photographs of, 140-41, 153(f); as leader, 167; as singer, 172

audience. *See* visitors

authenticity, 75, 207; criteria for, 123-24; and tradition, 64

authority: and collecting, 16, 24; curatorial, 219; museums as sites of, 219, 233; sharing of, 29; and voice, 12-13, 24

backrest banners, 208-9, 208(f)

Barbeau, Marius, 73; and salvage ethnography, 64; and "vanishing race," 75

bead work, 65, 118, 169-70, 226

belief systems. *See* epistemology

Bigknife, Charlie, 167

Bigknife, Donald, 133

Bigknife, Florence, 177

Bill C-45, 242, 268*n*2

bison: decimation of, 37, 42

Black-Rogers, M., 164

Blackfeet Nation: repatriation and, 182-83

Blackfoot Digital Library, 251, 269*n*11

Blackfoot First Nations Sacred Ceremonial Objects Repatriation Regulation, 181

Blackfoot Indians of Alberta, 74

Blackfoot people: anthropological interest in, 179; and ceremonial bundles, 27, 179-80; experience of colonialism, 179; and museum work, 183-84; and repatriation, 181-83; representations of, 212-14; research visits to museums, 183, 191

Blackwood, Beatrice, 41, 48, 58, 92, 96, 263*n*54

Boas, Franz, 3; as collector, 69, 83; influence of, 65, 70, 72; museum work, 201; on role of museums, 64-65; use of photographs, 158

Boast, Robin, 227

British Association for the Advancement of Science (BAAS), 68-69, 79

British Museum, 31, 244-45

Bruised Head, Jenny, 188-89, 228, 236

Bull Plume, 50

Bureau of American Ethnology (BAE), 85

Burkinshaw, Jane, 243-44

Burlington Fine Arts Club, 229-31

Bushnell, Geoffrey, 81, 211, 262*n*42, 267*n*20

Cadzow, Donald A., 4, 5(f); as advocate, 57; biography of, 106-7; fieldwork for Museum of the American Indian, 35, 89, 107, 111, 114, 122-23, 135-36, 142; Franklin Motor Expedition plans of, 99, 109; personal collecting of, 128, 263*n*68; as photographer, 137-38, 141

Calgary Museum, 77

Calgary Stampede, 53-54, 125

Cameron, Sam, 36, 114, 160

Canada: ties with the United Kingdom, 24

Canadian Museum of Civilization, 6; name change, 253*n*2; repatriation and, 8, 68

Carpenter, Edmund (Ted), 119

Carrier, Lorne, 62-63, 156

ceremonial practices: and community divisions, 49, 57, 181; demonized, 49; and language, 49; modification of, 51; non-Native attendance at, 51, 143, 188; reconstruction of, 142-43; suppression of, 49-53, 58. *See also* Sun Dance

Christianity. *See* missionaries

Clarke, Louis Colville Gray, 79, 82(f), 133; biography of, 81; as curator, 199, 203, 208-9; support of North American research, 105

Clifford, James, 28

Cole, Douglas, 20

collaboration: in anthropology, 28; between museums, 110; in curatorship, 227, 240, 241, 248; international, 228-29, 247-48; vs non-collaborative display, 228

collaboration process: changes in, 11-12; protocols for, 240-41

collecting, of artifacts: by anthropologists, 18, 96, 135-36; by British museums, 78-79; by Canadian museums, 68-75,

95; of ceremonial objects, 93, 119, 122-23; and classification, 16, 68; and colonialism, 18-19; competitive aspects of, 135; contemporary, 223, 226; cost of, 170; Department of Indian Affairs involvement in, 94-96, 176; on expeditions, 18, 67, 85; by fur traders, 67, 71, 76, 93; by Indian agents, 94-96; indigenization of, 93; by indigenous people, 18, 86-87; indigenous perspectives on, 24; media criticism of, 71-72, 126; by missionaries, 67; for museums, 71; need for haste, 65, 108, 131; relationship with hunting, 136, 137; resistance to, 135-36; scientific, 67; by soldiers, 67; by United States museums, 83-90; value of histories of, 165
collectors: types of, 18, 123
colonialism: and anthropology, 59; and healing, 7, 239
colonization: effects on First Nations, 37, 39
contact zone, 28; critique of, 255*n*16
conversion: and destruction of cultural objects, 161; and sale of cultural objects, 161, 180
cultural area: as display strategy, 212, 214
cultural biography: and artifacts, 25-27; limits of, 26-27, 237
cultural centres, 8, 66. *See also* keeping houses
cultural performance: in historical pageants, 53; at Indian Days, 53. *See also* Calgary Stampede; Wild West shows
culture: language and, 15, 19; loss vs survival/revival, 156; revitalization, 8, 182, 239, 248, 250; transmission of, 65
cultures, Aboriginal: anti-potlatch legislation and, 49-50; attacks on, 49-57; protocols of, 30, 93, 159, 164
curators/curatorship: classificatory processes of, 196, 199, 201-3; and exclusion of indigenous perspectives, 157, 196; as experts, 210. *See also* museums: and traditional care
Curtis, Edward: photographs of, 182
Cuthand, Josie, 122-23
Cuthand, Stan, 122-23

dancing: persistence of, 55-56; prohibitions on, 54-55

Daniels, Don, 163
Daniels, Minnie, 167-68
database projects, 192, 249-51. *See also* access; *specific database projects*
Dawson, George Mercer, 68, 69, 83
Dempsey, Hugh, 23-24
Department of Indian Affairs, 40; and agricultural policy, 43-44; and anthropological research, 35, 59, 92-96; and Indian agents, 40; and museums, 92-96, 176. *See also* Indian Act
Digby, Adrian, 230-31
digitization projects, 29, 248-51
Donaghy, James, 44, 45-46, 51, 115
Duvall, David C., 86-87
drums, 164, 172-74, 234

Eastman, Charles, 93
economy: of craft production, 45, 176-77; reserve-based, 41-45
education: and assimilation, 46-47. *See also* residential schools
Edwards, Elizabeth, 158, 159, 175, 197
epistemology, 27
ethnography: and representation, 12-13, 199; salvage, 63-65, 83, 135
Ethnologisches Museum (Berlin), 192
exhibitions: colonial displays in Britain, 80-81; display paradigms, 201-3, 210; permanent, criteria of, 224; permanent vs temporary, 229, 234, 245
exhibitions, museum: Annuraaq: Arctic Clothing from Igloolik, 245; The Art of Primitive Peoples, 229-31; Between Worlds: Voyagers to Britain, 1750-1850, 248; Extremes: Life in Subarctic Canada, 247; George Catlin: American Indian Portraits, 248; Home of the Brave, 232, 268*n*31; Hudson's Bay Company Historical Exhibit, 76; Image and Text, 232; Living and Dying, 245; Living Arctic, 246-47; Living Traditions: Continuity and Change, Past and Present, 173, 233-34; Niitsitapiisinni: Our Way of Life, 33, 183-84; Pikuni Blackfoot: Good Things Stay the Same, 184; Spirit Sings: Artistic Traditions of Canada's First Peoples, 6-7, 13, 246-47; Who Am I? 233; Wrapping the Globe: British South West Trade Cloth around the World, 232-33

expedixtions: and collecting, 18, 67; metaphor of, 34, and museums, 2-3, 81, 85, 109; sponsorship of, 2, 88; technology and, 2, 132; university related, 81, 104

File Hills Colony, 47, 118
File Hills reserves: artifacts from, 119, 166, 169-74, 176-77; ceremonial suppression at, 167-68; film and photographs from, 117, 139-44; Franklin Motor Expedition at, 116-20; resistance, 167; as a source for collectors, 118, 177
film: as evidence, 147; and Franklin Motor Expedition, 138; material qualities of, 158; meanings of, 158; as recording tool, 148; as representational medium, 149; as souvenir, 149, 152. *See also* photography and photographs
First Nations Sacred Ceremonial Objects Repatriation Act, 181
Franklin Motor Expedition: documentation relating to, 103, 153, 195; funding of, 109-10; symbolism of car, 151-52
frontier, concept of, 108, 154

Gennahmodhi (George Tanner), 114, 197-98, 262*n*38, 266*n*7
Geological and Natural History Museum, 68
Geological Survey of Canada: Anthropological Division, 5, 68-70, 72-75; collecting activities, 5-6
gifting, 50, 134. *See also* value: ceremonial distribution
Giigido Asin (John Talking Stone), 114, 138, 161, 262*n*38
Glasgow Museums, 232
Glenbow Museum, 6-7, 33, 181, 183-84, 246, 257*n*12
Godsell, Phillip, 90
governance, reserve: and elective system, 41; traditional forms of, 41
Graham, William, 40-41, 95, 118, 121(f)
Great Lakes Research Alliance for the Study of Aboriginal Arts and Cultures (GRASAC), 190, 249, 250, 251

Haddon, Alfred Cort, 1, 198, 201; museum work of, 202-3, 253*n*1
Harper, Stephen, 59

Head-Smashed-In Buffalo Jump, 184
Herle, Anita, 224, 227
heroism, in fieldwork/expeditions, 122, 132, 136, 154-55
Heye, George, 65; as collector, 87-88, 123-24
Heye Foundation, 87-90. *See also* National Museum of the American Indian (Smithsonian Institution)
H.H. Franklin Manufacturing Company, 111, 264*n*12
historical media: fieldwork accounts, 122, 136; film and photography, 137, 149, 158-59; museum archives, 137; newspaper stories, 120; photographs, 224
historical record: limitations of, 11
history: contested, 158; and historical commemorations, 53
Hodge, Frederick Webb, 208-9
Hooke, Samuel H., 96, 259*n*46
Horniman Museum and Gardens, 202, 268*n*3

Idle No More movement, 242, 268*n*2
Immoyiikimii (Grassy Water), 130, 130(f), 151-52
Indian Act, 39; amendments to, 49-50, 54-56, 92; potlatch prohibition, 49, 256*n*11; protection of cultural property, 91
Indian Notes, 90, 111, 142
Indian problem, 40, 54
indigenous arts: assumed death of, 65, 77; commissioned by museums, 95; legislation to protect, 91; marginalization of, 16, 71, 224; production of, 176-77; revival of, 250; as souvenirs, 124; and tourist trade, 91, 124-25; value of, 91. *See also* bead work
indigenous peoples: as tourist attractions, 53, 80, 124; as "vanishing race," 63, 144, 151
Ingold, Tim, 26

Jenness, Diamond, 73, 79; strategies for collecting, 90-91, 95

Kainai First Nation: ceremonial revival at, 182; and museum work, 183; residential school, 48

kâ-mostoswahcâpêw (Buffalo Bow), 117;
arrest of, 168; engagement with Franklin
Motor Expedition, 142-43, 143(f), 149,
150
kâ-pimohtêt, 117, 150-51, 167
keeping houses, 8, 66. *See also* cultural
centres
King, Jonathan C.H., 245
kîwisk, 108, 117, 261*n*23
knowledge, indigenous: objects and, 24;
residential schools and, 47, 180; restricted, 34, 159; transmission of, 65,
161-62, 180
k-owîkit (One Who Dwells), 117, 173
Kopytoff, Igor, 25-26. *See also* cultural
biography

Labrador Inuit Land Claims Agreement, 8
land: expropriation of, 39; legal concepts
of, 39. *See also* treaties
land claims: repatriation and, 8
Little Black Bear First Nation, 171-72
Little Pine First Nation, 122; and collectors,
122
loans: of artifacts, 171-72, 247-48
Lubicon Lake Cree, 7, 246
Lupson, Arnold, 126

mahkistikwân (Big Head), 135-36
Mandelbaum, David: as advocate, 57; as
collector, 118, 119; fieldwork of, 85-86,
144
Manitoba Museum, 76
material culture: clothing, 124; ethnicity
and, 18, 233; as ethnographic representation, 19, 199; theory and, 14; value of,
19, 170. *See also specific items of material
culture*
material culture studies, 19, 26. *See also*
anthropology
Matoas, Campbell, 57, 255*n*1
McIlwraith, Thomas F., 79-80
memory: anti-colonial, 169; and photographs, 159, 174-75; and portraiture, 169,
176
Midewiwin: artifacts associated with, 161,
164
mihkostikwân (Red Head), 150, 169, 170(f)
Miller, Daniel, 25

missionaries: attitudes toward ceremony,
51-52, 115; effect of, 161; opposition to
cultural expression, 54
Mitchell, Thomas, 104-5
mostâhtik (Simply Wood): headdress of,
120, 121(f)
Museum Ethnographers Group (MEG),
241
Museum of Archaeology and Anthropology (MAA) (University of Cambridge):
association with academic anthropology,
200; ceremonial objects, 173, 190, 214;
collaborative projects, 227, 249; collections of, 13, 105; community involvement in, 228; contemporary fieldwork
of, 223; dedicated interest in North
America, 81, 211; displays of, 203, 207-8,
211-16, 219-28; First Nations research
visits to, 190, 191; institutional challenges at, 198; links with Museum of the
American Indian, 103, 208-9; name
change, 266*n*11; online catalogue, 10;
organization of space in, 200-1, 211;
origins of, 105, 200; staffing of, 13;
teaching and, 201; temporary exhibitions
in, 233-34
Museum of Man and Nature, Winnipeg.
See Manitoba Museum
Museum of Mankind, 245-46
Museum of the American Indian, 87-90,
128-29; links with MAA, 103, 208-9
museums: as cabinets of curiosities, 67;
as collaborative spaces, 11, 241; colonial
institutions, 13, 239; community visits
to, 191, 192; cross-cultural education and,
184, 187; and Department of Indian
Affairs, 92-96, 176; display paradigms,
64, 201-3, 210; documentation conventions, 120; and ethnographic present,
210; in Europe, 11; financial resources
of, 81, 83, 84, 91; First Nations criticism
of, 164, 192; and First Nations researchers, 9-10, 11, 24; natural history, 77;
networks, 109-10; policies and policy-
making, 11, 241; as prisons, 164; relations
with indigenous people, 28-29, 185, 187,
189, 237, 239, 243, 249-50; responsibilities of, 187, 191; role of, 77, 185, 186; as
sites of authority, 219, 233; tensions

between US and Canadian, 83, 90; theories of presentation in, 201-3, 210, 214; and traditional care, 30, 165, 198; in the United Kingdom, 11-14, 229. *See also specific museums*

national identity: museums and, 78, 91; nationalism and, 23, 71; Native arts excluded from, 16; Northwest Coast art and, 91
National Museum of Canada: funding limitations of, 90-91. *See also* Canadian Museum of Civilization
National Museum of the American Indian (Smithsonian Institution), 88
National Museums Scotland, 247
Native American Graves Protection and Repatriation Act (NAGPRA), 13, 183
new museology, 19
Nisg̱a'a Final Agreement: repatriation and, 8

objects, ceremonial, 27; attempts to collect, 122-23, 135-36; demonized, 161; genealogies of, 173, 189; photography of, 30, 31; rights to ownership of, 164, 172-73, 185-86; as teachers, 189; transfer of, 119, 180, 185
objects, cultural: control of, 12; destruction of, 135; impact of access to, 171; repatriation of, 11, 171-72, 242 (*see also* repatriation). *See also* objects, ceremonial
Ojibwe Cultural Foundation, 248-49
Old Sun School, 47-48
oral histories: cultural interpretations of, 238; and images, 169
ownership: legislation and, 8; rights, 164

Pard, Allan, 86, 180-81, 182, 184, 185
pass system, 56, 60
Paul, Tim, 243-44
Pearce, Susan, 17
Peers, Laura, 11-12, 31, 250, 255*n*18
Perry, William, 96, 259*n*46
Pettipas, Katherine, 168
Phillips, Ruth B., 18, 20
Pitt Rivers Museum (University of Oxford), 201, 241, 247, 248-49, 250
photo-elicitation: as research method, 157-58, 159

photography and photographs, 224; anthropological conventions, 138; as evidence, 144; genres of, 137; material qualities of, 158; meanings of, 158; and memory, 159, 175; as representational medium, 149; as souvenir, 149, 152-53. *See also* film
Piikani Nation: artifacts in MAA, 129-30, 184-87; film and photographs from, 117, 138, 145-48; Franklin Motor Expedition and, 129-31; and museum work, 184; religious expression at, 181; repatriation and, 181-82
Pinay, Mike, 99, 171, 236
political activism, 56, 242
portraiture, 169, 176, 248
Potts, Jerry Jr., 24, 182, 185, 187
power: of ceremonial objects, 27, 30, 165, 185; and collecting, 16-17; museums as symbols of, 2; power-control, 164-65; shifts in, 9, 15, 28-29, 240
Pratt, Mary Louise, 25
Pratt, Stephanie, 248
primitive art: defined, 230; display of, 230-31
Provincial Museum of Alberta. *See* Royal Alberta Museum
Provincial Museum of Natural History, Regina. *See* Royal Saskatchewan Museum
Provost, Pat, 189

Racette, Sherry Farrell, 9-10, 16, 124
Reciprocal Research Network (RRN), 190, 249, 250, 251
Red Dog Singers, 172
repatriation, 8; of ancestral remains, 241; community expectations of, 11; conditions of, 186; of cultural property, 171; of foreign holdings, 11, 183, 242; impact of, 188; land claims process and, 8; of Nisg̱a'a artifacts, 8
representations, 199; of First Nations in contemporary media, 242. *See also* stereotypes
residential schools: attendance rates, 46; conditions in, 48; curriculum, 47; government apology for, 59; impact of, 49, 59, 180; management of, 47; survivors of, 59. *See also specific schools*

resistance: to anthropological research/anthropologists, 92, 135-36; to assimilation policies, 55-56; strategies of, 54-55, 65. *See also* political activism

rights, Aboriginal: to dance, 55; indigenous copyright, 29; of ownership, 8; religious, 49

Rochester Museum and Science Center, 126-27

Royal Albert Memorial Museum, 191, 232, 243-44

Royal Alberta Museum, 77, 181, 257*nn*2-3

Royal Commission on Aboriginal Peoples, 7, 9, 242

Royal Saskatchewan Museum, 75-76, 95

Rymill, John Riddoch, 4, 5(f); connection with MAA, 195-96; early life of, 105; as photographer, 138; as polar explorer, 106

Rymill, Robert Riddoch, 4, 5(f), 143(f); connection with MAA, 195-96; early life of, 105; expedition stories, 153; field notes of, 102-3; photograph album of, 153

Rymill Collection, 31; documentation of, 100-2, 112, 119, 166, 195-99, 204; loans from, 229-33; sketches of, 196, 197; and type specimens, 197, 224, 233

Sant Cassia, Paul, 219-20

Sapir, Edward, 1, 65, 72-73, 79; collaboration with Department of Indian Affairs, 93-94; as critic of government policy, 94

Saulteaux people: artifacts in MAA from, 122; Franklin Motor Expedition and, 120, 122

Scott, Duncan Campbell, 40, 92; support of Anthropological Division, 93-94

Scott, Rosie, 51-53

Scott, Wayne, 36, 62-63, 162-63, 165-66

scrolls, birch bark, 124, 197-98

Select Committee on Aboriginal Tribes, 66

Sign of the Goat Trading Post, 125, 136

Siksika Nation: artifacts in Canadian Museum of Civilization from, 128; artifacts in MAA from, 128; ceremonial revival at, 182; Franklin Motor Expedition at, 128

Skinner, Alanson, 89, 107; collecting activity of, 136

Smith, Harlan I., 58; artifact collecting of, 128; fieldwork of, 74, 128

songs, 173

St Mary's Roman Catholic Residential School, 48, 48(f)

Stanley, Grace, 226

Star Blanket First Nation, 117

Starblanket, Noel, 139, 167, 228, 265*n*8

Starr, Gilbert, 173-74, 177

stereotypes, 187, 199-200, 215, 246, 258n

Stewart, Susan, 17, 152

Sun Dance: prohibition on, 52, 58, 96

Swallow, Deborah, 216, 219

Swan Lake First Nation, 36; artifacts in MAA, 37, 115, 161, 197-98; attitudes to museums/cultural centres, 163, 166; band farm, 44; ceremonial practices at, 50-51, 115, 161; film and photographs from, 117, 138; Franklin Motor Expedition at, 114-16; religious freedom at, 57-58; research visits to museums, 161; Sun Dance, 58

Task Force on Museums and First Peoples, 7, 9

Thirst Dance: repression of, 167-68

Thomas, Nicholas, 20, 32

Thornton, Mildred Valley, 169

Tłı̨chǫ, 247

totem poles: commissioned by museums, 232, 243-44, 268*n*3; legislation to protect, 91; removal/destruction of, 91, 256*n*27; as tourist attractions, 91

trade: collecting as extension of, 134; with Europeans, 134; intertribal, 134; in Native handicrafts, 124-25

treaties: First Nations perspectives on, 38; museums and, 8; negotiation of, 38; obligations of, 42, 46. *See also* land

Truth and Reconciliation Commission of Canada, 59

Tsuu T'ina people: artifacts in MAA, 126; artifacts in Rochester Museum and Science Center, 126-27; and Franklin Motor Expedition, 125-26

Tylor, Edward Burnett, 69, 83

value: ceremonial distribution and, 50, 52; of film and photographs, 148, 154

Victoria Memorial Museum, 5, 70, 72, 79. *See also* Canadian Museum of Civilization

virtual repatriation. *See* digitization projects

visitors, 214-15, 267*n*21
visual anthropology, 134, 148
von Hügel, Anatole, 200, 220

Wahpeton Dakota people: artifacts in
    MAA, 122, 230; Franklin Motor
    Expedition and, 122
Watch (television programme), 215-16
Watcheston, Hortence, 168, 170(f)
Wellcome, Henry, 110

Wild West shows, 53, 80
Willmott, Cory, 23, 71, 73
Wilson, Robert N., 94-95
Wintemberg, William, 74-75
Wissler, Clark, 86-87
writing: of anthropologists/collectors, 108,
    136; contrast between public and private
    accounts, 136; contrast with images, 144;
    explorers/collectors, 108; and limitations
    of sources, 111

Printed and bound in Canada by Friesens

Set in Myriad and Garamond by Artegraphica Design Co. Ltd.

Copy editor: Deborah Kerr

Proofreader: Helen Godolphin

Cartographer: Eric Leinberger